Public Management Reform in the Gulf Cooperation Council and Beyond

This book offers an understanding of the current state of public management in the Gulf Cooperation Council (GCC) region, highlighting the region's institutional and human capital constraints. Drawing on case studies from GCC states and beyond, the book provides a policy-oriented analysis of these challenges and a set of recommendations on how to address them. *Public Management Reform in the Gulf Cooperation Council and Beyond* utilizes several theoretical frameworks to explore three themes: first, how the quality of government and efficiency of its bureaucratic machinery can offer a business-friendly environment for the private sector; second, how public-private partnerships can foster stronger collaboration and exchange of knowledge and expertise between the public and private sectors; and finally, how the existing human capital constraints may be addressed through the effective implementation of talent management, knowledge management, and training programs.

A comparative approach is taken throughout the book, contrasting the performance of GCC states with other Middle East and North Africa (MENA) countries or the Organization for Economic Cooperation and Development (OECD) member countries in key governance, public sector performance, and business competitiveness indicators—to identify what the GCC states need to do to enhance the quality of government and the capacity to deliver services more efficiently.

This book will appeal to academics, students, practitioners, policymakers, and private sector consultants, as well as those interested more broadly in the Middle East and the Gulf region.

Mhamed Biygautane is Assistant Professor of Public Policy and Management in the School of Social and Political Sciences at the University of Melbourne in Australia. He is the author of *The Institutional Context of Public–Private Partnerships: Lessons from the Arab States of the Gulf Cooperation Council* published by Edward Elgar Publishing in 2022. He specializes in public sector reform and explores topics such as privatization, infrastructure public-private partnerships, business-society relations and knowledge management, and public sector training in the context of the Gulf Cooperation Council (GCC) states. Mhamed holds a PhD in Public Management and a Master of Public Policy and Management from Monash University in Australia.

Public Administration and Public Policy
PUBLIC ADMINISTRATION AND PUBLIC POLICY
A Comprehensive Publication Program

EDITOR-IN-CHIEF
DAVID H. ROSENBLOOM
Distinguished Professor of Public Administration
American University, Washington, DC

RECENTLY PUBLISHED BOOKS

Building the Compensatory State
An Intellectual History and Theory of American Administrative Reform
Robert F. Durant

Social Equity and LGBTQ Rights
Dismantling Discrimination and Expanding Civil Rights
Lorenda A. Naylor

Handbook of Public Administration
Fourth Edition
W. Bartley Hildreth, Gerald J. Miller and Evert Linquest

The Public Productivity and Performance Handbook, Third Edition
Edited by Marc Holzer and Andrew Ballard

Cost and Optimization in Government, Third Edition
An Introduction to Cost Accounting, Operations Management, and Quality Control
Aman Khan

Contracting for Services in State and Local Government Agencies,
Third Edition
Best Practices for Public Procurement
William Sims Curry

Public Management Reform in the Gulf Cooperation Council and Beyond
Mhamed Biygautane

For more information about this series please visit: www.routledge.com/Public-Administration-and-Public-Policy/book-series/AUEPUBADMPUP

Public Management Reform in the Gulf Cooperation Council and Beyond

Mhamed Biygautane

NEW YORK AND LONDON

Designed cover image: Getty Images

First published 2023
by Routledge
605 Third Avenue, New York, NY 10158

and by Routledge
4 Park Square, Milton Park, Abingdon, Oxon, OX14 4RN

Routledge is an imprint of the Taylor & Francis Group, an informa business

© 2023 Mhamed Biygautane

The right of Mhamed Biygautane to be identified as author of this work has been asserted in accordance with sections 77 and 78 of the Copyright, Designs and Patents Act 1988.

All rights reserved. No part of this book may be reprinted or reproduced or utilized in any form or by any electronic, mechanical, or other means, now known or hereafter invented, including photocopying and recording, or in any information storage or retrieval system, without permission in writing from the publishers.

Trademark notice: Product or corporate names may be trademarks or registered trademarks, and are used only for identification and explanation without intent to infringe.

ISBN: 978-1-032-21307-1 (hbk)
ISBN: 978-1-032-45945-5 (pbk)
ISBN: 978-1-003-26774-4 (ebk)

DOI: 10.4324/9781003267744

Typeset in Times New Roman
by Newgen Publishing UK

Contents

List of figures vii
List of tables x
Preface xii
Acknowledgments xiv
List of abbreviations xv

1 Introduction: Public management reform and its importance for the GCC states 1

PART I
Quality of government and the public sector in the GCC region 27

2 Assessing the quality of government, governance, and public service delivery in GCC states: MENA comparisons and lessons 29

3 Global insights for Saudi Arabia's economic development: The role of effective machinery of government in revitalizing the private sector 66

4 Strategies for enhancing good governance and quality of government in the GCC states: Addressing corruption in the public sector 104

PART II
Importance of partnerships between the public and private sectors 135

5 The prospect and utility of infrastructure public-private partnerships in GCC states: Cases of Kuwait, Saudi Arabia, and Qatar 137

Contents

6 International review of public-private partnerships for school infrastructure development: Lessons and recommendations for Saudi Arabia   163

PART III
Importance of effective human resource development   199

7 Talent management in the GCC: MENA comparisons and recommendations   201

8 The impact of training on public sector organizations: Insights from the United Arab Emirates   225

9 Knowledge management in the public sector: Empirical insights from the United Arab Emirates   254

10 Conclusion: Translating institutional and human constraints into opportunities   301

Index   306

Figures

2.1	Government effectiveness	35
2.2	Inefficient government bureaucracy index	36
2.3	Public sector expenses (% of GDP)	37
2.4	Wage bill as % of public expenditure in 2017	38
2.5	Wage bill as % of GDP in 2017	39
2.6	Human Development Index	39
2.7	Global rankings of GCC and MENA countries in the Human Development Index	40
2.8	Regulatory quality	41
2.9	Control of corruption	42
2.10	Corruption Perceptions Index (2015–2018)	43
2.11	Voice and accountability	44
2.12	Political stability and absence of violence	45
2.13	Rule of law	46
2.14	Ease of doing business score	47
2.15	Ease of doing business global rankings in 2018	48
2.16	Start-up procedures to register a business	48
2.17	Time required to start a business (in days)	49
2.18	Total tax and contribution rate (% of the profit)	50
2.19	Quality of overall infrastructure	51
2.20	Quality of port infrastructure	52
2.21	Efficiency of customs and border management	53
2.22	Global innovation index ranking	54
2.23	Research and development expenditure (% of GDP)	55
2.24	University-industry collaboration in research and development	56
2.25	Researchers in R&D (per million people)	57
2.26	Skillsets of graduates	57
2.27	Availability of scientists and engineers	58
2.28	Capacity to retain talent	59
3.1	Oil rents (% of GDP)	76
3.2	GDP growth (% annually)	76
3.3	General government final consumption expenditure (% of GDP)	77

viii   *List of figures*

3.4	Services, value added (% of GDP)	78
3.5	Industry, value added (% growth)	78
3.6	High-technology exports (% of manufactured exports)	79
3.7	Research and development expenditure (% of GDP)	80
3.8	Turkish exports versus imports between 2012 and 2022 (in US$ billions)	94
3.9	Share of Turkey's exports in GDP (%)	95
3.10	FDI Confidence Index scores in 2020	98
6.1	Common school PPP models	176
6.2	Governments' reasons for school infrastructure delivery via PPPs	177
6.3	Essential requirements to support Saudi Arabia's school PPP project	189
7.1	Unemployment rates around the world	209
7.2	Percentage distribution of total employment by nationality in GCC countries (first quarter of 2020)	215
8.1	Role and involvement of the organizational leadership in preparing training strategies	234
8.2	Involvement of all staff in preparing training strategies	237
8.3	Tools used to develop training strategies	237
8.4	Involvement of staff and supervisors in identifying training needs	240
8.5	Training and employee development	242
8.6	Quality of training materials, subjects, and trainers	243
8.7	Impact of training strategy and methods on training effectiveness	244
8.8	Positive outcomes of effective training on employee performance	245
8.9	Effective training and organizational performance	246
8.10	Benefits of effective training on the overall performance of public sector entities	247
9.1	Evolution from data to knowledge	257
9.2	Awareness of KM in Dubai's public sector	267
9.3	Terms used for KM in Dubai's public sector	267
9.4	Challenges of knowledge sharing in Dubai public organizations	268
9.5	Mobility of staff in Dubai's public sector	273
9.6	Temporary staff with limited period contracts in Dubai government entities	274
9.7	Staff turnover	275
9.8	KM is one of the top five priorities of the organizations	275
9.9	Existence of written KM policy or strategy	276
9.10	KM policy/strategy focus areas	276
9.11	Sources of information for government entities in Dubai	277
9.12	Sources of knowledge for Dubai government entities	278
9.13	Methods of capturing knowledge and forms of documentation	279

List of figures   ix

9.14	Means of sharing knowledge within Dubai's public sector	280
9.15	Goals of implementing KM programs in Dubai's public sector	281
9.16	Factors that would facilitate the implementation of Dubai's public sector	282
9.17	Overall results of implementing KM in Dubai's public sector	283
9.18	Factors influencing the management of knowledge	283
9.19	Role of leadership in Dubai's KM programs	284
9.20	Assessment of KM performance in Dubai's public sector	285
9.21	Protection of employees and data	286
9.22	IT systems for KM in Dubai's public sector	288
9.23	Training effects on staff skills and knowledge	289
9.24	Utilization of staff skills, abilities, and experience by organizations	289
9.25	Techniques for transferring knowledge	290
9.26	Incentives for sharing knowledge within organizations	291
9.27	Governmental influences on KM programs in Dubai	292
9.28	Important factors for improving KM programs	293
9.29	Groups resisting KM and knowledge sharing	294

Tables

2.1	Differences in theory and practice of public administration and public management	33
3.1	Demographic data of benchmark countries and reasons for comparison with Saudi Arabia	72
3.2	Economic rankings	81
3.3	GCC countries' global Knowledge Index ranking from 2000 to 2021	96
3.4	UAE inward FDI stock, 2000–2020	98
4.1	Economic indicators of the GCC states in 2020	111
4.2	Transparency International's Corruption Perceptions Index	112
4.3	World Bank's Worldwide Governance Indicators	113
4.4	Government effectiveness indicators	115
4.5	Example cases of corruption in the GCC states	117
4.6	Anti-corruption agencies in the GCC	124
5.1	Selected indicators of governance	144
5.2	Ease of doing business	145
5.3	Length of the procurement process in Kuwait (in days)	147
5.4	The most problematic factors for doing business in selected GCC states	147
5.5	*Addressing* PPP constraints and *introducing* reform	156
6.1	Comparing advantages and disadvantages of PPPs	167
6.2	Factors contributing to the success or failure of PPP projects	169
6.3	Explanations and financial models of school PPPs with examples from international experience	170
6.4	PPP models in the education sector	174
6.5	Contractual forms of school partnership programs	175
6.6	Impact of partnership types on performance indicators	186
6.7	The prospects of various PPP initiatives in Saudi Arabia	191
7.1	Rankings of GCC and MENA regions in key Global Knowledge Index indicators in 2020	208
7.2	Brain drain index and unemployment rates in the GCC and MENA regions	210

7.3	Rankings of GCC and MENA regions in key Global Knowledge Index indicators	211
7.4	Comparison of results of tests in business administration	213
8.1	The role of leadership and the central government in preparing training strategies	235
8.2	Methods and measures taken to implement effective training strategies	238
8.3	Training needs measurement and assessment	241
8.4	Impact of training on organizational performance in Dubai public sector entities	248
9.1	Tacit and explicit knowledge	258
9.2	Knowledge management processes	261
9.3	Rationales for KM implementation among Dubai's government entities	271

Preface

The underlying ambition of writing this book is to document my experience, observations, and knowledge about the key challenges that face the Gulf Cooperation Council (GCC) region (Bahrain, Kuwait, Oman, Qatar, Saudi Arabia, and the United Arab Emirates (UAE)) in its efforts to modernize and reform its public sector organizations. Since 2008, I have lived and worked in numerous public sector organizations, universities, and consultancy firms in the GCC states of Bahrain, Kuwait, Oman, Qatar, Saudi Arabia, and the United Arab Emirates. Why is public management reform necessary for the GCC region? I think a practical way to answer this question is by highlighting the striking differences in public sector development levels and service delivery efficiency among the GCC states. Public management is close to the hearts of everyone because the quality of services we get from government departments affects the quality of our lives in numerous dimensions. For example, straightforward bureaucratic procedures such as converting one's international driver's license, which usually takes a matter of minutes to complete in the UAE, can unsurprisingly take a few days, if not weeks, in Kuwait due to the heavy bureaucratic procedures that underpin the international license conversion process.

The chapters of this book offer a general understanding of the current state of public management in the GCC region, highlighting particularly the region's institutional and human capital constraints. The book's ambition is to offer a policy-oriented analysis of the main public management-related institutional and human capital challenges the GCC region faces and provide recommendations on how to address them. To achieve this objective, the book draws on several theoretical frameworks that explore three themes that center around: a) how the quality of government and efficiency of its bureaucratic machinery can enhance economic development; b) how public-private partnerships can foster stronger collaboration and exchange of knowledge and expertise between the public and private sectors; and, finally, c) how to address the existing human capital constraints through the effective implementation of talent management, knowledge management, and training programs. The book draws on several case studies from different GCC states, which were selected mainly based on the availability and accessibility of data. The book adopts a comparative approach, often comparing the performance of GCC states in key governance, public sector performance, or business competitiveness indicators with other Middle East and North Africa (MENA) countries or the OECD member countries. Such comparisons help understand how well GCC states are doing or how much they still need to do to enhance the quality of government and its capacity to deliver services more efficiently.

I cannot think of a better time to write this book that synthesizes several topics that I have researched over the past 12 years such as public management reform, public-private partnerships, talent management, knowledge management, and training in the public sector. I lived in the GCC region during the advent of the financial crisis in 2007, and also during the drastic rise and fall of oil prices in the first and second half of 2014, and I am now spending my sabbatical leave form the University of Melbourne in Abu Dhabi in 2022 when the GCC region is recovering from the repercussions of COVID-19. Finalizing the chapters of this book in the heart of the GCC region offers a remarkable opportunity to observe the administrative reforms the book discusses in real life, but more importantly, to reflect on how far some GCC states, such as the UAE, have gone in improving the machinery of their government and streamlining their services. My hope is this book offers PhD students, scholars, and practitioners interested in understanding the depth and breadth of public management reforms undertaken in the GCC region a glimpse of how these reforms are carried out, and how GCC states compare to other countries of the MENA region and to a larger extent globally.

22 February 2023
Abu Dhabi, United Arab Emirates

Acknowledgments

This research would not have been possible without the input of several individuals from different government entities in Dubai, Doha, Kuwait, and Riyadh who so generously dedicated their time to participate in my interviews, and fill in the long surveys that were used to collect data for chapters Eight and Nine from Dubai government entities. I am thankful for their time and support for my research, and importantly, for their honest and invaluable insights that they offered on the raw material. I would also like to acknowledge the permission of previous outlets where earlier versions of three of the chapters in this book were published. These include Routledge which published "Anti-corruption Strategies in the Gulf Cooperation Council's States: Lessons Learnt and the Path Forward," which appeared in Zhang, Y. & Lavena, C. (eds.), *Government Anti-Corruption Strategies: A Cross-Cultural Perspective*, 2015, 187–214, an earlier version of Chapter Four; *Thunderbird International Business Review* which published "The Prospect of Infrastructure Public-Private Partnerships in Kuwait, Saudi Arabia, and Qatar: Transforming Challenges into Opportunities," 2018, 60(3), 329–346, an earlier version of Chapter Five; and Springer International Publishing which published "Talent Management in the MENA and GCC Regions: Challenges and Opportunities," which appeared in Al Ariss, A. (ed.), *Global Talent Management Challenges, Strategies, and Opportunities*, 2015, 197–215, an earlier version of Chapter Seven. I am incredibly appreciative of the support of the School of Social and Political Sciences at the University of Melbourne which generously provided the space and resources that made this work possible. I want to also express my gratitude to Professor David Rosenbloom for including my book in the "Public Administration and Public Policy" series. I am extremely grateful to the Taylor Francis Group's staff especially Editorial Assistants Ella Halstead and Elizabeth Hart for their incredible support during the publication process of this manuscript, and their reminders that kept me constantly on my toes till I delivered the full manuscript of this book. Finally, I cannot thank enough my wife Fatima for all her incredible support that has made researching, thinking and writing this book possible.

Abbreviations

ACTA	Administrative Control and Transparency Authority
APQC	American Productivity and Quality Center
BOO	Build, Own, and Operate
BOOT	Build, Own, Operate, and Transfer
BOT	Build, Operate, Transfer
CPC	Confederation for Production and Commerce
CPI	Corruption Perceptions Index
DBFO	Design, Build, Finance, and Operate
DBFOM	Design, Build, Finance, Operate, and Maintain
DBFOT	Design, Build, Finance, Operate, Transfer
DCM	Design, Construct, and Maintain
DGEP	Dubai Government Excellence Program
EDMS	Electronic Data Management System
FÁS	Foras Áiseanna Saothair
FDI	Foreign Direct Investment
FKI	Federation of Korean Industry
FSP	Future Schools Partners
FTZs	Free Trade Zones
GAB	General Auditing Bureau
GCC	Gulf Cooperation Council
GDP	Gross Domestic Product
HCIDP	Heavy Chemical and Industry Development Plan
HDI	Human Development Index
HRD	Human Resource Development
ICT	Information and Communication Technology
IMF	International Monetary Fund
IWPP	Independent Water Power Plant
KES	Kuwait Economic Society
KHDA	Knowledge and Human Development Authority
KM	Knowledge Management
KMS	Knowledge Management Systems
KT	Kuwait Transparency Society
L/ODO	Lease or Own, Develop, and Operate
MBRHE	Mohammed Bin Rashid Housing Establishment

MEED	Middle East Economic Digest
MENA	Middle East and North Africa
MOF	Ministry of Finance
MPs	Members of Parliament
NAZAHA	National Anti-Corruption Commission
NEAC	National Economic Action Council
NEP	New Economic Policy
NGOs	Non-governmental Organizations
NHRC	National Human Rights Committee
NPM	New Public Management
NSC	National Software Centre
NSW	New South Wales
OECD	Organization for Economic Cooperation and Development
OSD	Automotive Manufacturers Association
PAAC	Public Authority for Anti-Corruption
PCC	Polish Chamber of Commerce
PDC	Penang Development Corporation
PFI	Private Finance Initiative
PIC	Prosecution and Investigation Commission
PILOT	Payment In-Lieu of Taxes
PPPs	Public-Private Partnerships
PSC	Public Sector Comparator
QFC	Qatar Financial Center
R&D	Research and Development
RTA	Road & Transport Authority
SAB	State Audit Bureau
SAGIA	Saudi Arabian General Investment Authority
SAI	State Audit Institution
SAMA	Saudi Arabia Monetary Agency
SFAAI	State Financial and Administrative Audit Institution
SMEs	Small and Medium-sized Enterprises
SPDC	State Planning and Development Committee
SWOT	Strengths, Weaknesses, Opportunities, and Threats
TDI	Technology-Delivered Instruction
TIMSS	Third International Mathematics and Sciences Studies
UAE	United Arab Emirates
UNCAC	United Nations Convention against Corruption
UNDP	United Nations Development Programme
UNECE	United Nations Economic Commission for Europe
VfM	Value for Money
WTO	World Trade Organization

1 Introduction

Public management reform and its importance for the GCC states

Introduction

The past 50 years have witnessed impressive developments in many areas within the six Gulf Cooperation Council (GCC) states (Bahrain, Kuwait, Oman, Qatar, Saudi Arabia, and the United Arab Emirates (UAE)) that have managed to catch up with, and sometimes exceed, the countries of the Organization of Economic and Cooperation Development (OECD) in major global rankings and indicators of social development and ease of doing business. Over the past 50 years, the GCC governments have been the main providers of infrastructure and public goods, thanks to abundant oil and gas resources, and created, from scratch, the rudiments of modern states ranging from buildings, roads, and airports to investment in human capital. Moreover, as part of their social contracts and sharing of oil revenues, GCC states continue to provide free education and social benefits to all their citizens. This necessitated a bigger role of government in financing such projects, which required substantial financial investments.

However, this state-led economic and social development trajectory has started to change in response to various factors. First, GCC states have realized that pressure on governments to reduce the accelerating public spending, uncertainty over fluctuating oil prices, and the implications of the 2007 global financial crisis on their budgets necessitate new financing strategies. Furthermore, the drastic fluctuations of global oil and gas prices since 2014, and the implications of COVID-19 on GCC economies revealed the vulnerability of GCC economies to global financial and health crises and the fragility of local economies that largely depend on rents from oil exports. Second, the encouragement of the World Bank and other intergovernmental agencies for the GCC governments to reduce public spending is one of the key drivers for GCC governments' need to embrace administrative reforms that reduce the size of government and enhance efficiency in public service delivery. Third, GCC states have recognized that enabling the private sector to provide infrastructure and services is inevitable if they wish to lessen the financial burden on the government. Fourth, human capital challenges such as the concentration of the GCC states' local workforce

DOI: 10.4324/9781003267744-1

in the public sector, and their unpreparedness and sometimes reluctance to join private sector jobs, pose numerous challenges to GCC governments. These factors necessitate introducing and implementing public management reforms that will address any shortcomings in the machinery of the government as well as the human capital challenges that can inhibit GCC states from embracing a larger spectrum of public management reforms.

The GCC are now determined, more than ever before, to minimize their reliance on natural resources, and use their oil and gas revenues to build the foundations of economically competitive market economies. Since natural resources are no longer the main drivers of economic growth and competitiveness in a world that is becoming increasingly digitalized and information-driven, the GCC states certainly do not wish to be left behind. Hence, they are investing heavily in implementing reforms that will help them establish the rudiments of knowledge and information-driven economies.

This book aims to offer a general understanding of the current state of public management in the GCC region, highlighting particularly the region's institutional and human capital constraints. The book's ambition is to advance the theoretical debates on public management reform by offering a policy-oriented analysis of the main public management-related institutional and human capital challenges the GCC region faces, and provide a set of recommendations on how to address them. This book's underlying research question asks: how can GCC states reform their public sector and improve the quality of their government services by fostering collaboration with the private sector and enhancing the quality of their local human capital? To answer this research question the book draws on several theoretical frameworks that explore three main themes that center around: a) how the quality of government and efficiency of its bureaucratic machinery can offer a business-friendly environment for the private sector; b) how public-private partnerships can foster stronger collaboration and exchange of knowledge and expertise between the public and private sectors; and finally, c) how to address the existing human capital constraints through the effective implementation of talent management, knowledge management, and training programs. The book draws on several case studies from different GCC states, which were selected mainly based on the availability and accessibility of data. Furthermore, to better articulate the position of the GCC states in key governance and public management indicators, the chapters of the book will benchmark GCC states either with MENA countries or undertake global benchmarks to draw lessons that GCC states can learn from these global experiences.

This chapter offers a brief introduction to the key theoretical frameworks underpinning this book and is structured as follows. It starts by presenting the numerous definitions of public management reform and how it has evolved over the past few decades, and then explores the emergence of new public management (NPM) and how it has shaped debates around public sector reform. The chapter then discusses the relationship between the quality of government and economic growth, corruption, and the rule of law. The chapter then sheds light on the potential collaboration between the public and private sectors via the PPP route to enhance the quality and efficiency of delivering public services. Finally, the chapter discusses the importance of managing talent and knowledge as important levers for enhancing the overall quality of the public sector, and addressing the human capital challenges that face the GCC states.

What is public management reform?

This section begins by presenting the numerous definitions underpinning public management, and describes how public management reform has evolved to become the underpinning feature of NPM. This section then reflects on why public management reform is important, and briefly touches on post-NPM reforms. This section begins by presenting the numerous definitions underpinning public management, and describes how public management reform has evolved to become the underpinning feature of NPM. This section then reflects on why public management reform is important, and presents post-NPM arguments and why critics think NPM led to some adverse implications for the public sector.

Defining public management

Public management constantly evolves, and no single definition can capture its intricacy and scope. A comparative approach to the definitions of public management is, therefore, more appropriate to capture the varying meanings and dimensions of the field. Pollitt and Bouckaert (2004) discuss five competing definitions, progressing from the narrowest to the broadest conceptualizations in their public management literature review. The first definition, advanced by Perry and Kraemer (1983), views public management as "a merger of the normative orientation of traditional public administration and the instrumental orientation of general management" (p. x). In this definition, which focuses on institutional and organizational values and techniques, public management retains traditional public administration's focus on public sector values while incorporating managerial techniques from the private sector.

While Perry and Kraemer (1983) examine institutional values and techniques, Metcalfe and Richards (1987), in the second definition, highlight the management of systems of organizations. Public management, for Perry and Kraemer, is characterized by "the effective functioning of whole systems of organizations" and "explicit acknowledgment of the responsibility for dealing with structural problems at the level of the system as a whole" (1983, pp. 73–75). The third definition by Pierre (1995), examines the "output linkage of the state towards civil society" (p. ix). Output linkage refers to the information and resources that the state transfers to civil society (Bouckaert & Peters, 2002; Pierre, 1995). This interface, which Pierre argues is a two-way street, concerns "policy demands from private actors towards policymakers and policy implementation" (Pierre, 1995, p. ix).

Another definition of public management examines the underlying values, ideas, cultures, and ideologies underpinning the public service. Clarke and Newman (1997) conceptualize managerialism "as a cultural formation and a distinctive set of ideologies and practices which form one of the underpinnings of an emergent political settlement" (p. ix). A broader definition, put forward by König (1996), defines public management as a social system regulated by its own principles and constantly changing social conditions. It also distinguishes between the strategies that inform public and private sector decisions on the production, supply, and distribution of goods; while individual preferences inform the private sector in the context of the free market. Meanwhile, the public sector is influenced by "a collective, i.e., politico-administrative, development of objectives" (König, 1996, pp. 4, 59).

As these definitions demonstrate, public management is a contested domain, with the link between public and private management constituting a core point of disagreement. While one end of the spectrum argues for the separation of public management from commercial management due to the inherently different values informing the two, the other end supports borrowing the managerial tools of the private sector to increase efficiency and efficacy in the public sector (Ganguli, 2016; Gunn, 1987). Metcalfe and Richards (1987) are situated in the middle of this spectrum when they point out the utility of business sector managerial tools at the micro level of management in the public sector but not at the macro level which, according to these authors, is fundamentally unique. In comparison, Metcalfe and Richards (1987) highlight micro- and macro-variations in managerial tools, and Bouckaert and Peters (2002) point out variations in the technical and political features that characterize public sector activity. As Pollitt and Bouckaert (2004) argue, one common denominator between these various definitions is the idea that public management is an activity embedded in certain political, legal, and social contexts and guided by individuals informed by certain values and ideologies, as opposed to an objective, technical process (Ganguli, 2016).

The evolution of public management "reform"

The word "reform" refers to organizational changes in the public sector emanating from introducing business-like management techniques to the public sector and creating quasi-market government organizations to increase public organizations' efficiency and effectiveness (Hughes, 2017; Lapuente & Van de Walle, 2020). Pollitt and Bouckaert (2004) define public management reform as "deliberate changes to the structures and processes of public sector organizations to get them (in some sense) to run better" (p. 8). Public management reforms aim to improve the traditional Weberian approach or bureaucratic public administration model that emphasizes predictability, hierarchy, and obedience over innovation, efficiency, and efficacy.

The origins of public management reform can be traced to the 1980s in OECD countries when discontent with government performance in social and economic programs began to rise (Keating, 2001). By the early 1980s, scholars started to document trends in reforms in the public sector, which they referred to by various names, including NPM (Pollitt, 1990; 2018). In the mid-1990s, major intergovernmental organizations and institutions, including the OECD and the World Bank, began to adopt and promote NPMs as the "'way forward' for all governments" (Pollitt, 2018, p. 18). Critical scholarship subsequently dismissed early scholars' characterization of NPM as a coherent global trend and instead stressed the idea that NPMs encompass diverse sets of approaches and ideas (Pollitt, 2018).

Defining NPM

Outlining the definitional boundaries of NPM is still a disputed endeavor (Dunleavy et al., 2006). Pollitt (2018) tries to delimit the boundaries of NPM by defining it as a two-level phenomenon; the higher level captures the foundational idea that public sector efficiency can be enhanced by borrowing business sector tools and techniques, while the mundane level refers to specific sets of business-derived ideas and practices, such as performance and compartmentalization of tasks (Pollitt, 2018). Dunleavy et al. (2006) limit NPM to three specific business sector elements: disaggregation, competition, and incentivization. Disaggregation denotes separating public agencies into smaller and mission-focused agencies to improve performance monitoring and accountability (Dunleavy & Hood, 1994). The fostering of competition in public services seeks to reduce cost and increase efficiency in the public sector by, for example, outsourcing tasks and tying funding to performance (Boston, 1994). Incentivization rewards specific, as opposed to diffuse, performances, thereby breaking with the low-incentive traditional approaches in the public sector (Lapuente & Van de Walle, 2020; Miller, 2000). Most contemporary public administrations have incorporated NPM's efficiency and efficacy objectives and implemented measures encouraging competition, incentivization, and disaggregation (Pollitt, 2018).

However, this importation of private sector ideas and practices to the public sector has been criticized. Critics often stress the inapplicability and, thus, the inefficiency of these reforms due to the fundamentally different values and concerns defining the public (i.e., with its focus on public services and goods) and private (with its focus on profit maximization) sectors (Pollitt, 2018). These waves of criticism fueled the post-NPM debates that sought to put forward reform models that recognized the nuances of the boundaries between the private and public sectors.

Why is public management reform important?

The public management literature provides numerous explanations for the importance of public management reform. Pollitt and Bouckaert (2004) offer several justifications, including public management reform's utility not as an objective in itself but as a means to multiple ends for the public sector. Some outcomes that public management reforms help the public sector achieve include reducing public expenditure and increasing savings, enhancing the quality of the overall public services, increasing efficiency in government operations, and improving the effectiveness of policymaking and policy implementation (Bouckaert & Peters, 2002). Other more specific reasons for the importance of public management reform include improved policy capacity, better-performing machinery of government, improved budgetary performance, and better regulatory reform (Keating, 2001).

Pollitt and Bouckaert (2004) point out that public management reforms can achieve copious intermediate ends. For instance, public management reform can strengthen politicians' control over bureaucracy and reduce the bureaucratic barriers that traditionally hinder government officials' ability to manage effectively. Public management reform can also improve the accountability of government policies and programs to the legislature and the public. Additionally, public management reform serves symbolic and legitimacy functions. Engaging in public management reform policies and programs can create the symbolic image of "doing something" for politicians (Fryer et al., 2009). The acts of declaring or promoting new public management reforms and critiquing old ones can generate positive attention for public officials. The process of public management reforms can also enhance the legitimacy and reputation of politicians as partaking in "modernizing" and "streamlining" public sector activities (Pollitt & Bouckaert, 2004, p. 6). Among the various routes to improving governmental performance, such as political reforms or substantive policy changes, public management reform remains the only viable route to pursue the objectives of the public sector, despite the many challenges that may confront public management reform (Melo & Mota, 2020).

Keating (2001) establishes a clearer link between public management reform and economic and social development and underscores the contribution of the public management reform paradigm to economic and social development in several governmental areas. Regarding policy capacity, as Keating (2001) notes, public management reforms that improve policymaking capacity are the most consequential because they lead to more efficiency in integrating social and economic policies. Reforms in policy capacity are not confined to the internal organization of management processes but can also be extended to broader governance issues and relations within/between governments and the public (Lodge & Gill, 2011). While countries—especially, OECD states—differ in their approaches to the development of policy capacity, two generalizable lessons emerge; these consist of public management reforms that (1) aid the ministers and central government in focusing on development and policy coordination by reducing unnecessary workload, and (2) improve the quality and thoroughness of incoming information that informs policymaking (Lapuente & Van de Walle, 2020).

If implemented successfully, public management reform can improve the performance of the machinery of government (Miller, 2000). For instance, public management reform in countries like Canada and Australia enhanced policy coordination and reduced the burden of internal disputes within the Cabinet by decreasing the number of government ministries or merging the ones that are separate but related (Lodge & Gill, 2011). Similar changes that seek to enable the government to focus on strategic issues and setting policy directions include separating policy development and service delivery. Popular in Nordic states and, recently, in the United Kingdom and New Zealand, this separation of service delivery into distinct agencies allows the ministries to concentrate on effective policymaking. The disaggregation of delivery functions by moving them to lower levels of government or by increasing regional governments' authority are other ways of allowing the central government to concentrate on strategic policy (Rothstein & Teorell, 2012).

Another central area where public management reforms gain importance is in budgeting and financial management systems. The fact that the government's annual budget plays a key role in policy design and implementation renders budget and financial management systems as either capable of aiding or hampering the efficient allocation of government resources in line with strategic policies (Melo & Mota, 2020). For instance, the financial management system, which defines the government budget, influences the structures, processes, and cultures of management in government organizations (Fryer et al., 2009). Keating (2001) discussed two public management reforms contributing to budgetary improvements. First are reforms that intend to improve the quality of budgetary decision-making by, for example, reorganizing spending, savings, or tax proposals within one decision-making process and incorporating them into one annual budget framework (Miller, 2000). Processing proposals about spending and savings simultaneously increases merit-based competition among bidders for service delivery, reduces the number of off-budget financing, and ensures that individual decisions align with the government budget targets. The overall objective is that budgetary decision-making is accurately informed about program costs, thereby informing the efficient allocation and management of resources (Lapuente & Van de Walle, 2020).

The second type of public management reform that Keating (2001) examines focuses specifically on improving resource allocation and management. In order to disaggregate central agencies and foster effective program management, government agencies need to establish strict forward estimates of the running costs of each of their programs. Government control can still be exercised not by involving central agencies in program details but rather by ensuring that program managers adhere to performance targets and measurements. In OECD countries where these financial management reforms have been implemented, significant changes ensued in public service culture (Keating, 2001).

Regulation is one of the key tools of governing, and because of the centrality of regulation to the government, government processes, institutions, and culture form an integral part of any regulatory reform. Lukea and Garavan (2016) highlight two concerns that incentivize regulatory reforms: the dependency of economic development on more flexibility and competitiveness in markets and the cost of compliance with regulations on business. To address these concerns, public management reforms focus on reducing unnecessary regulations and enhancing the quality of new regulations by creating a systematic regulation review process. This process aids in identifying the objectives of the regulations and conducting a clear costs-benefits analysis of these regulations. While the traditional approaches to regulation tended to be concerned with control over certain processes, the new public management reforms use the intended outcome of interest as their point of departure when designing regulations.

The post-NPM reforms

The post-NPM reforms are best viewed as continuing and complementing NPM ideas rather than substituting or breaking with them (Lodge & Gill, 2011; Pollitt, 2018). Post-NPM reforms attempt to reintroduce traditional public administration values and redress the limitations of NPM (Pollitt, 2018). They maintain the business-derived tools and techniques introduced by NPM (e.g., specialization, marketization, and fragmentation) and stress fostering the capacities of collaboration, coordination, and centralization (Christensen & Lægreid, 2008; Pollitt, 2018). Post-NPM, therefore, integrates the managerial elements in the early waves of NPM with Neo-Weberian and traditional public administration features (Pollitt & Bouckaert, 2004). Nonetheless, critics argue that the public sector's adoption of NPM generates negative impacts that are not currently mitigated (Black & Upchurch, 1999). Key challenges and impacts will be explored below.

Budgetary cuts

Due to the cost-effective practices within NPM, many public agencies have faced budget cuts, which reduce the quality and diversity of employees. For example, Hudson (2017) reported that policy around salaries creates a barrier to attracting talented employees, as public sector jobs may pay up to 30% less than the private sector. Furthermore, Dougherty and Van Gelder (2015) found that employee engagement and trust in government have decreased because of NPM-related cuts. Subsequently, Clarke and Scurry (2017) contend that the public sector is facing a staffing crisis, particularly as long-standing public servants retire and new staff need to be sourced (Quinn & Warren, 2017).

Competition

As a result of budget cuts in the public sector, competition is exacerbating between public service providers. Brown (2004, p. 307) argues that competition can be detrimental to the health and wellbeing of civil society, as some agencies might receive funding for popular services while other less popular services are under-recognized and marginalize people with unique issues. Brown and Ryan (2003) find that this increased competition also forces public agencies to be more stringent with staffing decisions and benefits.

Slow recruitment processes

Critics argue that human resources in the public sector are lacking (Black & Upchurch, 1999). Van den Brink and Fruytier (2013) found that HR professionals face challenges navigating recruitment processes' "political gamesmanship". This refers to potential bias or favoritism within the hiring process, which conflicts with the public sector's commitment to equal opportunity and treatment. In addition, some recruitment processes are designed to attract high-performing and high-achieving individuals. For example, some public service graduate programs in Australia require candidates to undertake skill-based tests, provide high university and tertiary education results, and demonstrate prior experience. Hudson (2017) notes that these recruitment processes are often time-consuming and costly, which creates an accessibility gap. Critics argue that this recruitment process again conflicts with the public sector's values of inclusivity and equality (Thunnissen & Buttiens, 2017).

Rule-bound culture

The public sector has separate outcomes from the private sector, which are sometimes intangible and challenging to measure (Kock & Burke, 2008). For example, performance in the private sector can be measured by financial targets and profit margins, but the public sector might be evaluated using customer experiences as public services aim to provide an improved quality of living. As a result, performance measurement in the public sector has been a critical challenge over the past decade. In the past, performance in the public sector was based on a "rule-bound" culture, which often ignored staff potential and achievements (Shim, 2001). This rule-bound culture was entrenched in the bureaucratic nature of public agencies, which often have long and challenging approval processes. Critics argue that rewarding innovative thinking should be encouraged in the public sector to motivate staff and incentivize performance (Rana et al., 2013).

Quality of government and its impact on economic growth, corruption, and the rule of law

This section discusses the key features of the quality of government as they relate to public management reform. It starts with defining what is meant by quality of government, if there is a clear correlation between democracy and quality of government, how economic development shapes the quality of government, and how governance-related factors such as corruption and existence/absence of the rule of law affect the quality of government.

Defining the quality of government

Many scholars have attempted to define the "quality of government" since the concept rose to popularity in the mid-1990s (Rothstein & Teorell, 2012, p. 13). Public policy literature often uses the quality of government and good governance interchangeably. Holmberg et al. (2009) found that the most popular notion of quality of government derives from the World Bank's definition of governance:

> the traditions and institutions by which authority in a country is exercised. This includes (1) the process by which governments are selected, monitored and replaced, (2) the capacity of the government to effectively formulate and implement sound policies, and (3) the respect of citizens and the state for the institutions that govern economic and social interactions among them.
>
> (Kaufmann et al., 1999, p. 1)

The definition above evaluates the capacity of government to conform to different standards in three areas. All three areas have a best practice measurement that the World Bank prefers. For example, in section (2) of its definition, the World Bank would be more likely to rank policies that treat civil society equally than policies that attempt to discriminate against certain subgroups. To provide a fair and balanced evaluation of a country's governance, the World Bank draws on certain indicators to measure good governance. These indicators are referred to as the Worldwide Governance Indicators, which consider countries based on the following criteria: political stability, the rule of law, control of corruption, accountability, regulatory quality, and government effectiveness. Many critics doubt these contemporary indicators and global standards used to measure the quality of government. The World Bank is perceived to lack impartiality and judge countries based on deterministic ideas of how a country should be governed (Holmberg et al., 2009, p. 137). Rothstein and Teorell (2012) contend that the World Bank cannot distinguish good governance from liberal democracy and pro-Western ideals. From this perspective, countries that lack well-established democracies would perform poorly in section (1) of the above definition.

Introduction 11

There are alternate ideas about how the quality of government should be defined. Rotberg (2007, p. 154) argues that the quality of government should be measured by the effectiveness of a country's social services. However, Holmberg et al. (2009, p. 137) warn that equating the quality of government with good outcomes might overlook other elements that would undermine it. Rothstein and Teorell (2012, p. 23) offer a different definition of quality of government that considers normative theory. The normative theory allows different contexts to have reasonable expectations for what constitutes "good" governance. Furthermore, Rothstein and Teorell (2012, p. 23) emphasize the concept of impartiality and outline that quality of government can be seen where governments and countries act reasonably and impartially towards all people. These different definitions show that the quality of government can be interpreted in many ways. The following sections of this literature review provide an overview of the debates around key indicators that global governance institutions might overlook, such as political systems and economic development.

Is democracy a prerequisite for quality of government?

Scholarly research on the quality of government is divided on the concept of democracy leading to good governance. Global governance institutions, such as the United Nations, the World Bank, and the International Monetary Fund, consider democracy as a solution to eradicating corruption. For example, the 2000 United Nations Human Development Report focuses on democracy as an integral element of good governance (UNDP, 2002, p. 1). Deininger and Mpuga (2005, p. 171) explain that this idolization of democracy stems from its link with principles of accountability, which holds individuals and public officials responsible for actions. Many studies capture the link between democracy and the quality of government. For example, Li et al. (1998) and Chong and Gradstein (2007) found that the civil liberties granted in democracies are associated with greater prosperity and equality.

Alternatively, many critics argue that democracy can lead to bad governance and poor quality of government. Diamond (2007, p. 119) found that many countries that recently adopted democracy slipped further into corrupt practices, such as favoritism and political propaganda. For example, Peru began transitioning from military-led authoritarian rule to civil democracy in 1978. However, Peru's party system collapsed in the 1990s due to former President Fujimori's actions that dismantled democratic institutions (McMillan & Zoido, 2004). In addition, some critics highlight that countries perceived as anti-democratic often have sound governance systems. For example, Singapore and Hong Kong demonstrate high levels of quality of government according to the Worldwide Governance Indicators, especially on measurements such as government effectiveness and the rule of law (Holmberg et al., 2009, p. 138; Uslaner, 2008). Similarly, Holmberg et al. (2009, p. 138) argue that no empirical measurement or criteria can justify the link between democracies and better societal outcomes. The uncertainty around whether political systems, such as democracy, can lead to quality of government, has led academics to explore other ways of measuring the quality of government, such as economic development and the rule of law (UNDP, 2002).

Economic development and quality of government

Holmberg et al. (2009, p. 141) argue that there is a consensus in academia on the link between economic development and the quality of government. However, academics are divided over the causality between economic growth and good governance. Some scholars find that good governance systems can increase a country's wealth. For example, Kaufmann et al. (1999, p. 15) found that an improvement in governance by one standard deviation leads to a gain in per capita income that ranges from 2.5-fold to 4-fold. In addition, Chong and Calderón (2000) argue that the prosperity of a society is often linked with solid government social service delivery. Chong and Calderón (2000) found that the more effective and far-reaching a country's institutions are, the lower level of poverty. This rationale is often used to explain why regional groupings of people are often considered low socioeconomically, as public services often exclude remote locations (Krishna, 2007).

In contrast, some critics highlight that good governance cannot be established without economic growth. Grindle (2004) argues that it is challenging to establish good governance institutions, such as anti-corruption agencies and public services, without economic prosperity and public funds. For example, Goldsmith (2007, p. 165) outlines that economic growth in the United States and Argentina began to increase before governance reforms occurred. From this perspective, economic growth and capital are prerequisites for good governance systems. Additionally, scholars have shifted away from the assumption that economic growth derives from introducing capitalist ideals. The Washington Consensus model focused on methods, such as maintaining fiscal discipline over public spending and liberalizing trade, to promote economic growth (Serra & Stiglitz, 2008). Like the democratic debate, critics outline that neoliberal and pro-Western market systems are often inaccurately connected to good quality of government. Many critics outline that the Washington Consensus model is a one-size-fits-all method that should not be applied to developing countries that lack the means to institutionalize divergent market ideologies.

Corruption and quality of government

Scholars are divided on the impact of corruption on the quality of government. Corruption is "the abuse of public power for private gain" (Rothstein & Teorell, 2012, p. 19). Holmberg et al. (2009, p. 141) consider good governance as the absence of corruption and other practices related to corruption, including clientelism, nepotism, cronyism, patronage, and discrimination. On the other hand, Rothstein and Teorell (2012) argue that the absence of corruption cannot measure the quality of government, as corruption is difficult to define. Rothstein and Teorell (2012) draw on Kurer's (2005) argument that "the abuse of public power" is relativistic and depends on a country's political norms.

The link between bad governance and corruption rose to popularity when Transparency International founded its Corruption Perceptions Index in 1996 (Rothstein & Teorell, 2012, p. 15). As a result, many critics find that corruption is a manifestation of poor quality of government (Gupta et al., 2000; Mauro, 1995; Transparency International, 2008). The impacts of corruption are often tied with human development and economic growth. For example, Akçay (2006, p. 33) contends that corruption can negatively impact human development by reducing individuals' participation in the economy. Moreover, Mauro (1995) found that government spending on education declines when corruption exists in countries. This ties into the idea that corruption results in the inaccurate distribution of public resources, whereby large infrastructure and defense projects are likely to receive more funding, and public welfare services decrease. From this perspective, it is within a government's best interest to implement governance systems that implement anti-corruption policies.

Alternatively, some critics contest the link between corruption and bad governance. Some scholars argue that specific types of corruption can yield positive outcomes, such as economic development (Khan, 1996; 1998; Nye, 1967). For example, corrupt practices can circumvent systems that delay trade transactions, or "grease the wheels" of the economy. Corruption can also inspire governance reform, or signal the capacity of governance systems, such as strong anti-corruption policies and agencies, to identify and combat corruption. Despite different perspectives on how corruption can influence the quality of government, there is a recognized link between the quality of government and the implementation of anti-corruption policies.

The rule of law and quality of government

The rule of law is used as a critical indicator to measure the quality of government. The rule of law refers to creating and implementing policy-making and legal systems within a country. The concept of the rule of law also includes society's awareness and capacity to abide by legislated rules (Rothstein & Teorell, 2012, p. 20). Some critics argue that the rule of law is effective in evaluating the quality of government. For example, Costa (2008) identified a correlation between weak rule of law and weak socio-economic performance, as some individuals and subgroups might be subject to harsher or discriminatory practices under the rule of law. Moreover, developed and wealthy countries score well on the World Bank's Worldwide

Governance Indicators, as these countries have good institutions that monitor and mandate the rule of law (Economist, 2008, pp. 95–96).

However, the rule of law cannot measure the quality of government in all contexts. For example, China has the second largest economy in the world and is perceived as a very prosperous nation, and China achieved this wealth without scoring highly on the World Bank's rule of law indicator. As a result, Messick (1999) questions the causality between the quality of government and the rule of law. For instance, instead of using the rule of law to improve the quality of government, wealthy countries can inject more capital and development into their judicial institutions to strengthen the rule of law. This contrasts with the World Bank's indicator that assumes the rule of law leads to more development and better governance structures.

Collaboration between the public and private sectors via public-private partnerships (PPPs)

This section highlights the pros and cons of PPPs and their potential to deliver efficient and effective services and projects. The section begins by defining PPPs and articulating why governments adopt them, and reflects on the backdrop of adopting PPPs and the challenges associated with their use for infrastructure delivery.

PPPs are a recent extension of the NPM "agenda" for changes in how public services are provided (Broadbent & Laughlin, 2003). Given the tight budgets that governments worldwide have had to operate with since the advent of the financial crisis of 2007, PPPs are again becoming a more common strand of public policy, as they offer better efficiency for funding public services through appropriate allocation of risks, rewards, and responsibilities, which all promise better value for money and expand the dimensions of doing more with less (Teicher et al., 2006). The conceptual dialogue surrounding PPPs in the available literature demonstrates the vagueness of the meaning of the term PPP, which has been used to signify various things for different people (Broadbent & Laughlin, 2003).

In a PPP project, both the government and the private sector are involved in the different stages of service provision. While the private sector takes care of the design, construction, operation, maintenance, finance, and risk management operations, the government is responsible for strategic planning and industry structure, obtaining permits, regulating, and community service obligations (NSW Office of Financial Management, 2002). PPPs take various forms: design, construct, and maintain (DCM); build, own, and operate (BOO); and build, own, operate, and transfer (BOOT) (Grimsey & Lewis, 2000; Webb & Pulle, 2002). The private contractor owns the infrastructure for the contract term and provides contracted services that are paid for directly by the government or by customers. Thus, the government's role sometimes shifts from being the supplier of infrastructure services to the buyer from the private sector.

Governments adopt PPPs for a variety of reasons. First, they provide value for money. This is usually defined as getting "the best possible outcome at the lowest possible price" (English, 2006, p. 254). Grimsey and Lewis (2000) state that the principal aim of the public sector's involvement in PPPs is to achieve value for money from the services provided when the private sector meets contractual obligations "properly" and "efficiently". This takes many forms, such as "lower construction costs, lower operating costs and more efficient maintenance in the long run" (Webb & Pulle, 2002, p. 5). The private sector has to perform very well to earn profits from their projects, which enhances the quality of services and minimizes their costs. Another source of value for money arises from the "bundling" of services. The obligation to build, operate, maintain, and transfer the asset to the state at the end of the contract is an additional incentive to minimize the project's costs (English, 2006). Therefore, the efficiency of the service provided is maximized through effective and efficient design and construction of infrastructure projects, and its costs are kept to the minimum.

Another significant reason for adopting PPPs is risk transfer. This is the driver of value for money and the government's key justification for engaging in PPPs because, without significant risk held by the private sector, PPPs would not be worth taking on (English, 2006). These risks could be related to construction, market size, cost of operations and maintenance, delays in finishing projects, force majeure, and any changes to laws and regulations. In fact, the rationale behind implementing PPPs is that the bureaucratic structure of governments does not provide the necessary mechanisms and incentives to provide efficient and effective infrastructure services that can be finished on time. Moreover, any extra costs caused by time delays or performance failures that are not priced into government borrowing are borne by taxpayers (NSW Office of Financial Management, 2002). The private sector; however, is restricted by a tight budget and limited sources, and cannot levy any extra charges on its citizens. This obliges it to perform its services with minimal costs and higher quality to generate as much profit as possible. The Public Sector Comparator (PSC) assumes the responsibility of determining which sector provides better value for money with fewer risks. It predicts the costs of the project when the public and private sectors undertake it. It then determines which sector would provide better value for money.

While there are numerous advantages to adopting the PPP model, there are also disadvantages. PPPs do not work all of the time. When they do not work, both the private and public sector enter into a long legal process to settle their disputes, and try to identify who will bear the costs of the failure of the PPP. A review of global experiences with PPPs demonstrates the major failures of some PPP initiatives that were not carefully designed and implemented. In most cases, the taxpayers are the ones that bear the cost of these failures. Hence, it is essential not to enter into a PPP agreement until risks are carefully measured and assessed.

16 *Introduction*

Other challenges associated with using the PPP model involve the technicalities involved in designing and implementing such a project. Transparency is an important factor in the entire process and lifespan of a PPP. However, too much transparency creates many disadvantages for the private sector, especially when it comes to disclosing confidential information that would hinder a private company in its competitiveness, especially during the bedding period. At the same time, too little transparency affects citizens' access to public information, and this ultimately requires maintaining a balance between the interests of the two parties involved in PPPs. Other issues, such as the complexity of the contractual structure, can result in longer negotiation periods, and the up-front costs of PPP projects often become much larger than those of conventional procurement methods (Darvish et al., 2006). Furthermore, critics of transferring the provision of public infrastructure to the private sector argue that it makes the services more expensive than if the government provided them.

Talent and knowledge management in the public sector

This section offers working definitions and a brief discussion regarding the importance of talent and knowledge management in the public sector. It particularly emphasizes the need to develop effective knowledge management mechanisms that capture, organize, store, disseminate, and retain knowledge within public organizations in the GCC region.

In the past two decades, the concept of talent management has emerged as a strategy to improve employees' experience in the public sector. Since NPM was introduced to governments in the 1980s, public services have operated similarly to the private sector. For example, NPM focused on cost-efficiency strategies, performance-based management, and competition between providers (Shaw, 2012, p. 119; Waheduzzaman, 2019, p. 691). Critics highlight that NPM creates challenges for governments in attracting and maintaining talented staff due to cost-efficient measures (Brown, 2004, p. 307; Kravariti & Johnston, 2020, p. 86). As a result, researchers are refining and adapting the private sector's use of talent management to suit the public sector. This literature review will examine definitions of talent management in the public sector. The benefits of talent management in improving public services, mainly through the retention and empowerment of staff, will also be discussed.

Talent management initially emerged in the private sector, as private entities found many benefits in empowering and retaining high-performing employees that serve the company's interests. Talent management is commonly defined as a method to enhance the performance and talent of employees to improve organizational performance (Creelman, 2004). Talent management is also conceptualized as the use of tools and procedures to improve working conditions for employees, such as recruitment and selection processes, career development and training opportunities, and employee retention schemes (Al Ariss et al., 2014; Crowley-Henry & Al

Ariss, 2016; Meyers & Van Woerkom, 2014; Rigg, 2015). This investment in staff is designed to create a supportive and innovative environment that enriches the organization. This benefits the private sector, as high-quality candidates invest their talents in the organization after feeling supported.

Alternatively, talent management in the public sector focuses on adopting strategies that align strategic objectives with the organization's culture, employee aims, and structure (Garrow & Hirsh, 2008). Thunnissen and Buttiens (2017) find that individuals drawn to the public sector share the public sector's core values of equal treatment and transparency. The definitions of talent management differ between the public and private sectors due to each sector's separate values. The public sector aims to provide good services that benefit civil society, attracting employees with similar values of delivering services to the public. In contrast, the private sector is profit-oriented and does not have the fundamental values of serving the public for the common good (Kravariti & Johnston, 2020, p. 80).

Importance of managing knowledge in the GCC region

The economic and institutional performance problems GCC states have faced in the past 30 years have triggered a serious debate about the capacity of government entities and private sector firms to develop, incorporate, and manage human capital and knowledge resources more strategically and sustainably (Ganguli, 2016). The GCC states have historically faced critical challenges related to the formation and management of knowledge: the shortage of national skills and knowledge resources, the continued need for investments in these resources, and the reliance on a large number of foreign workers and firms to fill the national skill-knowledge gap and to shoulder the implementation of ambitious economic development goals. The region could afford this partly due to abundant financial resources, improved working and living conditions, and greater integration into the global economy (Al-Musali et al., 2019).

However, conditions have changed regarding shrinking budgetary allocations to significant expansion projects and human resource development, departure of talent from many sectors, and the quest for local workforce nationalization and employment opportunities. This highlighted the limitations of previous organization and management development approaches adopted by public and private sectors in the GCC region. These new conditions raise many questions about how knowledge—in its different forms and sources—is captured, organized, stored, disseminated, and used to achieve strategic developmental goals. As illustrated in the UNDP Arab Knowledge Development Report (2022), knowledge is a pivotal lever in the service of growth and development. Hence, effective knowledge management is a necessary vehicle for realizing and maximizing the potential of knowledge for sustainable performance for work organizations and society at large.

The discovery of oil and accumulation of abundant revenues dramatically changed the shape of GCC states and demanded urgent employment of foreign employees to run important institutions and organizations in these countries. Since the late 1980s, the UAE and other Gulf states, in general, have embarked on an unprecedented wave of constructing modern states, building state-of-art infrastructure, and attracting foreign financial institutions to have branches in these countries. Nevertheless, since GCC states lack sufficient local human capital with the necessary skills to run these institutions, they have heavily relied on the expertise and knowledge of foreign consultants, experts, and advisors (Alsaadi et al., 2018; 2019). The main challenge from this over-reliance on foreigners to run local businesses is that they take the experience and knowledge they have created and utilized while performing their jobs once they leave the country. Thus, their institutions lose significant knowledge and experience that could have been stored, documented, and made available for everybody to use within the organization. Accordingly, implementing knowledge management has become an inevitable necessity for these countries, especially after the advent of the global financial crisis and the mobility or even permanent departure of significant numbers of skilled employees.

Summary of this book's chapters

This book is divided into three parts. In Part One which explores the quality of government and public sector, Chapter Two explores the quality of government and the current state of public management in the GCC states which are benchmarked against the performance of other Middle East and North Africa (MENA) countries in key governance and public management indicators. The chapter finds mixed results regarding the performance of GCC and MENA countries in key governance and public management indicators. GCC states have ranked higher than the world median in performance indicators relating to government effectiveness, human development index, and other indicators demonstrating an effective and friendly business environment within GCC states. The chapter also shows that MENA countries differ markedly in their capacity to deliver public services efficiently. Furthermore, some Gulf states—such as Bahrain, Qatar, and the UAE—offer a sound regulatory environment for the private sector, and have managed to control corruption and enforce the rule of law more than their GCC and MENA counterparts. Nonetheless, this chapter argues that four main challenges hinder the governance and administrative capacity in MENA countries. This chapter offers four recommendations that would address these challenges.

Chapter Three demonstrates that effective state-business relations can support the Saudi government's efforts to implement the goals and objectives of Vision 2030. The chapter shows how effective state-business relations can significantly enhance economic growth and industrial development within Saudi Arabia. By extracting lessons from the experiences of

Chile, Korea, Malaysia, Ireland, Poland, Turkey, and the UAE, the chapter discusses what Saudi Arabia can learn from these benchmark countries to gradually transform itself into an industry-based economy in line with the objectives of its Vision 2030. Four main aspects of effective state-business relations are focused on: 1) the importance of bureaucratic institutions in developing effective economic policies, 2) the role of public-private dialogue through business and peak associations in supporting economic policymaking on the one hand, and voicing the interests and needs of the private sector to the government on the other, 3) ways in which the government can guide industrial planning based on cooperation and dialogue with the private sector, and 4) how a favorable business environment can facilitate economic and industrial growth and attract foreign direct investment (FDI).

Chapter Four's central argument is that, despite numerous anti-corruption institutions and legislation and anti-corruption strategies in all the GCC states, the outcomes of these states' efforts to curb corruption in the public sector differ considerably. Qatar and the UAE rank higher than their GCC counterparts in government and institutional effectiveness, boasting annually improving rankings in the most popular corruption indices. However, the rest of the GCC states still struggle to enhance their global images as corruption-free and investment-friendly environments. The chapter discusses some strategies existing literature considers important to curb corruption, particularly in the public sector. It illustrates the current state of corruption within the government sector of the six GCC states, and it demonstrates the uneven performance of these states in curbing corruption. The data is based on well-established and globally trusted indices that reflect regulatory and business environments, such as the World Bank Worldwide Governance Indicators, Transparency International's Corruption Perception Index, and the World Economic Forum's index. The chapter presents the various mechanisms each GCC state adopted to address and combat corruption in the public sector. These include enacting legislation and anti-corruption laws, establishing various anti-corruption agencies, formulating national anti-corruption strategies, and forming regional networks and collaborations to share best practices in controlling corruption.

In Part Two, which sheds light on the importance of strengthening partnerships between the public and private sectors, Chapter Five examines the prospect of using infrastructure public-private partnerships (PPPs) within Kuwait, Saudi Arabia, and Qatar, considering the fluctuating oil prices of their economies. It is argued that, while PPPs appear to be a strategic policy option for the three GCC states to tackle growing fiscal deficits, these states are constrained by numerous governance-related, administrative, and regulatory challenges that make PPPs problematic. Effective implementation of the inherently complex and contractual PPP policy requires addressing the existing institutional, economic, bureaucratic, and cultural constraints within the three states. The chapter recommends mitigating these challenges, which will require serious political will and sufficient time to yield positive results, and attract international investors and contractors to the Gulf region.

Chapter Six explores Saudi Arabia's ambition to embark upon a transformative economic journey under the umbrella of its Vision 2030 and National Transformation Plan. The Saudi government plans to implement various initiatives to engage the private sector in meeting new national development goals, including the provision of 1,600 schools through the PPP route. This chapter provides an international outlook and review of the use of PPPs to deliver school infrastructure and analyzes Saudi Arabia's potential to implement this promising program. Effective use of the PPP model can support the timely provision of schools and other infrastructure projects that could fulfill the vision of Saudi Arabia's political leadership, potentially serving as a catalyst and blueprint for other Gulf states. The chapter argues that, while Saudi Arabia's schools' program enjoys significant political support, its government must simultaneously pursue the parallel objective of developing the necessary institutional, legal, regulatory, and supervisory frameworks that are essential for successful PPP projects globally. The chapter concludes with a set of recommendations aiming to mitigate existing challenges and foster the involvement of the private sector in education sector development.

In Part Three, which addresses the human capital challenges within the GCC region, Chapter Seven shows that despite the growing literature on the challenges and opportunities that talent management offers public and private organizations globally, the GCC states and the MENA region have not attracted ample attention from researchers. This chapter addresses the paucity of research on talent management in these regions and provides insights and strategic recommendations for tackling this important subject. It examines the challenges GCC and MENA countries face in maximizing talent management. This chapter sheds light on the dichotomy that exists between the topic of talent management in a global setting and that in the GCC and MENA regions. Various socioeconomic and educational factors hinder not only the management of talent, but also its formation, preparation for the market, and development.

Chapter Eight is based on comprehensive fieldwork that assesses the effectiveness of training programs in the public sector of Dubai in the UAE, and their impact on the sector's overall performance. The role of public sector organization leadership in Dubai is crucial as they can secure necessary training budgets and be directly involved in the building and implementation stages of a training strategy. Moreover, the chapter analyses the methods and measures implemented to ensure effective training strategy implementation and assesses staff involvement in exercises to evaluate training needs. The chapter also examines the factors and elements that Dubai public sector entities relied upon to design such training strategies, and elucidates how the government has achieved successful training that positively impacts its output and effectiveness. The chapter concludes with specific recommendations for human resources and training directors in the Dubai government.

Chapter Nive covers three topics in exploring knowledge management in the public sector. First, it highlights the importance of creating, capturing, documenting, and disseminating knowledge within public organizations. Second, it assesses the extent to which Dubai's public sector relies on flexible and fixed-term employees and the policy measures adopted to protect and document their knowledge in the UAE. Since knowledge management is a protective mechanism that prevents loss of employee knowledge and knowhow, the chapter evaluates the techniques used for obtaining, capturing, and storing staff knowledge and how this affects the current state of knowledge management in Dubai's public sector, as well as its overall outcomes. Third, it presents the factors influencing the implementation of knowledge management within public organizations. Specifically, the chapter assesses the clarity of the knowledge management concept among Dubai's public sector entities, their ability to capture and store knowledge, and the rationales and expected benefits of knowledge management program implementation. A set of recommendations are then addressed to policymakers and heads of knowledge management departments in Dubai, the UAE, and the entire region. This study can offer numerous lessons to guide future initiatives or programs. The study confirms that it is in the UAE's best interests, particularly Dubai's governmental entities, to focus on knowledge development and management.

Chapter Ten concludes the book and provides a set of policy prescriptions that can potentially facilitate the implementation of public management reforms in the GCC. Furthermore, the chapter offers solutions that can address the institutional and human capital challenges that constrain the region's efforts to transform their economies from over-reliance on revenues from oil and gas exports to creating vibrant hubs that encourage FDIs.

References

Akçay, S. (2006). Corruption and human development. *The Cato Journal*, 26(1), 29–48.

Al Ariss, A., Cascio, W., & Paauwe, J. (2014). Talent management: Current theories and future research directions. *Journal of World Business*, 49(2), 173–179.

Al-Musali, M., Qeshta, M., Al-Attafi, M., & Al-Ebel, A. (2019). Ownership structure and audit committee effectiveness: Evidence from top GCC capitalized firms. *International Journal of Islamic and Middle Eastern Finance and Management*, 12(3), 407–425.

Alsaadi, M., Ahmad, S., & Hussain, M. (2018). A quality function deployment strategy for improving mobile-government service quality in the Gulf cooperation council countries, *Benchmarking: An International Journal*, 25(8), 3276–3295.

Alsaadi, M., Ahmad, S., & Hussain, M. (2019). Improving the quality of mobile government services in the Gulf Cooperation Council: A quality-function-deployment approach. *Journal of Systems and Information Technology*, 21(1), 146–164.

Black, J., & Upchurch, M. (1999). Public Sector Employment in G. Hollinshead, P. Nicholls, and S. Tailby (eds.), *Employee Relations*, Financial Times Management, London.

Boston, J. (1994). Purchasing policy advice: The limits to contracting out. *Governance*, 7(1), 1–30.

Bouckaert, G., & Peters, B. (2002). Performance measurement and management: The Achilles' heel in administrative modernization. *Public Performance & Management Review*, 25(4), 359–362.

Broadbent, J., & Laughlin, R. (2003). Control and legitimation in government accountability processes: The private finance initiative in the UK. *Critical Perspectives on Accounting*, 14(1–2), 23–48.

Brown, K. (2004). Human resource management in the public sector. *Public Management Review*, 6(3), 303–309.

Brown, K., & Ryan, N. (2003). Redefining government–community relations through service agreements. *Journal of Contemporary Issues in Business and Government*, 9(1), 21–30.

Chong, A., & Gradstein, M. (2007). Inequality and institutions. *The Review of Economics and Statistics*, 89(3), 454–465.

Chong, A., & Calderón, C. (2000). Institutional quality and income distribution. *Economic Development and Cultural Change*, 48(4), 761–786.

Christensen, T., & Lægreid, P. (2008). NPM and beyond — structure, culture and demography. *International Review of Administrative Sciences*, 74(1), 7–23.

Clarke, J., & Newman, J. (1997). *The Managerial State: Power, Politics and Ideology in the Remaking of Social Welfare*. Sage, London.

Clarke, M., & Scurry, T. (2017). The role of the psychological contract in shaping graduate experiences: A study of public sector talent management programmes in the UK and australia. *The International Journal of Human Resource Management*, 29(13), 2054–2079.

Costa, A. (2008). Rule of law: A (missing) Millennium Development Goal that can help reach the other MDGs, United Nations Commission on Crime Prevention and Criminal Justice, 17th Sess., Vienna. Retrieved from: www.unodc.org/unodc/en/about-unodc/speeches/2008-04-14.html Accessed on 26 November 2021

Creelman, D. (2004). Return on investment in talent management: Measures you can put to work right now, Human Capital Institute, Washington, DC.

Crowley-Henry, M., & Al Ariss, A. (2016). Talent management of skilled migrants: Propositions and an agenda for future research. *The International Journal of Human Resource Management*, 29(13), 2054–2079.

Darvish, H., Zou, P., Loosemore, M., & Zhang, G. (2006). Risk management, public interests and value for money in PPP projects: Literature review and case studies. *The CRIOCM International Symposium on Advancement of Construction Management and Real Estate*.

Deininger, K., & Mpuga, P. (2005). Does greater accountability improve the quality of public service delivery? Evidence from Uganda. *World Development*, 33, 171–191.

Diamond, L. (2007). A quarter-century of promoting democracy. *Journal of Democracy*, 18(4), 118–120.

Dougherty, G., & Van Gelder, M. (2015). Public agency hiring, minimum qualifications, and experience. *Review of Public Personnel Administration*, 35(2), 169–192.

Dunleavy, P., & Hood, C. (1994). From old public administration to new public management. *Public Money & Management*, 14(3), 9–16.

Dunleavy, P., Margetts, H., Tinkler, J., & Bastow, S. (2006). *Digital Era Governance: IT Corporations, the State, and E-Government*. Oxford University Press, New York.

Economist. (2008). Economics and the rule of law: order in the jungle. Retrieved from: www.economist.com/briefing/2008/03/13/order-in-the-jungle Accessed on 28 November 2021.

English, L. (2006). Public private partnerships in Australia: An overview of their nature, purpose, incidence and oversight. *UNSW Law Journal*, 29(3), 250–262.

Fryer, K., Antony, J., & Ogden, S. (2009). Performance management in the public sector. *International Journal of Public Sector Management*, 6, 478–498.

Ganguli, S. (2016). An economic analysis of sustainability of a potential GCC economic and monetary union during 2005–2014. *World Journal of Entrepreneurship, Management and Sustainable Development*, 12(3), 194–206.

Garrow, V., & Hirsh, W. (2008). Talent management: Issues of focus and fit. *Public Personnel Management*, 37(4), 389–402.

Goldsmith, A. (2007). Is governance reform a catalyst for development? *Governance*, 20, 165–186.

Grimsey, D., & Lewis, M. (2000). Evaluating the risks of public private partnerships for infrastructure projects. *International Journal of Project and Management*, 20, 107–118.

Grindle, M. (2004). Good enough governance: Poverty reduction and reform in developing countries. *Governance*, 17, 525–548.

Gunn, L. (1987). Perspectives on public management in J. Kjell and A. Eliassen (eds.), *Managing Public Organizations*, Sage, London.

Gupta, S., Davoodi, H., & Tiongson, E. (2000). Corruption and the provision of health care and education services. International Monetary Fund, Washington, DC.

Holmberg, S., Rothstein, R., & Nasiritousi, N. (2009). Quality of government: What you get. *The Annual Review of Political Science*, 12, 135–161.

Hudson, P. (2017). Public sector talent management: The influence of the private sector. Retrieved from: https://pl.hudson.com/Portals/PL/documents/cee-articles-influence-of-private-on-publicsector-article.pdf Accessed on 6 September 2022.

Hughes, O. (2017). Public management: 30 years on. *International Journal of Public Sector Management*, 30(6–7), 547–554.

Kaufmann, D., Kraay, A., & Zoido-Lobaton, P. (1999). Governance matters, World Bank Policy Res. Work. Pap. 2196, Washington, DC.

Keating, M. (2001). Public management reform and economic and social development. *OECD Journal on Budgeting*, 1(2), 141–212.

Khan, M. (1996). The efficiency implications of corruption. *Journal of International Development*, 8, 683–696.

Khan, M. (1998). Patron-client networks and the economic effects of corruption in Asia. *European Journal of Development*, 10, 15–39.

Kock, R., & Burke, M. (2008). Managing talent in the South African Public Service. *Public Personnel Management*, 37(4), 457–470.

König, K. (1996). *On the Critique of New Public Management*, Speyer, Forschungsberichte.

Kravariti, F., & Johnston, K. (2020). Talent management: A critical literature review and research agenda for public sector human resource management. *Public Management Review*, 22(1), 75–95.

Krishna, A. (2007). Poverty and health: Defeating poverty by going to the roots. *Development*, 50, 63–69.

Kurer, O. (2005). Corruption: An alternative approach to its definition and measurement. *Political Studies*, 53(1), 222–239.

Lapuente, V., & Van de Walle, S. (2020). The effects of new public management on the quality of public services. *Governance*, 33(3), 461–475.

Li, H., Squire, L., & Zou, H. (1998). Explaining international and intertemporal variations in income inequality. *Economic Journal*, 108, 26–43.

Lodge, M., & Gill, D. (2011). Toward a new era of administrative reform? The myth of post-NPM in New Zealand. *Governance*, 24(1), 141–166.

Lukea, S., & Garavan, T. (2016). The empowering of public sector officers in the Mauritian public sector in the context of reforms: How far has management education helped? *European Journal of Training and Development*, 40(4), 262–283.

Mauro, P. (1995). Corruption and growth. *The Quarterly Journal of Economics*, 110, 681–712.

McMillan, J., & Zoido, P. (2004). How to subvert democracy: Montesinos in Peru. *Journal of Economic Perspectives*, 18, 69–92.

Melo, A., & Mota, L. (2020). Public sector reform and the state of performance management in Portugal: is there a gap between performance measurement and its use? *International Journal of Public Sector Management*, 33(6/7), 613–627.

Messick, R. (1999). Judicial reform and economic development: A survey of the issues. *World Bank Research Observer*, 14(1), 117–136.

Metcalfe, L., & Richards, S. (1987). Evolving public management cultures. *Managing Public Organizations*, Sage, London.

Meyers, M., & Van Woerkom, M. (2014). The influence of underlying philosophies on talent management: Theory, implications for practice, and research agenda. *Journal of World Business*, 49(2), 192–203.

Miller, G. (2000). Above politics: Credible commitment and efficiency in the design of public agencies. *Journal of Public Administration Research and Theory*, 10(2), 289–328.

NSW Office of Financial Management. (2002). Private provision of public infrastructure and services.

Nye, J. (1967). Corruption and political development: A cost-benefit analysis. *The American Political Science Review*, 61, 417–427.

Perry, J., & Kraemer, K. (Eds.). (1983). *Public Management: Public and Private Perspectives*, Mayfield Publishing Company, Palo Alto, Calif.

Pierre, J. (1995). *Bureaucracy in the Modern State: An Introduction to Comparative Public Administration*. Edward Elgar Publishing, Cheltenham.

Pollitt, C. (1990). *Managerialism and the Public Services: The Anglo-American Experience*. Blackwell, Oxford.

Pollitt, C. (2018). A review of public sector reform. *Public Sciences & Policies*, 4(1), 17–32.

Pollitt, C., & Bouckaert, G. (2004). *Public Management Reform: A Comparative Analysis-Into the Age of Austerity*. Oxford University Press, New York.

Quinn, M., & Warren, L. (2017). New public management a re-packaging of extant techniques? Some archival evidence from an Irish semi-state power company. *Qualitative Research in Accounting & Management*, 14(4), 407–429.

Rana, G., Goer, A., & Rastogi, R. (2013). Talent management: A paradigm shift in indian public sector. *Strategic HR Review*, 12(4), 197–202.

Rigg, C. (2015). Managing talented employees, in R. Carbery and C. Cross (eds.), *Human Resource Development: A Concise Introduction*, Palgrave, London, pp. 197–211.

Rotberg, R. (2007). On improving nation-state governance. *Dædalus*, 136(1), 151–155.

Rothstein, B., & Teorell, J. (2012). Defining and measuring quality of government', in Sören Holmberg and Bo Rothstein (eds.), *Good Government: The Relevance of Political Science*, Edward Elgar Publisher, Cheltenham, pp. 13–27.

Serra, N., & Stiglitz, J. (2008). *The Washington Consensus Reconsidered: Towards a New Global Governance*, Oxford University Press, Oxford.

Shaw, R. (2012). New public management in australia: Past, present and future. *Pouvoirs*, 141(2), 117–132.

Shim, D. (2001). Recent human resources developments in OECD member countries. *Public Personnel Management*, 30(3), 323–347.

Teicher, J., Alam, Q., & Gramberg, V. (2006). Managing trust and relationships: Some Australian experiences. *International Review of Administrative Sciences*, 72 (1), 85–100.

Thunnissen, M., & Buttiens, D. (2017). Talent management in public sector organizations: A study on the impact of contextual factors on the TM approach in flemish and dutch public sector organizations. *Public Personnel Management*, 46(2), 391–418.

Transparency International. (2008). Poverty and corruption. Working paper #02. Retrieved from: www.transparency.org/en/publications/working-paper-02-2008-poverty-and-corruption Accessed on 27 November 2021.

UNDP. (2002). Human development report 2002: Deepening democracy in a fragmented world. Retrieved from: http://hdr.undp.org/en/content/human-development-report-2002 Accessed on 26 November 2021.

UNDP Arab Knowledge Development Report. (2022). Middle East and North Africa: addressing highest rates of youth unemployment in the world. Retrieved from: https://news.un.org/en/story/2022/05/1118842 Accessed on 10 July 2022.

Uslaner, E. (2008). *Corruption, Inequality, and the Rule of Law: The Bulging Pocket Makes the Easy Life*, Cambridge University Press, Cambridge.

Van den Brink, M., & Fruytier, B. (2013). Talent management in academia: Performance systems and HRM practices. *Human Resource Management Journal*, 23(2), 180–195.

Waheduzzaman, W. (2019). Challenges in transitioning from new public management to new public governance in a developing country context. *International Journal of Public Sector Management*, 32(7), 689–705.

Webb, R., & Pulle, B. (2002). Public private partnerships: An introduction. Department of the Parliamentary Library.

Part I
Quality of government and the public sector in the GCC region

2 Assessing the quality of government, governance, and public service delivery in GCC states
MENA comparisons and lessons

Introduction

This chapter explores the quality of government and the current state of public management in the Gulf Cooperation Council (GCC) states as benchmarked against the performance of other countries within the Middle East and North Africa (MENA) region in terms of key governance and public management indicators to reveal a diverse range of results. It shows that GCC countries have ranked above the world median in performance indicators relating to government effectiveness, the Human Development Index (HDI), and other indicators demonstrating an effective and business-friendly environment within GCC countries. In contrast, other MENA countries differ markedly in their capacity to deliver public services efficiently. Furthermore, some Gulf countries, such as the United Arab Emirates (UAE), Qatar, and Bahrain, offer a sound regulatory environment for the private sector and have managed to control corruption and enforce the rule of law more than their GCC and MENA counterparts. Nevertheless, the chapter argues that four main challenges are hindering these countries' governance and administrative capacity, and offers four recommendations to address them. The four challenges are as follows.

First, most GCC and MENA countries have scored poorly in good governance measures, particularly the voice and accountability indicator. Because it hinders administrative reforms and blocks initiatives aiming to modernize the public sector and introduce purposeful managerial reforms, addressing the region's lack of sufficient accountability measures is essential. Moreover, several studies indicate that corruption and lack of political accountability are interlinked, thus further stymying any efforts in this regard by GCC and MENA governments or international organizations supporting administrative reform such as the Organisation for Economic Co-operation and Development (OECD), the World Bank, or the United Nations Development Programme (UNDP) (Barsoum, 2018; Bhuiyan & Farazmand, 2019). The weak role of political accountability in the region can only be tackled by strong political leadership that implements grassroots reforms to tackle corruption, waste of government resources, and nepotism (Dixon et al., 2018).

DOI: 10.4324/9781003267744-3

Second, corruption and lack of transparency in procuring government contracts within the MENA region can be tackled by introducing rigorous budgetary reforms and implementing initiatives that combat the exploitation of public budgets. There are various features of an efficient budget and numerous ways GCC and MENA governments can implement them. Performance budgeting (Kong, 2005), for example, is a results-driven, cost-effective system of budgeting that links sources used for a particular project to the results and outputs derived from it (Carlin & Guthrie, 2003; OECD, 2008). It also presents the purposes and objectives for which funds are required and the total costs of programs, allows flexible use of fiscal resources, shifts the focus from input to results, and monitors whether such results are achieved (Shah & Shen, 2007).

Third, apart from a handful of GCC states, such as Bahrain, Qatar, and the UAE, most MENA countries' bureaucracies are sluggish, lack meaningful performance indicators, and seem content to merely absorb unemployed youth rather than produce efficient public services. In contrast, some GCC states have developed effective bureaucratic structures that enable a business-friendly environment, particularly in registering a business or offering attractively low tax thresholds for startups. Furthermore, Gulf countries surpass the rest of the MENA region and the world median with their quality of infrastructure and investment in creating a favorable business environment. Meanwhile, other MENA countries straggle behind the rest of the world and lack the rudimentary regulatory and institutional capacity to establish proper institutional frameworks and attract foreign investment (Jreisat, 2018).

Fourth, and finally, aside from a handful of Gulf states, most MENA countries rank considerably below the rest of the world in their innovation indices, since they do not invest in research and development (R&D) nor create collaborations and synergies among universities and the public and private sectors. In this regard, transitioning from the traditional form of public administration to a managerial one requires managers with the relevant educational backgrounds, skills, and training to be innovative. This will only be possible if GCC and MENA governments increase their spending on R&D.

In exploring these challenges and offering recommendations to address them, this chapter is structured as follows. The next section provides a theoretical analysis of the evolution of the traditional form of public administration and how several factors have led to the emergence of the public management model. Following that, the current state of government and good governance in the Arab world is evaluated, and government efficiency, public sector spending, and other measures of accountability, as well as the regulatory environment, corruption, and the rule of law, are analyzed. The following section identifies the characteristics of business environments in the Arab world, especially in terms of ease of doing business and efficiency of infrastructure. The chapter then examines the barriers that lower the capacity of GCC and MENA countries to drive innovation forward, such as lack of R&D and insufficient investment in talent. Finally, the chapter offers four recommendations that the GCC and MENA governments should adopt when addressing the challenges associated with their efforts to introduce wider public management reforms.

Shifting from public administration to public management models

This section briefly discusses the differences between the traditional model of public administration and the new public management (NPM) reforms that emerged in the UK during the 1980s. It discusses why and how these administrative models have evolved and sheds light on the key theoretical and practical differences between the traditional public administration and management models.

The traditional model of public administration was effective from the early 19th century until the end of the 1970s, when economic, political, and social changes proved that this administrative form could no longer offer effective and efficient public services (Bougan, 2008). More specifically, hierarchal bureaucratic systems in the 1970s were criticized for producing "staff who is corrupt, unreliable, incompetent, inefficient, lazy, rigid and unresponsive" (Olsen, 2005, p. 6). The monopolistic structure of public service, absence of valid indicators of organizational performance, the large size of many government agencies, and the costs of running such organizations all weighed heavily upon the public sector and instigated a call for change across the entire system of government administration (Boyne, 1998; Mascarenhas, 1993). It was clear that there was a pressing need to improve transparency, enhance staff responsiveness, and move away from a "one size fits all approach" (Sedgwick, 1994). In sum, the traditional public administration model no longer corresponded with the rapidly changing global economy and the budgetary and public pressures facing the world's governments (Hood, 1991).

The 1970s were thus witness to an era of economic challenges that required a new administrative model (Farazmand, 2001b). Global economic recessions in that decade and the 1980s coincided with the prevailing perception that public services were ineffective in meeting the needs of the people, as governments were dominated by bureaucrats and had become inflexible and unresponsive (Johnsen, 2005). Caiden (1991) summarizes this situation, stating that "the inherited administrative systems were proving to be sluggish, inflexible and insensitive to changing human needs and novel circumstances" (p. 1). Furthermore, both developed and developing countries faced considerable budgetary pressures during the 1970s and 1980s due to economic crises emanating from Asia, Europe, and North America, all calling into question the effectiveness of outdated administrative systems and their capacity to cope with challenging global economic realities (Farazmand, 2001a). At the same time, such large administrative systems became a significant budgetary burden on governments, which began formulating ways to restructure and downsize their public sectors to reduce costs.

These financial and performance-related challenges paved the way for the emergence of a wide range of administrative reforms under the label of NPM that aimed to tackle the new challenges of the 20th century and achieve higher levels of efficiency in service delivery and greater responsiveness to public needs (De Laine, 1997; Johnsen, 2005). To help resuscitate a declining global economy and reform government bureaucracies for greater efficiency, the emergence of NPM was essential (Eklund, 2008; Orchad, 1998). Table 2.1 illustrates the key differences between the traditional public administration and public management models. Proponents of the public management model propose the adoption of market-like practices that can introduce competition in the provision of public services by, for example, privatizing public entities, outsourcing public services to the private sector, and creating synergies between the public and private sectors via public-private partnerships (PPPs) (Osborne, 2006). The hierarchical command and control paradigms of traditional public administration ought to be replaced by new forms of management that emphasize outcomes rather than processes and focus on total quality management, team building, motivation, performance measurement, and accountability (Hughes, 2002a; Jreisat, 2004; Mulgan, 2000).

From a practical perspective, the differences between public administration and management are numerous. The bureaucratic system produced an inefficient administration model characterized by rigid hierarchy, the limited potential of public servants, unresponsiveness to public needs, high costs, and bureaucrats for life who abused their powers to cause numerous financial and social problems as a result of policies they implemented. Public management, meanwhile, promised greater efficiency in managing public resources, a focus on outcomes and results rather than processes, and encouraged the privatization of unproductive state-owned companies (Halligan, 2004). Furthermore, the traditional model of public administration suffered from a lack of long-term planning, as the role of administrators was simply to carry out bureaucratically specified roles and abide by them. In contrast, the public management paradigm introduced new mechanisms adopted from business environments to enhance the public sector's effectiveness and efficiency (Halligan, 2007), including the introduction of strategic and performance-oriented planning that enabled public managers to break bureaucratic rules and become innovative in delivering public services (Osborne, 2006).

The introduction of NPM meant that the role of government had shifted from its traditional role as caretaker of its citizens to acting as a facilitator to promote market capitalism and monitor public service delivery (Hughes, 2002a). NPM practices also changed the roles of public administrators from bureaucrats performing specific duties within a rigid hierarchical system to managers attempting to do more with less by innovatively adopting and applying market and managerial practices to the public sector. This radically altered the previous role of government from a provider of essential services equitably and affordably to its citizens to a regulator that monitors

Table 2.1 Differences in theory and practice of public administration and public management

	Public Administration	*Public Management*
Theory	• Bureaucracy. • Rational/legal authority = rigid adherence to rules. • Strict system of hierarchy. • Exam scores as criteria for appointment of officials/ appointment for life. • Political control / strict separation of politics and administration. • Scientific management: "One best way of Working". • Main focus on processes and obeying the rules among administrators. • Short-term goals within the organization. • Government monopoly on service provision.	• Market principles= competition = prices = choice. • Economic rationality / public choice theory. • Manager appointment based on training and experience = the best person in the best position / appointment by contract. • Close relationship between politicians and public managers. • Managers are free to adopt the strategies they think would generate better outcomes. • Main focus on results / managers must perform in a progressive way to keep their jobs. • Long-term goals and relationship between the organization and external environment. • Government reliance on the private sector to deliver services / increase contracting.
Practice	• Bureaucracy = conflicts with democracy / breeding of timeservers rather than innovators. • Adherence to rules more important than achieving results. • Hierarchy imposes more costs than benefits and preventing creativity and innovation • Appointment for life leading to unproductivity. • Inefficiency / no incentive to perform better. • Public servants only follow rules and manuals (processes) rather than solving problems and achieving results. • Poor relationship with the public leads to unresponsiveness to their needs and ultimately their dissatisfaction.	• Managers focusing on achieving progressive performance and results by being innovative and productive for long-term outcomes • Reliance on private services to deliver services by increasing competition, lowering costs, and offering more choice to the public. • Ministers directing and controlling their departments more effectively / public officers enjoying more flexibility • Substantial reduction in staffing/ reduction of federal government departments = less public spending • Strategies to measure performance and progress in the public sector • Stronger relationship with the public = more responsive government.

Sources: Adapted from Hughes (2003); Sedgwick (1994); Gregory (1998); Kastbeg and Siverbo (2008); Stewart (1993); Mulgan (1998; 2002)

the delivery of public services via the private sector. (Farazmand, 1999; Halligan, 2008).

The current state of government and good governance in the GCC and MENA regions

This section illustrates the current state of government and good governance practices across the countries of the GCC and MENA regions. Measures of government and good governance practices are benchmarked against those from OECD countries and the average rates of MENA countries. The section begins by defining governance and highlighting the importance of good governance practices to boost business and investment environments within the MENA region. It then measures how various GCC and MENA countries perform in terms of government performance indicators, such as government effectiveness, inefficient government bureaucracy, the expense of the public sector, wage bill as a percentage of public expenditure, wage bill as a percentage of Gross Domestic Product (GDP), and HDI, as well as the global rankings of GCC and MENA countries for HDI, regulatory quality, control of corruption, Corruption Perceptions Index, voice and accountability, political stability, absence of violence, and the rule of law.

Importance of good governance for administrative reforms

This chapter adopts the World Bank's definition of good governance as a country's capacity to offer "efficient, independent, accountable and open public service" (Leftwich, 1993, p. 371). The first official appearance of "good governance" was in the 1989 World Bank Report on Africa, which articulates that "underlying the litany of Africa's development problems is a crisis of governance" (World Bank, 1989, p. 60). Development agencies like the World Bank and the International Monetary Fund (IMF) soon realized that, despite the provision of financial aid, loans, and advice on how to design and implement sound economic policies, structural adjustment programs were failing to reduce poverty or improve economic conditions, particularly in Africa. The agencies realized that "bad governance" was behind the constant failure of such reform efforts (Ardouille, 2000). As Goldsmith (2007) puts it, "civic institutions that lack transparency, accountability, and inclusiveness generate perverse incentives that are said to hold down economic growth and perpetuate poverty" (p. 165).

Therefore, the emphasis shifted from the direct provision of financial aid to reforming administrative structures among the institutions that managed those aid programs. In 2007, the World Bank provided a more refined definition of good governance practices (Crowley & Coffey, 2007), describing them as the traditions and institutions by which authority in a country is exercised. This includes how fairly the government is selected, its capability to independently make and implement policies that serve its

Quality of government, governance, and public service delivery 35

public, and the respect of citizens and the state for the institutions that regulate economic and social affairs (Barrett, 2003).

The current state of government in the GCC and MENA regions

This section analyzes the performance of MENA countries across a broad range of government and governance indicators. How effectively public management reforms have been adopted can be reflected in higher rankings in government effectiveness and other indicators measuring the performance of the public sector. In contrast, lower rankings can indicate the dominance of the models and systems of traditional public administration that shackle the innovation and effectiveness of service delivery (Schomaker & Bauer, 2019).

An important indicator that assesses the quality of public service and policy formulation and implementation, as well as the government's commitment to attending to public needs, is the government effectiveness indicator, and Figure 2.1 demonstrates how the GCC and other MENA governments differ markedly in this regard. The UAE scored the highest in government effectiveness at 90% in 2018, having achieved considerable progress since its score of 83% in 2008. Its current ranking is double that of the average MENA ranking, and comes close to the average OECD country ranking of 92%. Saudi Arabia also improved this indicator by scoring 65% in 2018 compared to 58% in 2008. Meanwhile, other GCC countries experienced a decline in this indicator, including Kuwait, which dropped from 52% to 49%, and Qatar, which fell from 81% to 74%. Nevertheless, these numbers are still far higher than other MENA countries such as

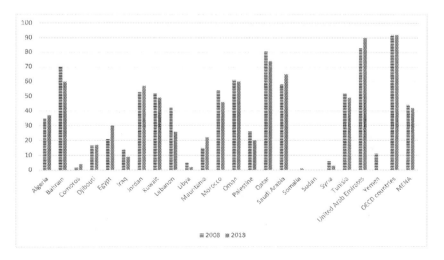

Figure 2.1 Government effectiveness
Source: *World Bank Data Bank (2019)*

Egypt, Algeria, and Mauritania, which in 2018 hovered below the MENA average at 30%, 37%, and 22%, respectively. Meanwhile, war-torn countries such as Syria, Libya, and Yemen stood far below the MENA and OECD averages, scoring 3%, 2% and 0%, respectively, in 2018.

Another indicator measuring government quality is the inefficient government bureaucracy index, which examines how excessive bureaucracy, lack of transparency, and legal frameworks can affect a country's business environment, with higher percentages indicating greater inefficacy. As shown in Figure 2.2, Kuwait scored 21.7% in 2017 compared to 24.7% in 2008, but this score still renders it the most inefficient government bureaucracy within the entire MENA region. Most GCC governments also managed to improve their performance in this indicator between 2008 and 2017 and overall scored much lower, such as Saudi Arabia, which ranked 13% in 2008 but improved in 2017 with 7%. Qatar also enhanced its performance by scoring 7.7% in 2017 compared to 10.8% in 2008. Meanwhile, Bahrain slightly improved its performance by dropping from a score of 13.8% in 2008 to 12.9% in 2017. The UAE maintained a relatively good index over the past ten years, scoring an average of 4% in 2017 compared to 5.6% in 2008, making it the most efficient government bureaucracy in the region. Nevertheless, Oman's performance in this indicator deteriorated, scoring 8.2% in 2008 but then ranking 13.4% in 2017.

Most MENA countries scored above the world median of 10.2% in 2018—a clear testament to the burden of inefficient government bureaucracy on their public sector performance. For example, Tunisia's inefficient

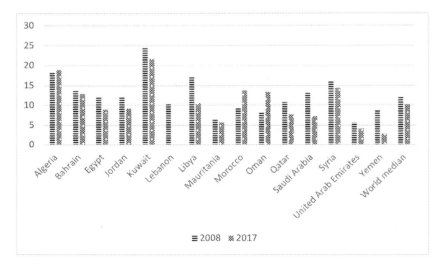

Figure 2.2 Inefficient government bureaucracy index *(0 = extremely efficient, 30 = extremely inefficient)
Source: *World Bank Data Bank (2019)*

Quality of government, governance, and public service delivery 37

government bureaucracy index spiked from 14.6% in 2008 to 18.1% in 2017. Similarly, Morocco's performance deteriorated from 9.2% in 2008 to 13.8% in 2017. Several other MENA countries, however, managed to slightly improve their scores, such as Egypt, which improved from 12% in 2008 to 9% in 2017, Jordan, which went from 12.1% to 9.2%, and Libya, which dropped from 17.1% to 10.6%.

The capacity of GCC and MENA governments to deliver efficient services is also reflected in the expenses of their public sectors as a percentage of GDP. As Figure 2.3 shows, the UAE managed to maintain a low level of public sector spending as a percentage of GDP since 1990 (between 4% and 6%), while Kuwait held the highest level at 43% in 1990. Since that time, however, Kuwait has followed a positive trajectory in lowering its spending on the public sector, which decreased considerably to 26% in 2018. Nonetheless, all MENA countries exceeded this indicator's world median of 22% in 2018. For example, Lebanon spent 52% of its GDP on public sector expenses—the highest rate in the Arab world—followed by Tunisia, which spent 35% of its GDP on public sector expenses, and then Egypt, which spent 30%. These rates are markedly higher than the world average. Morocco, meanwhile, is an example of a MENA country that experienced a steady but sharp increase in public sector expenses as a percentage of GDP, as it nearly doubled from 16% in 1990 to 30% in 2010

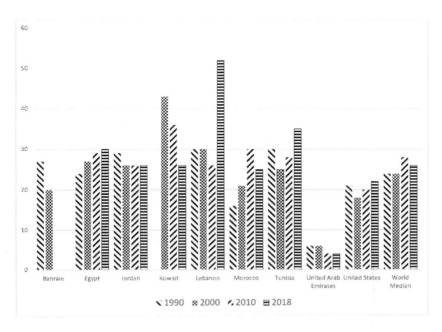

Figure 2.3 Public sector expenses (% of GDP)
Source: World Bank Data Bank (2019)

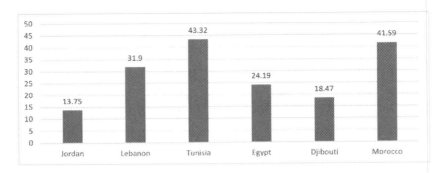

Figure 2.4 Wage bill as % of public expenditure in 2017
Source: *World Bank Data Bank (2019)*

despite efforts to curb public spending through its ultimately failed Early Retirement Program (El Massnaoui & Biygautane, 2021).

With the high interest in public sector employment among the MENA countries' young graduates as their largest employer of choice, the region's wage bill as a percentage of public expenditure is also among the highest in the world. Figure 2.4 shows that the wage bill represented 43% of all public expenditures in Tunisia in 2017, making it the highest, followed by Morocco (41%) and Lebanon (32%). Despite the World Bank's efforts to implement drastic economic and administrative reforms to decrease wage bills in the MENA region, the weak role of the private sector in generating job opportunities and absorbing unemployed youth has rendered such policies ineffective.

Furthermore, the impact of these high wage bills is reflected not only in their consumption of a significant portion of overall government public expenditures, but also in their exhaustion of a considerable amount of GDP. As illustrated in Figure 2.5, 12.65% of Morocco's GDP is dedicated to its wage bill, making it the highest country in the MENA region despite attempts by the Moroccan government to introduce an Early Retirement Program in 2005, which ultimately resulted in adverse outcomes costing the government its most talented employees while simultaneously failing to control government spending on the wage bill (El Massnaoui & Biygautane, 2021). The wage bill also consumed a significant portion of the GDP of Tunisia and Lebanon at 12.13% and 9.16%, respectively.

Nonetheless, despite their liberal government spending, MENA countries still trail behind the rest of the world in the HDI, which measures the capacity of a government to provide the necessary educational and health services to its citizens at an accessible price and acceptable level of quality. Figure 2.6 shows that, thanks to abundant oil and gas revenues, several Gulf countries scored above the Arab states' median of 0.70 and close to the OECD median of 0.89 in 2018. For example, the UAE scored 0.86 in

Quality of government, governance, and public service delivery 39

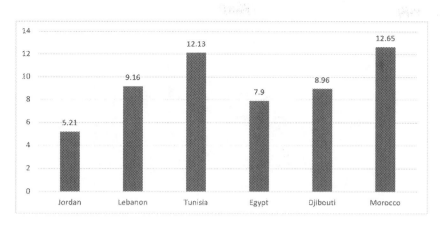

Figure 2.5 Wage bill as % of GDP in 2017
Source: *World Bank Data Bank (2019)*

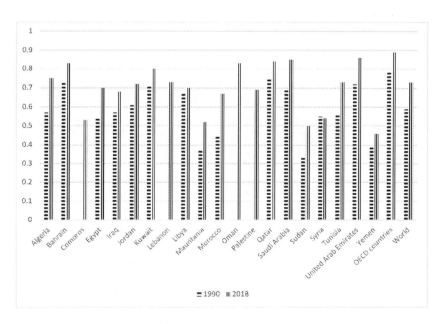

Figure 2.6 Human Development Index
Source: *World Bank Data Bank (2019)*

2018, while Saudi Arabia achieved 0.85 in the same year. Qatar scored 0.84, Bahrain and Oman ranked 0.83, and Kuwait achieved 0.80. In contrast, Morocco, Mauritania, Iraq, and Jordan stood below the world median of 0.73, with scores of 0.67, 0.52, 0.68, and 0.72, respectively. As may be

40 *Quality of government and the public sector in the GCC region*

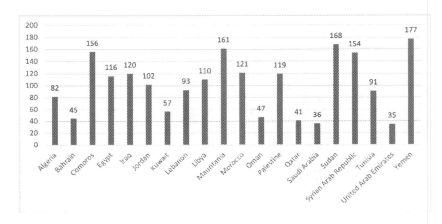

Figure 2.7 Global rankings of GCC and MENA countries in the Human Development Index in 2018 *(1= best, 177 = worst)
Source: World Bank Data Bank (2019)

expected, conflict-ridden countries, such as Yemen, Syria, and Sudan, scored far below the Arab states' average of 0.70, ranking at 0.46, 0.54, and 0.50, respectively.

Figure 2.7 illustrates the global ranking of GCC and MENA countries in the HDI. The UAE topped other MENA countries, ranking 35th globally in 2018, followed by Saudi Arabia, which ranked 36th. Meanwhile, all other Gulf countries were among the top 60, such as Qatar, which ranked 41st, Bahrain at 45th, and Kuwait at 57th. Other MENA countries, including Yemen, Sudan, Mauritania, and Morocco, ranked 177th, 168th, 161st, and 121st, respectively. Such low rankings demonstrate the vast gap between the GCC and other MENA countries in providing essential services to the public and the varying degrees of financial and administrative capacities of MENA countries to fulfill social obligations toward their citizens.

The current state of good governance in the GCC and MENA regions

One of the critical prerequisites for productive and successful administrative reforms is having sound governance mechanisms. When governments institutionalize the values of good governance and transparency and stress the importance of involving the public in policymaking, the task of introducing effective policies and reforms that can yield positive outcomes is facilitated. At the heart of good governance is the ability of governments to establish business-friendly regulatory frameworks. The World Bank's regulatory quality indicator assesses a country's ability to develop and implement regulatory functions that support and facilitate businesses and startups.

Quality of government, governance, and public service delivery 41

For this indicator, the UAE topped the GCC and MENA countries by having the most efficient regulatory environment, which has improved steadily over the past years. In 2008, the UAE's regulatory quality score was 75%, which improved by 5% in 2018, thus bringing its regulatory environment ranking closer to that of OECD countries. The UAE's ranking was followed by Qatar, which scored 71% in 2018, Bahrain at 68%, and Oman at 65% in the same year. Meanwhile, Saudi Arabia and Kuwait scored below other Gulf countries at 53% and 54%, respectively. Most other MENA countries also remained firmly below the OECD average score of 88%, which has been maintained over the past ten years, as shown in Figure 2.8. The average score for MENA countries in regulatory quality was 44% in 2008, and this performance slightly deteriorated as they reached an average score of only 42% in 2018. Most MENA countries generally performed below the average score for the region, and their scores have worsened over the past few years. For example, Mauritania scored 27% in 2008, but this score fell to 19% in 2018. Similarly, Egypt scored 29% in 2008 but deteriorated to 18% in 2018. Algeria exhibited a considerably poorer regulatory environment, falling from 12% in 2008 to 8% in 2018. The lowest-scoring countries in the MENA region were those ravaged by conflict, such as Yemen with a score of 22%, Iraq with a score of 9%, and Somalia with a score of 1%. Other MENA countries, including Libya and Syria, scored continuously low in the regulatory quality indicator at 2% and 4% in 2008, and 1% and 3% in 2018, respectively.

Meanwhile, GCC states have consistently performed better than other MENA countries in the control of corruption indicator as shown in Figure 2.9. The UAE, for example, continues to be ranked higher than any other MENA country, scoring similarly to OECD countries at 87%

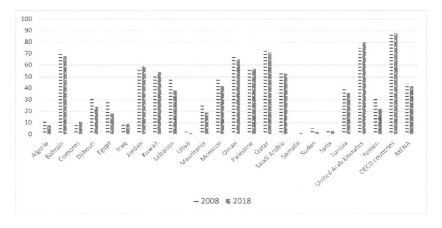

Figure 2.8 Regulatory quality *(0% = worst, 100% = best)
Source: World Bank Data Bank (2019)

42 *Quality of government and the public sector in the GCC region*

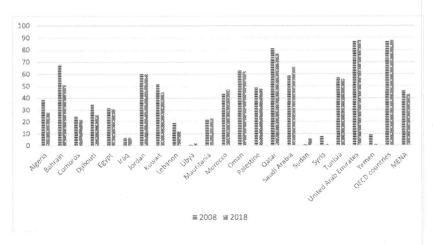

Figure 2.9 Control of corruption *(0% = worst, 100% = best)
Source: World Bank Data Bank (2019)

in 2008, but dropping to 83% in 2018. This was, however, still considerably higher than the MENA average of 43% during the same year. Qatar achieved a score of 82% in 2008 but earned a lower score in 2018 of 77%, followed by Saudi Arabia, which reached 66% in 2018, improving seven percentage points from 2008. Nevertheless, other Gulf countries scored much lower, including Bahrain, which plunged from a score of 68% in 2008 to 51% in 2018, and Kuwait, which fell from 52% in 2008 to 45% in 2018.

Such corruption has been an endemic feature of the MENA region that has hindered attempts to introduce broader public management reforms. Despite the efforts of the World Bank, Transparency International, and other governmental and non-governmental agencies to decrease corruption in the region, controlling it remains a persistent challenge that most MENA countries must seriously address to enhance their performance in terms of quality of government and good governance. For example, the average score for OECD countries in the control of corruption indicator was 88% in 2018, while the MENA average was 43% in the same year, deteriorating from a relatively higher score of 46% in 2008. While a few countries, such as Jordan, Morocco, and Palestine scored higher than the MENA average (60%, 47%, and 48%, respectively), the remainder scored far below the average median in the region. For example, Algeria dropped from 39% in the control of corruption indicator in 2008 to 28% in 2018, while Egypt has remained at an average of 30%. Meanwhile, Iraq, Libya, Sudan, Syria, and Yemen have scored below 10%. Such low performance is a strong indicator of the impact of corruption on the machinery of government and its devastating consequences for administrative reform and business environments in the region.

Quality of government, governance, and public service delivery 43

The Corruption Perceptions Index also provides a stronger indication of the disparities among GCC and MENA countries in controlling the spread of corruption throughout government and private sector entities. At 70%, the UAE scored highest among MENA countries as the least corrupt administrative environment, as shown in Figure 2.10. It is followed by Qatar, which scored 62% in 2018, and Oman, which scored 52%. Meanwhile, the remaining Gulf countries scored lower, including Bahrain, which deteriorated from 51% in 2015 to 36% in 2018, followed by Kuwait, which dropped from 49% in 2015 to 41% in 2018. Other MENA countries scored even lower compared to the Gulf countries. For example, Egypt scored 35% in 2015, followed by Morocco at 43% and Lebanon at 28%. Iraq, Syria, and Yemen all scored equally with 18% in 2018, while Libya reached only 17%.

Although Gulf countries outperformed the rest of the MENA region in terms of several government efficiency and corruption control indicators, virtually all MENA countries performed significantly below the OECD average of 90% in the voice and accountability indicator, which measures the involvement of citizens in policymaking and freedom of expression and association. Enabling citizens' involvement in government is crucial to facilitating participatory decision-making and the design of effective public policies. As Figure 2.11 shows, the MENA average for the voice and accountability score was 26% in 2018 (the same as 2008). Beginning with the GCC block which scored below the MENA average, Oman scored 20%

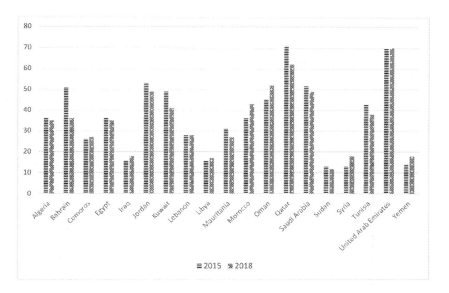

Figure 2.10 Corruption Perceptions Index (2015–2018)
*(1 = high corruption, 100 = low corruption)
Source: World Bank Data Bank (2019)

44 *Quality of government and the public sector in the GCC region*

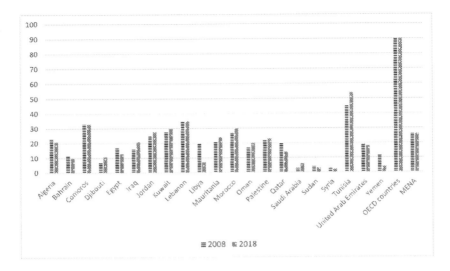

Figure 2.11 Voice and accountability *(0% = worst, 100% = best)
Source: World Bank Data Bank (2019)

in 2018, the UAE scored 18%, Qatar scored 14%, Bahrain scored 10%, and Saudi Arabia received the lowest score of 6%. Only a handful of countries scored above the MENA average of 26%. For example, Tunisia scored 54% in 2018, improving from 45% in 2008, Lebanon maintained a score of 35%, while Morocco and Kuwait reached 30%, and Jordan attained 28% in 2018. The remaining MENA countries scored below the MENA region's median score of 26%, with Egypt scoring 13% and Libya, Somalia, Syria, and Yemen all scoring below 10%.

In terms of political stability and absence of violence, GCC and MENA countries vary considerably, yet all remained below the OECD score of 74% in 2018. As Figure 2.12 shows, Gulf countries outperformed other MENA countries in this respect, with the UAE scoring 71% in 2018, followed by Qatar at 69%, and Oman at 68% in the same year. Bahrain scored the lowest among GCC countries with 17% in 2018, which is nonetheless significantly over its 9% in 2008. All other MENA countries were considerably below the MENA median (32%) in political stability and absence of violence, except for Morocco, which achieved a score of 34%, and Jordan, which was just slightly below it with 31% in 2018. Meanwhile, Algeria stood at 19% in 2018, Egypt was at 12%, and Lebanon, Palestine, Syria, and Yemen failed to break a score of 10%.

The rule of law is another essential indicator of good governance that measures the extent to which a government's institutions abide by existing

Quality of government, governance, and public service delivery 45

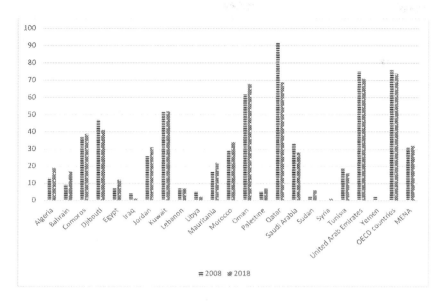

Figure 2.12 Political stability and absence of violence *(0% = worst, 100% = best)
Source: *World Bank Data Bank (2019)*

laws and the overall quality of contract enforcement measures, property rights, and police and court systems. Within OECD countries, the median score for the rule of law among each country's averages over the past ten years is 90%. Meanwhile, as Figure 2.13 illustrates, the GCC states achieved rankings much lower than the OECD average median, yet considerably above the MENA average of 42%. For example, in 2018 the UAE achieved a ranking of 77%, followed by Qatar, which scored 75% (5% lower than its score in 2008). Next in line were Bahrain at 66%, Kuwait at 60%, and Saudi Arabia at 58% in the same year.

On the other hand, only a few MENA countries scored above the region's median in the rule of law indicator. In 2018, Jordan achieved a ranking of 62%, while Morocco scored 49%. The remainder in MENA scored lower than the regional median, as was the case with Mauritania's score of 26%, Algeria's ranking of 22%, and Libya, Iraq, Syria, and Yemen again below 10%, ranking as the lowest performers in the indicator not only within the MENA region, but globally as well.

To sum up, MENA countries all vary considerably in their capacities to develop and implement good governance and government practices. However, compared to OECD countries' scores, only a few Gulf countries, such as the UAE, offer the kind of robust governance and regulatory environment that can be favorable to the private sector.

46 *Quality of government and the public sector in the GCC region*

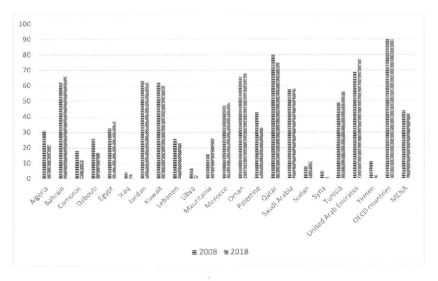

Figure 2.13 Rule of law *(0% = worst, 100% = best)
Source: World Bank Data Bank (2019)

The capacity of MENA governments to provide a business-friendly environment for the private sector

This section provides a more in-depth analysis of the capacity of GCC and other MENA governments to offer a robust business-friendly environment for the private sector. Specifically, it measures the performance of MENA countries in terms of ease of doing business scores, ease of doing business global rankings, number of start-up procedures to register a business, the time required to start a business in days, total tax and contribution rates (as percentage of profit), quality of port infrastructure, efficiency of customs and border management, and efficiency of the clearance process. The global median in these indicators is used as a benchmark to measure where GCC countries stand compared to the rest of the MENA region.

For ease of doing business, the Gulf states seem to have surpassed their peers in the MENA region. As shown in Figure 2.14, the UAE scored 76 in 2013 which improved to 81 in 2019. Similarly, Oman, and Qatar scored 68, Bahrain and Saudi Arabia scored 67, and Kuwait scored 61 in 2013, and while all these countries maintained their rankings, Saudi Arabia dropped to 63 in 2019. A few MENA countries outside the GCC also achieved high scores in 2013: Tunisia scored 68 and Morocco at 65, while Lebanon scored 61. Nonetheless, while Morocco improved its 2019 ranking to 71, Lebanon dropped to 54 and Tunisia 66. The remaining MENA countries such as Algeria and Iraq scored 48 in 2013 (Iraq dropped to 44 in 2019), Mauritania scored 46 in 2013, but improved its ranking in 2019 when it

Quality of government, governance, and public service delivery 47

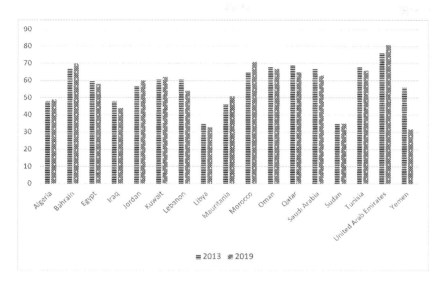

Figure 2.14 Ease of doing business score *(0 = worst performance, 100 = best performance)
Source: *World Bank Data Bank (2019)*

ranked 51. Also, in 2013, Libya and Sudan scored 35, which remained the same in 2019. These indicator scores reflect how challenging it can be to attract foreign direct investment in the MENA region and the resultant hardships local private sectors face in contributing to economic development in their countries. The indicators should also serve as a wake-up call encouraging their governments to enhance business environments and initiate reforms that address such challenges.

Global rankings for doing business can also provide a robust indicator of business environments in the MENA region. As Figure 2.15 shows, the UAE was recognized as the 16th best environment for ease of doing business globally (out of 190 countries), and ranked above all other MENA countries. The closest contenders to the UAE's position were Bahrain, which ranked 43rd globally, followed by Morocco at 53rd. The remaining Gulf and MENA countries have maintained lower rankings, with Oman ranking 63rd and Kuwait placing 83rd globally. Other MENA countries performed particularly poorly in this ranking, such as Egypt, which ranked 114th, and Mauritania, which ranked 152nd. Meanwhile, Iraq, Sudan, and Yemen ranked 172nd, 171st, and 187th, respectively, while Sudan bottomed out the list at 190th, making it the most poorly ranked country in the region for ease of doing business.

A critical indicator of ease of doing business is the number of procedures required for a startup to register a new business. The world average in 2018 was six procedures, and this is the same number of procedures required to

48 *Quality of government and the public sector in the GCC region*

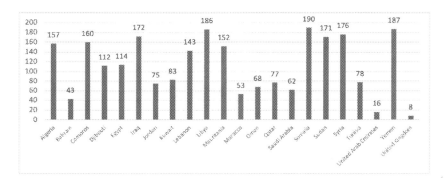

Figure 2.15 Ease of doing business global rankings in 2018 *(1 = best, 190 = worst)
Source: World Bank Data Bank (2019)

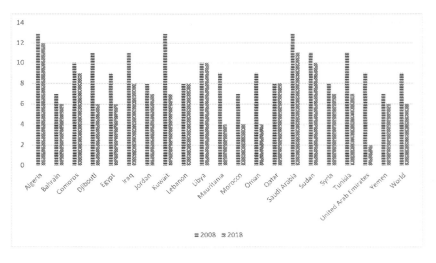

Figure 2.16 Start-up procedures to register a business *(1 = fewer procedures, 13 = more procedures)
Source: World Bank Data Bank (2019)

register a business in the USA, while only four are required in the UK, and both economic powerhouses attract considerable investments. Meanwhile, the GCC and MENA countries vary significantly regarding the number of procedures that their regulatory and administrative frameworks require for business startups (see Figure 2.16). For example, the UAE only required two procedures to start a business in 2018, improving drastically from the nine that were demanded in 2008. Oman required just four procedures in 2018, while Sudan demanded 10 and Saudi Arabia needed 11. Algeria

Quality of government, governance, and public service delivery 49

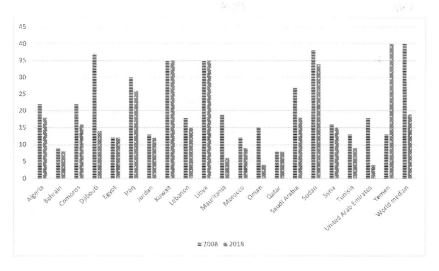

Figure 2.17 Time required to start a business (in days)
Source: *World Bank Data Bank (2019)*

had the highest number of procedures to start a business, requiring 12 procedures in 2018 (compared to 13 in 2008).

Regarding the number of days required to start a business, the world has experienced considerable improvement in its median over the past ten years. Figure 2.17 shows that 40 days were required to start a business in 2008, while this number dropped by more than half to only 19 days by 2018. Among MENA countries, the UAE topped the region and exceeded the world median in this indicator in 2018, requiring only 4 days to start a business—an immense improvement over 2008, when it required 18 days. In Oman, just four days are needed to start a business and is followed closely by Qatar, where it takes a total of eight days to commence a new business. However, other countries within the MENA region have not performed as effectively as the Gulf states in providing a business-friendly environment that facilitates starting new businesses. In 2018, for example, Egypt, Jordan, Lebanon, and Mauritania ranked below the world median by requiring 12 or 15 days to start a business, whereas in Libya and Kuwait it took 35 days, and in Yemen 40 days.

Factors determining the reliability and attractiveness of a country's business environment are also linked to administrative and regulatory systems and the broader ecosystem pertinent to taxation schemes and ease of handling customs and clearance processes. For example, the total tax and contributions rate as a percentage of profit is an essential indicator and reflection of a country's business environment. This indicator measures taxes and any other mandatory payments businesses must make as a share of their profits, typically after deducting any fees, expenses, and employee salaries. Such information is important, since businesses are most attracted to countries that offer tax exemptions and lower tax rates on profits. As Figure 2.18 illustrates, the world median for total tax and contribution rate as a percentage of profit was 40% in 2018. In this respect, GCC and MENA countries vary widely regarding their capacity to provide accessible taxation systems. Qatar had the lowest rate of total tax and contribution rate as a percentage of profit over the past ten years with a rate of 11%. It was followed by Bahrain and Kuwait, which required only 13% of profit for taxation purposes, and then Saudi Arabia with slightly more at 15%. Other MENA regions, such as Jordan, Libya, and Oman, offered 30% or less attractive tax rates. However, some MENA countries levy tax rates considerably higher than the world average. For example, standing at the high extreme are Algeria, Mauritania, and Tunisia, which require more than 60%, while others like Morocco and Egypt also exceed the world median with tax rates of 50% and 47%, respectively.

The quality of overall infrastructure is another important aspect that reflects a country's business environment and the government's commitment to investing resources in providing reliable infrastructure to the public and business actors. The world median for quality of overall infrastructure was 67 in 2018. Meanwhile, several Gulf states have outperformed much of the world in building state-of-the-art infrastructure. As a case in point, the UAE ranked 4th in its quality of infrastructure in 2018, improving from an earlier, but still high, ranking of 11th in 2008 (see Figure 2.19).

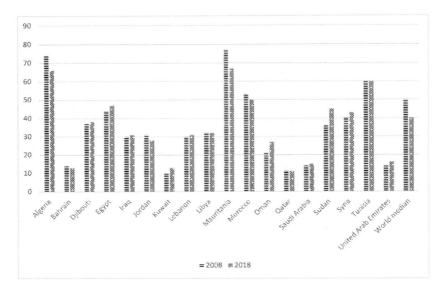

Figure 2.18 Total tax and contribution rate (% of the profit)
Source: World Bank Data Bank (2019)

Quality of government, governance, and public service delivery 51

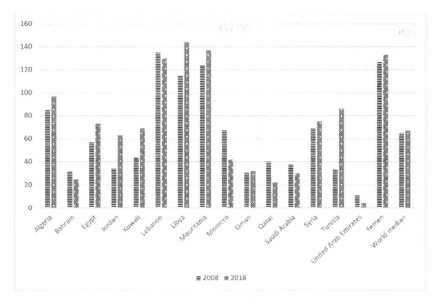

Figure 2.19 Quality of overall infrastructure *(1 = best performance, 137 = worst performance)
Source: World Bank Data Bank (2019)

Next in line among the GCC states is Qatar, which ranked 22nd in 2018, improving by nearly 20 places compared to 2008. Bahrain came in next at 25th in 2018. Some other Gulf countries were also ranked above the world median, including Oman at 32nd and Saudi Arabia at 30th; however, Kuwait came in slightly below the world median at 69th. Only Morocco and Jordan placed above the world median among the MENA countries, ranking 42nd and 63rd, respectively. The remaining MENA countries were far below the world median rank, including Tunisia at 86th and Algeria at 97th. Lebanon ranked 130th in 2018, Mauritania ranked 137th, and Libya ranked 144th. Lower quality of infrastructure is a stronger disincentive for the private sector when choosing to invest in a country, and a significant burden on the governments that must invest more in developing reliable and higher-quality infrastructure.

The quality of port infrastructure is also an essential determinant of the capacity of a country to attract foreign direct investment and encourage trade. Specifically, this indicator measures business executives' perceptions of the quality of port facilities and how efficiently and promptly they process imports and exports. As illustrated in Figure 2.20, the world median in 2017 was 65. As with most business indicators, Gulf countries topped their MENA peers in terms of the quality of port infrastructure. Specifically, the UAE ranked 4th in 2017, demonstrating a notable improvement from its 8th

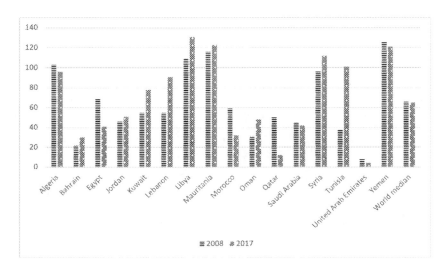

Figure 2.20 Quality of port infrastructure *(1 = best performance, 137 = worst performance)
Source: World Bank Data Bank (2019)

ranking in 2008. Qatar has also made considerable strides in modernizing and upgrading its port facilities, ranking 52nd in 2008 but leaping drastically to 12th by 2017. Bahrain followed with a ranking of 30th in 2017, deteriorating from its higher ranking of 22nd in 2008. Kuwait, meanwhile, has not performed as well as its Gulf counterparts. In 2017 it ranked 78th, having deteriorated from its better ranking of 55th in 2008. Similar trends could be observed in other MENA countries, as Lebanon's ranking deteriorated from 55th in 2008 to 91st in 2017 and Mauritania fell from 116th in 2008 to 123rd in 2017.

Meanwhile, most GCC and MENA countries appear to have efficient customs and border management systems, as border control agencies in each country adopt international best practices in processing imports and exports (see Figure 2.21). For example, the UAE scored 3.63 in 2018, considerably higher than the world median of 2.67. This ranking is followed by Qatar's score of 3 in the same year, and the remaining Gulf states also maintained levels higher than the world median. However, several other MENA countries fell below the world median in 2018, including Morocco (2.33), Mauritania (2.2), Lebanon (2.38), Jordan (2.49), and Algeria (2.37).

In summary, the capacity to provide a business-friendly environment differs markedly between GCC states and other MENA countries. While abundant income from natural resources has enabled GCC countries to provide the necessary funding, infrastructure, and knowhow that earn higher rankings in competitiveness indices, several MENA countries lag

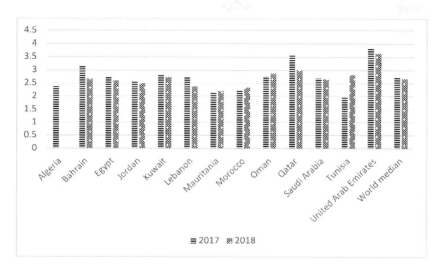

Figure 2.21 Efficiency of customs and border management *(1 = very low, 5 = very high clearance)
Source: World Bank Data Bank (2019)

considerably behind the rest of the world in numerous critical rankings. Addressing the performance gap among MENA countries through sharing knowledge, expertise, and financial support is essential to lift their lagging capacity and attract more foreign direct investments. In this regard, easing bureaucratic burdens, streamlining services, and issuing permits are all steps that can improve government machinery and attract more local and international business opportunities.

The capacity of MENA governments to drive innovation

The transformation from the traditional public administration into a public management model requires governments to continuously innovate solutions to pressing problems and adopt business-like practices to meet the public's needs. However, the capacity to drive such innovation requires them to start reforming existing public administration models, make fundamental changes to existing educational systems, and forge bridges among universities, research centers, and government institutions.

Considering the above, this section evaluates the GCC and other MENA countries' capability to drive innovation within the public sector and as part of their national strategies that aim to encourage R&D and prepare future leaders to facilitate innovation from a grassroots level. Therefore, this section will evaluate the performance of the GCC and MENA countries across several indicators, namely the global innovation index, R&D

54 *Quality of government and the public sector in the GCC region*

expenditure (as a percentage of GDP), university-industry research collaboration, graduate skillsets, availability of scientists and engineers, R&D researchers (per million people), country capacity to retain talent, and scientific and technical journal articles. These indicators will provide an initial assessment of where GCC countries stand compared to each other, the rest of the MENA region, and the world median.

As shown in Figure 2.22, Gulf states have blazed a trail among MENA countries in the global innovation index, with the UAE ranking 39 in 2019, followed by Kuwait at 60. Qatar's performance, however, declined in this indicator, deteriorating from a ranking of 43 in 2013 to 65 in 2019. Similarly, Saudi Arabia dropped from 42 in 2013 to 68 in 2019, sitting squarely on the world median of 68. Other Gulf countries, such as Bahrain and Oman, ranked lower than the world median at 78 and 80, respectively. The remaining MENA countries, meanwhile, scored considerably below the worldwide median of the global innovation index, reflecting the significant gap in capacity and performance of these countries relative to the Gulf countries and the rest of the world. Specifically, only 4 MENA countries—out of 14 with the available data—scored well in the global innovation index compared with the world median of 68. Nevertheless, despite ranking lower than the world average, it is important to acknowledge that some MENA countries have improved their rankings over the past few years. For example, Algeria ranked 138 in 2013, but managed to enhance that ranking in 2019 by achieving 113. Similarly, Egypt ranked 93 in 2019, up from 108 in 2013, while Morocco improved from 92 in 2013 to 74 in 2019. In contrast, some countries deteriorated, including Jordan,

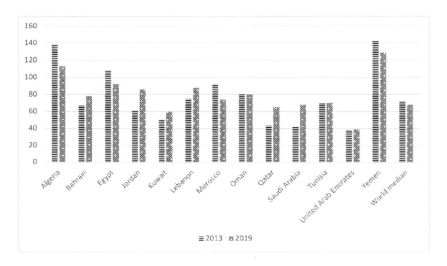

Figure 2.22 Global innovation index ranking *(1 = best, 142 = worst)
Source: *World Bank Data Bank (2019)*

Quality of government, governance, and public service delivery 55

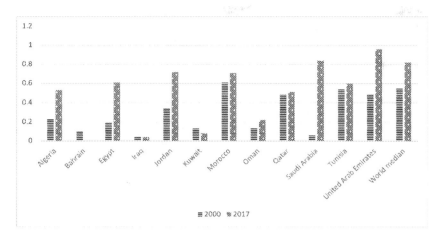

Figure 2.23 Research and development expenditure (% of GDP)
Source: *World Bank Data Bank (2019)*

which fell from 61 in 2013 to 86 in 2019, and Lebanon, which shifted from 75 in 2013 to 88 in 2019.

Figure 2.23 shows that only the UAE and Saudi Arabia exceeded the world median in their expenditure on R&D as a percentage of GDP, spending 0.96% and 0.84% of their GDP on research, respectively. The lower rankings of other GCC and MENA countries in the global innovation index described above can be attributed to various factors, among the most important of which is their investment in R&D, which is considered a key driver of innovation. For example, although it brands itself as a host of major international universities, Qatar dedicates a mere 0.51% of its GDP to R&D, while Kuwait invests only 0.08%. Similarly, Bahrain aims to diversify its economy and build a knowledge-driven economic structure, yet its spending on R&D in 2017 did not exceed 0.1% of its GDP. This is extremely low compared with advanced industrial countries, such as the USA, which dedicated 2.8% of its GDP in 2017 to R&D, or Germany, which allocated 3.03%.

Furthermore, an essential factor supporting innovation in the public sector is the creation of collaborative bridges among academic and research institutions and government and private entities. Such collaborations can foster the exchange of knowledge and best practices and enable the transfer of knowhow and development of technical capacity within the public sector. As Figure 2.24 shows, Qatar topped the rest of the MENA countries by ranking 12th in this indicator and scoring considerably higher than the world median of 67 in 2017. For Qatar, this represented a drastic improvement from its previous ranking of 42nd in 2007. The UAE was the second highest-ranking country within the MENA region at 25th in

56 *Quality of government and the public sector in the GCC region*

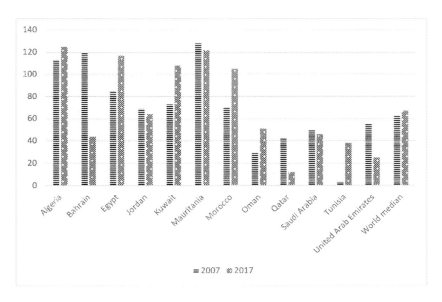

Figure 2.24 University-industry collaboration in research and development
*(1 = best performance, 137 worst performance)
Source: World Bank Data Bank (2019)

2017, improving from its 55th place ranking in 2007. Meanwhile, Kuwait ranked 73rd in 2007, but dropped to 108th in 2017. Ultimately, despite their purported centrality of university-industry collaboration to foster innovation, MENA countries are trailing considerably behind the rest of the world in this indicator. Morocco ranked 70th in 2007 but fell considerably to 105th in 2017, while Egypt dropped from 85th in 2007 to 117th in 2017.

Although the data show that little collaboration occurs across industries and universities, it is important to note that several GCC countries have a higher number of researchers in R&D per million people compared to the world median. While Gulf countries can easily attract foreign researchers by providing them with the financial and technical incentives they desire to work in the region, other MENA countries also have almost double the world median in this indicator. As shown in Figure 2.25, the UAE holds 2,410 researchers in R&D per million people, exceeding the world median of 604 in 2017 by a factor of four, but Tunisia and Morocco also boasted high numbers in that same year, with 1,960 and 1,007, respectively.

Collaboration among the university and industry sectors also necessitates having graduates with the relevant skillsets and knowledge required to support the private sector's initiatives and plans. As Figure 2.26 reveals, only a few MENA countries have graduates with adequate skillsets. The world median for this indicator in 2009 was 4.09, and in 2019 Qatar topped all other MENA countries and exceeded the world median by scoring 5.25,

Quality of government, governance, and public service delivery 57

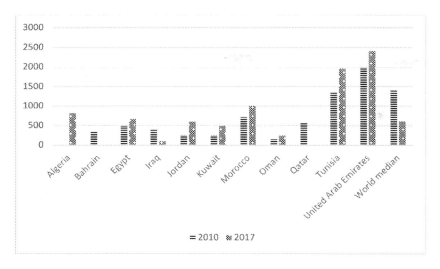

Figure 2.25 Researchers in R&D (per million people)
Source: *World Bank Data Bank (2019)*

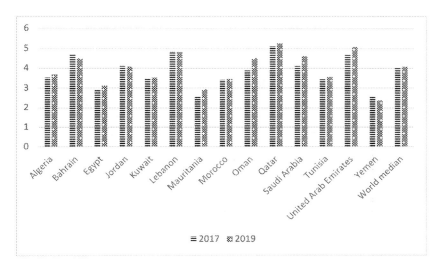

Figure 2.26 Skillsets of graduates *(1 = worst, 7 = best)
Source: *World Bank Data Bank (2019)*

followed by the UAE with a score of 5.08. The remaining MENA countries clustered below the global median in the skillsets of their graduates, except for Lebanon, which scored 4.82 in 2019. Meanwhile, Yemen scored 2.73, Mauritania scored 2.93, and Egypt scored 3.12 in 2019. These low rankings

58 Quality of government and the public sector in the GCC region

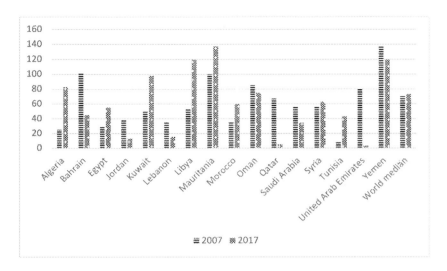

Figure 2.27 Availability of scientists and engineers *(ranking: 1 best–138 worst)
Source: World Bank Data Bank (2019)

indicate the lack of proper development of educational programs to reflect the market's requirements, harness students' critical thinking, and prepare them to play a critical role in their respective countries' administrative and economic development.

In addition to having higher skillsets among graduates, Gulf countries attract more scientists and engineers than their MENA counterparts (see Figure 2.27). The world median for the availability of scientists and engineers was 73 in 2017, and the UAE ranked 3rd while Qatar ranked 5th globally. Other Gulf countries stood far off in their rankings, with Saudi Arabia ranking 34th and Bahrain 45th in 2017. Kuwait, meanwhile, was below the world median, ranking 98th in 2017, dropping considerably from its higher ranking of 50th in 2007. All other MENA countries, such as Algeria, Libya, Mauritania, and Yemen ranked lower than the world median as they ranked 83rd, 119th, and 137th, respectively.

Furthermore, while the availability of scientists in the MENA region is important, the capacity of governments to retain them is even more critical. As Figure 2.28 demonstrates, Gulf countries have managed to exceed the world median in their capacities to retain talent. As cases in point, the UAE scored 5.85 in 2017, exceeding the world median of 3.41, followed by Qatar at 5.17, and then Bahrain at 4.43. Meanwhile, other MENA countries were not as successful in retaining their talent pools and ranked below the world median. For example, Yemen scored 2.13 in 2017, followed by Algeria with 2.46 and Mauritania with 2.64. Morocco's ranking dropped from 3.62 in 2013 to 3.15 in 2017, while Jordan's fell from 3.66 to 3.42.

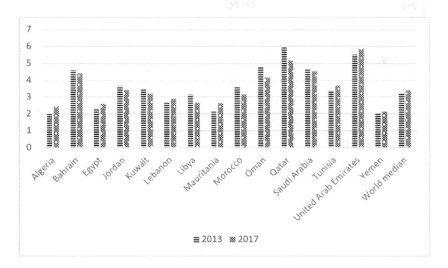

Figure 2.28 Capacity to retain talent *(1 = worst, 7 = best)
Source: World Bank Data Bank (2019)

Developing effective strategies to retain talent is a critical factor in driving innovation and both administrative and economic development and growth, and the brain drain and migration of talent from these MENA countries to the Gulf region or European and North American countries is a severe challenge depriving them of much-needed talent.

Recommendations and conclusions

While the administrative challenges facing GCC and MENA countries are often drastically different, this section offers four recommendations that can broadly address some of the issues hindering the capacity of their governments to adopt broader public management reforms and strengthening the capacity of the public services that can foster economic growth and development.

Addressing the weak role of political accountability in the GCC and MENA region through a managerial model of accountability

One major shortcoming in governance and government performance among GCC and MENA countries is the weak role of political accountability, which is a prerequisite for good governance (Cameron, 2004). Accountability denotes being "answerable" for certain decisions or actions to avoid the misuse of power and any other "inappropriate" behavior (Cameron, 2004). In this regard, Hughes (2002b) asserts that providing efficient administrative services necessitates a suitable system of accountability, as government organizations "are created by the public, from the public, and need to be accountable to the public" (p. 240). Lack of accountability will ultimately undermine any efforts to reform public administration or implement new managerial reforms that could lead to higher levels of efficiency.

At first glance, it would appear problematic to implement complex public management reforms within GCC and MENA countries, given the substantial differences in the relationship between the state and market in Western countries—from which public management reforms emanated—and that in the import destinations of the MENA region. In Western countries, the boundaries between the public and private sectors are comparatively clear and transparent, enabling government officials to implement measures that ensure the exercise of political accountability. However, such clear-cut demarcations among the public sector, market sector, and bureaucracy are not nearly as evident in the contexts of the GCC and MENA regions. Instead, these three dimensions are inextricably intertwined, making any questions of political accountability more difficult to address. Nonetheless, it is still possible for the managerial model of public management to enhance the GCC and MENA countries' levels of transparency and accountability.

Another aspect of managerial accountability lies in strengthening the government's relationship with citizens. Under the current traditional system in the GCC and MENA regions, there is no direct interaction between administrative systems and the public, as there has never been any perceived (institutional) need for that. The essential role of public servants has always been to follow the rules and processes, not to necessarily be responsive to the needs of the public. This is typically the case in most developing countries, and Hughes (2002c) makes this point clear by stating that "the traditional model of administration was not equipped to deal with the outside, while a formal model of bureaucracy allows no role for public servants in dealing with outside groups or improving responsiveness" (pp. 148–249). Meanwhile, using a business-like model, the managerial form of accountability considers citizens as clients and requires satisfying their needs and strengthening ties with them to become as responsive and interactive as possible.

Initiating administrative reforms to enable efficient public budgeting

Most MENA countries have inefficient government budgets and face challenges in balancing them. Public budgets are powerful "political tools" (Bloj, 2009) that enable governments to manage their finances and fulfill their political and economic policy objectives; conversely, they can also be misused to channel public finances in ways that line pockets and serve personal interests. Public budgets have several goals, including distributing and allocating resources in a way compatible with the government's political strategy and fiscal discipline (Devasy, 2003; Diamond, 2006). Moreover, public budgets are intended to serve various functions such as the setting of budget priorities consistent with government mandates, planning of expenditures to pursue a long-term vision for development, maintaining financial control over inputs, and managing operations to secure the efficiency of government operations (Shah & Shen, 2007). Moreover, a public budget serves as evidence of whether government targets have been achieved and realized and, as the OECD (2008) states, "the budget is the central tool through which development results and priorities are realized" (p. 3). Therefore, budget documents can be significant instruments to ensure accountability to legislative bodies, taxpayers, and even the press.

Implementing processes for strategic and performance planning

It is further recommended that GCC and MENA countries incrementally adopt processes of strategic and performance planning to enhance the quality of their public policies and services they offer to the public. Strategic planning is a "disciplined effort to produce fundamental decisions and actions that shape and guide what an organization is, what it does, and why it does it" (Bryson, 2003, p. 4–5). The private sector uses such planning when it prioritizes long-term and "external objectives" rather than focusing on immediate and internal problems (Hughes, 2002c). In this regard, it is important to mention four stages in the evolution of strategic planning: 1) budgeting and financial control, 2) business planning, 3) corporate strategic planning, and 4) strategic management.

Public organizations within OECD countries have increasingly adopted these strategic planning approaches that were developed in the private sector because they found them effective in dealing with their changing environments. Similarly, public organizations adopting strategic planning "can facilitate communication and participation, accommodate divergent interests and values, and foster orderly decision making and successful implementation" (Hughes, 2002c, p. 5). Gallop (2007) further argues that strategic planning has emerged as a necessity in response to various issues that have arisen in tandem with the new public management model and calls for governments to take a more strategic role in coping with such issues. He observes how several European and American government agencies have adopted numerous measures of performance to improve the mechanisms of realizing goals out of a desire to be more comprehensive and responsive to the needs of their citizens. The new role of the state has thus become to regulate and supervise the process by which society's needs are met by a "self-governing" and market-driven public sector where ministers are encouraged to let managers manage, and those managers are encouraged to let the market work independently from state intervention or unnecessary restrictions (Brown, 1992). It is the new challenges of the globalized world that NPM reforms are attempting to address, and this requires a government using strategic planning to provide supportive services to its citizens (Gallop, 2007).

Investing in research and development to enable a shift from hierarchical administrative bureaucracy to managerial government

Finally, GCC and MENA countries should rely heavily on R&D to further investigate factors hindering administrative reform and change. Informed by scientific and evidence-based research, the GCC and MENA governments must gradually shift from the hierarchical systems of bureaucratic governance to managerial practices, which have provided better results and higher returns for both the public and private sectors. Many factors contribute to the lethargic development of some GCC and MENA public administration and the lack of progress in major governance and public performance indicators. The key hindrance to implementing such reforms is the old mentality underpinning current administrative systems and perpetuating the endless bureaucratic procedures that slow down, if not block completely, economic growth in Arab countries. In this regard, Schomaker and Bauer (2019) state that the transition to public management must first address the following six major weaknesses in the existing models of administration: 1) high levels of centralization of public authority, 2) religious and cultural elements in the governance system, 3) cronyism, nepotism, and corruption, 4) autocratic leadership and unclear or unstable succession models, 5) gridlock of administrative reforms, and 6) mistrust within the public-administrative system and state-citizen nexus.

References

Ardouille, N. (2000). The transformation of governance paradigms and modalities: insights into the marketization of the public service in response to globalization. *The Round Table*, 353, 81–106.

Barsoum, G. (2018). Egypt's many public administration transitions: Reform vision and implementation challenges. *International Journal of Public Administration*, 41(10), 772–780

Barrett, P. (2003). Corporate governance in the public sector context. *Canberra Bulletin of Public Administration*, iss. 107, May, pp. 7–27.

Bhuiyan, S., & Farazmand, A. (2019). Society and public policy in the Middle East and North Africa. *International Journal of Public Administration*, 43(5), 373–377.

Bloj, C. (2009). The budgeting process and implications on social policies and poverty reduction: Alternative to traditional models. UNRISD working paper.

Bougan, J. (2008). The future of public service: A search for a new balance. *Australian Journal of Public Administration*, 67(4), 390–404.

Boyne, A. G. (1998). Public service under new labour: Back to bureaucracy? *Public Money and Management*, 43–50.

Brown, S. (1992). *International Relations in a Changing Global System: Toward a Theory if World Polity*, Westview Press, Boulder, CO.

Bryson, J. (2003). Strategic Planning and Management, in Peters, B, Guy & Pierre, J (eds.) *Handbook of Public Administration*, Sage Publications, London, Chapter 3, pp. 38–47.

Caiden, G. (1991). *Administrative Reform Comes of Age*. Walter de Gruyter, New York.

Cameron, W. (2004). Public accountability: effectiveness, equity and ethics. *Australian Journal of Public Administration*, 63(4), 59–67.

Carlin, T., & Guthrie, J. (2003). Accrual output based budgeting systems in Australia: The rhetoric-reality gap. *Public Management Review*, 5(2), 145–162

Crowley, K., & Coffey, B. (2007). New governance green planning and sustainability. *Australian Journal of Public Administration*, 66(1), 23–37.

De Laine, M. (1997). International themes in public service reform, background paper 3, Parliament of Australia, Canberra.

Devasy, D. (2003). The 4Ps of effective government budget offices: Essential tools for hard times. *Performance Oriented Government*. Centre for Accountability and Performance.

Diamond, J. (2006). Institutional framework for budget system reform, in Budget system reform in emerging economics: the challenges and the reform agenda, International Monetary Fund, Occasional Paper 245, pp. 75–89

Dixon, J., Bhuiyan, S., & Ustuner, Y. (2018). Public administration in the Middle East and North Africa. *International Journal of Public Administration*, 41(10), 759–764.

Eklund, N. (2008). *Globalization, Europeanization, and Administrative Reform*, Taylor and Francis Group, London.

El Massnaoui, K., & Biygautane, M. (2021). Downsizing the Public Sector: Re-evaluating the Achievements and Performance of Morocco's Voluntary Retirement Program, in Beschel, R., & Yousef, T. (eds.), *Public Sector Reform in the Middle East and North Africa: Lessons of Experience for a Region in Transition*, Brookings Institution Press, Washington, DC, 1–24.

Farazmand, A. (2001a). *Administrative Reform in Developing Nations*, Greenwood Press, Westport, CT.

Farazmand, A. (2001b). Globalization, the state and public administration: A theoretical analysis with policy implications for developmental states. *Public Organization Review*, 1, 437–463.

Farazmand, A. (1999). Globalization and public administration. *Public Administration Review*, 59(6), 509–522.

Gallop, G. (2007). Strategic planning: is it the new model? *Public Administration Today*, 10, January–March, pp. 28–33.

Gregory, R. (1998). Political responsibility for bureaucratic incompetence: Tragedy at Cave Creek. *Public Administration*, 76(3), 519–538.

Goldsmith, A. (2007). Is governance reform a catalyst for development? *Governance*, 20(2), 165–186.

Halligan, J. (2004). The Quasi-autonomous agency in an ambiguous environment: The Centrelink case. *Public Administration and Development*, 24, 147–156

Halligan, J. (2007). Advocacy and innovation in interagency management: The case of Centrelink. *Governance: An International Journal of Policy, Administration and Institutions*, 20(3), 445–467.

Halligan, J. (2008). *The Centrelink Experiment: Innovation in Service Delivery*, Australian National University E Press, Canberra.

Hood, C. (1991). A public management for all seasons? *Policy Administration*, 69, 3–19.
Hughes, O. (2002a). Accountability in Hughes, O., *Public Management and Administration: An Introduction*, Palgrave Macmillan, New York, 236–255.
Hughes, O. (2002b). Public Policy and Analysis in Hughes, O., *Public Management and Administration: An Introduction*, Palgrave Macmillan, New York, 113–131.
Hughes, O. (2002c). Strategic Management in Hughes, O., *Public Management and Administration: An Introduction*, Palgrave Macmillan, New York, 132–148.
Hughes, O. (2003). *Public Management and Administration: An Introduction* (3rd ed.), Palgrave Macmillan, New York.
Johnsen, A. (2005). What does 25 years' experience with performance management tell us about the state of performance measurement in public policy and management? *Public Money and Management*, 25, 9–17.
Jreisat, J. (2004). Governance in globalizing world. *International Journal of Public Administration*, 27(13), 1003–1029.
Jreisat, J. (2018). Public administration reform in Jordan: Concepts and practices. *International Journal of Public Administration*, 41(10), 781–791.
Kastbeg, G., & Siverbo, S. (2008). The impossible split? A study of the creation of a market actor. *International Advanced Economic Research*, 14, 65–75.
Kong, D. (2005). Performance based budgeting: The US experience. *Public Organization Review*, 5(91), 91–107.
Leftwich, A. (1993). Governance, democracy, and development in third world. *Third World Quarterly*, 14(3), 605–624.
Mascarenhas, R. (1993). Building an enterprise culture in the public sector: Reform of the public sector in Australia, Britain, and New Zealand. *Public Administration Review*, 53(4), 319–328.
Mulgan, R. (2000). Comparing accountability in the public and private sectors. *Australian Journal of Public Administration*, 59(1), 87–97.
Mulgan, R. (1998). Identifying the "core" public service. *Canberra Bulletin of Public Administration*, 87, 1–7.
Mulgan, R. (2002). Public accountability of provider agencies: the case of the Australian "Centrelink". *International Review of Administrative Sciences*, 68, 45–59.
OECD. (2008). Performance budgeting: A user's guide, *Policy Brief*, March. Retrieved from: www.oecd.org/dataoecd/32/0/40357919.pdf Accessed on 30 June 2022.
Orchad, L. (1998). Managerialism, economic rationalism and public sector reform in Australia: Connections, divergences, alternatives. *Australian Journal of Public Administration*, 57(1), 19–32.
Osborne, P. (2006). The new public governance? *Public Management Review*, 8(3), 377–387.
Olsen, J. P. (2005). Maybe it is time to rediscover bureaucracy. *Journal of Public Administration and Theory*, 16(4), 1–24.
Schomaker, R., & Bauer, M. (2019). Public governance in the MENA region: Reform trends and patterns, *International Journal of Public Administration*, 43(5), 378–391.
Sedgwick, S. (1994). Evaluation of management reforms in the Australian public service. *Australian Journal of Public Administration*, 53(3), 341–347.

Shah, A., & Shen, C. (2007). A premier on performance budgeting. Retrieved from: https://pdf4pro.com/cdn/shah-and-shen-a-primer-on-performance-budgeting-200dd2.pdf Accessed on 20 August 2022.

Stewart, J. (1993). The limitations of government by contract. *Public Money and Management*, 7–12.

World Bank. (1989). *Sub-Saharan Africa: From Crisis to Sustainable Growth*, World Bank, Washington, DC.

World Bank Data Bank. (2019). Retrieved from: www.worldbank.org Accessed on 2 September 2022.

3 Global insights for Saudi Arabia's economic development

The role of effective machinery of government in revitalizing the private sector

Introduction

This chapter shows how effective state-business relations can significantly enhance economic growth and industrial development within Saudi Arabia. By extracting lessons from the experiences of Chile, Korea, Malaysia, Ireland, Poland, Turkey, and the United Arab Emirates (UAE), the chapter discusses what Saudi Arabia can learn from these benchmark countries to gradually transform itself into an industry-based economy in line with the objectives of its Vision 2030. Four main aspects of effective state-business relations are focused on: 1) the importance of bureaucratic institutions in developing effective economic policies, 2) the role of public-private dialogue through business and peak associations in supporting economic policymaking on the one hand, and voicing the interests and needs of the private sector to the government on the other, 3) ways in which the government can guide industrial planning based on cooperation and dialogue with the private sector, and 4) how a favorable business environment can facilitate economic and industrial growth and attraction of foreign direct investment (FDI).

Literature review: The important roles of the state, institutions, and state-business relations in economic and industrial development

This section lays out the theoretical framework supporting the chapter's proposition that effective state-business relations are critical for economic and industrial development. This contradicts other arguments, which propose that the state's role in the economy should be limited to providing regulatory functions and ensuring macroeconomic stability while minimizing intervention in the private sector's activities. The section highlights important theoretical insights that not only guide the analysis of benchmark countries, but also enumerate the prerequisites that the Saudi government should implement to support the effective implementation of Vision 2030.

DOI: 10.4324/9781003267744-4

Definition and characteristics of effective state-business relations

State-business relations can either be active when the government intervenes in directing specific sectors or industries, or passive when it collaborates with private sector actors to set up economic policies but does not engage directly with those actors (Sen, 2015). Such relations can also have a significant positive or negative impact on economic growth and industrial development (Schneider & Maxfield, 1997). For example, when the relationship between the two sectors is collusive, the interests of the private sector are concentrated on accumulating rents from the government to satisfy specific interests rather than focusing on using government resources for the collective and public good. However, as stated by Evans (1997), the key to a developmental state's effectiveness is when its governance system allows bureaucrats to keep strong ties with the business sector while still maintaining their autonomy, and this form of "embedded autonomy" allows the two sectors to communicate and collaborate to set up effective policies that can be instrumental for economic growth and industrial development. For this to happen, the "analysis of government-business collaboration must be grounded on a vision of economic transformation" (Evans, 1997, p. 63). Such a vision can set the public and private sectors toward specific strategic objectives they need to reach within a certain timeframe.

Drivers of effective state-business relations

Political commitment to creating a harmonious relationship with the business sector is essential to align the government's bureaucratic structure and institutions, along with the prerequisites of a vibrant private sector and business environment. The factors for developing such a relationship are described below.

Strong meritocratic bureaucracy

The primary vehicle that will ensure efficient and effective collaboration between the state and businesses is a strongly meritocratic bureaucracy. When merit and competence-based appointments to the government bureaucracy are the norm in selecting public servants (Moynihan & Roberts, 2010), government machinery becomes an enabling factor for economic development. Bureaucrats whose promotion and remuneration are based on performance are incentivized to devise policies targeting the achievement of the common good instead of serving their interests. Such a system also rewards them for reaching out to the business community to assess the utility of government policies on the ground and investigate ways to enhance their effectiveness. Effective administrative systems enable swift decision-making, reduce red tape, and remove unnecessary hurdles for investors, diminishing chances of corruption. However, such efficient bureaucracy is often absent in countries where excessive public employment is used for patronage or to reduce unemployment (Schneider & Maxfield, 1997).

Effective public-private dialogue

If the exchange of reliable information is a feature of constructive state-business relations, the creation of channels for effective dialogue between the two sectors enables this flow of information in the first place. Bettcher et al. (2015) define public-private dialogue as "a structured, participatory, and inclusive approach to policymaking directed at reforming governance and the business climate, especially where other policy institutions are underperforming" (p. 2). This form of dialogue creates the basis for business-friendly policies that can strengthen economic competitiveness, since policies will reflect the needs and requirements of business actors. Furthermore, such dialogue strengthens bonds of trust between the two sectors and establishes an ecosystem of participatory, constructive, and evidence-based economic policymaking. It also raises the rate of investment by minimizing the chances of rapid and unpredictable changes in government policies that might disadvantage or negatively influence investors' interests. This kind of dialogue works best if it is institutionalized, regular, transparent, and representative, leading to binding and enforceable agreements.

Business and peak associations

Business associations can form powerful networks that connect government officials with private sector firms (Moore & Hamalai, 1993). When such associations are free from government influence and their mission is to convey the business sector's concerns directly to state officials, they can "minimize transactions and coordination costs and ensure that investments that its members make have the highest returns" (Cali & Purohit, 2011, p. 1544). Another, and more important factor, is the role of business and peak associations in lobbying governments to enact legislation and regulations that support the interests of the private sector entities they represent. When private sector companies' voices are communicated as part of a collective and united front to the government through an institutional channel, there are higher chances that their concerns will be acknowledged and addressed. Moreover, the role of peak associations is not only to lobby for or against government policies, but also to act as a platform by which government and private sector entities can negotiate the implementation of legislation and laws to ascertain that they are mutually beneficial to both parties. These peak associations are most effective when they represent all businesses (e.g., through compulsory membership), have their own policy research capacities, and can incentivize or discipline members who do not adhere to agreements negotiated with the government.

Investment climate reforms

The World Bank (2015) defines investment climate reforms as the institutional and regulatory changes governments undertake to support their business environments. In this vein, the World Economic Forum measures global competitiveness by assessing existing institutional setups' readiness to deliver efficient services, and recommends reforms that address short-, medium-, and long-term reform goals. The basic short-term and medium-term reforms focus on building the institutional capacities of governments and private sectors, decreasing red tape and bureaucratic impediments, providing necessary infrastructure, and creating an effective and stable macroeconomic environment. The long-term reforms, however, target enhancement of the private sector's efficiency by providing specialized higher education and training programs in alignment with the private sector's labor needs, and aim to develop financial and technological readiness. When successful, these reforms can eventually lead to more innovation-driven economies.

The link between effective state-business relations and successful industrial policies

This sub-section briefly presents how effective state-business relations influence the outcome of industrial policies. In doing so, it enumerates the political and institutional prerequisites for successful industrial policies and what the state and the private sector should do to ensure their effective implementation.

The Organization for Economic Cooperation and Development (OECD, 2013) uses a comprehensive definition of industrial policy that emphasizes the importance of effective state-business relations in drafting supporting policies for industrial development. The definition states that:

> industrial policy is any type of intervention or government policy that attempts to improve the business environment to alter the structure of economic activity toward sectors, technologies or tasks that are expected to offer better prospects for economic growth or societal welfare than would occur in the absence of such intervention.
> (OECD, 2013, p. 16)

The key objective behind implementing most industrial policies is to promote and enhance the growth of the manufacturing sector in the economy by targeting certain subsectors, firms, or regional clusters (Warwick, 2013). This seems straightforward in theory, so how can one explain the success of industrial policies in some countries, but their failure in others?

Altenburg (2011) associates the success of industrial policies in achieving their objectives with a set of preconditions that must exist before their implementation. The capacity of political leadership is necessary to secure these pre-conditions, which are as follows:

a) **Strategic capability**: It is necessary to have the capacity to design policies that lead to sustainable and inclusive productivity growth.
b) **Clear rules**: The government must enforce laws that facilitate the entry and exit of foreign firms and protect against monopolies.
c) **Service delivery**: Effective service delivery is important to ensure investors find an environment conducive to business development. This is particularly the case when the machinery of bureaucracy cannot meet the demands of the private sector, and thus the government needs to establish new agencies to deliver such services.
d) **Protective policies**: The government must establish a system of checks and balances to ensure minimum protective requirements are in place to prevent cartels.

How then can a government build and implement these preconditions? Altenburg (2011) argues that the main requirements are effective state-business relations and collaboration to formulate an enabling environment for industrial policy. Again, returning to the importance of a strong meritocratic bureaucracy, governments cannot implement effective policies or communicate effectively with the private sector without a bureaucratic system that is staffed with trained civil servants recruited based on their merits.

Governments that implement effective industrial policies have several specific features in common. For example, they invest in developing an effective bureaucratic system that can monitor the progress of their industrial strategies. Another feature especially salient within the context of developing countries is the crucial capacity to generate evidence-based policymaking to steer and guide government decisions and policies. A well-informed government that coordinates with private sector institutions and the public at large will be capable of devising policies that address existing regulatory challenges, target certain industries, and foster an enabling environment for its industrial policies. Such effective industrial policies are always those that are aligned with existing laws and related policies. Conversely, when industrial policies are developed in a top-down manner rather than through systematic collaboration with the private sector, there is a risk of them being ineffective or even non-operational.

What are the key features of effective state-business relations as illustrated in the existing literature? Maxfield and Schneider (1997) enumerate several characteristics that allow bureaucrats and capitalists to build upon their embedded autonomy to communicate, collaborate, and formulate effective economic policies that support the state's developmental objectives.

a) **Information**: The first pillar and feature of effective state-business relations as seen in all the benchmark countries is the exchange of reliable and accurate information. The flow of information from the private sector

to the government allows bureaucrats to better design economic policies and consider the best policy options. Furthermore, when the government shares information with the private sector about which sectors to invest in locally and which international markets to target, it demonstrates its credibility and willingness to support the private sector's goals.
b) **Transparency**: When government decision-making is transparent and sharing reliable information in its strategy to effectively engage with the private sector, this reduces political uncertainty for investors. It assures them that government rents will be distributed to those with the best capacity to deliver services, rather than those enjoying stronger (informal) relations with bureaucrats.
c) **Reciprocity**: The government ensures that the subsidies it provides to the private sector are used as intended and the private sector is doing something in return, such as performing highly in line with clear, pre-defined targets. Meanwhile, when private sector entities misuse subsidies to achieve their gains, the government must divert the funds to more deserving ones.
d) **Credibility**: Credible government policies send strong signals to private sector actors about the intentions of the government to create a favorable business environment in which the private interests of bureaucrats do not influence policies and government promises are reliably adhered to.
e) **Trust**: Another key ingredient for effective state-business relations is trust. When trust connects the bureaucrats who set up policies with the managers who implement them and the investors whose businesses are influenced by them, it makes the whole economy work better. When trust informs their actions, they can perform better than only pursuing materialistic gains. This drives more sustainable and long-lasting relationships to achieve the state's overall developmental goals.

By building on these pillars, governments can markedly enhance their relationship with businesses and improve the quality of bureaucracy and the productivity of the private sector. The key requirements for establishing these pillars are reliable and effective communication channels, as well as coordination between the state and businesses. For coordination to be effective, business associations need to be truly representative of their members, provide appropriate incentives, and possess substantial policy research capacity. This is only possible if the government is willing to empower business associations, consult with them on all key economic reforms, and even selectively delegate policymaking and regulatory powers to them.

Benchmarking the macroeconomic and industrial performance of Saudi Arabia against Chile, Turkey, Ireland, Malaysia, South Korea, and the UAE

This section begins by explaining the rationales for choosing the benchmark countries referred to in this chapter and the lessons that Saudi Arabia can learn from them. It then provides a selection of those countries' macro-economic and business environment characteristics and describes where Saudi Arabia currently stands in comparison with them. Table 3.1 offers demographic data of the benchmark countries and the reasons for their inclusion in this chapter.

Table 3.1 Demographic data of benchmark countries and reasons for comparison with Saudi Arabia

Country	Population (million)	GDP per capita (USD)	GDP (billion USD)	Reasons for inclusion in benchmarking chapter
Chile	19.12	13,221	252.7	Chile experimented with numerous models for driving its industrial sectors, ranging from import substitution and state-directed development to creating the institutional frameworks necessary to drive industrial growth and innovation.
Turkey	84.34	8,536	719.9	There is a strong link between the phenomenal economic growth of Turkey since the 1960s and the institutional change that took place within it during this period. Amicable and constructive state-business relations through effective institutions created the conditions for a strong track record of economic growth.
Ireland	4.985	85,423	425.8	Ireland's rapid transformation into a "knowledge economy" was largely driven by effective state-industry relations. It is a late developer that offers many lessons to Saudi Arabia.
Poland	37.89	15,742	596.6	In contrast to other benchmark countries, Poland's efforts to develop an industrial base faced additional challenges due to the absence of mature and well-functioning business associations. As a post-communist country, Poland's successful journey to create a strong industrial base commenced only in the 1990s.

Table 3.1 Cont.

Country	Population (million)	GDP per capita (USD)	GDP (billion USD)	Reasons for inclusion in benchmarking chapter
Malaysia	32.36	10,412	337	Malaysia successfully transformed its economy from a poor, commodity-based one into one befitting an industrialized middle-income country. This was achieved through an active industrial policy that targeted specific sectors, skills development, R&D, and attraction of FDIs through tax and subsidy reductions.
Saudi Arabia	34.81	20,204	703.3	Saudi Arabia can learn some lessons from the other countries in this table and create institutions to strengthen partnerships with the private sector, issue policies to encourage targeted industrial sectors, and begin initiatives to drive economic growth.
South Korea	51.83	31,597	1.637 (trillion)	In response to the economic crisis of 1997, the South Korean government enforced the "Big Deal" policy to prioritize sectors it viewed as important for industrial development. This meant creating new institutional channels and strategies to communicate economic reform to the local business conglomerates.
UAE	9.89	36,284	358.8	The UAE represents a unique case among other GCC states for its economic diversification and development of industrial policies since the 1980s. Creation of Free Zones (especially in Dubai) and strong collaboration and cooperation between the public and private sectors have led to the UAE economy becoming the most diversified in the GCC. Given the socio-political and economic similarities between Saudi Arabia and the UAE, many lessons can be learned from the case of the UAE and Dubai, in particular.

Source: World Bank Data (2022)

The basis for benchmark countries' selection

There are two key reasons for benchmarking Saudi Arabia against the countries in this chapter. First, some benchmark countries represent examples of "late developers" that successfully diversified their economies from resource-dependent countries into more industrial-based ones like Malaysia and the UAE. Second, while Turkey, Ireland, and South Korea have never been resource-dependent economies, they provide excellent examples of how effective state-business relations resulted in successful industrial policies that transformed their economies into globally competitive ones. Ireland, meanwhile, represents the most advanced country among the selected group of late developers. Chile is an interesting case in this regard, as it experimented with different political regimes (from a military government to a democratic one) and varying development models that ranged from import substitution to direct state intervention in guiding its industrial growth. More than these, effective state-business relations and effective policies negotiated by strong business and peak associations were among the key factors facilitating Chile's economic transformation. Like Chile, Turkey also had a military government for a certain period, and Turkey's business sector was dominated by certain business families with strong but informal links to the government. Then, the emergence of strong business and peak associations in the 1960s inaugurated a period of effective policymaking that contributed significantly to Turkey's phenomenal industrial growth. It is important to indicate that while this chapter focuses on the unique lessons each country can provide for the case of Saudi Arabia, the depth of analysis relies quite substantially on the availability and accessibility of data.

Although the "Irish miracle" of lifting Ireland's economy, which was described as a "continuous failure" in late 1995 (Guiomard, 1995), into a "Celtic Tiger" in 1999 (Brezntiz, 2012) was a direct result of effective state-industry relations, it also adopted a neoliberal economic approach and focused on creating the educational and technical foundations of a strong IT sector. As such, the Irish success story of transforming its economy that was never resource-reliant into a knowledge-based one with the highest GDP per capita among the benchmark countries in this chapter offers several clear lessons that Saudi Arabia can learn from.

In contrast, Malaysia was a poor, resource-dependent economy with rubber and palm oil as its main natural resources, until the government's New Economic Plan (NEP) in 1970 set a roadmap toward economic transformation with both short- and long-term objectives. While the short-term objectives translated into the state's direct intervention in targeting the development of certain sectors in the economy, the longer-term objectives focused on human capital development, increasing spending on R&D, providing incentives to attract FDIs, and ensuring a harmonious relationship between the state and businesses.

In South Korea, as in Turkey, the business sector was dominated by powerful family conglomerates controlling key economic sectors. However, the economic crisis faced by the country in 1997 resulted in government intervention targeting specific industries that generated economic growth. This "Big Deal" economic policy was enacted through effective dialogue and communication between the government and private sector via business associations.

The UAE was selected as a benchmark country because it is the only GCC state with a significantly diversified economy—at least in Dubai—and less reliant on oil resources to balance its budget. The UAE's economic diversification policies began in the 1980s and were not guided by fluctuations in global oil prices but by the political leadership's vision of using oil resources to construct the necessary infrastructure for industrial development. The UAE case thus offers Saudi Arabia many lessons that it can build upon to guide its industrial sector and pave the way toward translating the optimistic objectives of Vision 2030 into reality.

Select macroeconomic indicators

This sub-section aims to provide a comparative overview of macroeconomic indicators in Saudi Arabia and the benchmark countries. Analysis of these indicators is important to understand where Saudi Arabia is currently positioned in comparison with these countries, and also what it can learn from their experiences to transform itself from an oil-based economy into a production-based one.

To begin with, compared with the benchmark countries, Saudi Arabia is making relatively good progress in reducing its dependency on oil resources. As Figure 3.1 shows, the UAE had the highest percentage of oil rent contributions to GDP in the late 1970s, when it exceeded 60%, but this steadily decreased to less than 11.5% in 2020. Similarly, Malaysia decreased oil rents as a percentage of GDP from 18% in the late 1970s to 1.6% in 2020. Meanwhile, the Saudi government's efforts to diversify its economy away from oil dependence have been successful, as oil rents decreased to 17.7% in 2020 as compared to 50.5% in 2011.

Nevertheless, the Saudi government's dependence on oil revenues is still high, which is reflected in the fluctuations of its annual GDP growth that correlate with international oil price changes. As Figure 3.2 shows, the drastic plunge in oil prices since the late 1970s saw GDP growth plummet from 12% in that period to around 3.2% in 2020. Similarly, spikes in GDP growth were witnessed in the UAE, although to a lesser extent, and even less so in Malaysia. While GDP growth in other benchmark countries, except for Turkey and Chile, witnessed relative stability from 1979 to 2020, their economies were nonetheless affected significantly by the 2009 global financial crisis and the 2020 COVID-19 pandemic. Among the benchmark countries, the countries least affected by the pandemic were Ireland and Turkey, while Chile and the UAE were the most heavily impacted.

76 *Quality of government and the public sector in the GCC region*

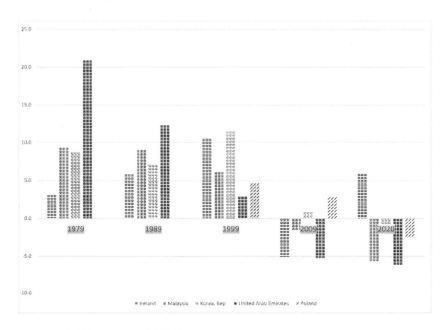

Figure 3.1 Oil rents (% of GDP)
Source: *World Bank Data (2022)*

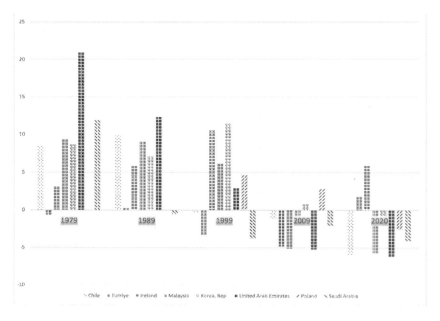

Figure 3.2 GDP growth (% annually)
Source: *World Bank Data (2022)*

Global insights for Saudi Arabia's economic development 77

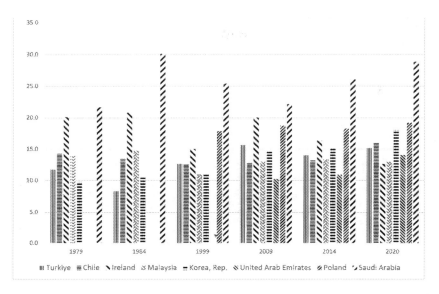

Figure 3.3 General government final consumption expenditure (% of GDP)
Source: World Bank Data (2022)

Regarding general government consumption as a percentage of GDP, Saudi Arabia exceeds other benchmark countries. As shown in Figure 3.3, Saudi Arabia's final consumption expenditure reached 24.4% in 2020, almost double that of Turkey, Malaysia, Chile, the UAE, or Ireland. This large expenditure was poured mostly into government subsidies for energy and other social benefits and public sector wages. Such data are evidence that its economy remains quite reliant on state spending.

Value-added services as contributions GDP and industrial growth

Value-added services as a percentage of GDP has witnessed significant growth in Saudi Arabia from approximately 34% in 1979 to 54% in 2020, and Malaysia has also seen a steady growth from 44% in 1989 to 55% in 2020, as shown in Figure 3.4. Similarly, Chile, Turkey, and South Korea also experienced a gradual increase in value-added services as a percentage of GDP. Nonetheless, from 1999, Ireland and Poland emerged as stronger examples of late developers transforming service-oriented economies, as the contribution of services to GDP exceeded 65% in Ireland and 56% in Poland in 2014.

In contrast to Saudi Arabia's value-added services as a percentage of GDP, which has seen relatively modest growth since 1979, its annual growth of value added from industry fell dramatically from its 83.1% growth in 1974 down to 45.5% in 2021 (see Figure 3.5). In contrast, Malaysia saw

78 *Quality of government and the public sector in the GCC region*

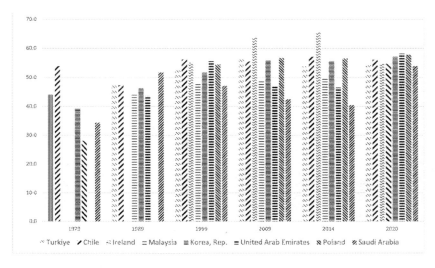

Figure 3.4 Services, value added (% of GDP)
Source: World Bank Data (2022)

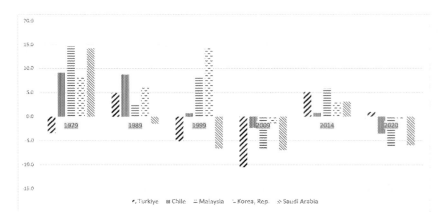

Figure 3.5 Industry, value added (% growth)
Source: World Bank Data (2022)

a gradual increase from 24.7% in 1960 to 37.7% in 2021. Turkey also witnessed a steady rise from 17.3% in 1960 to 31.1% in 2021. Nevertheless, all benchmark countries except Poland experienced negative growth due to the global financial crisis in 2009. Similarly, all but Ireland witnessed negative numbers in 2020 due to the global pandemic.

Global insights for Saudi Arabia's economic development 79

Overall, there is an urgent need for Saudi Arabia to diversify its industrial sectors away from oil and dependence on state spending. The current composition of Saudi industrial exports is dominated largely by chemical and plastic products linked to the oil sector. Furthermore, from 1995 to 2015, "other industrial" exports generated less than SAR40 billion, while oil-related chemical and plastic exports generated more than SAR180 billion.

The close link between high-tech exports as percentage of manufactured exports and R&D expenditure

Saudi Arabia needs to invest in technology-intensive production, which requires mid-skilled and highly skilled employment, to attract large numbers of Saudi youth. However, as Figure 3.6 shows, high-tech exports as a percentage of manufactured exports remains extremely low in Saudi Arabia, standing at 1.1% in 2009 and falling to 0.61% in 2020. The UAE's percentages were 10.17% in 2014 and 5.17% in 2020, which contrasts with Malaysia, where the percentage of high-tech exports relative to manufactured exports reached 54% in 2020. Meanwhile, in Ireland and Korea the rate exceeded 20% in 2020.

Crucially, it must be noted that there is a clear correlation between expenditure on R&D as a percentage of GDP and the percentage of high-tech exports. As Figure 3.7 shows, the three leading benchmark countries in terms of such exports—Ireland, Malaysia, and South Korea—are also

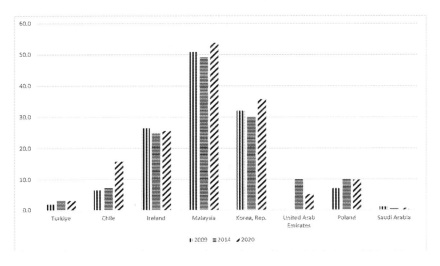

Figure 3.6 High-technology exports (% of manufactured exports)
Source: World Bank Data (2022)

80 *Quality of government and the public sector in the GCC region*

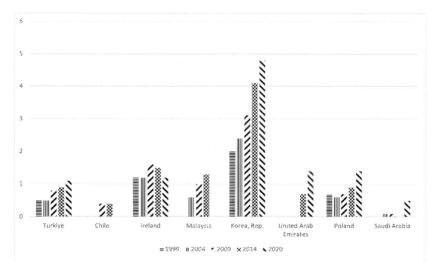

Figure 3.7 Research and development expenditure (% of GDP)
Source: World Bank Data (2022)

those most heavily invested in R&D, particularly South Korea, where expenditures exceeded 4% of the GDP in 2020. In Chile, high-tech exports are lower and expenditure on R&D has consistently fallen below 1%. In the UAE, this figure exceeded 1% for the first time in 2018 and reached 1.45% in 2020. Saudi Arabia remains the lowest investor in R&D, as it has yet to break 1% of GDP to date (0.52% in 2020 compared to its highest expenditure of 0.9% in 2011). Furthermore, it is equally important to invest in R&D to create a culture conducive to innovation and technological development.

Selected business environment indicators

One of the key factors for attracting FDI is how business-friendly the regulatory and institutional environment is. In this regard, Table 3.2 presents the findings from the Doing Business Report, which ranks countries based on regulatory, institutional, and business readiness indicators. For ease of doing business, South Korea stands as the most business-friendly environment among the benchmark countries, ranking 5th globally in 2020. Malaysia ranked 12th, followed by the UAE (16th) and Ireland (24th) in 2020. Saudi Arabia, meanwhile, ranked the lowest among the benchmark group, placing at 62nd globally in 2020, which nonetheless represents considerable progress since 2013, when it ranked 94th. In starting a business, the UAE topped the benchmark countries at 17th globally in 2020, making significant strides from 2013 when it ranked 53rd. Trailing behind all other benchmark countries was Poland, which ranked 128th globally in 2022. However, Poland, Malaysia,

Table 3.2 Economic rankings (1 = best, 190 = worst)

	Ease of Doing Business		Starting a Business		Getting Credit		Trading across Borders		Enforcing Contracts		Resolving Insolvency	
	2013	2020	2013	2020	2013	2020	2013	2020	2013	2020	2013	2020
Chile	57	59	59	57	82	94	65	73	56	54	55	53
Malaysia	12	12	54	126	1	37	11	49	33	35	49	40
Poland	24	40	107	128	20	37	1	1	55	55	27	25
Ireland	18	24	10	23	32	48	47	52	90	91	17	19
Turkey	69	33	79	77	82	37	70	44	33	24	126	120
Saudi Arabia	94	62	147	38	82	80	158	86	105	51	169	168
South Korea	5	5	11	33	44	67	32	36	1	2	4	11
United Arab Emirates	26	16	53	17	101	48	85	92	25	9	104	80

Source: Doing Business World Bank Data (2022)

and Turkey were among the easiest places to get credit, all ranking 37th globally in 2020, while Saudi Arabia stood in 80th place and Chile ranked 94th as the most difficult country to obtain credit among the benchmark nations. Poland ranked 1st globally in trading across borders, followed by South Korea at 36th. Saudi Arabia, meanwhile, ranked second to last among the benchmark countries at 86th globally. South Korea again topped the list of benchmark countries by ranking 2nd globally in enforcing contracts (in comparison, Ireland ranked last at 91st), and also ranked highest in resolving insolvency at 11th place globally, followed by Ireland and Poland at 19th and 25th, respectively. Saudi Arabia scored the lowest in resolving insolvency compared to all other benchmark countries. In sum, these rankings suggest that the regulatory and bureaucratic challenges for investment and diversification in Saudi Arabia are substantial, and the high rankings of the most successful cases suggest that, to achieve the greatest degrees of diversification and growth, a world-class administrative system is necessary.

How the benchmark countries developed effective state-business relations

This section illustrates how the benchmark countries developed effective state-business relations that enabled them to achieve considerable economic and industrial developments within a relatively short period, emphasizing four interlinked features of state-business relations. First, it examines how the selected countries invested in building the institutional and human capabilities to create an effective business environment. Second, it reveals how business and peak associations played an instrumental role as bridges between the government and private sector to enact policies and laws that facilitated the capacity of the private sector to drive economic growth. Third, it shows how institutional capacity and joint policymaking allowed successful industrial planning within the benchmark states. Fourth, and finally, it focuses on how the UAE managed to create a business-friendly environment that has attracted considerable FDI to achieve the highest levels of economic diversification in the Gulf region.

Building the institutional and human capabilities for an effective business environment

This section presents the experiences of Malaysia, South Korea, Ireland, and Chile in building effective institutions and human capacity to drive their successful economic transformations. Such experiences offer several valuable lessons for Saudi Arabia to learn from.

Role of efficient bureaucratic systems in Malaysia's economic development

Malaysia transformed from reliance on agriculture and natural resources during the 1960s into an industrialized and diversified economy by the

1990s. Since its independence in 1957, the country's path to industrialization was largely guided by the motivation to become an industrial hub in its region and enhance living standards through sectors such as technology and knowledge-based economic activities. To achieve this, from as early as 1967 the Higher Education Planning Committee prioritized the fields of science, math, engineering, and technology, and set a 60:40 ratio of science to arts students (Cherif et al., 2016). Since then, each government's five-year development plans have prioritized education and its role in supporting Malaysia's economic transformation.

Meanwhile, the 1971 New Economic Policy (NEP) set out Malaysia's long-term economic and industrial objectives toward freeing its economy from dependence on natural resources. However, the true journey of economic diversification began in 1981, when Mahathir Mohamad was elected as the country's fourth prime minister. One of the first actions he took was to reform the country's sluggish bureaucracy, which he believed was an essential vehicle for facilitating economic growth. Accordingly, he introduced strict discipline to the public sector and demanded higher productivity and efficiency from civil servants. Furthermore, to enhance the quality of services provided in the public sector, he recruited a cadre of capable technocrats with extensive experience in the private sector to bring the business sector's dynamism into the government's machinery. To enable the newly recruited technocrats, who had undergone extensive training in economics and business at top Western universities, Mohamad ensured that their policymaking was autonomous from political influence or interference (Khalid & Abidin, 2014).

After establishing a functional and well-equipped bureaucracy, Mohamad's next step was to create government institutions that could effectively improve an ailing economy, and the National Economic Action Council (NEAC) was one of the key institutions established to streamline economic growth in Malaysia. While the council's objective was to attain economic and financial stability, its key achievement was to bring "together all the relevant ministries and interest groups to overcome the problem of inter-agency areas responsibility" (Khalid & Abidin, 2014, p. 397). This ensured that all government entities worked toward achieving a single vision guided by a clear strategy. Because the prime minister personally chaired it, the NEAC had the power to implement its policies and decisions with little resistance from other government entities. Other government institutions, such as Khazanah Nasional Berhad and Tenaga Nasional, were then created and staffed with young professionals from the business sector to create economic investment opportunities and privatize certain government entities (Khalid & Abidin, 2014).

Furthermore, from the mid-1980s, Mohamad introduced the concept of "Malaysia Incorporated", showing both the public and private sectors that the country was akin to a "business entity" that they should jointly and collaboratively strive to make successful (Cherif et al., 2016, p. 88). In 2010, a new National Transformation Program was introduced to continue the journey of economic development and increase the national GDP per capita from $6,700 to $15,000 by 2020, thus making Malaysia officially a high-income country. New government institutions, such as the Malaysia External Trade Development Corporation, the Malaysia Production Corporation, and SME Corporation Malaysia, were then created to support the National Transformation Program's objectives.

Role of efficient bureaucratic systems in South Korea's economic development

Like Malaysia, South Korea presents another story of a country that shifted from a poverty-stricken economy dependent on foreign aid into an industrialized and self-sufficient one in less than three decades. Specifically, between 1962 and 1989, income per capita jumped from US$87 to US$5,199 and GDP in current prices increased from US$2.3 billion to US$220.7 billion (Harvie & Lee, 2003).

Efficient bureaucracy was an essential enabler in South Korea's success story. Among the first steps taken by General Park Chung-hee after assuming power in 1961 was to establish "an autonomous state capable of guiding economic development" (Fields, 1997, p.127). General Park created strong and independent bureaucratic institutions in a true spirit of meritocracy, as the recruitment of civil servants was based on the ability and capacity to implement the economic policies he had envisioned to lift South Korea from poverty into prosperity. In doing so, General Park's mission to streamline the bureaucratic machinery was not as difficult as it was, for example, in Malaysia. This is because South Korea had inherited the tradition of a well-disciplined and functional bureaucracy from the Japanese occupation and other neighboring countries. Furthermore, education was culturally very important in South Korea, hence the efforts of its government were not as strenuous as those of Malaysia's. South Korea's government also prioritized specific educational sectors that prepared future generations of citizens for high-tech jobs to meet increasing demands in the market for this talent (Fields, 1997).

To facilitate and centralize economic decision-making and achieve South Korea's developmental goals, General Park gave all relevant powers to the Economic Planning Board and Council of Economic Ministers (Fields, 1997). These two institutions were empowered to make all fiscal, monetary, industrial, and trade decisions. This removed the burden of cooperation or conflict among various government entities and situated all economic decision-making under a single umbrella. Since merit was the only criterion for admission of civil servants to key bureaucratic agencies according to Evans (1997), only 2% of individuals who sat for the annual higher civil service exam were accepted, the result was the high quality of public services and the capacity of bureaucrats to implement effective economic policies matching the needs and interests of the private sector.

Role of effective institutions and educational reforms in Ireland's developmental trajectory

During the 1970s, Ireland was one of the poorest countries in Europe, yet it managed to become one of its wealthiest nations by 2006. It took the country only a single decade to catch up with the rest of Europe's economic powers, thus becoming an exemplary European late developer. What was the secret behind this phenomenal transition?

First, numerous institutions played a key role in Ireland's ascent. Spiraling unemployment in the country during the late 1970s and early 1980s necessitated the urgent intervention of the Irish government to revamp and restructure its industrial policy. In response, the National Economic and Social Council (NESC) published the Strategy for Development 1986–1990, which was drafted in consultation with employers, unions, and even the opposition party in government. The report recommended reducing the size of the government and prioritizing the industrial sector as an engine for economic growth and job creation in Ireland. Furthermore, the NESC issued the Telesis report in 1982, which outlined the support necessary for the private sector to create a thriving IT industry and build on the country's capacity in that field. The government then created the National Centre for Partnership and Performance to become the R&D arm of the private sector and stimulate innovation. When the National Software Centre (NSC) was established, the serious commitment of the government to focus on the IT industry and build its industrial base was on full display.

Then, to serve as a bridge between local and foreign IT companies, the Irish government established Forfás, its national policy advisory body focusing on issues such as innovation, science and technology, and trade and industry development. This institution was vital for the industrial success of Ireland, not only because it facilitated communication and flow of information between both local and foreign private sector entities and international industrial firms, but also because it addressed the regulatory and legal challenges facing industries in Ireland and proposed solutions to address them as well. It further offered attractive tax holidays and financial incentives for foreign companies to invest in Ireland's growing industrial market. Another important institutional change was the merger of the Department of Industry and Commerce and the Department of Employment into one institution: The Department of Enterprise and Employment. This facilitated decision-making regarding industrial development and simultaneously eliminated numerous bureaucratic hurdles. Furthermore, Ireland believed that aligning the labor market with its new industrial policies was essential, so it created the Foras Áiseanna Saothair (FÁS) in 1987 to serve as a liaison between industries and job seekers. The agency provided policy advice to the government regarding skills the industry required and participated in designing training programs and preparing the skills of job seekers to match those offered by the market.

Second, education stood at the core of the economic transformation witnessed by Ireland during the second half of the 20th century (Brezntiz, 2012). In 1966, an OECD report underlined the weaknesses in the Irish educational system, the need to modernize it, and, more importantly, the necessity of providing equal access to education for all Irish citizens (O'Hearn, 2001). The government responded to the recommendations of this report by providing free education throughout Ireland, building more educational institutions, and providing financial support to students. In 1980, a white paper published by the Irish government highlighted that the existing educational systems produced mostly students with agricultural and manufacturing skills. Accordingly, the government shifted the focus of its tertiary education curriculum to engineering and technology. Efforts were also made to encourage student enrollment in vocational training, especially in technology-related jobs. In 1970, less than 3% of young people between the ages of 25 and 30 had a third-level qualification, but this number rose to almost 30% by the late 1990s (Kirby, 2008). The government also introduced the Leaving Certificate Vocational Programme in 1989, which provided high school dropouts the opportunity to join the workforce by apprenticing in industries in high demand in the private sector. As a result, Ireland became a favored destination for foreign firms, particularly among the US IT and engineering companies. While FDI represented only 23% of the country's GDP in the 1980s, that figure jumped to 63% in the late 1990s (OECD 2015).

All these factors supported Ireland's vision of becoming a powerful industrial IT base. By the mid 1990s, Irish companies like Insight Software and Real-Time Software ranked among the most prominent IT firms globally, and the industrial landscape of Ireland changed from relying on basic industries to being supported by technology-related ones. Ireland also increased its investment in R&D at the university and industry levels, and new IT companies like Iona were able to emerge and prosper internationally.

Role of Chile's effective state institutions in economic development

If effective government institutions and educational reforms were the keys to transforming Ireland into a vibrant economy, in Chile, it was the role of effective state institutions that was responsible for the country's metamorphosis from a state-centered society into a market-centered one (Wormald & Brieba, 2012). To transform itself, the Chilean government adopted a "top to bottom" approach in implementing institutional reforms that aimed to introduce free market principles and shift economic activities from government-centered to market-oriented. For example, from 1973 to the 1990s, the government implemented a privatization program that saw major services deregulated and sold to the private sector. The size of the state accordingly began to shrink, the bureaucracy was modernized and reformed to enhance the efficiency of services, and the quality of public administration was improved (Wormald & Brieba, 2012). These changes were reflected in overall government performance, which witnessed significant change, as many sluggish government entities were substantially downsized, quality measures were enforced, and, like in Malaysia and South Korea, bureaucratic machinery was transformed into an effective and productive system. Furthermore, numerous free trade agreements were signed with foreign governments, eventually leading Chile to become the first South American country to join the OECD in 2010.

Enabling joint policymaking through business and peak associations

Building necessary human and institutional capacity on the government side is critical for supporting effective state-business relations. Meanwhile, information exchange and proper institutional communication channels are vital for economic policymaking. This section highlights how the benchmark countries achieved joint policymaking through business and peak associations. The role of these associations was not solely to lobby against government policies but, as the various cases show, they became instrumental in ensuring that the private sector's needs were communicated properly to the government, and vice-versa.

Role of South Korea's peak associations in facilitating dialogue between the government and private sector

The case of South Korea presents several useful lessons that illustrate the importance of dialogue between the government and private sector and the critical role of business and peak associations in facilitating and enabling such dialogue. Before General Park seized power, business groups could not lobby or influence economic policymaking, as the state did not depend on the private sector's expertise due to its reliance on simple technologies for industrial development (Shafer, 1997). However, when General Park took control amid dwindling economic growth, he shifted the "sectoral base of the economy from light to heavy manufacturing" (Shafer, 1997, p. 109). The government adopted a top-down approach to achieve this shift successfully by involving the elite *chaebol* (business families owning large conglomerates). General Park's strategy was thus to transform the nation into "Korea, Inc.", and this first required creating state-funded industrial associations to ensure the flow of reliable information between the public and private sectors on the one hand, and clear reception by the government of the voices, concerns, and issues of the private sector in achieving the state's objectives on the other (Chu, 1989).

More than 200 associations operated under the umbrella of the Ministry of Trade, but they simply reacted to government policies rather than initiating policies that reflected their own needs (Fields, 1997). Only a few independent organizations representing the private sector were relatively free from government pressure, including the Korean Chamber of

Commerce and Industry, the Korean Traders Association, and the Korean Federation of Textile Industry (Fields, 1997). The most influential among such institutions was the Federation of Korean Industry (FKI) which has been described as a "self-defense interest and lobbying organization for the Chaebol to protect their own interests" (Fields, 1997, p.136).

The FKI's role in negotiating with the government and protecting the interests of the business elites was important. Although some argue that the FKI operated in an "information up, orders down" fashion (Fields, 1997, p. 138), many examples demonstrate its representation of business groups' interests. To begin with, the FKI changed its function from a lobbying organization into an institution advocating policy change and implementation. To achieve this, the FKI created numerous policy research groups that provided advice on issues concerning commerce, taxation, and foreign trade (Fields, 1997). The FKI's capacity to generate reliable and evidence-based policy proposals that represented and reflected business groups' needs then brought it closer to the government bureaucracy. The government ended up implementing around 40% of the policy proposals it received from the FKI (Fox, 1992), and it "accepted" 90% of the FKI's recommendations (Fields, 1997, p. 138).

General Park's belief that dialogue between the government and private sectors was essential for economic development led him to initiate monthly meetings personally chaired by himself and attended by all key ministers in charge of commerce, business, and economy to discuss any issues related to local and foreign trade (Fields, 1997). Furthermore, among the 176 policy recommendations proposed to the government by the Korean Traders Association (in charge of promoting Korean exports and revisiting trade regulations to facilitate the movement of goods across borders), 76% were implemented, and at the same time, other business associations were no longer receiving orders from the government, but rather negotiating which sectoral policies best served the interests of the business and government sectors (Fields, 1997). In addition, these associations conducted industry surveys to better understand the private sector's challenges and how they could be mitigated through government intervention and policies. This was particularly true in the case of the auto industry, which was supported and energized by the direct involvement of the president's office (Fields, 1997).

Role of Chile's business associations in communicating business interests to policymakers

If the case of Korea demonstrated the strength of the state over business associations, Chile by contrast represents a bottom-up approach, as its business associations played an instrumental role in representing the interests of the business sector and forcing the government to issue policies that reflected their interests. Silva (1997) states that there were two ways through which businesses represented their needs: the first was through large business associations, such as the Confederation for Production and

Commerce (CPC), which oversaw monetary policy issue negotiations, and the second was through sector-specific peak associations honing in more closely on issues regarding their respective sectors. These two types of associations would threaten to join the political opposition if their preferred policy reforms were not implemented. Through lobbying and pressure on the government and relevant ministries by the CPC and sectorial associations, they communicated their challenges and needs directly to the government, which facilitated the country's recovery from its economic crisis in 1982 and 1983 (Silva, 1997). Furthermore, allowing the private sector to participate in policy formulation led to creating an environment conducive to investment and attracting greater foreign investments. Key government institutions, such as the Ministry of Finance, the Ministry of Economy, the central bank, and the budget office worked closely with the private sector, particularly with huge firms like BHC, the Edwards conglomerates, and the Grupo Cruzat-Larraín (Silva, 1997). The government institutions always consulted with private sector entities before major economic policies were drafted and implemented.

The CPC's role was thus critical in establishing effective communication channels between the government and private sector. Moreover, peak business associations were directly involved in negotiating drafts of legislation before finalization, and negotiations between the business associations and bureaucrats over policy issues were based on technical assessments of the potential impact of policies on economic and industrial growth (Silva, 1997). The CPC also made substantial reforms in taxation and social policy issues. First, they negotiated with the government to keep taxes as low as 14% from 1990 to 2001, 17% from 2002 to 2009, and 18.5% between 2009 and 2013 (UNRISD, 2014). These figures were considerably lower than those in other Latin American countries, which ranged between 30% and 40% (UNRISD, 2014). Policies in favor of businesses were also enacted, such as reducing business contributions to social welfare and increasing workers' contributions to their retirement funds. Furthermore, the CPC encouraged political and economic elites to enact a strategic economic plan to inform and guide the country's economic policies over the upcoming 35 years.

Role of foreign businesses in creating peak organizations in Poland

As an example of a post-communist country that experienced an abrupt economic recession, Poland was the first to recover from it with a strong and growing economy during the 1990s (Gardawski et al., 2012). Poland did not have strong business associations to support the private sector's policy preferences, and instead the European Union had a direct influence on the creation of Polish business associations, which it empowered to force the government to open its heavy industries market to international investors. As a result, there was significant pressure from foreign investors, who created associations to lobby against certain government policies in

Poland that stood against their business interests (Schoenman, 2005). This bottom-up approach adopted by foreign business associations then saw the emergence of Polish business associations, which attempted to direct government policies to support their businesses. Among the most influential of these business associations was the Polish Chamber of Commerce (PCC), which comprised 150 member organizations representing approximately 150,000 businesses. In contrast to South Korea and Chile, business associations in Poland represented the interests of its political and economic elites (Schoenman, 2005); nevertheless, businesses were able to voice their concerns and issues to the government, and to some extent managed to influence policy decisions pertinent to Poland's business environment.

The weaker role of business associations in Turkey

In the case of Turkey, until the 1970s it was quite difficult to establish a "peak all-encompassing umbrella organization able to aggregate various interests, shape policy, and function as a conflict resolution mechanism among business firms" (Biddle & Milor, 1997, pp. 286–287). This was ultimately the result of the private sector's development under the direct control of the government and the political leadership's refusal to allow such institutions to evolve. However, the 1980s saw the birth of numerous associations at the industry level, which pressured the local and central governments to implement specific policies and requested subsidies to help their businesses to grow. Many of these associations served as links between the government and various industries, and even intervened on many occasions to solve conflicts between the two sectors (Biddle & Milor, 1997).

The business associations were even more influential in lobbying the government to issue numerous investment incentives for Turkish businesses. In the 1980s, for example, the government agreed to provide two sets of incentives: investment-related and export-related ones. These included certain tax incentives, such as exemptions from customs, investment taxes, VAT refunds, social security, and foreign exchange allocations. Furthermore, the government offered other trade incentives, including foreign exchange allocations and import permits. In terms of direct subsidies, businesses were offered preferential credits, land allocations, and investment, transportation, and energy subsidies (Biddle & Milor, 1997). It is crucial to note that many of these incentives were not doled out indiscriminately, but rather were linked to export performance. In some cases, incentives and licenses were administered directly by the business associations acting on behalf of the government.

Nevertheless, Turkey also represents an example of business associations working against the private sector's interests. Such was the case with the Automotive Manufacturers Association (OSD), which was created in 1974 to fix the prices of goods that the industry needed (Biddle & Milor, 1997). In this instance, the informal networks connecting government officials with some of the OSD's leaders compromised its integrity and undermined the trust of other auto industry dealers. Due to the influence of business leaders on its decision-making, conflicts arose between the demands of old and new car dealers, who viewed the OSD as blocking the interests of new car dealers and lobbying for a cap on car imports. Car dealers therefore "bypassed" the OSD when they wished to communicate with the state, especially when they knew that their interests conflicted with those of the association (Biddle & Milor, 1997).

Successful industrial planning through institutional change and effective state-business coordination

This section will demonstrate how Malaysia, South Korea, and Turkey achieved effective state-business coordination through industrial planning and institutional change. Saudi Arabia can draw many lessons from the trajectories followed by these countries and the institutional reforms they underwent to facilitate industrial development.

Lessons from Malaysia

Malaysia managed to transform itself from an agricultural economy into an industrial one, and this was ultimately the result of direct state involvement in the creation of institutions and drafting of industrial policies developed in close conjunction with industrial and private sector bodies. One example of a successful industrial transformation within Malaysia occurred in the district of Penang (located on the northwest coast of the Malaysian Peninsula), which was the poorest in natural resources among the country's districts. Its case demonstrates how industrial success often relies on state intervention in drafting purposeful policies and aligning educational curricula and training with market needs.

The path to industrialization in Penang began in 1969, when the central government drafted an economic master plan benchmarking the district against regional economic powers such as Hong Kong, Japan, and South Korea. At the heart of the plan was establishing an export-led economy through reliance on training unemployed youth and equipping them for the jobs needed by the private sector. The government aimed to turn "the socially disturbing high unemployment rate in Penang…into a socioeconomic advantage through the promotion of labor-intensive industries" (Lim, 2005, p. 64). The government thus prioritized the electronics industry, which it wanted to develop into a niche within the region, and created the legal and regulatory structures for free trade zones (FTZs) to attract international firms specializing in electronic devices.

The first concrete step the Penang government took toward realizing its industrialization plan was restructuring its government institutions to avoid policy conflicts and streamline public decision-making. To accomplish this, the Penang Development Corporation (PDC) was established as a focal point for communicating between the local and federal governments while maintaining full independence from the bureaucracy. Then, the State Planning and Development Committee (SPDC) was created within the PDC to make all decisions related to assigning land for development and overcoming the bureaucratic hurdles that often hamstrung the private sector's involvement in industrial development. The PDC also created one-stop shops for investors, coordinated with local companies, shared information about which international markets could be attractive for Penang, and provided financial incentives to local companies to promote their industrial services and capacities to neighboring countries. It furthermore held extensive individual meetings with both large and small businesses in Penang to understand their challenges, and worked closely with them in drafting industrial policies.

The Penang government also understood that a successful industrial policy relied on training and development of local skills. Therefore, it created the Industrial Training Institute, which attracted high school dropouts and trained them in electronics and related skills required by the industry. Meanwhile, the PDC worked closely with local factories, designed special training programs to develop the exact skills those factories needed, and launched the Young Entrepreneur Program to enhance high school dropouts' entrepreneurial skills.

The efforts of the Penang government reached fruition by the mid-1980s, when it hosted some of the world's largest electronics firms in competition with Japan and the USA. At the time, the Penang industrial zone hosted reputable electronics companies like Sony, Sanyo, and NEC, and soon moved into more sophisticated electronic production to become associated with companies such as Dell and Motorola. As a result, the export of manufactured goods from Penang jumped from US$90 million in 1973 to US$4.5 billion by the late 1980s, and its growth remained stronger than any other region in Malaysia (World Bank Data, 2022). In 2005, foreign firms accounted for over 70% of all manufactured exports in Penang, which itself was responsible for more than half of all Malaysian electronics exports. This industrial success story significantly impacted Penang's GDP per capita, which was 10% lower than the national average in the 1970s, but rose to 57% higher than the national average in 2010. By 2000, manufacturing accounted for more than 47% of Penang's GDP (World Bank Data, 2022).

Lessons from South Korea

South Korea also provides an excellent case study of a country that managed to become a powerful industrial hub within a few decades. For South Korea, the government was directly involved in redirecting and shifting the country's economy into heavy industry, announcing in 1973 the Heavy Chemical and Industry Development Plan (HCIDP) to establish a well-designed institutional and regulatory framework for the country's future industrial development, one in which General Park played a direct personal role. Then, the government created the National Investment Fund to provide businesses with financial incentives such as access to low-interest loans for growing industrial firms, tax holidays for firms investing in heavy industry, reduced tariffs, and subsidized prices of heavy machinery and equipment. Importantly, the provision of such incentives and subsidies was accompanied by strict follow-up on where subsidies were spent and the outcomes they yielded for the economy and businesses. As a result, between 1977 and 1979, more than 80% of all investment in manufacturing was spent exclusively on heavy industry (Shafer, 1997). The government also worked closely with the *chaebol* and designed policies to facilitate their industrial activities, which the government forced them to align with the aims and goals of the HCIDP. In contrast to Ireland or Malaysia, for example, South Korea did not rely heavily on FDI as a source of financing or transfer of knowhow during its industrial growth, relying only on external borrowing and technology licensing.

Lessons from Turkey

In contrast to South Korea, Turkey serves as an example of a late industrialized nation that adopted two forms of industrialization policies. From 1923 up until the 1980s, the country relied on an import-substituting industrialization program with heavy protection that aimed to foster the local industrial capacity to produce capital goods. From the 1980s, the Turkish government shifted toward trade liberalization through a structural adjustment program to enhance export-oriented industrialization. Accordingly, Turkey substantially reduced tariffs and embarked on a journey toward diversifying its economy and increasing its industrial capacity. Therefore, the Turkish government directed investment into specific sectors that it highlighted in its "positive list" and focused primarily on promoting exports by providing generous incentives and tax holidays for exporters. The government also created the Resource Utilization Support Fund to provide loans with low-interest rates to new export companies.

When Turkey joined the World Trade Organization (WTO) in 1995, more institutional and legal reforms were made to facilitate industrial development and exports. Figure 3.8 shows exports rose from the mid-1990s and picked up further after 2000 (Atiyas & Bakis, 2013). This exponential rise in exports was a result of industrial policy shifting away from the old sectoral preference toward regional initiatives and instead encouraging and supporting the creation of small and medium-sized enterprises (SMEs), investing in research centers that provided useful industrial policy analysis to the government, and establishing channels of communication between the private and industrial sectors. Furthermore, important institutions like the Turkish Industry and Business Association and the Union of Chambers and Commodity Exchanges of Turkey were instrumental in lobbying for the private sector's interests and coordinating the economic and industrial policymaking process between that sector and the government.

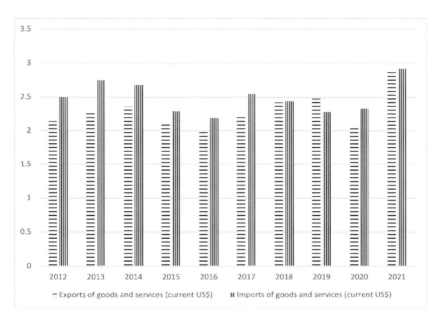

Figure 3.8 Turkish exports versus imports between 2012 and 2022 (in US$ billions)
Source: *The Economic Policy Research Foundation of Turkey (2014)*

In 2004, the Turkish government issued Law 5084, which stressed the importance of developing industrial clusters and cities outside the regions of Istanbul and Ankara to provide job opportunities for those in regional areas, especially those where income per capita was less than US$1,500 in 2001. The law specified several incentives for the private sector to encourage job creation and provided opportunities for stimulating industrial growth. For example, it exempted workers earning minimum wage in industrial zones from taxes and reduced their employers' taxes and social obligations, which the state then subsidized. Furthermore, land was allocated free of charge within industrial zones to companies that employed at least 10 workers for five years (Atiyas & Bakis, 2013).

The government also introduced innovative schemes to target certain industrial sectors. For example, in 2009, Turkey was divided into four regions based on socioeconomic characteristics, and on that basis, the government decided which industrial sectors it would focus on. In regions whose populations had higher income and educational backgrounds, the government targeted high-tech industries, while in other regions light manufacturing industries and agricultural activities were the focus (Atiyas & Bakis, 2013). Government industrial policies have since had a clear impact on the growth of exports as a percentage of GDP. As shown in Figure 3.9, since 1978 the share of exports in GDP has increased drastically from 5% to 20% in the mid-1980s and then 28% in 2020.

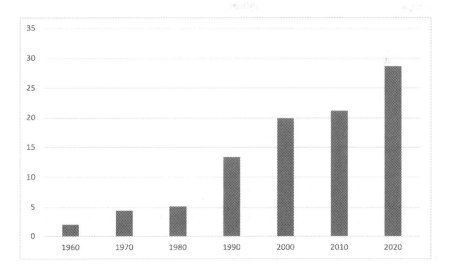

Figure 3.9 Share of Turkey's exports in GDP (%)
Source: *World Bank Data (2022)*

The UAE's transition to a knowledge economy

This section discusses the successful journey of the UAE in its transition into a knowledge economy. In this regard, the experience of the UAE can offer Saudi Arabia several lessons on how to build on its existing institutional and human capacity to achieve the objectives of its Vision 2030.

One important strategic priority for the UAE has been shifting its economy from reliance on natural resources toward being driven by innovation. To realize this goal, its government attracts talent from across the globe and invests in educating its Emirati population. In recent years, the UAE government has also embarked upon a promising program for fostering its national capacity by providing free education, granting scholarships to nationals to study abroad, and facilitating integration into the workforce. In addition, many government-backed funding institutions have been established to provide low-interest loans to nationals for investment in SMEs.

Table 3.3 compares the progress the UAE and other GCC countries have made in generating the key prerequisites and conditions for shifting toward a knowledge-based economy. The rankings demonstrate the readiness of a country to generate economic activities based on innovation and information technology in terms of institutional and human capacity. In 2000, the UAE ranked 48th in the Knowledge Economic Index and progressed to 12th place in 2021, ranking 1st among the GCC. Saudi Arabia, meanwhile, is among the GCC countries that witnessed a substantial upgrade, moving from 76th in 2000 to 40th in 2021.

Table 3.3 GCC countries' global Knowledge Index ranking from 2000 to 2021

Country	2000	2012	2021
UAE	48	42	12
Bahrain	41	43	54
Oman	65	47	52
Saudi Arabia	76	50	40
Qatar	49	54	58
Kuwait	46	64	47

Source: UNDP & MBRF (2021)

Thus, the UAE has been making remarkable progress in its shift to a knowledge economy, and its rankings in key indicators have been improving since 2000. For example, it ranked 12th in the World Bank's Global Knowledge Index in 2020, having risen 36 positions since 2000. It also ranked 21st on the Information and Communication Technology (ICT) Index for telephone, computer, and Internet penetration (rising 11 places since 2000). Nonetheless, it only ranked 79th in the Education and HR Index (still 15 places higher than 2000), which calculates average adult literacy and secondary and tertiary enrollment (World Bank Data, 2022). Despite this, Dubai has developed a reputation as a financial and education hub in the GCC and MENA regions, and prestigious American, British, and Australian universities have opened branches in the UAE to attract both local and international students from the GCC and the rest of the Arab world. Furthermore, the Education Zone and the Academic City were established in Dubai to centralize the provision of education and attract more universities to open branches in the emirate. Abu Dhabi, meanwhile, has also attracted world-class universities such as INSEAD, New York University in Abu Dhabi, and the Sorbonne.

Sultan Al Mansouri, the UAE Minister of Economy, confirmed the strategic direction of his government in supporting a knowledge- and innovation-driven economy. He stated:

> The Ministry of Economy is committed to attracting international expertise to support economic development by focusing on introducing advanced technologies. These are aimed at boosting the efficiencies of various industrial and economic sectors. We also focus on promoting a culture of innovation and research and development.
>
> (Gulf News, 2011)

This government commitment has facilitated the shift from dependence on oil revenues, and the UAE has gradually yet successfully been moving away from its oil-based economy. For example, oil revenues accounted for over 60% of the GDP in 1979, but in 2008, oil-based utilities accounted

Global insights for Saudi Arabia's economic development

for only 27%. By 2020, this had dropped even further to just 11.5% (World Bank Data, 2022).

The UAE, particularly in Dubai, has achieved significant economic transformation over a short period despite considerable obstacles. To broaden Dubai's economy beyond mere resource extraction, the emirate's former ruler, Sheikh Rashid, poured oil revenues into investments. For example, Dubai built port facilities and drydocks at Jebel Ali Port and Port Rashid in the 1970s and 1980s, which greatly exceeded projected demand at the time and transformed Dubai's economy and relations with other nations. Petroleum and gas now account for less than 1% of Dubai's GDP, and the US Navy docks more ships at Jebel Ali than any other port outside of the USA.

Attracting foreign businesses and FDI inflows to the UAE

The rankings of the UAE as a flexible and business-friendly country, with its stable political environment and excellent logistical hub, all serve to attract and encourage investors to come and open businesses in the country. As Figure 3.10 below shows, the UAE is among the top 15 countries globally in the business confidence index for investment, scoring above Singapore, Belgium, Norway, and several advanced OECD countries in 2020.

The government of the UAE also makes the influx of FDI one of its top strategic objectives as it aims to sustain its economic growth, diversify economic activities, and entice businesses to operate in the country. The UAE's stock of inward FDIs grew at an average rate of 49% per year from US$1.1 billion (1.5% of GDP) in 2000 to US$85.4 billion (23.7%) in 2011. This makes the UAE the next largest recipient of FDIs after Saudi Arabia. Such FDIs are essential for building knowledge-based economies, as they offer a rich source of expertise, knowledge, and technology transfer, provide employment opportunities for the host countries, and import significant amounts of hard currency. Hence, the UAE considers FDIs to be an important element as they veer away from dependence on oil resources and establish an environment of private sector competition and investment in service-based industries. Looking at the performance of the UAE's inward FDI stocks thus reveals its progression toward reaching the strategic objectives of fully diversifying its economy from reliance on oil and natural resources. As Table 3.4 shows, the contribution of FDIs to the UAE's GDP has increased considerably over the past couple of decades. From 2000 to 2010, the FDI growth rate witnessed a sharp uptick of more than 300%, rocketing from 0.5% to 3% of GDP. From 2010 onward, FDI stock accounted for 5.5% of its GDP.

Recommendations and conclusions

The Saudi economy is still heavily reliant upon oil revenues, and driven by state spending, which has been shrinking since the fall of oil prices in

98 Quality of government and the public sector in the GCC region

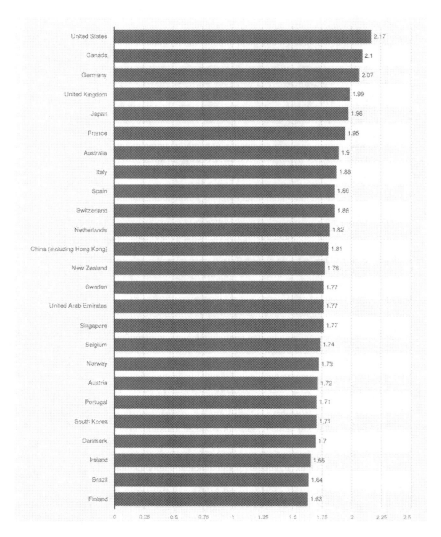

Figure 3.10 FDI Confidence Index scores in 2020
Source: *World Bank Data (2022)*

Table 3.4 UAE inward FDI stock, 2000–2020

	2000	*2010*	*2020*
Foreign direct investment, net inflows (% of GDP)	-0.5	3.0	5.5
Foreign direct investment, net inflows (BoP, current US$)	-506,329,999.9	8,796,769,641.0	19,884,468,660.0

Source: *UNCTAD (2022)*

mid-2014 and the ramifications of the COVID-19 pandemic since early 2020. The benchmark cases discussed above reveal that transforming a resource-dependent economy into one that is industrially based is possible, but requires strong political commitment, institutional reforms, and capacity development. What reforms does the Saudi government need to implement to make the achievement of its Vision 2030 possible?

The need for more effective bureaucratic systems

The experiences of Malaysia, South Korea, and Chile reveal the importance of effective bureaucratic systems and their role in facilitating the flow of information and communication between the public and private sectors. The leaders of those three countries began by selectively recruiting qualified technocrats for key government positions and then ensured their autonomy from political influence, thereby empowering leading agencies that enjoyed special developmental mandates. This was often accompanied by a streamlining of general administrative structures. Such efforts facilitated the implementation of economic policies to address the private sector's needs, allowed governments to make support for businesses conditional on clearly measured performance indicators, and provided focal points for effective and credible state-business coordination.

In Saudi Arabia, the government has already begun reforming its bureaucracy and restructured some of its key ministries to align their objectives and performance with Vision 2030. Providing effective training programs to government officials will better support their efforts to implement policies that serve the private sector's needs, especially given Vision 2030's focus on facilitating dialogue and cooperation between the public and private sectors. Furthermore, a streamlined and efficient public sector will mean a faster and more accountable decision-making process that will assist the private sector's operations.

Effective dialogue between the public and private sectors

Chile and South Korea's cases demonstrated how effective state-business relations can be instrumental for the private sector's growth and development. Peak business associations in the two countries supported and advocated for the interests of the private sector and voiced the concerns and needs of specific businesses. In Chile, business associations not only acted as liaisons between the state and the private sector, but also went so far as to support the capacity development of specific businesses by providing customized training programs to address the capacity challenges facing firms in competing internationally. In Turkey, on the other hand, the involvement of politicians in business association operations during the 1980s prevented certain sectors from relying on them to voice their concerns to the government. In all cases, however, associations have been the most effective in coordinating economic policy when they represent all national businesses rather than only segments of it, possess a profound research capacity and ability to gauge business interests and capabilities, and are entrusted by governments with regulatory tasks.

Meanwhile, Saudi Arabia does have some influential chambers of commerce that the government consults while drafting economic policies. Nonetheless, these chambers and other business associations could potentially play a bigger role in facilitating dialogue between the government and business sector to achieve the goals of Vision 2030. Now, chambers of commerce need to include smaller firms, especially SMEs, in economic decision-making and planning, and they must create think tanks to produce policy research in support of the private sector's growth. The private sector will benefit from more independent sectoral organizations as well. Furthermore, the public sector's ownership of large companies operating within the private sector can make it more difficult for smaller enterprises to operate and compete.

Industrial planning and development

The efforts and roles of the Irish, Malaysian, South Korean, Turkish, and the UAE governments were instrumental in guiding the shifts of their respective countries toward industrial development. In South Korea, the government redirected the focus of powerful business conglomerates through the policies of the HCIDP and incentives for investment in heavy industries. The Irish government, meanwhile, provided tax holidays and numerous other incentives for international electronics firms to establish their businesses in the country. Similarly, the government in Malaysia enacted business-friendly policies to attract international investors and closely coordinated with private companies to meet their infrastructure and training needs.

Saudi Arabia can learn many lessons from these countries to diversify its industrial base, which is currently centered on oil and petrochemicals as discussed in the literature review. Such diversification will require the government to support educational policies as Ireland did in the 1970s and imitate Malaysia's approach by prioritizing the fields of math, science, technology, and engineering. The Saudi government can also enhance its industrial sector by investing in high-quality vocational training, and reforming current educational systems to mirror the interests of Saudis in high-tech fields. Now, Saudi Arabia's share of high-tech among total manufacturing exports (0.26%) is below its neighboring states of Kuwait (0.52%) and Oman (0.30%) and far below the UAE (3.20%), OECD (17.40%), and East Asia (28.40%) averages (World Bank Data, 2022). To address this challenge, the government should increase its R&D investments in coordination with the private sector and provide more attractive vocational training options based on actual business needs so that Saudi youth can occupy jobs in the industrial sector.

Another challenge Saudi Arabia's industrial sector faces is its concentration in just a few administrative regions. Only four out of the thirteen administrative regions of Saudi Arabia attract finance and loans from the government and host the lion's share of its factories. In 2010, 48% of the total value in industrial investment was centered in Eastern Saudi Arabia, followed by 16.5% in Riyadh. Regarding the number of industrial factories operating, 93% are in the Eastern region, Riyadh, Madinah, and Makkah, while the remaining 7% are divided among the nine other regions. While this has occurred because most businesses are also concentrated within these regions, expanding the industrial base to other regions of the nation will considerably increase jobs for Saudis living in those areas and enhance overall economic development. The experiences of countries like Malaysia, which have successfully focused their development efforts on poorer regions, can guide this process.

Reforming the business climate

Among the benchmark countries, the case of the UAE best reveals the importance of the business environment in supporting economic growth and attraction of FDIs. Institutional development began there in the 1980s and the government continues to invest in enhancing key business indicator rankings as stated above. This has enticed foreign companies to establish their regional hubs in Dubai and elsewhere in the UAE. An increasing number of industrial zones also supports the UAE's shift to a knowledge-based economy.

References

Altenburg, T. (2011). Industrial policy in developing. Countries. overview and lessons from seven country cases. Retrieved from: http://edoc.vifapol.de/opus/volltexte/2011/3341/pdf/DP_4.2011.pdf. Accessed on 28th August 2022.

Atiyas, I., & Bakis, O. (2013). The regional dimension of productivity and exports in turkey: Evidence from firm-level data. Retrieved from: www.frbatlanta.org/-/media/documents/news/conferences/2013/caed/C2Atiyas.pdf Accessed on 28 August 2022.

Bettcher, K., Herzberg, B., & Nadgrodkiewicz, A. (2015). Public-private dialogue: The key to good governance and development. Retrieved from: www.cipe.org/publications/detail/public-private-dialogue-key-good-governance-and-development. Accessed on 28th August 2022.

Biddle, J., & Milor, V. (1997). Economic Governance in Turkey: Bureaucratic capacity, Policy Networks, and Business Associations. In S. Maxfield, B. Ross Schneider (eds.), *Business and the State in Developing Countries*, Cornell University Press, Ithaca.

Brezntiz, D. (2012). Ideas, structure, state action and economic growth: Rethinking the Irish miracle. *Review of International Political Economy*, 19, 87–1113.

Cali, M., & Purohit, S. (2011). Measuring state-business relations within developing countries: An application to Indian states. *Journal of International Development*, Washington, DC. 23(3), 394–419.

Cherif, R., Hasanov, F., & Zhu, M. (2016). *Breaking the Oil Spell: The Gulf Falcons' Path to Diversification*. IMF publications.

Chu, Y. (1989). State structure and economic adjustment of the East Asian newly industrializing countries. *International Organization*, 43(4), 647–672.

Evans, P. (1997). *Embedded Autonomy: States and Industrial Transformation*, Princeton University Press, Princeton.

Fields, K. (1997). Strong States and Business Organization in Korea and Taiwan. In *Business and the State in Developing Countries*, S. Mayfield and B. Ross Schneider (eds.), NYL Cornell University Press, Ithaca, pp. 122–151.

Fox, J. (1992). The nexus between the state and the Chaebok Brining Class Back in. Paper presented at the Annual Meeting of the Association for Asian Studies. Washington, DC. April.

Gardawski, J., Mrozowicki, A., & Czarzasty, J. (2012). *Trade Unions in Poland*. ETUI aisbl, Brussels.

Guiomard, C. (1995). *The Irish Disease and How to Cure it: Common Sense Economics for a Competitive World*. Oak Tree Press, Dublin.

Gulf News. (2011). Knowledge-based economy is UAE's strategic objective. Retrieved from: https://gulfnews.com/business/knowledge-based-economy-is-uaes-strategic-objective-1.808295 Accessed on 7 September 2022.

Harvie, C., & Lee, H. (2003). Export-led industrialization and growth: Korea's economic miracle, 1962–1989. *Australian Economic History Review*, 43(3), 256–286.

Khalid, K., & Abidin, M. (2014). Technocracy in economic policy-making in malaysia. Retrieved from: https://englishkyoto-seas.org/2014/08/vol-3-no-2-khadijah-md-khalid-and-mahani-zainal-abidin/ Accessed on 29 October 2022.

Kirby, P. (2008). Explaining Ireland's development: Economic growth with weakening welfare. *Social Policy and Development Paper* no 37. URISD, Geneva

Lim, C. (2005). Building on Penang's strengths: Going forward. Retrieved from: library.wou.edu.my/vertical/vf2011-1.pdf Accessed on 12 August 2022.

Moore, M., & Hamalai, L. (1993). Economic liberalisation, political pluralism and business associations in developing countries. *World Development*, 21(12), 1895–1912

Maxfield, S., & Schneider, B. (1997). *Business and the State in Developing Countries. Cornell Studies in Political Economy*. Cornell University Press, Ithaca, NY.

Moynihan, D., & Roberts, A. (2010). The triumph of loyalty over competence: The Bush administration and the exhaustion of the politicized presidency. *Public Administration Review*, 70, 572–581.

OECD. (2013). New approaches to industrial policy and the future of manufacturing. Retrieved from: www.oecd.org/about/membersandpartners/publicaffairs/NATO2013_New%20Industrial%20Policy.pdf Accessed on 12 November 2016.

OECD. (2015). OECD economic surveys Ireland: Overview. Retrieved from: www.oecd.org/eco/surveys/Ireland-2015-overview.pdf. Accessed on 10 November 2021.

O'Hearn, D. (2001). *The Atlantic Economy: Britain, the US and Ireland*, University of Manchester Press, Manchester.

Shafer, M. (1997). The Political Economy of Sectors and Sectoral Change: Korea Then and Now in S. Maxfield and B. Ross Schneider (eds.), *Business and the State in Developing Countries*, Cornell University Press, Ithaca, NY, pp. 3–35.

Schneider, B., & Maxfield, S. (1997). Business, the State and Economic Performance in Developing Countries in S. Maxfield and B. Ross Schneider (eds.), *Business and the State in Developing Countries*, Cornell University Press, Ithaca, NY, pp. 63–87.

Schoenman, R. (2005). Captains or pirates? state-business relations in post-socialist poland. *East European Politics and Societies,* 19(1), 40–75.

Sen, K. (2015). *State-Business Relations: Topic Guide*, GSDRC, University of Birmingham, Birmingham.

Silva, E. (1997). Business Elites, The State and Economic Change in Chile in S. Maxfield and B. Ross Schneider (eds.), *Business and the State in Developing Countries*, Cornell University Press, Ithaca, NY, pp. 63–87.

The Economic Policy Research Foundation of Turkey. (2014). Retrieved from: http://www.tepav.org.tr/en Accessed on 4 September 2021.

UNCTAD. (2022). Retrieved from: www.unctad.org/fdistatistics Accessed on 2 September 2022

UNDP & MBRF. (2021). Global Knowledge Index 2021. Retrieved from: www.undp.org/publications/global-knowledge-index-2021 Accessed on 30 July 2022.

UNRISD. (2014). State-business relations and the financing of the welfare state in argentina and chile: Challenges and prospects. Retrieved from: www.unrisd.org/80256B3C005BCCF9/(httpAuxPages)/B923648CA3C7A866C1257DB600617DDF/$file/Moudud,%20Perez%20and%20Delamonica.pdf Accessed on 12 December 2016.

Warwick, K. (2013). Beyond industrial policy: Emerging issues and new trends, *OECD Science, Technology and Industry Policy Papers*, No. 2, OECD Publishing.

World Bank Data. (2022). Available from: www.worldbankdata.org.

World Bank. (2015). Investment climate reforms: An independent evaluation of. World Bank Group support to reforms of business regulations. Retrieved from: https://documents1.worldbank.org/curated/en/989551468334811535/Investment-climate-reform-An-independent-evaluation-of-World-Bank-Group-support-to-reforms-of-business-regulations.pdf Accessed on 2 September 2022.

Wormald, G., & Brieba, D. (2012). Institutional Change and Development in Chilean Market Society in A. Portes and L. Smith (eds.), *Institutions Count: Their Role and Significance in Latina American Development*, University of California Press, Berkeley, pp. 60–84.

4 Strategies for enhancing good governance and quality of government in the GCC states

Addressing corruption in the public sector

Introduction

Since the discovery of oil, the Gulf Cooperation Council (GCC) states of Bahrain, Kuwait, Oman, Qatar, Saudi Arabia, and the United Arab Emirates (UAE) have achieved significant developmental and economic growth. Some of the GCC's non-oil sectors are growing exponentially and emerging as regional economic hubs, including Dubai in the UAE, Qatar, and Bahrain. However, the achievement of this rapid growth pace has been accompanied by numerous governance and institutional weaknesses. This is mainly due to factors such as the relatively recent formation of most Gulf countries, insufficiency of human resources, and the ineffectiveness of several regulatory institutions (Askari et al., 2010). Furthermore, GCC states have recently realized that oil resources are inadequate for securing long-term economic prosperity without effective anti-corruption strategies and government machinery tools.

Furthermore, while these states share common historical and geographical characteristics, their performance in annual worldwide corruption perceptions surveys have varied greatly, with some trailing significantly behind others. This poses a significant challenge considering the GCC states' ambition to transform their economies into knowledge-based ones that attract foreign direct investment (FDI) and skilled talent. Specifically, the UAE ranked 21st globally in Transparency International's 2020 Corruption Perceptions Index (CPI), making it the most corruption-free GCC state, while Saudi Arabia placed 52nd and Kuwait was 78th (out of 179 countries), thus indicating the serious challenges faced by these states in relation to corruption within the Gulf region.

The central research problem this chapter addresses is that, despite the presence of numerous anti-corruption institutions and legislation and the existence of anti-corruption strategies in all GCC states, the outcomes of their governments' efforts to curb corruption in the public sector differ considerably. Overall, Qatar and the UAE rank higher than their GCC counterparts in government and institutional effectiveness, boasting annually improving rankings in the most popular corruption indices. However, the remaining GCC states still struggle to enhance their global images as

DOI: 10.4324/9781003267744-5

Enhancing good governance and quality of government 105

corruption-free, investment-friendly environments. For the purposes of this chapter, corruption is defined as: "The promise, offering or giving to a public official, directly or indirectly, of an undue advantage... in order that the official act or refrain from acting in the exercise of his or her function" (UN Guide for Anti-Corruption Policies, 2003, p. 33). The chapter examines the initiatives and strategies that GCC states have implemented to curb corruption within their public sector organizations, and one of its main conclusions is that political will and leadership have played an instrumental role in Qatar's and the UAE's efforts to gradually reduce corruption in the public sector.

The chapter is organized as follows. After this introduction, the following section discusses some strategies highlighted as important by the existing literature for curbing corruption, particularly within the public sector. The next section then illustrates the current state of corruption within the governments of the six GCC states and describes their uneven performance in quashing corruption. The data referred to are based on well-established and globally trusted indices that reflect regulatory and business environments, such as the World Bank's Worldwide Governance Indicators, Transparency International's CPI, and the World Economic Forum's index. The section following that presents the various mechanisms each GCC state has adopted to address and combat corruption in the public sector. These include enacting legislation and anti-corruption laws, establishing various anti-corruption agencies, formulating national anti-corruption strategies, and forming regional networks and collaborations to share best practices for controlling corruption. The next section analyzes how Qatar and the UAE (viewed as the least corrupt countries in the GCC) have successfully implemented effective institutional and structural governance mechanisms that tackle corruption within their governments. What makes them unique in their approaches that allowed them to successfully tackle corruption, despite sharing political, cultural, and historical similarities with their neighboring states?

Strategies for enhancing government effectiveness: Anti-corruption strategies and policies

This section describes anti-corruption strategies encompassing regulatory frameworks (including legislation and enforcement), public sector reform, civil society education and engagement, and economic liberalization. The final part considers overarching principles for designing and implementing anti-corruption strategies.

Regulatory strategies

Legislative anti-corruption strategies typically involve some form of domestic legislation containing anti-corruption provisions and ratifying the United Nations Convention against Corruption (UNCAC) at the international level. Domestic legislative measures may take a variety of forms, including the following.

a) *Dedicated anti-corruption legislation* typically criminalizes various corrupt behaviors, including bribery, extortion, fraud, embezzlement, nepotism, cronyism, and the misappropriation, diversion, or concealment of assets. The legislation may also establish requirements for businesses and organizations to implement controls to prevent corruption, including fulfilling obligations under the UNCAC and maintaining accurate books and records.
b) *General criminal legislation* as a domestic complement to or substitute for dedicated anti-corruption legislation may contain provisions and perform functions similar to those described above (e.g., the Indian Penal Code).
c) *Whistleblowing legislation* establishes procedures for receiving and investigating complaints concerning potential corruption and puts into place safeguards against the victimization of those making such complaints.
d) *Public sector administration and procurement legislation* govern public sector agencies' use of public assets, accounting and financial management practices, auditing and recordkeeping, and procurement practices. Such legislation may also include probity, transparency, or performance requirements.

For both enforcement and deterrence purposes, legislative schemes rely on penalty regimes that may include imprisonment, fines, forfeiture or confiscation of profits and other proceeds of corruption, removal of directors from companies, and rescission of contracts affected by corruption (Brody et al., 2021). While the form of the legislative scheme may vary, it is vital that it adequately captures a comprehensive range of corrupt behaviors relevant to the particular jurisdiction and is capable of effective enforcement by the agencies responsible, and this includes sufficient empowerment of those agencies when and where it is appropriate (Mauro, 1995).

Regulatory policies and frameworks

Anti-corruption regulatory policies are the procedures and guidelines formulated by enforcement agencies to prevent corruption and unlawful acts (Brody et al., 2021). Many states consolidate multiple anti-corruption measures into overarching frameworks, like Uganda's National Anti-Corruption Strategy (Lubeck, 1992). In this regard, Transparency International's National Integrity System (see McCusker, 2006, p. 10–11) is among the most prominent best practice exemplars.

Preventive reform strategies

Public sector reform

Public sector reform is typically an essential component of effective anti-corruption strategies, particularly in developing states, where there is a high potential for public employees to accept bribes, embezzle or misappropriate public assets, or engage in nepotism (Gumisiriza & Mukobi, 2019). To that end, this section describes various anti-corruption strategies directed toward public sector reform.

Pay and benefits

Strategies incorporating public sector pay and benefits are vital in reducing the attractiveness of bribery, misappropriation, or embezzlement. Hay and Schleifer (1998) recommend that such strategies comprise two components: firstly, adequate pay for public sector employees to reduce the temptation to engage in corrupt behavior. Secondly, to prevent the bribes sought or amounts misappropriated from simply increasing to account for this. Quah (1999) suggests the removal of benefits, such as pension schemes and allied benefits, and the imposition of additional penalties like fines (potentially multiplied by the amount of the bribe / misappropriated funds) or employment termination as punishment (Kaufmann, 2005). A variation of this is rewarding or incentivizing non-corrupt behavior or whistleblowing by employees.

Appointment and rotation

Transparent, merit-based employee recruitment and promotion mechanisms underpinned by credible monitoring and enforcement are also vital to maintaining impartial public services and preventing cronyism and bribery (Shleifer & Vishny, 1993). Following Singapore's example, Quah (1999) also suggests the potential rotation of employees to reduce the propensity for individuals to establish themselves in entrenched patterns of corruption.

Limiting discretionary power

Another critical strategy is to remove or reduce opportunities for public sector employees to engage in corrupt behavior through such means as administrative process reforms to remove employees' discretionary powers or eliminate the state's authority to regulate certain types of conduct (e.g., export restrictions or licensing requirements) (Kumar, 2019). Privatization could form part of the solution where there is sufficient market competition in the provision of a public good or service, although this may end up simply transferring existing corruption risks to the private sector (McCusker, 2006, p. 13).

Organizational controls, monitoring, and oversight

Public sector agencies should maintain appropriately proportioned and resourced internal control, oversight, and auditing procedures and systems to detect corruption in its various forms, and should undertake regular risk assessments of such procedures and systems to ensure their continued efficacy (Kaufmann, 2005). Such measures may be significant for certain institutions whose independence and integrity are paramount, such as the judiciary, which may require additional controls, including professional ethics codes and inspection systems (Mauro, 1995). At a higher level of abstraction are overarching whole-government auditing, review, and investigative institutions and systems such as auditors-general, ombudsmen, watchdogs, and special commissions of inquiry (Shleifer & Vishny, 1993).

Education and cultural reform

Education campaigns are also essential to engage and mobilize the public to combat corruption. Specifically, such campaigns are designed to:

a) Educate the public about and raise understanding and awareness of the nature, varieties, and causes of corruption and the harms and costs it inflicts on citizens, institutions, and states;
b) Encourage broader cultural reform to embed attitudes and values that prioritize anti-corruption measures (over competing socioeconomic issues);
c) Increase and sustain public engagement with anti-corruption strategies and institutions to ensure intended results are achieved; and
d) Positively influence the behavior of corrupt, or potentially corrupt, individuals (Shleifer & Vishny, 1993).

Education campaigns can be delivered by one or more anti-corruption agencies (which often have dedicated education or community relations functions like Hong Kong's Independent Commission Against Corruption), media outlets, or civil society organizations such as NGOs (McCusker, 2006). The educative role of the media and civil society organizations can be supplemented by investigative or monitoring roles, which draw on relevant expertise to scrutinize public and private sector practices in relation to corruption (Hay & Schleifer, 1998).

Economic reform

Economic anti-corruption strategies typically comprise macroeconomic policy settings designed to enhance economic growth and trade openness through liberalization via such means as market-determined exchange and interest rates and lowering or removal of tariffs, subsidies, license requirements, and other barriers to international trade or market entrants. Such measures are intended to alleviate corruption's often inhibiting effects on economic growth while simultaneously reducing the discretionary power of the public sector (Ampratwum, 2008). Such economic strategies have been prominently advocated for by international organizations like the World Bank, which has attached conditions concerning reduced corruption to its lending and financial aid to developing states (Ampratwum, 2008).

Economic strategies have, however, attracted a range of significant criticisms, including the following:

a) They are structurally unsuitable in many developing state contexts, where a lack of strong government, financial systems, or other institutional support is likely to impede their successful introduction and undermine their efficacy once implemented.
b) They tend to reflect particular "Western" values that are often incongruous with a state's populace and fail to account for domestic cultural, social, and historical conditions or factors contributing to poor governance and government performance.
c) Their assumption that corruption impedes economic development and growth is not well supported by empirical data, which instead shows in many contexts that corruption is not necessarily a constraint on growth (e.g., in China and South Korea), and under the right circumstances, can drive economic change and increase efficiency.

Given the challenges in developing anti-corruption strategies that consider these criticisms, McCusker (2006) suggests that implementing economic measures may be most appropriate in Special Governance Zones (SGZs). Drawing from the concept of free trade and enterprise zones, SGZs involve significant reforms being implemented only within a particular city or region of a state, thereby allowing reversal if unsuccessful or acting as an exemplar exportable to the rest of the state if successful (Vadlamannati, 2015).

Designing and implementing governance reform programs

Given corruption's unique drivers and the social, cultural, and institutional settings in which it exists, effective anti-corruption strategies must necessarily be unique to their jurisdictional contexts. McCusker (2006) broadly outlines the following steps for designing anti-corruption strategies.

a) *Jurisdictional assessment* can identify and assess the relevant economic, educational, cultural, and political drivers of corruption in a particular jurisdiction, as well as the political and socioeconomic environments, thereby recognizing the potentially different manifestations

in, or impacts on, individuals, businesses, and organizations, the public sector, and society in general.
b) *Strategy determination* draws on the assessment described in a) above to determine the goals and focus of an anti-corruption strategy, including normative preferences (e.g., determining the extent to which the strategy should be preventive or retributive, or focused on a public sector office or individual officeholders).
c) *Measure evaluation* identifies relevant anti-corruption strategies and measures and evaluates their practical applicability in a jurisdiction, considering inter alia the prerequisites for implementation (notably, the need for public engagement and support), potential adverse or unintended consequences, and any disparate short- or long-term effects.
d) *Performance measurement* determines appropriate, quantifiable measures for determining the success of anti-corruption strategies and measures.
e) *Sequencing* determines the most effective implementation sequence to ensure reforms' long-term sustainability and effectiveness.

While implementation considerations will ultimately vary according to the specific anti-corruption measures, there are two universal considerations (Khan, 2002). The first is the importance of coordination between anti-corruption measures and strategies and the agencies that implement them. This involves the designation of a "focal point" coordinating agency, such as an independent anti-corruption agency, with overall responsibility for delivering and publicizing the anti-corruption strategy. The second critical consideration is that of political will and support, particularly at the highest levels of government, toward realizing the intended practical results of an anti-corruption strategy and raising public legitimacy, awareness, and ultimately support for it. Without sufficient political commitment and support, an anti-corruption strategy may not move forward and, even if it does, will be unlikely to attract the resourcing or public goodwill necessary to deliver its intended results.

The current state of government effectiveness in the GCC region

The GCC states are oil-rich countries considered among the richest and highest-income among countries outside of the Organization for Economic Co-operation and Development (OECD). Exploiting oil revenues has allowed them to build state-of-the-art infrastructure, skip the industrial phase of development, attract FDI, and compete with global economic powers to provide services. As Table 4.1 illustrates, according to the World Bank Data Bank (2020), Saudi Arabia constitutes the largest economy in the Gulf with a GDP of US$703 billion, followed by the UAE with US$358 billion, while Bahrain is its smallest economy with a GDP of only US$34 billion.

Table 4.1 Economic indicators of the GCC states in 2020

Country	Gross domestic product, current prices (US dollars – billions)	Gross domestic product per capita, current prices (US dollars – units)
Bahrain	34.723	20,406.50
Kuwait	105.96	24,811.77
Oman	73.971	14,485.39
Qatar	202.561	100,260.49
Saudi Arabia	703.367	20,203.67
United Arab Emirates	358.868	36,284.56

Source: World Bank Data Bank (2020)

Levels of perceived corruption, meanwhile, differ significantly among the GCC states, as do their levels of progress toward improving such rankings, as demonstrated by the CPI. A globally recognized indicator of the state of corruption in a country, the CPI provides a micro-level conception of the prevalence of corruption-related practices in each GCC state. Table 4.2 shows that the UAE tops the region, boasting a score of 6.9 (with a score of 1 meaning corruption is pervasive and 10 meaning it never occurs) and a global ranking of 26th (out of 177 countries) in 2013. This impressive performance marked significant progress since 2003, when it scored 5.2 and ranked 37th globally. The UAE then gradually improved its performance, ranking 21st globally in 2020. Qatar followed a similar positive trajectory, scoring 5.6 and ranking 32nd globally in 2003, results that it managed to improve in 2013 when it scored 68 (out of 100) and ranked 28th (only to decline slightly in 2020 to 30th).

On the other hand, the remaining GCC state's rankings seem only to have worsened with time. In 2003, for example, Oman, Bahrain, Kuwait, and Saudi Arabia were ranked 26th, 27th, 35th, and 46th, respectively, among the 133 nations taking part in the ranking that year. In 2013, they ranked 61st, 57th, 69th, and 63rd, respectively. Oman improved its ranking to become 49th globally in 2020, as did Saudi Arabia, which ranked 52nd, but Kuwait's and Bahrain's performance continued to deteriorate with a tied rank of 78th in 2020. In this respect, Kuwait has performed more poorly than all other GCC states.

Analysis of the GCC states' performance in the World Bank dimensions of good governance over time, such as voice and accountability, government effectiveness, rule of law, and control of corruption, also reveals quite insightful findings. Table 4.3 shows how both Qatar and the UAE substantially improved their control of corruption scores from 56% in 1996 to 84% and 83% in 2012, respectively. In 2020, the UAE maintained its 83% score while Qatar dipped slightly to 78%. This reflects the soundness of the corruption control measures they implemented and the effectiveness

Table 4.2 Transparency International's Corruption Perceptions Index *(global ranking with 1 being least corrupt and 180 most corrupt)

	2003 (133 nations)		2004 (146 nations)		2009 (180 nations)		2011 (183 nations)		2013 (177 nations)		2020 (179 nations)	
	Score	Rank	Score	Rank	Score	Rank	Score	Rank	Score	Rank	Score	Rank
Qatar	5.6	32	5.2	38	7	22	7.2	22	68	28	63	30
UAE	5.2	37	6.1	29	6.5	30	6.8	28	69	26	71	21
Saudi Arabia	4.5	46	3.4	71	4.3	63	4.4	57	46	63	53	52
Oman	6.3	26	6.1	29	5.5	39	4.8	50	47	61	54	49
Bahrain	6.1	27	5.8	34	5.1	46	5.1	46	48	57	42	78
Kuwait	5.3	35	4.6	44	4.1	66	4.6	54	43	69	42	78

Source: Transparency International (2020)

Enhancing good governance and quality of government   113

Table 4.3 World Bank's Worldwide Governance Indicators *(Percentile rank from 0 low to 100 high)

Country	Voice and Accountability				Government Effectiveness				Regulatory Quality				Rule of Law				Control of Corruption			
	1996	2004	2012	2020	1996	2004	2012	2020	1996	2004	2012	2020	1996	2004	2012	2020	1996	2004	2012	2020
Bahrain	25	28	11	9	73	73	69	68	68	74	74	73	53	72	62	67	63	72	68	53
Kuwait	44	39	29	30	60	61	51	46	55	69	52	63	65	65	63	63	78	82	53	54
Oman	33	27	20	17	70	69	61	58	49	71	67	67	67	68	67	72	61	72	61	62
Qatar	31	37	26	14	68	71	78	78	50	59	75	76	55	63	82	83	56	73	84	78
Saudi Arabia	8	10	3	5	46	45	57	59	47	56	55	62	59	57	61	60	28	46	57	63
UAE	36	26	19	16	73	77	83	88	75	76	73	83	67	65	67	79	56	85	83	83

Source: World Bank Data Bank (2020)

of their results. Nevertheless, such positive trends were not witnessed among the rest of the GCC states. While Bahrain slightly enhanced its performance from 63% in 1996 to 68% in 2012, it significantly plunged to 53% in 2020. Similarly, Kuwait achieved 78% and 82% in 1996 and 2004, respectively—far better than any of its neighboring countries—but considerably worsened its performance in 2012 when its score fell to 53%, making it the most corrupt country in the GCC that year, and it remained so in 2020 when its score stayed largely unchanged (54%).

Similar trends can be witnessed in the dimension of government effectiveness. Qatar and the UAE achieved remarkable progress, moving from 68% and 73% in 1996 to 78% and 83% in 2012, respectively. However, while the UAE's performance improved to 88% in 2020, Qatar's score dropped to 78%. Other GCC states also showed a negative trend, such as Kuwait, which dropped from 60% in 1996 to 46% in 2020, and Bahrain, which fell from 73% in 2012 to 68% in 2020. Similarly, Oman drastically declined from 70% in 2012 to 58% in 2020. In the dimension of voice and accountability, all six countries exhibited a negative trend. Specifically, their ranks plummeted from 1996 to 2020, falling substantially from 44% to 30% in Kuwait, from 36% to 16% in the UAE, and from 8% to 5% in Saudi Arabia, which had the lowest score of all GCC states.

In explaining such trends, research confirms a strong correlation between corruption's prevalence and government machinery's effectiveness. Heavily burdened bureaucratic institutions tend to encourage government officials to misuse their positions, demand bribes to facilitate complicated administrative processes, and conduct other unlawful practices in the public sphere. Table 4.4 provides a list of indicators that show the quality of government, and a careful examination of the rankings of GCC states in these indicators demonstrates the varying degrees of quality of government and governance within them. Qatar and the UAE ranked 15th and 10th, respectively, in "transparency of government policymaking" in 2017, putting them in positions commensurate with OECD countries. Meanwhile, Kuwait ranked 104th in this indicator in 2017, putting it at the bottom of the list among GCC states and globally. In "wastefulness of government spending", the UAE scored highest globally as the least wasteful government, while Qatar ranked 4th in 2017 and the other GCC states were among the top 22, except for Kuwait, which ranked 59th. Kuwait also ranked 78th globally in "favoritism in government officials' decision-making" in 2017, but this ranking marked a substantial improvement over 2013 when it ranked 100th globally while the rest of the states were among the top 30.

"Burden of government regulation" is an indicator that, when high, allows considerable room for utilization of government offices for private gains and allows the public to fall prey to the greed of bureaucrats. The institutional frameworks that Qatar and the UAE have in place demonstrate their effectiveness in reducing government regulations for the public, as testified by their 6th and 4th place positions, respectively, in 2019. In the same year, Saudi Arabia ranked 10th and Kuwait ranked 39th. Nevertheless,

Table 4.4 Government effectiveness indicators *(1st is the highest rank)

Country	Public trust in politicians 2013	Public trust in politicians 2017	Transparency of government policymaking 2013	Transparency of government policymaking 2017	Ease of doing business 2013	Ease of doing business 2017	Diversion of public funds 2013	Diversion of public funds 2017	Favoritism in government officials' decision-making 2013	Favoritism in government officials' decision-making 2017	Wastefulness of government spending 2013	Wastefulness of government spending 2017	Burden of government regulation 2013	Burden of government regulation 2019
Qatar	2	4	5	15	48	77	12	5	5	5	1	4	2	6
UAE	3	2	12	10	23	16	26	3	7	2	3	1	6	4
Saudi Arabia	10	12	21	48	26	62	26	20	18	19	7	7	37	10
Oman	13	19	22	37	47	68	15	30	12	35	5	10	7	17
Bahrain	31	24	36	26	46	43	32	22	28	25	19	22	9	12
Kuwait	56	68	113	104	104	83	59	54	100	78	102	59	145	39

Source: World Economic Forum (2020)

it is worth mentioning that Kuwait made considerable progress in this indicator compared to 2013, when it ranked 145th. Furthermore, public trust in politicians is lowest in Kuwait, ranking 56th in 2013, which deteriorated further in 2017 to 68th, making it the lowest-ranking GCC state. Public trust in politicians is highest in the UAE, which ranked 2nd, and Qatar, which came in 4th in 2017.

Since GCC states aim to diversify their economies, encourage the involvement of the private sector in the provision of services, and aspire to attract FDI, their ranking in "Ease of doing business" is a factor they should observe carefully. Establishing the necessary institutional and legal environments to become investment- and business-friendly are prerequisites for attracting businesses and convincing them to stay. The UAE topped the GCC region by ranking 16th globally in 2017, followed directly by Bahrain, which ranked 43rd. The other states of the Council were all in the 40 range, except for Kuwait, which ranked 83rd in 2017 (improved from its 2013 ranking of 104th).

Identification of significant types of corruption in the GCC public sector

Since the types and forms of corruption vary from country to country, it is crucial to identify what type of corruption prevails in a specific country to determine how to best tackle it. Riley (1998) discusses the three major types of corruption and their characteristics. "Incidental" corruption is considered "small scale", usually involving government officials in junior positions, and has little impact on macroeconomic costs, but is difficult to curb. "Systematic" corruption is entrenched within government departments, not only specific individuals. It can also potentially have a more considerable developmental impact on a country since government officials can utilize government revenues for private purposes. The third type is "systemic" corruption, which denotes a thoroughly corrupt government system. Corruption, in this case, is deeply rooted in the machinery of government and affects most of its transactions (Riley, 1998).

Table 4.5 exhibits some examples of corruption cases reported in national newspapers. From the analysis of this table and the previous indices and indicators, it is safe to argue that there are two major types of corruption within the GCC states: incidental corruption in the cases of Qatar, the UAE, and Bahrain, and systematic corruption in the cases of Saudi Arabia, Oman, and Kuwait. The parliament of Kuwait has been repeatedly criticized by local and international media for cases of corruption that occur mainly in public and involve high-ranking government officials. As the cases in the table illustrate, Kuwait, Saudi Arabia, and Oman saw government institutions and departments directly involved in the corruption, while in Bahrain, Qatar, and the UAE, individuals were mostly the key actors in corruption-related cases. Among the GCC states, Kuwait is the only country that could potentially run the risk of institutionalizing

Table 4.5 Example cases of corruption in the GCC states

Country	Year	Type	Description
Kuwait	2008	Bribery	Parliamentary elections rigged by buying votes with bribes.
	2009	Embezzlement	Money embezzlement from Kuwaiti Investment Organization dating back to 1988—US$1.2 billion in missing funds.
	2011	Graft	Corruption in parliament—suspicious US$92 million transferred into accounts of two MPs.
	2011	Bribery	Siemens involved with authorities, allegedly bribing to buy contracts.
	2014	Bribery	Kuwait Municipality loses more than KD14 million after a cleaning company illegally took over 10,000 square meters in Abdullah Port.
	2014	Embezzlement	Depletion of KD8 billion in public funds from oil company.
	2014	Embezzlement	Over US$50 billion disappears from public funds, transferred to foreign banks.
	2016	Graft	Investigation by the anti-corruption authority into a US$1.1 billion helicopter deal with France has begun.
	2020	Bribery	Anti-corruption authority NAZAHA investigates allegations of bribes in relation to Airbus.
Saudi Arabia	2009	Graft	Corruption reaches all-time high, especially among ministries in Jeddah.
	2012	Nepotism	Corruption within Saudi Arabia, as Internet and media are controlled not by the Ministry of Media but by the Ministry of Interior.
	2013	Bribery	Allegations of bribery over Saudi arms race.
	2013	Embezzlement	Financial and administrative corruption within Commission for the Promotion of Virtue and Prevention of Vice.
	2014	Bribery	Cases of bribes to high government officials to secure different contracts.
	2014	Embezzlement	Saudi officials forge deeds and embezzle money with no sources of income other than government salaries.
	2012–2013	Money laundering	Hundreds of money laundering and corruption cases reported by the Ministry of Interior.
	2016	Graft, bribery, and embezzlement	Authorities detain more than 200 officials and businessmen as part of corruption crackdown.
	2018	Bribery and embezzlement	More than US$100 billion recouped and as many as 56 high-profile royal family members and businessmen jailed

(*continued*)

118 *Quality of government and the public sector in the GCC region*

Table 4.5 Cont.

Country	Year	Type	Description
	2020	Bribery and embezzlement	Anti-corruption body arrests 298 on corruption charges.
UAE	2009	Money laundering	Charges of money laundering and forging and misusing official documents after investigation team collects evidence over two years.
	2011	Money laundering	68 laundering cases were reported by money exchange shops, insurance companies, and other companies operating in the UAE.
	2012	Bribery	47 cases of bribery registered in the federal courts for 2012.
	2020	Corruption	Two UAE cricket players charged for breaking cricket's anti-corruption rules.
	2022	Money laundering	UAE placed on money laundering "gray list" by the Financial Action Task Force
Bahrain	2013	Bribery	Different types of corruption cases occur in Bahrain.
	2013	Bribery	Corruption among businesses and senior officials, millions paid in bribes to secure contracts.
	2014	Bribery	US ALCOA: US$384 million to resolve US criminal and civil probes, admission of paying millions of dollars in bribes to Bahrain's government officials.
	2019	Bribery	Ministry of Justice, Islamic Affairs and Endowments employee and brother arrested for accepting bribe.
	2022	Corruption	Government employee sentenced to seven years in jail for corruption.
Oman	2013	Bribery	Ministry of Transport official accused by state prosecutors of receiving bribe from executives (CCC-Oman) to facilitate several projects.
	2014	Bribery	Former Commerce Minister Khusaibi was guilty of paying bribes worth US$1 million to former Transport Ministry officials to win contracts.
	2014	Graft	Oman Oil Company CEO's jail sentences total 23 years after being convicted of accepting bribes, money laundering, and abuse of office.
	2014	Graft	Prominent businessmen and officials, including former undersecretary of the Ministry of Housing, were accused of corruption.
	2014	Bribery	Petroleum Development Oman executive bribes employees to grant contract for Al Amal bloc and other projects.

Enhancing good governance and quality of government 119

Table 4.5 Cont.

Country	Year	Type	Description
	2016	Bribery	Oman's National Gas Company fires CEO over bribery.
	2022	Corruption	Oman sets up the Anti-Corruption Commission to combat financial and administrative violations.
Qatar	2014	Bribery	Controversial Qatari businessman allegedly bribes Thai FIFA executive and promises gas deals worth tens of millions of US dollars.
	2021	Corruption	Finance minister arrested over allegations of corruption, misuse of public funds, and abuse of power.

Source: Author's compilation from numerous newspaper articles and online sources

corruption within the entire machinery of its government. If strong political will and adequate and proper anti-corruption mechanisms are not thoroughly introduced and comprehensively implemented, Kuwait might ultimately become an example of a state with "systemic" corruption. Low public trust in government, the frequency and severity of corruption cases, and the failure of parliament to implement transparent and good governance practices among its members are vital signs of corruption becoming an institutionalized element within the government (Bertelsmann Foundation, 2014).

Strategies and institutions for combating corruption in the GCC states

Combating corruption has been at the top of GCC states' agendas over the past decade, as the political leadership of the entire region recognizes the negative impact of corruption within the public sector on their economic development. Since these states wish to veer away from reliance on oil and other natural resources to focus on diversifying their economies and creating a vibrant private sector, establishing a business-friendly, transparent, and corruption-free environment represents a major challenge in achieving their long-term goals and economic objectives. Attracting FDI, forming public-private partnerships (PPPs), and encouraging international corporations to invest and operate in the Gulf require investors' trust in the overall business climate of the region. This has been the impetus behind GCC leaders' motivation, urging them to ensure implementation of institutional and legal frameworks that will curb corruption and punish violators.

Fortunately, corruption is no longer a taboo topic in the GCC states. These days, corruption cases make the headlines in major national newspapers within the six states of the Gulf, and top government officials are summoned to courts to be questioned and tried for mismanagement of public funds. All GCC members also signed the UNCAC, which obliges its signatories to enhance integrity and combat corruption within their public sector entities. This strongly reflects their intentions to prevent corruption, prosecute violators, and raise public awareness about corruption's implications for economic growth and social welfare.

Nevertheless, GCC states' strategies and institutions created to combat corruption differ in their number and effectiveness. In their quest to compete with other service and financial hubs, such as Hong Kong and Singapore, Qatar and the UAE have recently intensified their efforts to rid their public sector institutions of corruption and top the MENA countries in global rankings related to government effectiveness and low levels of corruption. Other states, such as Saudi Arabia, Oman, and Kuwait, despite their relentless efforts to diminish the magnitude of corruption, are still plagued with its repercussions for government revenues and impact on business environments. To better understand why, this section illustrates the individual efforts of each GCC state to introduce mechanisms and tools that can potentially combat corruption within the government sector.

Bahrain

The Kingdom of Bahrain introduced Law No. 01/2013 to further expand Decree No. 15/1987, which enumerates its Anti-Corruption Articles. Bahrain's Penal Code further stipulates the severe punishments that any government official shall incur if found to take part in giving or receiving a bribe. Moreover, Bahrain signed the UNCAC in February 2005 and ratified it in October 2010. Under this treaty, the Bahraini government implemented several policies and strategies to tackle corruption within the public sector. In 2014, the Prime Minister of Bahrain then gave the directive to enact strict financial controls and introduce tougher anti-corruption laws.

In addition, the General Directorate of Anti-Corruption and Economic and Electronic Security is the leading organization in charge of anti-corruption mechanisms and strategies in Bahrain. It operates within the framework of the Ministry of Interior and reports corruption cases to the Public Prosecutor's Office. The Directorate was visited personally by the Crown Prince of Bahrain on many occasions as an indication of the political leadership's commitment to actively participate in the fight against corruption. Furthermore, a hotline was established to allow citizens to make anonymous phone calls and report corruption cases. This system, which falls under the Directorate, promises to uncover numerous corruption cases within public sector entities without compromising the callers' identities or endangering their safety.

Kuwait

The state of Kuwait is aware of the immense challenges it faces in combating deeply rooted corruption within its public sector, and has been attempting to curtail corruption-related practices among its highly ranked government officials by introducing a wide range of legislation, initiatives, and institutions. Its law to criminalize corruption was created in 1970 and covers numerous practices such as receiving or giving bribes, involvement in acts of corruption, and money laundering. Kuwait first signed the UNCAC in December 2003 and ratified it in February 2007. Furthermore, in September 2011, Kuwait passed an anti-corruption draft law, and in January 2013, the National Assembly passed the Anti-Corruption and Wealth Disclosure Decree, which calls for more transparency in decision-making and mechanisms to be put into place to control financial transactions of members of parliament and other government officials. These laws were backed by a National Anti-Corruption Strategy that strongly called for establishment of an independent entity that would investigate and follow up on corruption cases.

For more than 40 years, Kuwait has focused more on legislation and laws to combat corruption than on institutions. After passing Penal Law No. 31/1970, the state did not immediately establish an independent anti-corruption agency, and local courts handled all corruption-related issues. Table 4.6 shows that the three institutions dealing with corruption are the Kuwait Transparency Society, the State Audit Bureau of Kuwait, and the Kuwait Economic Society. None of these institutions' agendas are entirely focused on investigating cases of corruption within the public sector. Hence, the Emir of Kuwait made a speech ordering the creation of the Public Authority for Anti-Corruption as late as 2011, after witnessing the consequences of not having a fully dedicated anti-corruption agency within the machinery of government. Kuwait's Council of Ministers has been directly responsible for creating this entity and ensuring that it contributes to enhancing integrity and transparency within the public sector.

Oman

Oman has put into place several laws to address the issues of bribery and corruption in the public sector. Royal Decree No. 112, the "Law for the Protection of Public Funds and Avoidance of Interest" (Anti-Corruption Law), stipulates the severe punishments awaiting public sector employees found guilty of involvement in corruption-related cases. The law defines such cases as "Any person who has accepted a bribe for himself or another person, be it in cash or as a present or promise or any other benefit, for performing a lawful act of his duties."[1] Oman was subject to a great deal of criticism for not signing the UNCAC until January 2014. Since it was the last GCC country to sign the agreement, this negatively impacted its ability to create the legislative and constitutional capacity to tackle corruption in the public sector. A report by the International Labor Organization (2011)[2] criticized not only the "poor governance and inefficient institutions" of Oman, but also the government's sluggishness in formulating a solid strategy to tackle corruption. Oman has the least number of anti-corruption institutions among GCC states, and the State Financial and Administrative Audit Institution (SFAAI), established in 1970, is the only organization to curb corruption in the public sector. Its mandate is to create more transparency, accountability, and fairness within the machinery of the Omani government.

Qatar

Qatar, meanwhile, has implemented a great deal of legislation, enacted laws, and built effective institutions to combat corruption within its public sector. Penal Code No. 11/2004 criminalizes any form of corruption and severely punishes any convicted public officer. The UNCAC was signed in December 2005 and ratified in January 2007, and serves as a comprehensive legal and institutional framework for the Qatari government to enhance its efforts to curb corruption. Furthermore, the Qatari government issued the National Strategy for Integrity and Transparency 2008–2012, which was a comprehensive platform that targeted three goals: 1) to prevent corruption, 2) to educate and raise awareness about anti-corruption measures, and 3) to establish processes for detecting and investigating corruption. This strategy was updated and complemented by the Second National Development Strategy 2018–2022 which aimed to build on the success of the first strategy and expand its mandate.

Effective anti-corruption institutions are also vital for implementing Qatari legal and strategic initiatives. The oldest such organization is the State Audit Bureau of Qatar, which was created in 1973 and reports directly to the Emir for the necessary political support to function effectively. One of its missions is to ascertain transparency in financial transactions within government machinery on all levels. Immediately after ratifying the UNCAC in 2007, the National Committee for Integrity and Transparency was created primarily to help with the implementation of all the convention's articles, provide guidance and practical advice on how to enhance the quality of government, and combat the various types of corruption through coercive and educational mechanisms. The creation of the Rule of Law and Anti-Corruption Centre in 2011 was also a milestone in Qatar's continuous efforts to combat corruption. According to the *Qatar Tribune* (2020), the organization was created to provide research and training support to Qatar's public sector and other neighboring Arab countries. Furthermore, the Emir of Qatar's role in providing political support for anti-corruption campaigns has been instrumental to their success, having approved the necessary funding for setting up the various

Enhancing good governance and quality of government 123

institutions and agencies to control corruption and empowering their missions to eradicate corruption.

Saudi Arabia

The government of Saudi Arabia has put into place various legislative and legal mechanisms to combat corruption. For example, the Regulations for Combating Bribery, which prohibits the involvement of public sector officials in acts of corruption, was passed in 1992 and consists of 23 articles that specifically address various cases and forms of corruption and indicates severe punishments for law violators. In addition, the Basic Law of Governance was passed in 1992, and it subjects all government entities to careful auditing to prevent public resource utilization for private purposes (Loughman & Siberry, 2012). This was further supported by the issuance of the Anti-Money Laundering Statute in 2003, which was aimed to detect and punish individuals involved in crimes related to money laundering. Although Saudi Arabia signed the UNCAC in January 2004, it did not ratify it until April 2013. Nevertheless, to further demonstrate its dedication to enhancing transparency and integrity within the public sector, Saudi Arabia set up a National Strategy for Maintaining Integrity and Combating Corruption approved by the Council of Ministers in 2007. This strategy now acts as a framework under which various government initiatives can be aligned to combat corruption and enhance integrity in the public sector.

Within Saudi Arabia, various institutions govern the fight against corruption. Perhaps the oldest institution (as shown in Table 4.6) is the Anti-Money Laundering Committee, established in 1952 under the Saudi Arabia Monetary Agency (SAMA) to detect government officials' misuse of public finances for private use. Similarly, the General Audit Bureau was established in 1971 and reports directly to the King of Saudi Arabia, being responsible for financial control and auditing activities throughout the whole of the Saudi government machinery. It also takes on the responsibility of "strengthening the principles of transparency, disclosure, and accountability; protecting integrity, and fighting corruption".[3] Furthermore, following a Royal Order in May 2011, the National Anti-Corruption Commission (NAZAHA), an acronym meaning "integrity" in Arabic, was established to combat all forms of corruption within the public sector. The Commission enjoys substantial administrative and financial independence and resulted from the merger of two former bodies tackling corruption in the Kingdom: The National Commission for Combating Corruption and the Oversight and Investigation Commission (Arab News, 2021). The role of NAZAHA was reinvigorated in 2017 under Crown Prince Mohammed bin Salman, who initiated a nationwide campaign against corruption. Hundreds of princes, prominent businessmen, and high-level government officials were arrested and questioned, some were even prosecuted (Arab News, 2022).

Table 4.6 Anti-corruption agencies in the GCC

Country	Anti-corruption agency	Nature and year of establishment	Affiliation	Agenda
UAE	State Audit Institution (SAI)	Governmental (1976)	Independent department	Dedicated to improving accountability and standards of governance across the UAE federal government.
	Anti-Money Laundering and Suspicious Cases Unit	Governmental (1980)	UAE Central Bank	Combats money laundering activities.
	Anti-Corruption Unit	Defense Ministry (1971)	Federal level	Dedicated to discovering corruption and dealing with it through Public Prosecution.
Kuwait	Kuwait Transparency Society (KTS)	Licensed NGO (2005)	National	Serves civil society.
	State Audit Bureau (SAB) of Kuwait	Ministry of Finance (1964)	Independent federal department	Aims to protect and trace public funds to prevent any misuse or manipulation.
	Kuwait Economic Society (KES)	NGO (1970)	National	Established to sustain the growth and reform of Kuwait's economy, improve transparency, and curb corruption within public institutions.
	Public Authority for Anti-Corruption (PAAC)	Governmental (2012)	National	Works to enhance the transparency and integrity of public institutions and the conduct of civil servants.
Bahrain	Ministry of Interior's General Directorate of Anti-Corruption and Economic and Electronic Security	Governmental	National	Works with Public Prosecution to combat corruption.
	Public Prosecution Office	Ministry of Justice	National	Works toward cutting down on corruption among government, businesses, and individuals.

Enhancing good governance and quality of government 125

Saudi Arabia	National Anti-Corruption Commission (NAZAHA)	Governmental (2011)	National	Promotes transparency and fights against financial and administrative corruption.
	General Auditing Bureau (GAB)	Governmental (1971)	Council of Ministers	Aims to combat corruption as a public auditing bureau.
	Anti-Money Laundering Committee (within SAMA)	Governmental (1952)	Ministerial (within SAMA)	Conducts financial, compliance, performance, and EDP audit operations within government entities.
	Prosecution and Investigation Commission (PIC)	Governmental	Independent body reporting to the Council of Ministers	Investigates corruption cases against public service officials and reports to the Council of Ministers.
Qatar	Administrative Control and Transparency Authority (ACTA)	Governmental (2007)	Federal	Works on the federal level—especially in the resource commodity market.
	National Committee for Integrity and Transparency	Governmental (2007)	National	Charged with implementation of UNCAC articles.
	State Audit Bureau (SAB) of Qatar	Governmental (1973)	Independent federal department	Directly reports to the Emir of Qatar and prescribes financial, compliance, performance, and EDP audit operations in its scope.
	National Human Rights Committee (NHRC)	Ombudsman (2002)	National	Dedicated to dealing with citizen complaints over irregularities within government agencies.
	Rule of Law and Anti-Corruption Center	Governmental (2011)	In cooperation with the UNDP	Conducts studies, research, and training programs on how to tackle the burden of corruption within the public sector.
Oman	State Audit Institution (SAI) or State Financial and Administrative Audit Institution (SFAAI)	Governmental (1970)	National	Achievement of more accountability, transparency, and fairness in government performance through Public Prosecution.

(*continued*)

Table 4.6 Cont.

Country	Anti-corruption agency	Nature and year of establishment	Affiliation	Agenda
Regional	Anti-Corruption and Integrity in the Arab Countries Project	NGO—UNDP Democratic Governance	Regional	The UNDP Regional Bureau for the Arab States was responsible for implementing the four-year project (2011–2014).
	Arab Anti-Corruption and Integrity Network	Supported by UNDP	Regional	Combats corruption on various levels of the government sector.
	Arab Anti-Corruption Organization	NGO (2004)	Independent civil institution	Seeks to promote transparency and good governance in the Arab World.

Source: Author's compilation from numerous government documents and online sources

UAE

The UAE has implemented various legal practices and legislation to combat corruption. Article 62 of its constitution explicitly prohibits involvement of government officials in any commercial or financial occupations that conflict with their public sector occupations. UAE Federal Law No. 1 of 2004 on Combating Terror Crimes also contains some articles that deal specifically with bribery, embezzlement, and money laundering (Loughman & Siberry, 2012). Moreover, it signed the UNCAC in August 2005 and ratified it in February 2006 as the framework under which the first Federal Anti-Corruption Law was constructed in the UAE under orders from the President of the UAE in 2012. The law is intended to indicate the legal provisions that will enshrine anti-corruption practices within the country's government. Enhancing the transparency and accountability of government is also indicated in the UAE's Government Strategy of 2011–2013.

Moreover, several government institutions are responsible for combating corruption within the federal and local governments of the UAE. The State Audit Institution (SAI), established in 1976, is considered the key federal institution that detects and fights against corruption in the UAE. More specifically, it aims to "safeguard public funds and assist the Federal Government in improving public sector governance and performance standards and to grow Emirati professional capabilities" (State Audit Institution, 2014). It also enjoys full financial and organizational independence and reports directly to the Federal National Council. Its role has so far been immense in protecting public funds from misuse by public officials—in 2011, for example, the SAI adopted the UN's anti-corruption recommendations and developed "Best Practices Guidelines" to foster its existing strategies and practices to combat corruption. The Defense Ministry also hosts an anti-corruption unit that functions as an organ to detect cases of corruption within the public sector. Furthermore, the Anti-Money Laundering and Suspicious Cases Unit within the UAE Central Bank has been influential in dealing with money laundering cases in the country. The influence of these organizations was especially important during the 2007–2009 global financial crisis, when they identified violators of UAE law and brought them to justice. Meanwhile, police departments within the seven Emirates of the UAE each have a section responsible exclusively for dealing with corruption cases in the public and private sectors.

Regional institutions

Several region-wide anti-corruption institutions have formed regional frameworks that attempt to unite the 22 Arab League countries' efforts to reduce the magnitude of corruption within their public institutions, most of which function under the umbrella of the United Nations Development Programme (UNDP). For example, the Anti-Corruption and Integrity in the Arab Countries Project has worked to institutionalize a culture of anti-corruption among all Arab countries. Meetings are also regularly organized in various Arab countries to allow policymakers, anti-corruption agencies, and specialists to gather and discuss innovative methods and plans to curb corruption. Another initiative supported by the UNDP and the World Bank is the Arab Anti-Corruption and Integrity Network, which was established in 2008 as a network that combines the efforts of the UNDP's Program on Governance in the Arab Region, the OECD, the United Nations Office on Drugs and Crime, and the League of Arab States. The GCC states actively participate in these meetings and share their experiences and practices, especially concerning their utilization of e-government initiatives to provide public services.

What these regional institutions bring to the table is their knowledge and expertise in combating corruption internationally through various instruments and forms. It is true that international experts on corruption can share their views on the best possible options for GCC states in their quests to enact laws, implement organizational reforms, and establish independent bodies to ensure that the rule of law is respected. However, something that these international experts do not always consider are the numerous and specific contextual and cultural characteristics of the GCC states that differ vastly from those of other countries.

The GCC's collaborative approach

In March 2013, the heads of government entities in charge of curbing corruption in the GCC's public sector held their first meeting in Saudi Arabia to exchange ideas and best practices and to establish collaboration frameworks. The second meeting took place in February 2012 in Kuwait. Suppose these meetings' outcomes and agendas are well documented, and their recommendations are carried out. In that case, they promise to offer a rich learning experience for all GCC countries, as they hold the potential to transfer knowledge among the states and share best practices in institutionalizing an anti-corruption culture within the public sector. Countries like Oman and Kuwait need to improve their global rankings in indices like Transparency International's CPI and the World Bank's control of corruption indicator, and this will only be possible if they learn from other well-performing states, such as Qatar and the UAE, about how they can substantially reform their public sectors' ethical practices.

Lessons learned from anti-corruption initiatives within the GCC states

Although sharing religious, historical, cultural, linguistic, and institutional similarities, the GCC states differ noticeably in their ability to curb corruption within their public sector organizations. Qatar and the UAE have radically improved their international rankings in both effectiveness of government machinery and corruption control. International experts in combating corruption, who have repeatedly applauded the efforts of Qatar and the UAE to reduce corruption to a notable degree, are in full support of this initiative, and Tables 4.2 and 4.3 show their systematic and gradual progress in enhancing scores and international rankings across various globally popular and trusted indicators. The question remains, however, as to how they differ from the other four GCC states that significantly lag in these indicators, despite seeming to have all the same necessary legal frameworks, institutions, and levels of government commitment.

The experiences of the six GCC states together demonstrate that it is difficult to generalize the causes and consequences of corruption, or the best methods to address its challenges. Despite similarities with neighboring countries, each state has its unique environment that requires a specific approach toward tackling corruption. Overall, the role of anti-corruption agencies and legislation is minimal in curbing corruption in most GCC states, and other factors must be considered to identify causes, consequences, and best solutions. As Table 4.6 shows, various governmental, federal, ministerial, and independent agencies aim to curb corruption through either the investigation of corruption cases or policies and laws to govern corruption. Oman seems to be the exception, as it has only one agency: the SFAAI. It is also an exception because it was the last GCC country to sign the UNCAC, doing so only in 2014. Of course, Oman struggles with corruption, but not as much as Kuwait, which has as many as four different agencies to deal with corruption, has enacted a considerable amount of legislation and laws in this regard, and yet still has CPI scores lower than any other GCC state (tied with Bahrain). Similarly, Saudi Arabia has at least four anti-corruption agencies operating within various jurisdictions and affiliations, yet its performance is not so different from that of Oman. Bahrain's efforts to tackle corruption are also visible, as its laws that criminalize corruption date back to 1987 (amended in 2013) and two major anti-corruption agencies have strong political support. Nevertheless, it still trails behind other GCC states in terms of "Transparency of government policymaking", "Wastefulness of government spending", and "Favoritism in government officials' decision-making".

The effectiveness of these institutions and the applicability of laws and legislation are thus highly questionable. For example, there are no external audits or reports about the performance of these agencies and their equal application of the law, and high-ranking government officials and policymakers are those in charge of ensuring justice is served. In Kuwait, there have been many cases in which political leadership has provided immunity to some of its high-ranking officials charged with allegations of corruption. How valuable are these agencies then in curbing corruption? Without reliable openness of data that would allow government officials to share experiences, an affirmative answer to that question remains most likely impossible. The literature on combating corruption in developing countries generally indicates that three key patterns should be adopted to successfully deal with corruption. The first involves anti-corruption laws without a specific enforcement agency, the second is the implementation of anti-corruption laws by multiple agencies, and the third is creating a single specialized and fully independent agency that comprehensively and effectively implements anti-corruption measures throughout the government (Quah, 2007). The GCC states seem to possess a mixture or combination of these patterns, and their outcomes vary significantly. Analysis of the strategies and institutions that GCC states have adopted to combat corruption thus reveals interesting trends regarding more influential factors. All six states share the same motivations in their fight against corruption, as they are all primarily interested in diversifying their economies and attracting FDI and foreign investors. Without a proper and convenient investment landscape, this is not a possibility, so political leadership's role in achieving it is highly evident within those states. The key difference, however, seems to be in the way they attempt to transform their commitment and visions into reality.

The political leaders of Qatar and the UAE have succeeded in proactively translating their economic ambitions into reality. They do not confine their sentiments to rhetoric only, as in the other GCC states, but rather closely follow up on their governments' progress in enhancing the quality of services they provide to the public. They accomplish this not only through the various legislative and organizational channels that they oversee, but also by appointing young, able individuals to leadership positions and making them work toward achieving a specific vision. This aspect seems to be absent in the other four GCC states. Empowering those leaders and entrusting them with positions involved in decision-making encourages them to give it their best and deliver tangible results. What matters most in combating corruption is not simply having numerous agencies or high amounts of legislation to control corruption, but also having the genuine and visible commitment of political leadership to punish those charged with corruption, regardless of their links or positions within the government. Oman has recently begun to apply this principle, as many current and previous ministers have been charged with corruption crimes, and their trials were publicly announced and discussed in national newspapers, something that would have been unheard of in the past. Other countries, including Saudi Arabia, are also seriously applying anti-corruption laws and attempting to catch up with Qatar and the UAE in international rankings to attract FDI. International report rankings and findings have recently attracted the attention of GCC leaders who wish to compete with their neighboring states. Hence, the topic of combating corruption occupies a high place in their national strategies.

Another important lesson that can be drawn from the GCC experience is that it is a significant challenge to holistically transform the organizational culture of public sector institutions in a short period. It requires continuous and sustainable efforts from top leadership to curb corruption and create an environment of accountability, trust, and good ethics. The past few years have witnessed the birth of several anti-corruption institutions in the GCC, but this will not be a quick remedy for a long-existing epidemic, and those institutions should not be considered decisive or absolute instruments to eradicate corruption in the public sector. Reform is usually incremental and requires the simultaneous application of various educational programs, strategies, legal instruments, and incentives to yield long-term positive results. The GCC region has unique cultural, political, economic, religious, and organizational characteristics that differ significantly from the rest of the world, and therefore any attempt to learn from how other countries have dealt with their corruption problems must consider the unique contextual aspects of the region in question. Anti-corruption agencies can provide only a short-term solution, and so what is needed is a sustainable and long-term solution that considers the roles of the various stakeholders involved in the issue.

Conclusion

This chapter has provided a holistic view of corruption within the public sectors of the GCC states. It examined the current state of corruption among them and the institutions and strategies they have each implemented to curb and minimize its effects on their developmental plans. The chapter has demonstrated how, despite historical, religious, economic, and cultural similarities among the GCC states, levels of corruption and outcomes of instruments used to combat it differ substantially. One of the main lessons to be gleaned from this chapter is that the mere existence of anti-corruption agencies and legislation in a region does not suffice to curb corruption. In many an example, the personal connections of various public sector officials with high-ranking government officials have enabled them to escape prosecution under such legislation. Instead, what is instrumental is the role of top political leadership within the GCC states and their genuine interest in and commitment to stopping the epidemic from growing and consuming extensive government resources. The experiences of Qatar and the UAE can thus serve as catalysts of change for the rest of the GCC. Learning from their experiences will allow the other states in the region to embark upon a journey toward effectively reducing corruption. While this will require time, commitment, and patience, the results can dramatically enhance the quality of governments within the GCC and create transparent, coherent, and effective governance structures.

Notes

1 http://omanlawblog.curtis.com/2013/10/anti-bribery-laws-restrictions-on.html
2 www.ilo.org/wcmsp5/groups/public/@ed_emp/@emp_ent/@ifp_seed/documents/publication/wcms_167007.pdf
3 www.intosaijournal.org/highlights/saudi_bureau.html

References

Ampratwum, E. (2008). The fight against corruption and its implications for development in developing and transition economies. *Journal of Money Laundering Control*, 11(1), 76–87.

Arab News. (2021). 172 arrested in Saudi Arabia's anti-corruption efforts. Retrieved from: www.arabnews.com/node/1963521/saudi-arabia. Accessed on 11 July 2022.

Arab News. (2022). Saudi Arabia's anti-corruption campaign takes root. Retrieved from www.arabnews.com/node/2020831. Accessed on 11 July 2022.

Askari, H., Rehman, S., & Afraa, N. (2010). *Corruption and Its Manifestation in the Persian Gulf*, Edward Elgar, Cheltenham.

Bertelsmann Foundation. (2014).www.bfna.org/ Accessed on 17 September 2021.

Brody, R., Gupta, G., Ekofo, A., & Ogunade, K. (2021). The need for anti-corruption policies in developing countries. *Journal of Financial Crime*, 28(1), 131–141.

Gumisiriza, P., & Mukobi, R. (2019). Effectiveness of anti-corruption measures in Uganda. *Rule of Law and Anti-Corruption Center Journal*, 2, 1–8.

Hay, J., & Schleifer, A. (1998). Private enforcement of public laws: A theory of legal reform. *American Economic Review*, 88(2), 398–403

International Labor Organization. (2011). www.ilo.org/wcmsp5/groups/public/@ed_emp/@emp_ent/@ifp_seed/documents/publication/wcms_167007.pdf Accessed on 17 September 2022.

Kaufmann, D. (2005). Myths and Realities of Governance and Corruption in *Global Competitiveness Report 2005–06* (October 2005), 81–98.

Khan, M. (2002). Corruption and Governance in Early Capitalism: World Bank Strategies and their Limitations, in Pincus J & Winters J (eds.), *Reinventing the World Bank*, Cornell University Press, pp. 164–184

Kumar, P. (2019). Anti-corruption measures in India: A democratic assessment. *Asian Journal of Public Affairs*, 11(2), 1–17.

Loughman, B., & Siberry, R. (2012). *Bribery and Corruption: Navigating the Global Risks*, Ernst & Young LLP, Hoboken.

Lubeck, P. (1992). The crisis of African development: Conflicting interpretations and resolutions, *Annual Review of Sociology*, 18(1), 519–540.

Mauro, P. (1995). Corruption and growth. *The Quarterly Journal of Economics*, 110(3), 681–712.

McCusker, R. (2006). *Review of Anti-Corruption Strategies*, Australian Institute of Criminology, Canberra.

Qatar Tribune. (2020). Qatar has said that corruption harms the rule of law. Retrieved from: www.qatar-tribune.com/news-details/id/193682/corruption-harms-rule-of-law-ability-of-states-to-better-governance-qatar Accessed on 5 September 2022.

Quah, J. (1999). Comparing anti-corruption measures in Asian countries: Lessons to be learnt. *Asian Review of Public Administration*, 6(2),71–90.

Quah, J. (2007). Anti-corruption agencies in four asian countries: A comparative analysis. *International Public Management Review*, 8(2), 73–96.

Riley, S. (1998). The Political Economy of Anti-Corruption Strategies in Africa in Robinson, M. (ed.), *Corruption and Development*, Frank Cass Publishers, London, pp. 129–159.

Shleifer, A., & Vishny, R. (1993). Corruption. *The Quarterly Journal of Economics*, 108(3), 599–617.

State Audit Institution. (2014). Retrieved from: https://saiuae.gov.ae/en/Pages/default.aspx Accessed on 12 September 2022.
Transparency International. (2020). Retrieved from: www.transparency.org/ Accessed on 8 September 2022.
UN Guide for Anti-Corruption Policies. (2003). Retrieved from: www.unodc.org/pdf/crime/corruption/UN_Guide.pdf Accessed on 6 September 2022.
Vadlamannati, K. (2015). Fighting corruption or elections? The politics of anti-corruption policies in India: A subnational study. *Journal of Comparative Economics*, 43(4), 1035–1052.
World Economic Forum. (2020). Retrieved from: www.weforum.org/ Accessed on 8 September 2022
World Bank Data Bank. (2020). Retrieved from: www.worldbank.com Accessed on 10 September 2022.

Part II
Importance of partnerships between the public and private sectors

5 The prospect and utility of infrastructure public-private partnerships in GCC states
Cases of Kuwait, Saudi Arabia, and Qatar

Introduction

Modern governments are invariably pressured to reform their public sectors, which are often described as inefficient and unresponsive to their citizens' growing needs (Grossman, 2012; Sabry, 2015). Since the 1980s, the public administration literature has witnessed a mounting interest in public management reform and the introduction of public-private partnerships (PPPs) as an infrastructure delivery mechanism, particularly within the Anglo-Saxon context (Pollitt, 2015). However, international business and public administration scholars often overlook the experiences of the Gulf Cooperation Council (GCC) states, which comprise Bahrain, Oman, Kuwait, Qatar, Saudi Arabia, and the United Arab Emirates (Akoum, 2009). Investigation of the influence of tribal and Islamic heritages on the Gulf region's administrative practices (Common, 2008; Kinsinger, 2007; Rice, 2004) can offer new perspectives for theorizing and developing public sector reforms.

This chapter situates three GCC states—Kuwait, Saudi Arabia, and Qatar—within the international debate on infrastructure PPPs and assesses how their administrative and regulatory structures form receptive environments for such a complex policy instrument. These particular states were selected for comparative analysis for three reasons. First, their economies are substantially dependent on oil and gas revenues, and the constant fluctuations and declines in these resources has considerably impacted their ability to finance future infrastructure projects under rising budget deficits.

Second, the three states have planned mega-infrastructure projects vital for their socioeconomic development over the next ten years. Qatar missed the opportunity to deliver large-scale infrastructure worth $220 billion for the 2022 FIFA World Cup under the PPP scheme but has a massive pipeline of projects to deliver under the Qatar Vision 2030. Meanwhile, Saudi Arabia has planned mega-infrastructure projects worth more than $1.2 trillion, including the King Abdullah Economic City, power plants, a metro system, and rail projects (MEED Projects, 2015; The National, 2015). Likewise, Kuwait has a pipeline of infrastructure projects that exceed $100 billion as part of its 2035 Economic Vision which aims to

DOI: 10.4324/9781003267744-7

reduce its dependence on natural resources and transform its economy into a knowledge-based one. Since funding these projects through their budgets seems exceedingly complex, the three states exhibit considerable political will to seek private finance, as reflected in the recently published Kingdom of Saudi Arabia Vision 2030 (2016), which describes PPP as a vehicle for financing future infrastructure services. Third, although the three states are in the same geographical region, they each have different sociopolitical dynamics that have shaped their institutional structures. Realizing this diversity is beneficial when examining the potential of infrastructure PPPs within each state and drawing lessons from them for other GCC states.

This chapter begins by reviewing the academic and practitioner PPP literature to identify the key assumptions underlying the success of PPP contracts within developed and developing countries. Building upon this conceptual framework, it is argued that, while infrastructure PPPs appear to be a strategic policy option for GCC states and an attractive investment opportunity for international managers, the three states are shackled by significant constraints. These relate to governance and the rule of law, regulatory and legal structures, and the lack of a competitive private sector or professional capacity to deliver mega-infrastructure projects through the PPP route.

Particular attention is drawn to the Gulf's "traditional culture", which often undermines the official functions of the government bureaucracy and exacerbates the Gulf's already complicated business climate (Akoum, 2009; Ali, 2010; Rice, 2004). This is one of the factors leading to the conclusion that extending infrastructure PPPs to the GCC states will require substantive public administration and institutional reforms, as well as empowerment of the private sector's role in the economy. These reforms, albeit extensive and requiring committed political will and time to mature, can ultimately help to establish an attractive and competitive business environment for international business investors.

Empirical data for this chapter is based on the author's ten years of research and teaching within the GCC states, which provided access to interviews with senior government officials, business leaders, and academics. This experience also allowed direct observation and understanding of the factors that shape the administrative and business environments in the Gulf. Data from the World Bank's Worldwide Governance Indicators and Doing Business database were relied upon to show where the three GCC states stand comparatively in terms of key governance and business indicators and support the article's conclusions.

The following section examines the ambiguity associated with the PPP phenomenon, its complexity, and the assumptions underlying the success of PPP projects based on international experience. This conceptual framework is then applied to the context of the three GCC states to inform an analysis of the constraints that limit the prospect of implementing infrastructure PPPs. This is followed by a section on the managerial implications of these limitations and then a set of recommendations for policy reforms to address these shortcomings.

The concept and complexity of infrastructure PPPs

The PPP concept has been "contested" and "loosely" defined, encompassing many "approaches" (Weihe, 2008) with "overlapping" definitions that mean different things to different people (Linder, 1999). Scholars have also been divided between those who consider PPPs to be a type of language game (Teisman & Klijn, 2002), and those who view them as an emerging governance scheme for the delivery of public infrastructure services through new forms of institutional engagements (joint ventures) or contractual arrangements between the public and private sectors (Flinders, 2005). This chapter focuses solely on infrastructure PPPs, defined as "arrangements whereby private parties participate in, or support the provision of public infrastructure-based services" such as roads, bridges, airports, power stations, and railways (Grimsey & Lewis, 2004, p. 2). Although the PPP phenomenon is controversial, and is believed to achieve mixed results (Petersen, 2010), tapping into the private sector's finances and expertise in delivering infrastructure promises value for money (Rondinelli & Priebjrivat, 2000), sharing of risk or its transfer to the party best qualified to handle it, and delivery of projects in a timely fashion (Vining & Boardman, 2008).

Infrastructure PPPs are attractive in theory, but their complexity renders most projects controversial, risky, and "less ideal than the idea" (Klijn & Teisman, 2003, p. 137). The complexity of PPPs is an outcome of the long-term nature of partnerships that can exceed 30–40 years and the involvement of players from diverse sectors and networks with varying, and sometimes conflicting interests (Kanter, 1994). The multiple layers of intricacy underlying PPPs involve engineering, design, and implementation risks (Grimsey & Lewis, 2004), the need for sophisticated legal structures, and institutional and strategic barriers that resist the delivery of infrastructure outside traditional routes (Klijn & Teisman, 2003). Furthermore, technical impediments associated with calculating the Public Sector Comparator (PSC), risk evaluation, discount rates (Grimsey & Lewis, 2004), accountability and transparency mechanisms (Delmon, 2011), and difficulties in evaluating PPP projects' overall financial value and performance (Moore, 2000) add to the complexity of PPPs.

The debates surrounding infrastructure PPPs' complexity prove their implementation is problematic even within Western states' political and economic environments where the PPP concept originated. The literature on PPPs is rife with cases of disputes between the public and private sectors over contractual disagreements (Bloomfield, 2006), attempts to renegotiate contracts after commencement (Jooste et al., 2011), premature termination of multibillion-dollar contracts (Marin, 2009), scandalous cases of corruption leading to lawsuits against high-level government officials

(Greve, 2003), and even legal action by the private sector against the government for breach of contract. Therefore Flinders (2005) describes the complexity of the PPP phenomenon as "changing both the nature and structure of the British state and its governance frameworks within which it operates" (p. 218). The increasing involvement of the private sector in long-term infrastructure projects "further complicates the structure of the modern state" (p. 227) by creating extra autonomous entities within the state's administrative landscape to monitor the governance and progress of PPP projects.

Despite these complexities, it did not take long for PPP ideas to travel from Western jurisdictions to developing countries (Pessoa, 2009; Pollitt, 2015). International governmental organizations and consultancy firms have urged developing countries to embark on market liberalization-driven policies like PPPs, propounding their promise to deliver infrastructure projects with more value for money and superior levels of efficiency (Petersen, 2010; Rondinelli & Priebjrivat, 2000). Nonetheless, the failure of numerous PPP projects in developed and developing countries, along with their sluggish progress in many others, underscores the inherently complex nature of PPPs and the importance of first getting the governance and institutional "fundamentals right" (Awortwi, 2004). Therefore, it is essential to regard the PPP phenomenon not simply as an infrastructure delivery tool but as a governance mechanism that necessitates an enabling environment to achieve the desired goals (Sabry, 2015).

Assumptions underlying successful infrastructure PPPs

This section revisits the fundamental assumptions to the success of international PPP experiences, which serve as a framework to test the PPP readiness of Kuwait, Saudi Arabia, and Qatar.

Good governance and the rule of law

PPPs are contractual agreements that necessitate sophisticated institutional, legal, and legislative capacity to ensure PPP contracts' legitimacy, transparency, and accountability (Jooste et al., 2011). Infrastructure PPP projects have considerable upfront costs, which force international investors and managers to thoroughly examine the hosting countries' governance climates (IMF, 2006; Pongsiri, 2002). The existence of sound governance mechanisms is crucial to protect international investors' rights and businesses against the commercial risks incurred during the construction phase of a PPP, or during its life cycle that typically lasts up to 30 years (UNECE, 2008). Independence of the judiciary system from political influence enables international investors to use arbitration or local courts' systems in disputes that often arise in construction and contractual agreements.

Legal and regulatory institutions

The intricate networks linking actors from the public and private sectors that operate with competing, and often conflicting, interests require "a strong democratic state using its financial, institutional, or legislative muscle to level the playing field for all partners by regulating unequal power relationships" (Balasooriya et al., 2010; Miraftab, 2004, p. 93).

Savas (2000) argues that the most significant inhibitor of private participation in the delivery of services is uncertainty about the regulatory environment and the existence of transparent and accountable institutions that can monitor the conduct of bureaucrats and hold them accountable for their actions. Political will, however, remains a vital foundation upon which institutional effectiveness can be built, because international investors give more weight to the quality of legal and regulatory institutions than to mere laws on paper (Pistor et al., 2000). If the institutional preconditions do not exist, or do not function properly, PPPs are likely to fail to deliver their promised value for money (Awortwi, 2004). Such situations allow for rent-seeking and corruption, especially in environments where patronage and patron-client relationships are rampant (Beh, 2010).

Sound and well-defined legal and regulatory frameworks that clarify conditions for ownership of the private sector's projects, specify the types of PPP models that are authorized, and allow access to land are factors that demonstrate the public sector's commitment to attracting, retaining, and partnering with foreign businesses (Abdel Aziz, 2007; OECD, 2013; UN, 2007). International managers and investors require certainty and protection from expropriation or unexpected political or economic changes that could jeopardize a PPP agreement or infrastructure project (Pongsiri, 2002). Additionally, investors pay attention to how a country's institutions regulate issues related to investment laws, contract enforcement, ownership rights, and bankruptcy (IMF, 2006; UNECE, 2008). These elements are factored in when international companies calculate a country's risk ratio.

Competition-driven market economies

The acclaimed efficiency of PPP projects is principally derived from the market's competitive forces that empower the private sector to deliver high-quality services with fewer resources (OECD, 2013). Many mechanisms must be in place for the private sector to achieve this.

First, there should be a solid political will to involve the private sector in delivering services that have traditionally been the sole responsibility of the public sector (IMF, 2006; UNECE, 2008; OECD, 2013). This eases the legislative and bureaucratic barriers that usually hamper the private sector, and offers a friendly business environment for international investors (Al-Shareem et al., 2015). In countries where "civil society and/or the private sector are discriminated, the government remains the dominant supplier of social goods" (Pessoa, 2009, p. 20). Such political will is reflected in a country's involvement with the private sector through outsourcing infrastructure services or, on a larger scale, through successful privatization programs (Akoum, 2009; Al-Husan & James, 2007). Governments need to allow an "exchange of information between actors and [have] a willingness to look for solutions on a mutual basis" (Teisman & Klijn, 2002), which then builds a culture of mutual trust between the two sectors and allows a true spirit of partnership to develop.

Second, free market economies require adopting transparent tendering processes based on the bidders' quality and experience, rather than favoritism, corruption, or patronage (Beh, 2010; Hayllar, 2010). Such practices, commonly the result of ineffective regulatory institutions, have severely undermined the performance of numerous infrastructure PPP projects and ultimately led to their failure (Awortwi, 2004; Beh, 2010). Competition over contracts should be safeguarded by independent institutions that base the decision to award projects on the merit of each proposal and the capacity of the private sector entity to deliver within the required budget and timeframe (UNECE, 2008).

Professional capacity within the public and private sectors

The technical capacity of the government and private sector to deliver infrastructure projects through PPPs is commonly taken for granted when considering this delivery method (Grimsey & Lewis, 2004). Therefore, it is important to carefully match governments' capacity with the complexity of PPPs (Gestel et al., 2012; World Bank, 2014b). The public sector needs to operate at levels of efficiency and effectiveness closer to those of the private sector, enhance the quality of administrative systems, and minimize red tape and other bureaucratic processes surrounding the procurement of permits (Mouraviev & Kakabadse, 2015). Development of internal capacity and resources within the public sector, such as a dedicated PPP unit, helps to efficaciously "manage, monitor and enforce [PPP] contracts" more strategically (Bloomfield, 2006, p. 410).

Equally important to such technical capacity is the financial and practical capability of the local private sector to deliver the desired services with the promised quality, or at least the possibility of tapping into international experience in providing such services (Kanter, 1994). Zhang (2005) undertook an extensive survey that covered the public and private sectors in China and the UK, and identified a lack of mature financial markets, engineering techniques, and unfavorable economic and commercial conditions among the principal barriers to PPPs. However, it is imperative to note that, despite considerable efforts to deliver infrastructure services through the PPP method, some projects still fail to deliver on time or achieve the promised value for money (Dunleavy & Carrera, 2013).

To summarize, infrastructure PPPs involve highly complex contractual mechanisms. The quality of governance and regulatory structures and the

The prospect and utility of infrastructure PPPs in the GCC states 143

capacity within the public and private sectors determine the outcome of PPP contracts. With these factors in mind, it is appropriate to critically evaluate the characteristics underlying the governance, administrative, and private sector structures of Kuwait, Saudi Arabia, and Qatar. Such analysis provides an understanding of the contextual factors that affect the implementation and performance of infrastructure PPP projects within the three states.

Assessing the readiness of Kuwait, Saudi Arabia, and Qatar to adopt infrastructure PPPs

This section assesses the readiness of each of the three Gulf states to adopt infrastructure PPPs for their projects drawing on the performance of these states in major indicators of good governance, easiness of doing business, length of the procurement process and the most problematic factors for doing business in the three GCC states.

Kuwait

Kuwait possesses a unique political system among the dominantly autocratic GCC states. In 1961, it established the first constitution and parliament in the GCC (Al-Sabah, 1980). However, political parties are still banned in Kuwait, and the Emir maintains the power to dismiss the parliament—which Kuwait rulers have done six times between 2006 and 2022 (BBC, 2012; Reuters, 2022). The Emir also appoints the prime minister from the ruling family and forms the government after receiving the Emir's approval. Kuwait's ranking in the World Bank's "voice and accountability" indicator declined from 44% in 1996 to 29% in 2014 (Table 5.1), demonstrating the marginal role that parliament plays in Kuwait's semi-democratic political model. Furthermore, this performance did not improve in 2020 as it remained at 30%.

The role of the parliament as an arbiter dividing power between the Emir and Kuwaiti citizens has resulted in long-lasting political crises that have hamstrung the business climate since the 1980s (Kinninmont, 2012). Members of Parliament (MPs) have repeatedly voted against the government's investment plans and proposals, which they see as benefiting the traditional merchant classes, and voted for the direct distribution of oil revenues to Kuwaiti citizens (Herb, 2014). This makes "the legislative branch ... over the past eight years ... the most important factor hampering reform and disabling the role of the private sector" (Al-Monitor, 2014). It was not until 2013 that a pro-government policy parliament was elected, but its impact on improving the private sector has yet to materialize.

The role of the law in Kuwait is undermined by the lack of an independent judicial system, since the Emir "appoints all the judges", and the executive branch is responsible for approving judicial promotions (CIA World Factbook, 2015). As Table 5.1 shows, Kuwait's performance in the

Table 5.1 Selected indicators of governance *(1% = worst, 100% = best)

Country	Voice and Accountability				Government Effectiveness				Regulatory Quality				Rule of Law				Control of Corruption			
	1996	2004	2014	2020	1996	2004	2014	2020	1996	2004	2014	2020	1996	2004	2014	2020	1996	2004	2014	2020
Kuwait	44	39	29	30	60	61	47	46	55	69	48	62	65	65	60	63	78	82	50	54
KSA	8	10	3	5	46	45	62	58	47	56	53	61	59	57	65	60	28	46	59	63
Qatar	31	37	22	14	68	71	78	78	50	59	70	76	55	63	81	82	56	73	82	78

Source: World Bank Data (2020)

The prospect and utility of infrastructure PPPs in the GCC states 145

"rule of law" indicator remained the same since 1996 when it scored 65% and in 2020 this indicator slightly declined to 63%. This jeopardizes the sanctity of legal contracts, given the royal family's control over the judiciary system. Furthermore, despite the efforts of the parliament to institutionalize the decision-making process in Kuwait, there have been many instances of key ministerial members using their positions to bypass formal processes and achieve personal gains (Biygautane, 2015). This threatens the legitimacy of the regulatory environment and means that connections are essential to gain access to government contracts and navigate the complex state bureaucracy.

As Table 5.2 shows, Kuwait ranks 106th (out of 140) in terms of "legal rights" and 58th (out of 189) in "enforcing contracts", and its current bankruptcy laws do not meet international standards (US Department of State, 2015), and in 2020 it scored 1 in legal rights (0 weak to 12 strong). It also ranks 122nd (out of 189) in terms of "resolving insolvency" according to the World Bank Group Doing Business Database (2015), but that improved somewhat in 2020 when Kuwait ranked 115. The court system in Kuwait is notoriously slow and lengthy, and judges lack the necessary training to streamline their operations and effectively serve in the sluggish legal system (CIA World Factbook, 2015). The existing Judicial Arbitration Law in Kuwait has numerous shortcomings that make it unattractive to international businesses. In its current form, it "draw[s] a closer resemblance to the practice of litigation" and requires extensive reforms to meet the international criteria (Houti, 2015).

Although Kuwait was the first among the GCC states to attempt to establish the regulatory and institutional frameworks for PPPs, the involvement of the pre-2013 parliament in setting the PPP legislation resulted in many shortcomings that did not make Kuwait an attractive place for PPPs. The Build-Operate-Transfer (BOT) law (7/2008) was perceived by the Kuwaiti business community as an "inhibitor of PPPs", since most of its clauses were restrictive to both local and international investors (MEED Projects, 2015). However, the pro-government parliament passed the new

Table 5.2 Ease of doing business *(1= best, 189= worst, except legal rights where 1= best, and 140= worst)

	Starting a Business		Getting Credit		Enforcing Contracts		Resolving Insolvency		Legal Rights	
	2014	2019	2014	2019	2014	2019	2014	2019	2014	2019*
Kuwait	148	82	109	119	58	74	122	115	106	1
Saudi Arabia	130	38	79	80	86	51	189	168	106	3
Qatar	109	108	133	119	112	115	51	123	129	1

Source: World Bank Group Doing Business Database (2020); *0 = weak to 12 = strong

PPP Law 116/2014 to improve the legal landscape for PPPs in Kuwait and remedy the weaknesses of the previous law, but it nevertheless prohibits the sale of state land to the private sector. As a result of political resistance to the private sector's involvement in delivering public services, and the previously inadequate PPP law, the Kuwait Authority for Partnership Projects (Kuwait's PPP Unit) only managed to achieve financial close of one PPP project—Az-Zour North—in December 2014 since its establishment in 2008.

As in other rentier economies, excessive reliance on oil revenues makes the Kuwaiti government and its conglomerates the leading forces in the local market. The drop in oil prices since 2014 resulted in a deficit of more than $27 billion in the 2016 budget (IMF, 2015b), and increased pressure on the government to diversify the economy. Also, powerful merchant families dominate most sectors of the economy and profit from government contracts that they receive based on their closeness to members of the ruling family (Kuwait Times, 2014).

Family businesses have historically been supported by the government's "restrictive policies" that curtail competition from foreign investors (Al-Kuwari, 2012; Al-Sabah, 1980). For example, the outdated 1964 Public Tenders Law, which is still in force, stipulates that foreigners cannot bid for government contracts unless they partner with a Kuwaiti agent, who charges a fee simply for including their name in the bidding documents. Such factors make doing business in Kuwait "notoriously hard" (Herb, 2014), a fact that Kuwait's low ranking in the World Bank's Doing Business proves, where it stood at 148 out of 189 in "starting a business" in 2014, but that improved significantly in 2019 when it ranked 82. Nonetheless, the performance of Kuwait in "getting credit" declined from 109 in 2014 to 119 in 2019.

Kuwait's history is replete with cases of tendering processes for high-profile infrastructure services lacking in transparency and leading to corruption. A former Minister of Electricity, along with 11 other government officials, were accused of mishandling public funds while procuring 500 MW of electricity in 2007 (MEED Projects, 2015). Also, unlawful "connections between the administration and private companies, have resulted in [similar cases of] uneven market competition" (Business Anti-Corruption, 2015a). Nevertheless, given the limited levels of transparency and secrecy surrounding legal controversies involving high-ranking officials, information regarding the execution of court judgments is not always disclosed to the public (Biygautane, 2015). Kuwait's ranking in the World Bank's "control of corruption" indicator dropped from 78% in 1996 to 50% in 2014, and improved marginally in 2020 when it ranked 54 affirming widespread corruption in the country.

Kuwait suffers from excessive bureaucracy and red tape, along with an extremely lengthy procurement process (633 days) that is approximately four times longer than the world average (174 days) (Table 5.3). The situation is evident in its low ranking in the "inefficient government

The prospect and utility of infrastructure PPPs in the GCC states 147

Table 5.3 Length of the procurement process in Kuwait (in days)

Stage	Global average	Kuwait
Advertising to receiving bids	28	102
Receiving bids to award	80	128
Award to contract signing	28	266
Contract signing to notice to proceed	28	64
Total	174	633

Source: World Bank (2015)

Table 5.4 The most problematic factors for doing business in selected GCC states

Kuwait	Saudi Arabia	Qatar
• Inefficient government bureaucracy • Restrictive labor regulations • Restricted access to financing • Inadequately educated labor force • Corruption	• Restrictive labor regulations • Inadequately educated labor force • Inefficient government bureaucracy • Restricted access to financing • Poor work ethic in labor force	• Restrictive labor regulations • Inadequately educated labor force • Inefficient government bureaucracy • Inflation • Poor work ethic in labor force

Source: World Bank Group Doing Business Database (2020)

bureaucracy" indicator, which topped the World Bank's list of the most problematic factors for doing business in Kuwait (Table 5.4).

The public sector's lack of technical capacity and knowledge about delivering infrastructure projects through PPP is another obstruct for Kuwait. The chance of learning from the private sector's expertise is hampered by the government's restrictive labor regulations that require the private sector to recruit a majority of Kuwaiti nationals, who often do not possess the necessary expertise or skills to implement PPP projects.

Saudi Arabia

Similar to Kuwait's semi-democratic model, Saudi Arabia has its King nominate members of the Council of Ministers (the Cabinet), who "exercise supervision and control over the Saudi bureaucracy" (Jabbra & Jabbra, 2005, p. 135) and have the final say in the management of state affairs (Al-Ghanim, 2010). The limited participation of the general public in policymaking is perhaps responsible for Saudi Arabia's position as one of the low-ranking countries in the World Bank's voice and accountability indicator (Table 5.1), in which it scored 8% in 1999 and dropped to a mere 3% in 2014 and slightly improved to 5% in 2020.

The King of Saudi Arabia, much like the Emir of Kuwait, appoints Sharia-trained judges who maintain Islamic jurisdiction within the court system. Saudi Arabia still lacks a functional arbitration system, and international investors rely on international arbitration to solve their disputes. The Board of Grievances that forms a part of the Saudi bureaucracy is responsible for solving commercial disputes and oversees the arbitration process (Practical Law, 2014a). The current Arbitration Law is closer to litigation than arbitration, and does not allow government entities to engage in arbitration until it is approved by the Prime Minister (the King) (Ashurst, 2016). What lowers Saudi Arabia's World Bank Doing Business ranking is the resolving insolvency indicator, in which it ranked 189 out of 189 in 2014 although that ranking improved modestly when it was ranked 168 in 2019 (Table 5.2), which, among other factors, makes it a risky environment to conduct business. Furthermore, in legal rights, Saudi is similar to Kuwait with a ranking of 106 out of 140 in 2014, and a score of 3 in 2019, and stands lower in enforcing contracts, which scored 86 out of 189 in 2014 which improved when it scored 51 in 2019.

Although Saudi Arabia still lacks the legal and regulatory frameworks that Kuwait has to oversee PPPs, it nonetheless grants land to some private sector entities to establish PPPs, and new regulations also permit foreign investors to bid on government contracts without the need for Saudi agents (US Department of State, 2015). While the regulations allow 100% foreign ownership of businesses, joint ventures with local companies are considered by some international businesses as a must in order to operate within the Saudi business sector (The Economist, 2014). Saudi Arabia's Regulatory Quality has not improved in the past decade; in fact, it declined from 56% in 2004 to 53% in 2014 and improved slightly to 61% in 2020, reflecting the slow pace of regulatory reform.

If the procurement system in Kuwait is sluggish, in Saudi Arabia, many of the Government Tenders and Procurement Law provisions are problematic for PPPs. All public sector entities in Saudi Arabia are required to use a standard contract that is approved by the Ministry of Finance (MOF) for all infrastructure projects, which limits the private sector's ability to negotiate the terms of contracts based on the type and nature of a project (Ashurst, 2016). Furthermore, contracts that exceed 5 million Saudi Riyals and a period of five years need to be approved by the MOF, which entails a long, costly, and wearisome bureaucratic process for the private sector.

Saudi Arabia is the largest economy in the entire Middle East and North Africa (MENA) region and one of the largest exporters of oil in the world (Akoum, 2009). As a resource-dependent rentier state, government spending generates growth in the private sector (Rice, 2004). The significant drop in oil prices in the second half of 2014 left the Saudi government with a more than 20% budget deficit in 2016, and IMF predicts this deficit will persist till 2020 if the government continues its current spending while oil prices remain below $50 (IMF, 2015c).

The prospect and utility of infrastructure PPPs in the GCC states 149

Like that in Kuwait, the private sector in Saudi Arabia is primarily dominated by a few traditional family businesses that control approximately 90% of all private sector companies (Oukil & Al-Khalifa, 2012). These businesses contributed around 25% of the national GDP in 2012, and among the 5,000 registered businesses in the Chamber of Commerce, only 156 are listed on the stock market (Arab News, 2012). Their unwillingness to become publicly listed companies emanates mainly from a hesitance to adhere to the required levels of scrutiny and accountability, the risk of being forced to reveal the informal mechanisms that characterize their business models, and their preference to maintain full control over their family businesses (Oukil & Al-Khalifa, 2012). Although Saudi laws proclaim equal opportunities for all bidders, "rent-seeking and corruption are not uncommon in government procurement processes" (Business Anti-Corruption, 2015a). Saudi scored 59% in the control of corruption indicator in 2014, advancing from 28% in 1996, and improved slightly in 2020 when it scored 63%. However, the lack of comprehensive legislation to control corruption continues to make it one of the biggest barriers to operating in the Saudi private sector.

Family businesses' scale, influence on the private sector, and informal impact on economic decision-making hinder access to and doing business in Saudi Arabia. This fact is reflected in the country's rank of 130 out of 189 in the World Bank's starting a business indicator, but the Saudi government managed to drastically improve this ranking in 2020 when it scored 38% which is the best performance compared to Qatar and Kuwait (see Table 5.2). Because "family loyalty is the most powerful force in Saudi society ... rather than technical competence or management performance" (Rice, 2004, p. 74), international businesses have little faith that Saudi government officials will make fair decisions and "not favor well-connected companies or individuals when deciding policies and contracts" (Business Anti-Corruption, 2015b).

Another factor that hinders the business environment in Saudi Arabia is "restrictive labor regulations". The Saudi authorities oblige employers to hire large portions of Saudis under the *Intilaqat* Saudization program, which specifies size-based quotas private sector entities must meet to maintain their business licenses. International companies working for a Saudi government entity must devote 30% of work under contract to Saudi nationals (Practical Law, 2014b). The Saudi Arabian General Investment Authority (SAGIA) has already cancelled dozens of business licenses of entities that failed to meet the Saudi hiring requirements (The Economist, 2014). It has delayed issuing residency visa requests for businesses to obtain employees from other countries (US Department of State, 2015).

Like Kuwait, the overstaffed and inefficient government bureaucracy in Saudi Arabia is another factor complained about by local and international businesses (Table 5.4). Because "coordination between state bodies is often poor ... it is still necessary to have the right connections to negotiate the official bureaucracy" (The Economist, 2014). This forces individuals and businesses to either pay bribes or use their connections to overcome the bureaucratic hurdles (Rice, 2004). A survey by the Riyadh Chamber of Commerce (2007) showed that more than 77% of businessmen in Saudi "bypass" the law to obtain the necessary approvals for their businesses. A lack of merit-based recruitment practices and the absence of systems of accountability and performance measurements are largely to blame for this situation (Jabbra & Jabbra, 2005).

Qatar

Similar to Kuwait and Saudi Arabia, the ruler of Qatar nominates "all judges, many of them non-Qataris, making them vulnerable to deportation" if they make decisions that are unfavorable to the ruler (Fromherz, 2012, p. 127). Law 12/2008 established a new Supreme Court, but the Emir of Qatar also assigns its judges (US Department of State, 2015). Compared to the other two GCC states, Qatar scored highest in rule of law, achieving 82% in 2019 compared to 55% in 1996. Additionally, Qatar is among the highest-ranking states in the Middle East regarding control of corruption in the public sector (Biygautane, 2015).

The rankings of the Qatar government's legal and regulatory institutional capacities reveal conflicting results. It was ranked highest in the resolving insolvency indicator, which ranked 51 in 2014 compared to Saudi Arabia at 189 and Kuwait at 122. However, Qatar's scoring in resolving insolvency dropped considerably in 2020 when it scored 123. Furthermore, the Qatar Financial Center (QFC) has civil and commercial courts and a regulatory tribunal that serve as judicial arms. Unlike Kuwait and Saudi Arabia, Qatar relies more on arbitration than litigation to solve commercial disputes and has a dedicated entity for that purpose in the form of the Qatar International Center for Conciliation and Arbitration. However, similar to Saudi Arabia, the Tenders Law requires public sector entities to obtain high Ministerial approval before they agree to arbitration (Practical Law, 2014b). Qatar ranks lowest among the three GCC states in enforcing contracts, at 112 in 2014 compared to 58 in Kuwait and 86 in Saudi Arabia. However, this score deteriorated in 2020 when it ranked 115. Furthermore, it ranked lowest in legal rights, which stood at 129 compared to 106 in the other two states in 2014, but similar to Kuwait in 2019 with a score of 1 (Table 5.2).

Qatar also has restrictive government investment policies that protect traditional business families. Investment Law 13/2000 limits foreign investment to 49% of capital, with a Qatari partner holding at least 51%, but the law also specifies that, subject to the approval of the Cabinet, there are opportunities in certain sectors for foreigners to own 100% of their companies. Similar to the cases of Kuwait and Saudi Arabia, foreign firms wishing to bid for government procurement programs in Qatar must do so through a local agent (Practical Law, 2014b). Although more than 1,000 family businesses dominate the private sector in Qatar, only 5% of them have formal and transparent governance structures (Qatar Today, 2014). The lack of accessible data on these local businesses' performance or governance mechanisms could make foreign investors hesitant to partner with most of them.

Of the three GCC states, Qatar ranked as the least difficult place for starting a business, ranking 109 in 2014 compared to 148 in Kuwait and 130 in Saudi Arabia (Table 5.2). However, in 2019, Qatar became the most difficult place to do business when it scored 108 compared to 82 in Kuwait and 38 in Saudi Arabia. Meanwhile, Qatar is also the hardest place for getting credit, as evidenced by its ranking of 133 compared to 109 in Kuwait and 79 in Saudi Arabia in 2014, and continued to be the hardest place for getting credit even in 2019 when it ranked 112 compared to Saudi Arabia that ranked 86 and Kuwait that ranked 58 (Table 5.2). The public procurement system is equally problematic compared to the other two states. The lack of rigorous transparency measures and the prevalence of favoritism in granting government contracts to some traditional merchant families (Business Anti-Corruption, 2015c) are some issues lamented by foreign businesses in Qatar.

Similar to the cases of Kuwait and Saudi Arabia, the quality of public administration in Qatar hinders the growth of the business and private sectors. The bloated and inefficient state bureaucracy, which absorbs approximately 85% of the Qatari workforce (IMF, 2014), is considered the third most problematic factor for doing business in Qatar, as indicated in the World Bank Doing Business Database (Table 5.4). Nonetheless, the Qatari government has increased its pressure on the private sector to recruit Qatari citizens, who often lack the educational and technical skills required for their jobs (Biygautane, 2016). This can negatively impact the performance and efficiency of private sector companies that typically recruit employees based on their capacity to perform their tasks and deliver on time.

Managerial implications of governance, administrative, and business challenges related to infrastructure PPPs

This section discusses the managerial implications of governance and institutional challenges in implementing infrastructure PPPs. Awareness of these challenges is vital for policymakers in the three states, and international investors considering the investment in the region.

Governance, legal, and regulatory constraints

The principle challenges faced by Kuwait, Saudi Arabia, and Qatar in attracting private finance for infrastructure projects are their weak governance, legal, and regulatory capacities. The bankability of PPP contracts is determined by assessing risks involved during all phases of the project, and the absence of principles of good governance and the rule of law exacerbate these risks. The three GCC states scored low (by developed and developing country standards) in key World Bank governance and regulatory environment indicators such as voice and accountability, rule of law, enforcing contracts, resolving insolvency, and legal rights. These low scores have negative consequences for attracting foreign businesses, which find the business environment extremely risky. The abrupt changes in laws and regulations without prior notice exacerbate the levels of risk in the three GCC states, which frustrates both local and international investors. Furthermore, the lack of an independent judiciary system, an outdated and very slow legal system, and the limited scope of arbitration in solving disputes between public and private sector entities further discourage international businesses from considering the PPP market in the GCC.

The low scores of the three GCC states in regulatory quality raise questions about the capacity of government institutions to monitor PPP projects effectively. Transparency in the governance of projects after the implementation phase is critical for achieving value for money. The difficulty of controlling corruption, particularly within Kuwait and Saudi Arabia, might jeopardize the transparency of PPP projects and enable individuals with access to powerful bureaucrats to maneuver around rules and regulations to fulfill their goals.

The absence of a publicly centered decision-making structure in Saudi Arabia and Qatar casts the "public" component of PPPs in a dubious light. Given the concentration of political and economic decision-making among a small number of political elites and other senior government officials, PPPs might better be referred to as "government-private partnerships". In Kuwait, however, PPP law stipulates that 50% of the shares of the awarded project company must be accessible to Kuwait citizens through an Initial Public Offering. Nonetheless, restricting these shares to Kuwaitis alone discriminates against expatriates, who form the largest portion of "the public" and can contribute to the local share market.

Bureaucratic constraints

The inefficiency of government bureaucracies in the three states is another hurdle for infrastructure PPPs. Although legal and regulatory frameworks are essential, the implementation level of PPPs within the local bureaucracy is instrumental in their success (Sabry, 2015). A dearth of qualified public sector employees with sufficient experience and understanding of the technical requirements of PPPs is a recurrent complaint from private sector entities that attempt to engage in contractual relationships with the governments of Kuwait, Saudi Arabia, and Qatar. A lack of proper coordination and communication among government entities that are fragmented and occupied by individuals often chosen because of patronage rather than competence all lead to "excessive red tape that is hidden from public view" (Kinsinger, 2007, p. 539).

The complex and contractual nature of PPP agreements necessitates smooth, streamlined cooperation and collaboration among public and private sector entities. However, the lengthy bureaucratic processes in the three states lead to long delays in obtaining permits or gaining the necessary approvals to procure government projects (particularly in Kuwait). The outcome of these excessive delays, which come at a considerable cost to the private sector, is the cancellation of projects at different operational stages and jeopardizes the trust of international investors. The institutional challenges imposed by Kuwait's opaque and inefficient bureaucracy and political resistance toward private delivery of infrastructure have undermined the functions of its PPP Unit and PPP laws.

Private sector constraints

International experience has shown that PPPs work most effectively in environments with vibrant and active private sectors with a long history of competitive provision of infrastructure projects (Al-Shareem et al., 2015). In the three GCC states, several factors limit the capacity of their private sectors to carry out infrastructure services effectively.

First, public sector spending from oil revenues still drives economic growth, and the lack of mature and strong financial markets remains a challenge for these states. The private sector's dependence on government contracts and inability to generate economic wealth, coupled with restrictive policies that restrict foreign businesses' entrance into local markets, pose serious barriers to infrastructure PPPs. When oil prices fell in the second half of 2014, government spending went down significantly, and so did the private sector's growth performance, which led to shrinking liquidity and lending appetite within local banks. Consequently, the credit ratings of the three Gulf states have been lowered, especially in Saudi Arabia, which saw its ratings downgraded by the three major rating agencies of Standard & Poor's, Fitch Group, and Moody's (The National, 2016). This makes attracting finance for infrastructure PPPs even more difficult and expensive.

Second, it is difficult to properly estimate the actual size of the private sector and the capability of local markets to finance mega-infrastructure projects. The secrecy that surrounds SOEs' performance and the absence of mechanisms of transparency and good governance within most family businesses that dominate the sector prevents an accurate assessment of the readiness of these states' financial markets to support long-term projects. Furthermore, granting government contracts to prominent merchant classes with access to powerful political elites, regardless of their technical capacity, is problematic for foreign investors wanting to do business in the three GCC states. This generates mistrust between the local public and private sectors, as witnessed in Kuwait and Saudi Arabia. Another challenge is that family businesses invest primarily in low-risk projects with a short time frame of three to five years, and yield high returns on investments in such areas as real estate and other construction services. Shifting their focus to long-term projects with high risks and low returns on investments requires a fundamental alteration of the investment culture of the Gulf.

Third, since infrastructure has historically been provided through government funding and traditional procurement methods, the local private sector lacks the required experience and capacity to deliver infrastructure efficiently. The option of importing talent from international markets is limited by government policies that force the private sector to meet certain quotas for hiring citizens and restrict the issuing of residency visas to expatriates. Fourth, the difficulty of leasing land in Saudi Arabia and Qatar and the prohibition of private sector ownership of land in Kuwait are persistent barriers to forming a PPP-friendly environment. Without proper legislation that allows the private sector to use land, the prospect of PPPs remains bleak.

Cultural constraints

Numerous cultural dimensions obstruct the uptake of PPPs in the three states. First, since the discovery of oil and the creation of modern states, the public sector has been responsible for providing free infrastructure services to citizens. Any shift of this responsibility to the private sector faces severe resistance from the public, who view the private sector's involvement in delivering these services as "selling the country" (Arabian Business, 2014). Also, attempting to charge citizens for the use of public infrastructure requires revisiting the "social contract" between the state and society whereby the state is responsible for its citizens' welfare from "the cradle to the grave" in return for their political acquiescence.

Second, the tribal heritage of the Gulf region holds that "loyalty [is first] to the family, then the clan, the tribe, and the nation" (Rice, 2004, p. 73). Since "family" continues to "rival the state as the focal point of loyalty and security" (Jabbra & Jabbra, 2005, p. 144), GCC citizens often look for ways to maneuver around bureaucratic rules and legal regulations to grant favors to their friends, extended family, or fellow tribal members. These favors range from granting government contracts to unsuitable contractors (Ali, 2010) to facilitating bureaucratic transitions. Although this is perceived as nepotism, corruption, or patronage from a Western perspective, in these states, it is considered a duty to prioritize one's family in business deals before evaluating technical competency or financial competitiveness (House, 2013).

Such practices undermine the fundamental assumptions of efficiency that underpin PPP agreements, such as granting contracts to the most qualified bidders. In the absence of strong independent regulatory and auditing institutions to guarantee the transparency and fairness of the tendering process, international investors are likely to be disinclined to work in an environment where local cultural beliefs weaken competitive market mechanisms. For example, Beh (2010) highlighted the prevalence of a culture of patronage and granting government contracts to favored private sector entities as the main impediment to realizing the full potential of PPPs in Malaysia. Likewise, Adams et al. (2006) revealed that in the context of China, the widespread culture of corruption among government officials who monitor the tendering process, along with the difficulty of detecting their relations with individuals in the private sector, posed a serious challenge to the future success of PPPs in China.

Third, particularly in Saudi Arabia, religious influence on policy and decision-making is reflected in a conservative business environment (Rice, 2004). The implications of this on the prospect of PPPs must be accounted for. The court system in Saudi Arabia exercises the principles of Sharia law, which international investors find problematic as a means of resolving disputes. Furthermore, Islamic finance is becoming the favorite form of private finance in the Gulf. It will be useful for international managers to familiarize themselves with the principles of Islamic finance and build the necessary capacity to negotiate and enforce PPP contracts when needed.

Impact of these challenges on the existing infrastructure PPP market

The weak PPP environment in Kuwait, Saudi Arabia, and Qatar is reflected in the embryonic stage of their infrastructure PPP market. Existing PPP projects are centered on the Independent Water Power Plant (IWPP) industry and not on core infrastructure (except Saudi Arabia's Medina airport). The PPP models being used in the IWPP sector do not involve significant risk from the private sector's side, and although they raise project finance, in the longer term, these models could be costly for the governments, especially when there is less demand for electricity (Strategy&, 2010). In this type of PPP, the government operates as a single buyer of electricity and water generated by a private sector company through fixed-term power and water purchase agreements (Deloitte, 2013). Foreign companies' hesitation in tackling the high risks associated with investing huge amounts of capital in the GCC region, and their preference for dealing with the government as a single buyer, is evident from the restriction of PPPs to only one low-risk industry. Tackling the challenges that presently inhibit the private sector from competitively delivering infrastructure services is a timely endeavor for GCC states to create the kind of business-friendly environment necessary for attracting private finance to a broader spectrum of projects. The next section offers some policy recommendations to enhance the PPP environment in the three GCC states.

Policy recommendations

For PPPs to be viable in GCC states, there is a need to strengthen the roles of regulatory and legal institutions to ensure that all parties involved in any kind of partnership respect the sanctity of legal contracts. As Table 5.5 shows, this can be achieved by establishing independent regulatory and

Table 5.5 Addressing PPP constraints and *introducing* reform

Strengthening the governance, legal, and regulatory capacity	Introducing more competition in the private sector	Enhancing the efficiency of bureaucratic systems	Reducing the impact of traditional culture
• Establishing independent judiciary and regulatory institutions • Reforming and modernizing the legal systems and allowing the public sector to rely on arbitration to solve commercial disputes • Empowering state institutions to equally apply the rule of law to all individuals regardless of official status • Easing and simplifying regulations and laws regarding labor, solving insolvency, enforcing contracts, bankruptcy, and legal rights • Encouraging communication and exchange of information among government entities	• Empowering private sector growth and independence from natural resources • Creating a business-friendly environment and fair competition in the market • Establishing trust between the public and private sectors, and involving the private sector in economic decision-making • Reviving effective privatization of weak SOEs • Ensuring transparency and fairness of the bidding process • Enabling the private sector's access to land and capital • Easing labor regulations and laws and enabling the private sector to import needed skills	• Enhancing the quality of public administration • Introducing merit-based employment systems • Introducing performance evaluation techniques • Building government officials' technical and leadership skills • Building the public sector's internal legal, technical, and financial capacities to administer PPP projects • Strengthening cooperation, collaboration, information sharing, and communication among public sector entities • Streamlining and simplifying the PPP procurement process • Introducing effective one-stop shops for investors	• Empowering the role of formal institutions in society • Implementing independent bodies to conduct tendering of infrastructure projects • Reducing the influence of channels of informal decision-making • Spreading awareness of concepts such as business growth, efficiency, and prosperity • Teaching business elites the importance of competition and transparency in a globalized business environment • Educating the young owners of local businesses about the importance of good governance when competing internationally.

Source: Designed by the author

judiciary systems, which will assure foreign investors that their legal rights are protected when disputes arise. Being able to avail themselves of local arbitration and court systems in cases of breach of contract by the public sector is a key requirement for an attractive PPP environment. Simplifying laws regarding private ownership, labor, enforcement of contracts, and bankruptcy-related issues would send positive signals to international investors about the GCC governments' firm commitment to involving the private sector in the delivery of mega-infrastructure projects. This is particularly true for Saudi Arabia, as it ranks lowest in the resolving insolvency indicator and still lacks commercial courts that measure up to international standards.

Streamlining the machinery of government, creating channels of collaboration and cooperation among different entities, and encouraging one-stop shops to process all required documents can shorten delays in procurement that sometimes result in blockage of a project's progress or lead to its cancellation. This situation is most notable in Kuwait, where the current procurement system takes almost four times longer than the world average, and in Saudi Arabia, where international investors complain about their inability to penetrate the bureaucracy without relying on corruption, intermediaries, or bribes.

Empowering the role of the private sector in the local economy and creating a business-friendly environment for foreign investors is another essential requirement to successfully attract foreign capital. Saudi Arabia's Vision 2030 reflects the government's willingness to relinquish dependence on natural resources, but committed political will is necessary to make structural reforms and create regulatory regimes to ensure fair and equal treatment of all players in the private sector. Moreover, fostering trust between the public and private sectors and creating more alliances and joint ventures between local private entities and international ones can facilitate knowledge transfer and enhance local capacity-building. In Kuwait, the prospect of PPPs remains reliant on establishing a parliament that passes business-friendly policies and laws, and a political climate that fosters the private sector's growth.

Issuing laws that allow full foreign ownership of businesses and access to capital without needing a local agent can improve the low scores of Kuwait, Saudi Arabia, and Qatar in the starting a business and "getting credit" indicators. More importantly, transparency in tendering and awarding contracts should be guaranteed and practiced to harness the powers of creativity and efficiency in the private sector. Infrastructure PPPs can only deliver the promised value for money and superior quality of services in a private sector environment driven by competition (Marin, 2009). Furthermore, one key to the success of PPP projects is allowing the private sector to hire the needed talent, and own land, especially in Kuwait and Qatar, particularly when building green field projects.

Cultural challenges may be the hardest to overcome to create a PPP-friendly environment in the three states. However, a competitiveness-based approach toward the private sector's involvement in delivering infrastructure services will show the public the higher quality and the value of harnessing the private sector's expertise. Also, facilitating the role of formal government bureaucracy in decision-making and enforcing the role of regulatory agencies can reduce the impact of favoritism in distributing government contracts. Spreading awareness about the values and concepts of competition, ethical business behavior, and the importance of transparency and governance structures in a globalized business environment can potentially yield positive results to ameliorate the culture of favoritism in the region.

Conclusion

Infrastructure PPPs are highly complex contractual agreements that necessitate the existence of solid governance, regulatory structures, and capacity within the public and private sectors. This chapter has attempted to fill a significant gap in the existing PPP literature by analyzing the prospect of infrastructure PPPs in Kuwait, Saudi Arabia, and Qatar. PPPs are a seemingly attractive policy tool for Gulf governments to compensate for their fiscal and infrastructure gaps and an opportunity for international investors to access the growing Gulf markets. However, the extension of PPPs to core infrastructure sectors in the three GCC states is contingent on whether or not considerable obstructions in these states' governance, legal, bureaucratic, and business environments can be addressed.

References

Abdel Aziz, A. (2007). Successful delivery of public-private partnerships for infrastructure development. *Journal of Construction Engineering and Management,* 133, 918–931.

Adams, J., Young, A., & Zhihong, W. (2006). Public-private partnerships in China: system, constraints and future prospects. *International Journal of Public Sector Management,* 19(4), 384–396.

Akoum, I. (2009). Privatization in Saudi Arabia: Is slow beautiful? *Thunderbird International Business Review,* 51(5),427–440.

Ali, A. (2010). Managing MNC-government negotiations in Saudi Arabia: The key role of elites. *Journal of Promotion Management,* 16, 494–521.

Al-Ghanim, M. (2010). Do elections lead to reform? Assessing the institutional limits of representative bodies in Bahrain, Kuwait and Saudi Arabia. *Contemporary Arab Affairs,* 3(2),138–147.

Al-Husan, F., & James, P. (2007). Multinational HRM in privatized Jordanian enterprises: An exploration of the influence of political contingencies. *Thunderbird International Business Review,* 49(6), 637–653.

Al-Kuwari, A. (2012). The visions and strategies of the GCC countries from the perspective of reforms: the case of Qatar. *Contemporary Arab Affairs,* 5(1),86–106.

Al-Monitor. (2014). Public sector reform in Kuwait key to economic development. Retrieved from at: www.al-monitor.com/pulse/business/2014/09/kuwait-econo mic-growth-reforms.html#ixzz3yQPaL433 Accessed on 29 April 2022.

Al-Sabah, Y. (1980). *The Oil Economy of Kuwait,* Kegan Paul International.

Al-Shareem, K., Yusof, N., & Kamal, E. (2015). External factors influencing the readiness for implementing public-private partnerships among public and private organizations in Yemen. *Journal of Science & Technology Policy Management*, 6(1), 56–75.

Arabian Business. (2014). Kuwait's new PPP law is 'selling' the country, says MPs. Retrieved from: http://m.arabianbusiness.com/kuwait-s-new-ppp-law-is-selling--country-says-mps-556260.html Accessed on 5 June 2022.

Arab News. (2012). Family businesses contribute 25% of GDP. Retrieved from: www.arabnews.com/family-businesses-contribute-25-gdp Accessed on 5 June 2016.

Ashurst. (2016). A review of the government tenders & procurement law in saudi arabia in the context of major projects. White Paper Ref. No. 983583.

Awortwi, N. (2004). Getting the fundamentals wrong: woes of public-private partnerships in solid waste collection in three Ghanian cities. *Public Administration and Development*, 24, 213–224.

Balasooriya, A., Alam, Q., & Coghill, K. (2010). State vs. market in search of good governance: The case of Sri Lanka telecommunications industry reforms. *Thunderbird International Business Review*, 52(5), 369–389.

BBC. (2012). Kuwait Emir al-Sabah dissolves parliament. Retrieved from: www.bbc.com/news/world-middle-east-19861587 Accessed on 6 June 2022.

Beh, L. S. (2010). Development and distortion of Malaysian public-private partnerships-patronage, privatized profits and pitfalls. *Australian Journal of Public Administration*, 69(S1), S74-S84.

Biygautane, M. (2015). Anti-Corruption Strategies in the Gulf Cooperation Council's States: Lessons Learnt and the Path Forward. In Y. Zhang & C. Lavena (eds.), *Government Anti-Corruption Strategies: A Cross-Cultural Perspective*, Taylor & Francis Group, Florida.

Biygautane, M. (2016). The Gulf Cooperation Council's Public Sector Executive Education: Importance, Trends, Challenges and Opportunities in T. Lepeley, E., Kimakwitz, & R. Bardy (eds.), *Human Centered Management in Executive Education: Global Imperatives, Innovation and New Directions*, Palgrave Mcmillan, London.

Bloomfield, P. (2006). The challenging business of long term public-private partnerships: reflections on local experience. *Public Administration Review*, 66(3), 400–411.

Business Anti-Corruption. (2015a). Kuwait. Retrieved from: www.business-anti-corruption.com/country-profiles/middle-east-north-africa/kuwait/snapshot.aspx Accessed on 6 June 2022.

Business Anti-Corruption. (2015b). Saudi Arabia. Retrieved from: www.business-anti-corruption.com/country-profiles/middle-east-north-africa/saudi-arabia/snapshot.aspx Accessed on 6 June 2022.

Business Anti-Corruption. (2015c). Qatar. Retrieved from: www.business-anti-corruption.com/country-profiles/middle-east-north-africa/qatar/snapshot.aspx Accessed on 6 June 2022.

Common, R. (2008). Administrative change in the gulf: Modernization in bahrain and oman. *International Review of Administrative Sciences*, 74(2), 177–193.

CIA World Factbook. (2015). Data. Retrieved from: www.cia.gov/library/publications/the-world-factbook/

Delmon, J. (2011). *Public-Private Partnership Projects in Infrastructure: An Essential Guide for Policy Makers*, Cambridge University Press, Cambridge.

Deloitte. (2013). *The Project Finance Compass: East and West*. Middle East Point of View.

Dunleavy, P., & Carrera, L. (2013). *Growing the Productivity of Government Services*, Edward Elgar, Cheltenham.
Flinders, M. (2005). The politics of public-private partnerships. *British Journal of Political and International Relations*, 7(2), 215–239.
Fromherz, A. (2012). *Qatar: A Modern History*, I.B.Tauris, London.
Gestel, K., Voets, J., & Verhoest, K. (2012). How governance of complex PPPs affects performance. *Public Administration Quarterly*, 36(2),140–188.
Greve, C. (2003). Public-private partnerships in Scandinavia. *International Public Management Review*, 4(2), 59–69.
Grimsey, D., & Lewis, M. (2004). *Public-Private Partnerships: The Worldwide Revolution in Infrastructure Provision and Project Finance*, Edward Elgar, Cheltenham.
Grossman, S. (2012). The management and measurement of public-private partnerships: Toward an integral and balanced approach. *Public Performance & Management Review*, 35(4), 595–616.
Hayllar, R. (2010). Public-private partnerships in Hong Kong: Good governance– The essential missing ingredient? *Australian Journal of Public Administration*, 69(S1), S99-S119.
Herb, M. (2014). *The Wages of Oil: Parliaments and Economic Development in Kuwait and the UAE*, Cornell University Press, New York.
House, K. (2013). *On Saudi Arabia: Its People, Past, Religion, Fault Lines-and Future*, Vintage Books, New York.
Houti, D. (2015). Arbitration in kuwait: Time for reform? Retrieved from: http://kluwerarbitrationblog.com/2015/02/20/arbitration-in-kuwait-time-for-reform/ Accessed on 7 May 2016
IMF. (2006). Determinants of Public-Private Partnerships in Infrastructure. WP/06/99.
IMF. (2014). Retrieved from: www.imf.org/en/Data Accessed on 6 June 2022.
IMF. (2015b). Kuwait: IMF Country Report No. 15/327.
IMF. (2015c). Saudi Arabia: IMF Country Report No. 15/251.
Jabbra, J., & Jabbra, N. (2005). Administrative Culture in the Middle East: The Case of the Arab World. In J. Jabbra & O. Dwivedi (eds.), *Administrative Culture in a Global Context*, de Sitter Publications, Canada, pp. 135–153.
Jooste, S. F., Levitt, R., & Scott, D. (2011). Beyond "one size fits all": how local conditions shape PPP-enabling field development. *Engineering Project Organization Journal*, 1(1), 11–25.
Kanter, R. M. (1994). Collaborative advantage: the art of alliances. *Harvard Business Review* (July–August), 96–108.
Kingdom of Saudi Arabia Vision 2030. (2016). Retrieved from: http://vision2030.gov.sa/en Accessed on 19 May 2022.
Kinsinger, P. (2007). The "business intelligence" challenge in the context of regional risk. *Thunderbird International Business Review*, 49(4), 535–541
Kinninmont, J. (2012). *Kuwait Parliament: An Experiment in Semi-democracy*, Chattam House, London.
Klijn, E.-H., & Teisman, G. R. (2003). Institutional and strategic barriers to public-private partnership: An analysis of dutch cases. *Public Money and Management*, 23(3), 137–146.
Kuwait Times. (2014). Kuwait family business at key transitional stage. Retrieved from: http://news.kuwaittimes.net/kuwaiti-family-business-key-transitional-stage/ Accessed on 1 June 2022.

Linder, S. (1999). Coming to terms with the public-private partnership: A grammer of multiple meaning. *American Behavioral Scientist*, 43(1), 35–51.
Marin, P. (2009). *Public-Private Partnerships for Urban Water Utilities: A Review of Experiences in Developing Countries*. The World Bank Publications.
MEED Projects. (2015). GCC Projects Market Report 2015. *Middle East Economic Digest*.
Miraftab, F. (2004). Public private partnerships: The Trojan horse of neoliberal development? *Journal of Planning Education and Research*, 24, 89–101.
Moore, A. (2000). Long term partnerships in water and sewer utilities: Economic, political, and policy implications. *Journal of Contemporary Water Research and Education*, 117, 21–26.
Mouraviev, N., & Kakabadse, N. (2015). Legal and regulatory barriers to effective public-private partnership governance in Kazakhstan. *International Journal of Public Sector Management*, 28(3), 181–197.
OECD. (2013). *Public-private partnerships in the Middle East and North Africa: A handbook for policy makers*.
Oukil, S., & Al-Khalifa, H. (2012). Managerial Weaknesses and Features of Family Businesses in the Eastern Region of Saudi Arabia. 2012 International Conference on Economics, Business and Marketing Management IPEDR, 29. 49–54.
Pessoa, A. (2009). Public-private sector partnerships in developing countries: Prospects and drawbacks. *FEP Working papers*. No.228.
Petersen, O. (2010). Regulation of public-private partnerships: The Danish case. *Public Money and Management*, 30(3), 175–182.
Pistor, K., Raiser, M., & Gelfer, S. (2000). Law and finance in transtion economies. *Economics of Transition*, 8(2), 325–368.
Pollitt, C. (2015). Towards a new world: Some inconvenient truths for Anglosphere public administration. *International Review of Administrative Sciences*, 81(1), 3–17.
Pongsiri, N. (2002). Regulation and public-private partnerships. *International Journal of Public Sector Management*, 15(6), 87–495.
Practical Law. (2014a). Construction and projects in Saudi Arabia: Overview. Practical Law Company. Publication No.2-534-0319.
Practical Law. (2014b). Construction and projects in Qatar: Overview. Practical Law Company. Publication No. 5-519-5882.
Qatar Today. (2014). GCC family businesses: Increased competition in local markets. Retrieved from: www.qatartodayonline.com/gcc-family-businesses-increased-competition-in-local-markets/ Accessed on 10 May 2022.
Reuters. (2022). Kuwait crown prince dissolves parliament, calls for early election. Retrieved from: www.reuters.com/world/middle-east/kuwait-crown-prince-dissolves-parliament-calls-early-general-election-2022-06-22/ Accessed on 27 July 2022
Rice, G. (2004). Doing business in Saudi Arabia. *Thunderbird International Business Review*, 46(1), 59–84.
Riyadh Chamber of Commerce. (2007). *Enhancing the Relationship Between the Public and Private Sectors in the Kingdom of Saudi Arabia* [In Arabic]. Riyadh Economic Forum.
Rondinelli, D., & Priebjrivat, V. (2000). Assessing privatization investment opportunities in Thailand. *Thunderbird International Business Review*, 42(6), 623–650.

Sabry, I. (2015). Good governance, institutions and performance of public private partnerships. *International Journal of Public Sector Management*, 28(7), 566–582.

Savas, E. (2000). *Privatization and Public-Private Partnerships*, Chatham House Publishers and Seven Bridges Press, New York.

Strategy&. (2010). The future of IPPs in the GCC: new policies for a growing an evolving electricity market. Retrieved from: www.strategyand.pwc.com/media/file/The-future-of-IPPs-in-the-GCC.pdf Assessed 27 July 2022.

Teisman, G. R., & Klijn, E. H. (2002). Partnership agreements: Governmental rhetoric or governance scheme? *Public Administration Review*, 62(2),197–205.

The Economist. (2014). Half-opening the gates: Foreign businesses are welcome—but only the right sort. Retrieved from: www.economist.com/news/business/21604176-foreign-businesses-are-welcomebut-only-right-sort-half-opening-gates Accessed on March 27, 2022.

The National. (2015). Qatar to have its first budget deficit in 15 years. Retrieved from: www.thenational.ae/business/economy/qatar-to-have-its-first-budget-deficit-in-15-years Accessed on 22 May 2022.

The National. (2016). Saudi Arabia, Oman and Bahrain credit ratings downgraded by Moody's. Retrieved from: www.thenational.ae/business/economy/saudi-arabia-oman-and-bahrain-credit-ratings-downgraded-by-moodys Accessed on 30 May 2022

UN. (2007). Seoul Declaration on Public-Private Partnerships for Infrastructure Development in Asia and the Pacific.

UNECE. (2008). *Guidebook on Promoting Good Governance in Public-Private Partnership*, United Nations, Geneva.

US Department of State. (2015). Country economic reports. Retrieved from: http://www.state.gov/r/pa/ei/bgn/5437.htm Accessed on 18 May 2022

Vining, A., & Boardman, A. (2008). Public-private partnerships in canada. Theory and evidence. *Canadian Public Administration*, 51(1), 9–44.

Weihe, G. (2008). Ordering disorder-on the perplexities of the partnership literature. *The Australian Journal of Public Administration*, 67(4), 430–442.

World Bank. (2014b). *A Checklist for Public-Private Partnership Projects*. The World Bank Group.

World Bank (2015). Infrastructure development in MENA and the State of Kuwait. Presented at MEED Kuwait Projects Conference. November 24, 2022.

World Bank Data. (2020). Accessible from: data.worldbank.org/

World Bank Group Doing Business Database. (2015). Accessible from: www.doingbusiness.org/data. Accessed on 6 June 2022.

Zhang, X. (2005). Critical success factors for public-private partnerships in infrastructure development. *Journal of Construction Engineering and Management*, 131(1), 3–14.

6 International review of public-private partnerships for school infrastructure development

Lessons and recommendations for Saudi Arabia

Introduction

Public-private partnerships (PPPs) are no longer adopted exclusively to deliver economic infrastructure projects, such as airports, tunnels, and roads, and their use is now increasingly being extended to social services like healthcare and education. A 2009 report by the World Bank argued that PPPs have the potential to incorporate innovative ways of improving services related to education, economic development, healthcare, and social work (World Bank, 2009). This can be realized through their construction of a business model guaranteeing access to such services at an affordable price while simultaneously delivering them with high efficiency. Since then, governments worldwide have gradually set up regulatory and legal frameworks and policies that would allow PPPs to operate effectively and become an integral part of their service delivery.

In Saudi Arabia, the last 50 years have witnessed impressive developments in many areas, with the country managing to catch up with and, in some cases, even exceed the developed world in many global human development rankings. When it comes to offering infrastructure and public goods, the Saudi government has been the primary provider since it discovered oil and gas, since it needed to create, from scratch, the rudiments of a modern state ranging from buildings, roads, and airports to investments in human capital. Moreover, as part of its social contract and distribution of oil revenues, the government was compelled to provide free education and social benefits to all its citizens, and this necessitated the government's leading role in financing the substantial investments required by those projects.

Over the last few years, this system has started to change in response to various factors. First, Saudi Arabia has realized that pressure on its government to put the brakes on public spending and uncertainty over fluctuating oil profits, combined with the impact of 2014's dramatic plunge in global oil prices on its budget, are all necessitating new financing strategies that match global best practices. Second, it has been noticed that, in Western nations, implementing new public management (NPM) practices within the public sector has been a key driver in changing governments' attitudes toward public spending. NPM proposes new service delivery

DOI: 10.4324/9781003267744-8

methods that assume many forms, including introducing policies like contracting out, privatization, and PPPs, and Saudi Arabia has begun adopting some of these models to varying degrees over the past few years. Third, the Saudi government has recognized that the involvement of the private sector in providing infrastructure and other social services is an ineluctable reality if it wishes to ease the financial strain on its budget, which has been negatively affected by dwindling oil prices. Furthermore, Saudi Arabia has become determined to gradually minimize its reliance on natural resources and aims to use its oil and gas revenues to build the foundations of an economically competitive market that can provide services previously dominated by the public sector. Since natural resources are no longer the main drivers of economic growth and competitiveness in a world that is becoming increasingly knowledge-driven, Saudi Arabia is investing heavily in sectors that will help establish a knowledge economy's rudimentary basis.

To shed light on that process in Saudi Arabia, this chapter provides an international review of the performance of PPPs as a vehicle for delivering school infrastructure and other educational services and analyzes Saudi Arabia's readiness to adopt PPPs as the policy of choice in making good progress on its ambitious plan to build 1,600 schools. It highlights the critical role that the PPP model can play in fulfilling this objective and helping provide schools on time and within budget, thereby attaining the vision of Saudi Arabia's political leadership. Such a model could serve as a catalyst and blueprint for other Gulf states wishing to follow Saudi Arabia's example. Reflecting upon the Saudi context, this chapter argues that, while Saudi Arabia's school program enjoys significant political support and boasts ambitious plans for the sustainable growth of Saudi Arabia, the country has yet to develop the necessary institutional, legal and regulatory, and supervisory frameworks that serve as the essential foundations for any successful PPP project. While numerous PPP projects have been conducted in Saudi Arabia in the past, they were implemented on an ad hoc basis with varying contractual arrangements and results.

Meaning(s) of PPPs

This section discusses the arguments and debates surrounding PPPs as a concept and highlights theoretical discussions concerning the meanings and pros and cons of PPPs.

PPPs are a recent extension of the NPM agenda, which incorporates the managerial skills of the private sector into the more bureaucratic government structures through which public services have been provided in the past (Broadbent & Laughlin, 2003). Promising better value for money and the ability to do more with less, PPPs have now become a common strand of public policy, offering better efficiency for funding public infrastructure services through appropriately allocating risks, rewards, and responsibilities (Teicher et al., 2006). A PPP can be broadly described as a relationship through which the government collaborates with the private sector to finance, design, deliver, and maintain infrastructure services. Other commonly used definitions for PPPs are:

- "An arrangement between two or more parties who have agreed to work cooperatively toward shared and/or compatible objectives and in which there is shared authority and responsibility; joint investment of resources; shared liability or risk-taking; and ideally mutual benefits" (European Commission, 2003, p. 16);
- "A cooperative venture between the public and private sectors, built on the expertise of each partner, that best meets clearly defined public needs through the appropriate allocation of resources, risks and rewards" (Canadian Council for PPPs, 2022); and
- "Long-term contract between a private party and a government entity, for providing a public asset or service, in which the private party bears significant risk and management responsibility and remuneration is linked to performance" (PPP Knowledge Lab, 2022).

In a PPP project, the government and the private sector collaborate throughout the various stages of service provision. While the private sector assumes responsibility for the design, construction, operation, maintenance, financing, and risk management operations, the government is responsible for strategic planning and industry structure, obtaining permits, and regulating and meeting community service obligations (NSW Office of Financial Management, 2002). PPPs take various contractual forms, including Design Construct and Maintain (DCM), Build, Own, and Operate (BOO), and Build, Own, Operate, and Transfer (BOOT) (Grimsey & Lewis, 2000; Webb & Pulle, 2002). Under such terms, the private contractor owns the infrastructure for the contract term and provides contracted services paid for directly by the government or customers, and the government's role sometimes shifts from supplying infrastructure services to buying services from the private sector.

Rationale(s) behind adopting PPPs for infrastructure development

This section explains the rationale(s) for adopting infrastructure PPPs and outlines the benefits for the private and public sectors of adopting the PPP model to deliver services. After this, another subsection analyzes factors leading to the successful or unsuccessful implementation of PPPs based on existing academic and practitioner-oriented literature. Such an analysis is essential, since Saudi Arabia can benefit from the broader international experience with multifarious factors affecting the performance of PPPs in general (Caldwell & Keating, 2004; Ernst & Young, 2013).

In most Western countries, PPPs only appeared after years of contracting out and privatization, and have been driven largely by the search for efficient and competitive infrastructure delivery methods (Teicher et al., 2006).

Governments adopt PPPs for multifarious reasons, but since most PPP-adopting governments face budgetary constraints that limit their capacity to finance infrastructure services, cost-effectiveness is often foremost among them. When their contractual arrangements are designed correctly, PPPs provide value for money and ensure "the best possible outcome at the lowest possible price" (English, 2006, p. 254). This value can take many forms, including "lower construction costs, lower operating costs and more efficient maintenance in the long run" (Webb & Pulle, 2002, p. 5). The private sector must perform well to earn profits from projects, which enhances the quality of services and can minimize costs. Another source of value for money arises from the "bundling" of services. The obligation to build, operate, maintain, and transfer an asset to the state at the end of the contract term provides an additional incentive to minimize the project's costs (English, 2006). The efficiency of the service provided is thus maximized through effective and efficient design and construction of infrastructure projects with costs kept to a minimum.

Another reason for adopting PPPs is the transfer of risk to the private sector, or the party that can best handle the risks associated with a project (Grimsey & Lewis, 2000). Risk transfer is one of the critical drivers of value for money and justifies a government's reliance on PPPs, since without a significant risk being borne by the consortium, PPPs would be unable to achieve the desired levels of efficiency and value for money (English, 2006). Such risks could be related to construction, market size, cost of operations and maintenance, delays in finishing a project, force majeure, or any changes to existing laws and regulations. PPPs are ultimately adopted because government bureaucracy does not provide the necessary mechanisms and incentives to encourage efficient and effective infrastructure services that can be delivered on time. Moreover, any extra costs caused by time delays or performance failures that are not priced into government borrowing are then borne by taxpayers (NSW Office of Financial Management, 2002). On the other hand, the private sector is restricted by a tight budget and limited resources, and cannot levy extra charges on citizens. This then forces the private sector to perform its services with minimal costs and higher quality to generate higher profit.

Advantages and disadvantages of PPPs

Despite the positive outcomes that PPP projects promise to achieve, failure to deliver the expected outcomes can result when their implementation is not carefully designed. For instance, Bovaird (2004) states that one of the major problems of the partnership approach—when it is not well planned—is the concomitant fragmentation of structures and processes, which then leads to a "blurring" of responsibilities and accountability (p. 203). Bovaird (2004) goes further to explain how PPPs had caused governance and accountability problems when they failed to reveal important performance-related information to the public on the grounds of "commercial confidentiality" or "data protection" (p. 203). In the same context, Sands (2006) argues that commercial confidentiality clauses reduce transparency and limit the public's access to the previously available information. This then "leaves the door open" to undesirable practices, such as corruption, patronage, and "kickbacks", which can ultimately undermine administrative processes and, to varying degrees, call into question the performance of the partnership agreement itself (Sands, 2006, p. 9). Furthermore, Sands (2006) states that too much transparency can result in many disadvantages for the private sector, while too little can affect citizens' access to public information, thus balancing the interests of the two parties involved in PPPs is essential to their success. Other issues, such as the contractual structure's inherent complexity, can result in more extended negotiation periods, and the upfront costs of PPP projects can balloon much higher than those of conventional procurement methods (Darvish et al., 2006).

Table 6.1 summarizes both the advantages and disadvantages of PPPs. Critics have often stressed the difficulty of achieving their functional and service specifications, which are usually set relatively high. Furthermore, the costs incurred in contracting, the difficulty of transferring all risks

Table 6.1 Comparing advantages and disadvantages of PPPs

Advantages of PPPs	Disadvantages of PPPs
• Facilitation of creative and innovative approaches. • Access to skills, experience, and technology. • Functional brief finalized prior to tendering. • Complete integration of design, construction, operation, maintenance, and refurbishment costs with the potential to achieve value for money. • Greater risk transfer is enabled in each phase, including costs to the private sector. • Assumption of "whole of life" cost risk encourages efficient design and attention to materials used in the construction and operation of the entity. • Payment of services depends on delivery services and facilities to agreed-upon standards.	• Well-defined functional and service specifications may be difficult to achieve. • Several designs developed simultaneously can translate into a need for significant stakeholder resources. • Complexity of contracting requires specialist skills from the public sector. • High contracting costs rule out many projects. • Not all risks can be cost-effectively transferred to the private sector. • Financing arrangements and risk pricing can potentially increase costs once construction has begun. • Transparency and accountability are often limited.

Source: Adapted from Grimsey and Lewis (2005), English (2006), Darvish et al. (2006), and Sands (2006)

Factors behind PPP success or failure: Lessons from international experiences

This section explores some of the factors behind the success or failure of PPPs based on international experiences.

Western countries have primarily used PPPs to construct large-scale infrastructure and public assets, such as freeways, tunnels, bridges, and social projects like hospitals, schools, and prisons. While some such projects accomplished the desired outcomes through their implementation, numerous factors have been responsible for the failure of other projects, and these can provide lessons on how to manage PPPs' associated risks better and achieve superior value for money (Darvish et al., 2006; Grimsey & Lewis, 2007). In Australia, for example, the New South Wales government has enjoyed the successful delivery of many social infrastructure projects under the PPP model. These include the redevelopment of the Newcastle Mater Hospital, the Long Bay Prison and Forensic Hospitals, and the New Schools Phases 1 and 2 (Kozarovski, 2006). According to Kozarovski (2006), these projects delivered value for money, particularly in the case of the New Schools Phases 1 and 2, because the government managed to secure savings of 7% and 23%, respectively. Even more significantly, these projects were delivered on time and within budget (Kozarovski, 2006). Another example of a successful PPP project is Melbourne's City Link Road infrastructure project, one of Australia's largest BOOT projects. Most of the project's commercial risks were borne by the private sector, which managed to finish the project within the anticipated timeframe and budget. Careful analysis of factors leading to the achievement of such projects reveals that accountability and transparency throughout the process, the competitiveness of bids, appropriate risk management, and other factors contributed to their successful delivery.

Nevertheless, not all PPP projects in Australia have been so successful (Forward, 2006), and Sydney Airport Rail Link is one example of a failure to achieve anticipated results or meet the performance targets indicated in a contract. Darvish et al. (2006) investigated the reasons behind this PPP project's nonsuccess to develop recommendations on how to avoid repeating similar mistakes in the future. They found that the misfire of the Airport Rail Link project was due to various factors, including the "unusual" and "careless" division of responsibilities between the public and private sectors, which did not adequately take into consideration the project's inherent risks (Darvish et al., 2006, p.24). Even worse, the government signed the PPP contract without clearly specifying the risks that would be transferred to the private sector. Ultimately, the risk allocation structure of the project was "inappropriate", as the private partner had

Table 6.2 Factors contributing to the success or failure of PPP projects

Factors leading to successful PPPs	Factors leading to unsuccessful PPPs
• Accountability and transparency of the process • Competitiveness of bids • Effective procurement • Appropriate risk management • Stable policy regime • Available financial market • Reputation, trust, and motivation	• Poor accountability and transparency measures • Differences in interests and expectations • Lack of government commitment and objectives • Complex decision-making • Low credibility of government policies • Lack of competition

Source: Adapted from Darvish et al. (2006)

to shoulder very few risks while it became the government's responsibility to handle most hazards associated with the project's design and implementation. This risk allocation structure, which left the public sector handling most of the project's liabilities, stands in contradiction to the primary objective of a PPP in this regard, which is to transfer risks to the party best prepared to handle them. Table 6.2 breaks down the factors found contributing to the success or failure of PPP projects. Among other factors, transparency of the process, the competitiveness of bids, risk management techniques, and reputation will ultimately decide the fate of any PPP project.

PPPs in the education sector: Initiatives, models, and contractual agreements

This section presents the initiatives, models, and contractual agreements that PPPs in the education sector may take up and offers a wide range of modalities that Saudi Arabia could consider in pursuing its school projects, mainly since infrastructure PPPs are only one component among several other options that its government could consider.

Involvement of the private sector in delivering economic infrastructure services, such as bridges, railways, and airports, has long been a common practice in developed and developing countries. On the other hand, private sector involvement in social infrastructure service delivery, including hospitals and schools, is a relatively recent phenomenon (Fennell, 2010; World Bank, 2009). PPPs in the education sector can be classified into five initiatives, with the public and private sectors playing different roles in each (see Table 6.3).

Private sector philanthropic initiatives

This type of initiative is considered the most common partnership between the public and private sectors in the educational arena, and it takes the

Table 6.3 Explanations and financial models of school PPPs with examples from international experience

PPP type	Explanation and financial model	Examples
Private sector philanthropic initiative	• In the USA, foundations provide funding for basic education • The most common form of PPP in US basic education • In the UK, educational academies are established by sponsors ranging from businesses to volunteer groups in partnership with the government to provide free education to children • Funds provided by state or private donors to some schools	• Philanthropic foundations (USA) • Academies Programme (UK) • Philanthropic venture funds (USA)
School management initiative	• Educational authorities partner directly with private providers to operate public schools • Schools are privately managed, but publicly owned and funded and free of charge to all students • The private sector sometimes pays for infrastructure costs, but the government pays teachers' salaries based on student enrollment	• Contract schools (USA) • Charter schools (USA and Canada) • Independent schools (Qatar)
Purchase of educational services from private schools	• The government pays a subsidy for each student enrolled in an eligible private school • In New Zealand, AE schools are funded on a per-student basis. • Schools cannot charge students extra fees	• Alternative Education (AE) in (New Zealand) • Financial assistance per child enrolled (Pakistan)
Vouchers and voucher-like programs	• Parents can use government vouchers to pay for either public or private schools • In the Netherlands, the voucher system incentivizes schools to offer better education to attract more students	• School funding system (Netherland) • Targeted individual entitlement and independent school subsidies (New Zealand)

Table 6.3 Cont.

PPP type	Explanation and financial model	Examples
School infrastructure initiative	• The most common forms are BOT or Design, Build, Finance, Operate, Transfer (DBFOT) • The government provides land for building schools on nominal lease rent • The private sector bears capital costs upfront for infrastructure, and provides non-core services • The government retains responsibility for education delivery and teaching • The government often provides lower capital subsidies and viability gap funding up to 20% of project cost • Arrangements for 25–30 years with contracts specifying exact services that vary by country	• Private Finance Initiative (UK) • PPP New Schools Project (Alberta, Canada) • New Schools PPPs (South Australia) • PPP for New Schools (Egypt) • Schools PPP project (Spain)

Source: Education International (2009), World Bank (2009), CfBT (2008), and McKinsey & Company (2014)

form of donations of money or goods to public schools by organizations or individuals on an ad hoc basis or under the umbrella of corporate social responsibility (UNICEF, 2011). In 2006, over 70,000 corporate, private, and community-based foundations in the USA distributed US$41 billion worth of grants to the education sector (CfBT, 2008). The Bill and Melinda Gates Foundation is a prominent organization leading educational and philanthropic initiatives in the USA.

This philanthropic model is certainly not exclusive to the USA and can be found in Asia and the Gulf region. In India, for example, the Bharti Foundation donated US$50 million to establish non-profit private schools in remote areas of the country, and the Philippines and Pakistan have also used donations from corporate foundations to construct schools (World Bank, 2009). In Singapore, an investment company called Orient Global donated more than US$100 million to build schools and improve infrastructure in developing countries that needed it. In 2007, the Dubai-based Mohammed bin Rashid Al-Maktoum Foundation was established with an endowment fund of US$10 billion to enhance educational systems in the

Arab world and provide scholarships to needy students wishing to pursue their education. Furthermore, in 2015, the Al-Ghurair Foundation in Saudi Arabia was formed with an endowment of US$1.13 billion from Abdullah Al-Ghurair to provide financial support for local and regional schools and scholarships for students to enroll in the region's top universities.

School management initiative

Under this form of collaboration, the public sector remains the owner and the financier of schools, which it contracts to either a private sector entity or not-for-profit, non-governmental organizations (NGOs) that operate, manage, and run them. The government pays either a yearly management fee or a fixed sum per student to the school operator, and payments are based strictly on performance measures and benchmarks in a concession contract lasting approximately 25 years. This model includes US contract schools, which have existed since the 1990s and have the private sector operator running a school under management or operational contract (World Bank, 2009; CfBT, 2008).

A second example can be found in charter schools, namely, secular schools for which performance measures are specified in the charter contract that establishes them. Management contracts for this type range from three to five years with the financing body that funds their educational activities held accountable. Since their introduction, the number of charter schools in the USA has increased exponentially, from 253 schools in 1995 to 4,147 in 2007 (Vanourek, 2005).

Purchase of educational services from private schools

This demand-driven initiative involves the government (often the ministry of education) purchasing places for students in private schools to increase student enrollment, particularly in remote areas, and enhance the quality of educational systems. To qualify for government contracts to fund students, schools must meet the minimum criteria regarding infrastructure and quality of their teachers and programs. Schools are then accountable for student performance, which is the critical criterion for government contract renewal. This initiative is prevalent in many developing countries such as Uganda, Côte d'Ivoire, the Philippines, and developed countries like New Zealand.

Vouchers and voucher-like programs

A school voucher is a certificate parents can use to enroll their children in a school of their choice. This is more commonly used than the previous model, in which the government pays schools directly based on the number of students enrolled, and it allows parents to choose the school that they believe offers the type of educational quality desirable for their children.

Therefore, such a model encourages competition among schools to offer superior performance and attract higher numbers of students and is widely used in rural areas of developing countries, but also in New Zealand, the Netherlands, and the USA.

School infrastructure initiatives

Since the 1990s, PPPs have become an essential delivery route for school infrastructure development worldwide. Although the contractual structures of school PPPs can vary significantly, BOT is the most adopted form of partnership wherein the private sector raises the necessary finances for building a school, operates it, and then transfers it to the public sector upon expiration of a contract period ranging from 25 to 30 years (Patrinos, 2005). The UK has primarily taken this route via the Private Finance Initiative (PFI) since 1992 and, in October 2007, more than 115 PFI deals worth US$6.5 billion have been signed between the UK private sector and the Department of Children, Schools and Families to construct infrastructure for schools in various parts of the UK (HM Treasury, 2007). Other countries with PPPs commonly used for schools are Australia, Canada, Germany, and the Netherlands (see the individual sections on these countries for a detailed account of the structures and models of their school PPPs).

Government purchases and contract types for education sector PPPs

While the previous section provided a general description of the various initiatives through which the public and private sectors collaborate to deliver different forms and types of services in the education sector, this section offers a detailed description of what these initiatives deliver and their contract types. Table 6.4 shows how the private sector can provide various general management (financial management, staff management, long-term planning, and leadership), support, and professional services under these arrangements.

Operational services may entail the operation of a single school or an entire system of public schools, particularly in remote regions. Under this type of operational contract, the private sector manages all processes related to maintenance of the schools, staff, and students, as well as delivery of educational materials, the design of which remains within the purview of the government. When governments purchase educational services using student vouchers, they ensure the competitiveness of the education sector by forcing private sector institutions to provide higher quality and affordable prices. This initiative thus expands student access to schools while obviating the upfront costs of constructing and operating schools.

Although the facility availability model is most common in North America, Europe, and Australia, it is also the most difficult to achieve, as it involves various contractual types (see Table 6.4). As indicated by the

Table 6.4 PPP models in the education sector

PPP model	What governments purchase	Contract type
Management, professional, and support services (input)	• School management (financial and human resources management) • Support services (meals and transportation) • Professional services (teacher training, curriculum design, textbook delivery, quality assurance, and supplemental services)	• Management contract • Professional services contract (curriculum design)
Operational services (process)	• Student education, financial and human resources management, professional services, and building maintenance	Operational contract
Education services (output)	• Student placement in private schools (by contracting schools to enroll specific students)	Contract for providing education to a specific number of students
Facility availability (input)	• Infrastructure and building maintenance	Provision of infrastructure services contract
Facility availability and education services (input and output)	• Infrastructure combined with services (operational or educational output)	Provision of infrastructure contract with education services contract

Source: Education International (2009); World Bank (2009); CfBT (2008); McKinsey & Company (2014)

World Bank (2009), this model requires the competitive selection of a private sector consortium to raise finances for the construction of a facility and its operation and management. The government, meanwhile, maintains full control over the provision of teaching materials, personnel, and other curriculum-related issues. One model that has not been tested sufficiently in the educational arena is the combination of facility availability and provision of services under one contract. While it has been proven extensively in the healthcare sector, the model has yet to be utilized in the education sector.

Range of contractual options in providing school infrastructure and risk transfer

The contractual forms assumed by school partnership programs are multifarious, ranging from a government's complete ownership of assets to their full privatization. As Table 6.5 illustrates, school projects can either be designed and built based on government-specified requirements, operated

Table 6.5 Contractual forms of school partnership programs

Contractual forms of school partnership program	Features
Traditional design and build	The government contracts a private partner to design and build a school facility to specific requirements.
Operation and maintenance	The government contracts a private partner to operate a publicly owned school facility.
Turnkey operation	The government provides financing while the private partner designs, constructs, and operates a school for a specified period with the public partner retaining facility ownership.
Lease-purchase	The private partner leases a school to the government for a specified period, after which ownership is vested with the government.
Lease or Own, Develop, and Operate (L/ODO)	The private partner leases or buys a school from the government and develops and operates it under contract with the government for a specified period.
Build, Operate, and Transfer (BOT)	The private partner obtains an exclusive contract to finance, build, operate, maintain, manage, and collect user fees from a school for a fixed period to amortize its investment and, upon franchise end, the title reverts to the government.
Build, Own, and Operate (BOO)	The government either transfers ownership and responsibility for an existing facility or contracts a private partner to build, own, and operate a new facility perpetually.

Source: Education International (2009), World Bank (2009), CfBT (2008), and McKinsey & Company (2014)

by the private sector as indicated previously, or fully funded by the government with turnkey school operations held by the private sector partner operations. Other standard contractual arrangements can take the form of Lease or Own, Develop, and Operate (L/ODO) arrangements, whereby the school is bought from the government and operated by the private sector for a certain period as specified in a contract. Similarly, the BOO model can transfer ownership and operation of a school facility to a private entity.

It is important to note that the levels of risk maintained by the public and private sectors can differ substantially depending on the contractual arrangements between the two sectors. In the case of complete privatization of school assets or concession agreements, the private sector bears all project risks. By contrast, when the project is wholly owned by the government or delivered on a traditional Engineering, Procurement, and Construction (EPC) basis, most of the project's risks reside with the public sector.

The PPP model, however, provides a middle ground for risk sharing through which risks are transferred to the party best suited to handle them.

176 *Importance of partnerships between the public and private sectors*

For example, risks associated with construction, operation, and maintenance can be borne by the private sector, while those pertaining to force majeure and unexpected regulatory, legal, or other changes in policy direction that could affect project continuity can be handled by the public sector. This risk-sharing approach to the management of infrastructure projects promises timely completion and facilitates efficient handling of the inherent risks of such projects.

Standard PPP models and rationale for school PPPs

In an extensive empirical research survey, Education International (2009) investigated the PPP models utilized to deliver school infrastructure in 57 countries. As Figure 6.1 below illustrates, nearly 70% of all survey respondents indicated that the most widely used PPP model in their respective countries was infrastructure PPP. This was followed by the outsourcing of support services (46.8%) and private operation of public schools (39.2%), with the least-used types being the outsourcing of curriculum design and outsourcing of delivery (29.1% and 27.8%, respectively). Regarding the regional concentrations of these PPP projects, they were primarily used in North America, Europe, and the Asia Pacific, with a smaller presence in Africa and Latin America (Asian Development Bank, 2010).

Findings from Education International (2009) also help to explain the motivations behind government use of PPPs to deliver school infrastructure. As shown in Figure 6.2, the three most cited reasons are budgetary constraints (78.5%), improvement of educational quality (57%), and provision of more innovative approaches to school asset management (50.8%). These reasons resonate with international research on PPPs showing that rising government fiscal deficits and the search for more efficient infrastructure service delivery encourage governments to pursue the PPP route.

In terms of utilizing private finance for infrastructure development, World Bank data (2020) show the Middle East and North Africa (MENA) region remaining the most reticent to employ such finance globally. Numerous reasons can explain the scant use of this model to finance

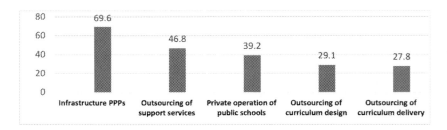

Figure 6.1 Common school PPP models
Source: *Education International (2009)*

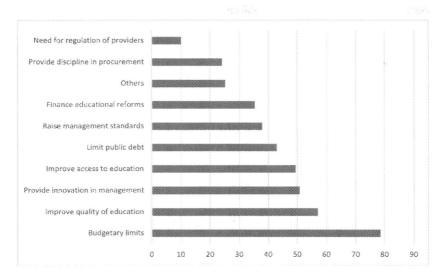

Figure 6.2 Governments' reasons for school infrastructure delivery via PPPs
Source: Education International (2009)

infrastructure services in the region, including a lack of local capital markets to generate necessary funds for such projects and weak regulatory and legal frameworks to govern and supervise PPP contracts. These factors can also make international investors reluctant to mobilize massive financial resources in MENA countries.

International examples of school infrastructure delivery via PPPs

This section provides an international review of school PPP programs' performance to date across an array of Western countries and their PPP experiences in the education sector, and it also reflects on some experiences within Middle Eastern and Gulf countries.

School PPPs in Australia

Australia has demonstrated an extensive track record of reliance on the PPP model to deliver its economic and social infrastructure services (Ross, 2004), and New South Wales (NSW) had its first experience with building schools via the PPP route when it constructed nine schools worth US$129 million (NSW Office of Financial Management, 2002; World Bank, 2009). The project was delivered through the NSW New Schools Project Concession Deed between the Minister of Education and the contractor, and the contract had two components, with Axiom Education Pty Ltd 1) financing, designing, and constructing the schools, and 2) providing facility management services such as building maintenance, security, and cleaning for 25 years. The Department of Education now pays a monthly fee based on the performance and availability of schools for classes, and the contract allows for upward or downward adjustments to reflect any amounts owed to the state or the contractor under the provisions of the Concession Deed. Debt finance has been provided to the contractor through bonds underwritten by ABN AMRO Bank NV in Australia under a private debt financing arrangement (Banks, 2008).

The success of this initiative resulted in the extension of the use of PPPs for school infrastructure to ten other schools completed between 2006 and 2009, with a net worth of US$168 million (Audit Office of New South Wales, 2006). In both cases, the Department of Education pays the private operator a monthly fee based on the availability of schools for classes. At the end of the contracts, which will last until approximately 2032, the contractor will transfer the buildings to the public sector. It is estimated that delivering these projects on a PPP basis saved 7% of their total project costs compared with delivery on an EPC basis (OECD, 2010).

Three other states in Australia are also implementing PPP projects in schools. For example, South Australia relied on PPPs for the financing, construction, and 30-year maintenance of six public schools while education services remain under the government's umbrella. Similarly, in 2013, the Queensland government announced the selection of the Plenary Schools Consortium to deliver ten schools. This consortium will be responsible for designing, constructing, commissioning, partially financing, and managing the schools' facilities. Six schools opened between 2015 and 2016, and another three opened in 2017. Furthermore, the state of Victoria engaged the private sector in building 15 schools delivered between 2017 and 2018 and refurbishing and fixing many other existing ones. Payments for all these PPP deals were based on the "availability and satisfactory operation" model.

School PPPs in New Zealand

Meanwhile, New Zealand's government only began adopting PPPs as a policy approach for delivering infrastructure services in 2010. The government stated that "it will use PPPs where they can be demonstrated to provide clear value for money (VfM) and where they will improve service delivery outcomes" (National Infrastructure Plan, 2010). Thus, due to a lack of funding to support projects requiring substantial upfront costs, the New Zealand government resorted to PPPs (Ernst & Young, 2013).

The first two projects to be delivered on a PPP basis were Hobsonville Point Primary and Secondary Schools, where Learning Infrastructure Partners was awarded a contract of 25 years for two schools on a Design, Build, Finance, and Operate (DBFO) basis. Since completion of construction, the contractor receives quarterly payments based on the availability

International review of PPPs for school infrastructure 179

of the schools for classes and agreed-upon standards of performance in maintaining and operating the schools. The project reached its financial close in 2012, and both schools were finished on time and within budget. The success of the Hobsonville Point schools raised the New Zealand government's interest in using PPPs for school projects, and in 2015 the government awarded a US$298 million contract to the Future Schools Partners (FSP) consortium to build and maintain four new schools.[1] Furthermore, in July 2016, three consortia were shortlisted to design, finance, build, and maintain six additional schools worth more than US$200 million on a PPP basis.[2] In all three PPP projects, the project contracts specified that the government retained ownership of the schools' facilities and land and indicated that deductions in payments could occur for the non-availability of teaching spaces or failure to meet specified performance indicators. The principal and a board of trustees would then be responsible for each school's governance and day-to-day running.

School PPPs in Canada

Nova Scotia was Canada's first province to utilize the PPP model to build schools. In the mid-1990s, its local government faced financial constraints owing to declining natural resource prices and a lack of sufficient funds to build urgently needed schools, and thus the province resorted to the PPP route to secure access to schooling for its rising number of students (Ronald, 2005). Thirty-nine schools were then designed, built, financed, and maintained by the private sector through the DBFMO model used in most Canadian school PPP projects (Boardman et al., 2016). The private sector owned the schools, which were leased for 20 years, while the development of curriculum and education delivery remained the government's responsibility (Infrastructure Ontario, 2015).

The government can decide whether to renew the lease (twice for a period of up to five years each), walk away, or buy the schools from the private sector upon the expiry of the PPP contract. Annual rent payments are equivalent to 85% of the capitalized cost of the project, meaning that the government can use facilities delivered more efficiently, on time, and cheaper by 15%. In order to make this deal more attractive to the private sector, the schools' buildings are rented to the school system from 8:30 AM to 3:30 PM, Monday to Friday, from September to June, and outside of these official hours, the facilities can be rented to approved organizations and businesses for commercially competitive prices. These additional revenues then help the private sector recoup the 15% of project costs it did not receive from the government. However, the performance of the Nova Scotia school PPP project was not as successful as expected. In February 2010, a report by the Auditor General pinpointed numerous weak points in implementing the school PPP contracts and concluded that the government could have saved more than $52 million had it delivered the projects via the EPC method.

The province of Alberta, meanwhile, had a more successful experience using PPPs to build 18 schools in Edmonton and Calgary in 2007, providing 12,000 new spaces for local students (OECD, 2010). The total cost of the project reached US$634 million, and when construction finished in 2010, the government paid a lump sum advancement payment of $125 million to the project company. The government then began the payment of capital and maintenance fees over 30 years, under the conditions that the schools be available for classes and well-maintained (Schmold, 2009). This project was a greater success, as the schools were delivered on time and within budget.

School PPPs in the USA

The USA lags significantly behind Europe and Canada in its implementation of school PPPs for two reasons: 1) the US government did not face the same fiscal challenges confronted by most local governments in Europe in the 1980s and 1990s, with the majority of US municipalities and public schools having sufficient funds to expand, renovate, or build new schools, and 2) US federal and state governments offer tax incentives to school facilities owned and operated by the public sector (PWHC, 2010; Ronald, 2005). As a result, school systems have not been an attractive investment target for the private sector. Furthermore, unlike in the UK, where the private sector can own school property for a certain number of years, private entities in the USA receive only a lump sum payment for financing, designing, and building public schools.

Nevertheless, there have been a few school PPPs delivered through innovative mechanisms. For example, two high schools in Houston, Texas, were constructed by Gilbane Properties in 1998, which created a not-for-profit corporation issuing tax-exempt bonds, managed the construction process, and kept the title for facilities when construction finished. Gilbane Properties' not-for-profit corporation receives an annual lease payment from the local government to repay its debt, and this arrangement resulted in saving more than US$20 million on the construction of the two schools, their delivery finished a year ahead of schedule.

A similarly innovative approach was adopted in 2001 to rebuild James F. Oyster Bilingual Elementary School in Washington, DC, when a national real estate development company called LCOR Incorporated partnered with the District of Columbia Public Schools to deliver the project. The cost of building the school was financed with a 35-year tax-exempt bond package worth US$11 million issued by the District of Columbia. The bonds would be fully repaid from revenues generated by a 211-unit apartment building LCOR Incorporated constructed for US$29 million on unused land belonging to the school. Taxpayers paid nothing for the newly built school, financed through Payment In-Lieu of Taxes (PILOT) from income generated by renting the newly built apartments. The school was thus constructed at no cost to taxpayers, and provided new apartment units offering better housing for the community at affordable prices.

School PPPs in Europe

England and Wales

Since the introduction of the Private Finance Initiative in 1992, the school partnership program in the UK has become the most extensive in the world, with over 700 projects reaching financial close and the private sector contributing more than $67 billion by 2012 (HM Treasury, 2012). In 2007, England had signed 115 PFI school deals at a value of more than US$11.6 billion under the DBFO model, with projections that this would increase to US$16 billion in the coming years (World Bank, 2009). Furthermore, more than 717 projects have been signed in England, with 648 already in various operational stages (HM Treasury, 2012). The Welsh government also signed more than 20 school-related PPP deals. Payment for all these projects has been made under an "availability-based" model, and this can take many forms, including monthly, quarterly, or annual rent payments based on contractual terms. School councils are also not obliged to rent the facilities beyond their initial lease terms, which incentivizes the private sector to keep the school facilities up to the highest standards (HM Treasury, 2005).

Scotland

Scotland has also adopted the PFI model for school PPP projects predominantly due to its lack of financial resources to provide them through public procurement (Accounts Commission, 2002). More than 130 existing schools needed refurbishment and renewal in 2002 due to inadequate and dilapidated school buildings at approximately US$554 million, with the government retaining control over educational policies and curriculum development. To meet this need, the Scottish government provided subsidies for local education authorities to meet their lease payments and operating costs. Performance reporting underpins the payment mechanism of PFI school contracts, with payment to the consortium dependent upon 1) timely completion and delivery of the new or refurbished schools and 2) delivery of services and maintenance over 25 to 30 years. Scotland's PFI financing is sometimes quite novel; for example, in the case of Balfron High School, 99% of its debt came from a bank and only 1% from equity. This reduced the overall interest costs with PFI contracts to 5% per year (World Bank, 2009). The PFI model in Scotland has delivered school projects on time and within budget, especially in the South Lanarkshire and Glasgow Schools Projects, which secured approximately US$800 million in private finance (HM Treasury, 2003).

The Netherlands

Education in the Netherlands has been decentralized and demand-driven for over 100 years, and the use of PPPs for school construction began in 2005 when the Ypenburg suburbs needed to accommodate 1,200 students (CfBT, 2008). The contract was for 30 years, including 1.5 years for construction and 28.5 years for maintenance, cleaning, furnishing, and ICT (World Bank, 2009). While payments for school PPP projects in the Netherlands are based on the availability of facilities for students, public and private schools are also funded by the government vouchers parents use to freely select which schools they wish to send their children to. Government funding for schools remains critical yet dependent on performance, and this system incentivizes schools to provide the best possible educational facilities to attract more students. While the government makes decisions and policies regarding educational systems, at the operational level, schools are governed by private boards, which manage the schools' quotidian administrative activities.

Germany

Germany's biggest PPP project was undertaken for the Offenbach Schools in 2005, in which the government contracted out financing, refurbishment, and operation of 88 government schools (a total of 450 buildings) at the cost of approximately €550 million (German Federal Ministry of Finance, 2010). The private sector partners operated the schools for 15 years and received monthly payments from the government based on the availability of schools and performance (World Bank, 2009). Another school-related PPP project was implemented in Frankfurt in 2007 and involved building new facilities, refurbishing existing ones, financing three schools, and then operating and maintaining them for 20 years. School Cologne-Rodenkirchen is another major PPP project in which the contract volume reached €127 million and involved financing, construction, and operation of the schools over 27 years.[3] Payments from the government in all these projects have depended upon the availability of buildings and services during school hours. Monthly payments can also involve penalties if the private partners cannot provide the agreed-upon performance standards.

Spain (Madrid)

Spain boasts some of the largest school PPP deals in all of Europe, as there has been a surging need for additional schools due to rapid population growth in its central capital of Madrid. Schools are privately owned and managed in that city, and the regional government pays teachers' salaries and half of all operating expenses. Between 2005 and 2012, the government awarded 56 PPP concessions to build and operate grant-aided schools with an investment of €650 million (Carpintero & Siemiatycki, 2015). These school projects were tendered one by one (around €10 to 15 million for each) rather than as a bundled concession to allow small companies to participate, and 53 of these schools are now running. As a result, small enterprises have played a significant role in delivering PPP projects for schools. The concession period for these PPPs is up to 50 years, and roughly 40% of contracts have been financed through project finance (Financier World Wide, 2012). The procurement process was simple, with standardized tender documents used in implementing the projects. Banks also required that schools be built at once rather than in stages to eliminate construction risks, with the consortia assuming construction, operational, financial, and demand risks (Carpintero & Siemiatycki, 2015).

School PPPs in the Middle East

Egypt

The country of Egypt implemented one of the Middle East's largest PPP deals in the education sector when the government provided land and the private sector designed, constructed, financed, furnished, and provided non-educational services under long-term agreements for 345 schools across 23 governorates in 2006 (CfBT, 2008). This successful initiative was expanded in 2007 to cover more than 2,210 new primary and secondary schools valued at more than US$1.2 billion (World Bank, 2009). The aforementioned 345 schools are currently under operation, and payment for these projects is based on the "availability and performance" model in line with international best practices for delivering PPP school projects.

United Arab Emirates

The government of Abu Dhabi in the United Arab Emirates has extensively used the PPP model, particularly in managing its many public schools. Many of its schools and universities, such as the Sorbonne Abu Dhabi, Zayed University, and several others, are managed and operated by a range of private sector entities (Financier World Wide, 2012). In 2008, a report by the Abu Dhabi Department of Economic Development (2008) on PPP use in the education sector indicated that PPP projects added 61 schools for the academic year 2007–2008 in Abdu Dhabi and Al Ain. These PPPs mainly took the form of contract management services. As a notable example, The United Arab Emirates University was constructed through a 30-year BOT agreement, including financing, construction, and management of campus facilities. The project was completed for US$410 million in 2009, and the contractual structure took the format of a performance-based contract, with the government paying a monthly charge for the availability of buildings and proper management of facilities.

Qatar

The government partly funds numerous schools and universities in Qatar, but is entirely operated by the private sector, and independent schools in Qatar have been run by government-selected operators and overseen by the Supreme Educational Council since 2005 (World Bank, 2009). Independent schools can be either new or converted from existing ones owned by the Ministry of Education, with operators being granted three-year agreements to run the schools dependent upon satisfactory performance. Independent schools operate on open admission policies and the curricula are designed by the Ministry of Education. The government then pays schools based on the number of enrolled Qatari students, while international students must pay tuition.

As of this writing, Qatar has yet to extend its use of PPPs to finance, construct, and maintain its schools. While there were several proposals to build numerous schools on a PPP basis, most were canceled, put on hold, or reverted to the EPC structure. Nonetheless, the Qatari government has recently announced the development of a PPP law and legal framework to enable school PPP projects.

Kuwait

Unlike some other Gulf countries, where the use of PPPs for education has been a relatively nascent phenomenon, in Kuwait, there have been numerous attempts by the Kuwait Authority for Partnerships Projects to procure nine schools (five kindergartens, three elementary schools, and one middle school) on a Design, Build, Finance, Operate, and Maintain (DBFOM) basis since 2013. Nevertheless, procuring these schools has been sluggish, and financial closure has not been reached for any projects.[4]

Saudi Arabia

All public schools in Saudi Arabia are delivered through the EPC model and are fully funded by the Ministry of Education. The abundance of oil revenues in recent decades has simplified the financing of infrastructure projects through public funding. PPPs have been restricted to independent water and power plants and have yet to be extended to social infrastructure.

Impact of school PPPs on educational outcomes

This section presents the findings of a few existing studies regarding the performance and impact of each PPP initiative or model on certain educational outcomes, which offer a clear picture that would allow the Saudi government to better determine which PPP model could best serve its interests and fulfill its policy objectives.

This chapter has presented several ways in which the public and private sectors can partner to provide educational services, with a primary focus on delivering schools through infrastructure PPPs. Overall, the four types of PPP models described have varying impacts on educational performance indicators, as shown in Table 6.6 below. School vouchers have a substantial effect on increased accessibility of schools for students and an equally powerful influence on improving the quality of educational outcomes, since the voucher model induces competition in the education market by allowing parents to choose schools that are reputed for high standards. This model also lowers the costs since schools wish to attract more vouchers.

Government subsidies for educational services also have considerable ramifications for increased enrollment in existing schools and reduction of educational inequality, yet they have little impact on competition. Private management of schools significantly influences lowering education inequality, a moderate impact on increased enrollment, and a low effect on competition. Meanwhile, the PFI model of delivering school infrastructure through the private sector has a high impact on reducing education inequality, as it increases the number of schools via private finance, reduces costs of infrastructure when delivered through a competitive consortium (and the bidding process is transparent), and allows project risks to be transferred to the party best suited to handle them.

Overall, growing evidence suggests that delivery of school infrastructure through private finance results in superior performance. A Treasury report in the UK examining the performance of 61 PFI school infrastructure projects showed that 88% of those projects were delivered on time and within budget (HM Treasury, 2007). Another study investigating the results of 37 PFIs demonstrated that 76% of the projects were delivered on time, with 79% completed within budget. Furthermore, only 27% of those projects would have been delivered within their timeframes and budgets had they been delivered under the traditional EPC model (CfBT, 2008). The HM Treasury (2003) report also showed that 76% of public sector school project clients expressed satisfaction with the private sector's performance in handling, operating, and maintaining school infrastructure. Likewise, for Australia's infrastructure PPP school projects, the Australian Department of Education and Training (2003) stated that projects delivered through the PFI model are often delivered two years ahead of those delivered using EPC and save the government 7% of the total project costs as well. As indicated by the cases of Australia and New Zealand, such positive outcomes are the primary motivation behind utilizing PPPs to construct a larger number of schools in both countries.

How essential is the PPP model for Saudi Arabia's future schools?

This section explains how essential the PPP model is for Saudi Arabia's school program, particularly considering the decline in oil prices and the

Table 6.6 Impact of partnership types on performance indicators

Contract type	Effect on increasing enrollment	Effect on improving educational outcomes	Effect on reducing educational inequality	Effect on reducing costs	Risk sharing	Competition
Vouchers	**Strong** for number of students who receive vouchers	**Strong** for school choice	**Strong** when targeted	**Strong** when the private sector is more efficient	Low	Significant
Subsidies	**Strong** when using existing private infrastructure	**Moderate** but limited by available places and quality of services delivered in the private sector	**Strong** when targeted	**Moderate**	Moderate	Low
Private management and operation	**Moderate** but limited by the supply of private school operators	**Moderate** but limited by available places in the private sector	**Strong** when targeted	**Moderate**	Low	Low
Private finance initiatives	**Moderate** but limited by financial constraints	Low	**Strong** when targeted	**Strong**	Significant	Low

Source: *World Bank (2009) and McKinsey & Company (2014)*

shift of government policies toward broader involvement of the private sector in the provision of public services. More importantly, the readiness of Saudi Arabia to effectively construct its school program through the PPP model is assessed, and the requisite tools to adequately achieve it are pinpointed.

To create 1,600 schools over the next ten years, the Saudi government needs to seek mutual collaboration with the private sector using the PPP model. In its search for sustainable development, greater civic engagement in decision-making, and transformation into a knowledge- and innovation-based economy, it would behoove Saudi Arabia to actively engage the private sector in effectively addressing its shortage of financial resources, which are vital to the delivery of its much-needed school infrastructure. This has been clearly articulated in both Vision 2030 and the Saudi National Transformation Plan. Local or international private sector entities and banks can provide the Saudi government with the financing necessary to establish its urgently needed public and private schools and the skills required to operate and sustain them. The public sector must therefore facilitate the processes involved in creating and establishing the legal and institutional capacity to provide an ecosystem where the private sector can operate effectively. This will bring about numerous opportunities for Saudi Arabia in its school projects and further stimulate innovation and strategic partnerships in other infrastructure-related areas.

The proper utilization of PPPs to build schools can also afford numerous advantages to Saudi Arabia and minimize any disadvantages that could arise from delivering a national program of such magnitude through the EPC model. Topping the list of such advantages is the generation of creativity and innovation, as the local or international private sector service providers can enjoy access to the talent, human capacity, and tools necessary to provide services more imaginatively and transfer their knowledge to the local workforce. Moreover, engagement with the private sector in delivering schools can, to some extent, guarantee that the government of Saudi Arabia will achieve value for money, proper transfer of risks, and higher quality of services and products associated with the schools' design, construction, and maintenance.

How prepared is Saudi Arabia to successfully deliver schools via the PPP model?

While the political leadership of Saudi Arabia fully supports the adoption of PPPs in both its Vision 2030 and the National Transformation Plan, the country nevertheless faces several institutional, governance, and legal hurdles in making PPPs an operational tool to achieve its newly set policy goals. Over the past decade, numerous infrastructure projects have been developed throughout the Kingdom using the PPP model (particularly in independent water and power plants), but without reliance on legal frameworks or models, being simply conducted on contractual and ad hoc bases. Furthermore, while PPPs have been used in several cases in Saudi Arabia, the absence of policies or laws to govern them makes the private sector hesitant to enter further and more complex forms of partnerships with the public sector. As such, scrutinizing Saudi Arabia's contextual factors and customizing the importation of PPP policies to meet the local context is essential for their success. It is, therefore, imperative to develop a PPP model that is pertinent to Saudi Arabia and fits its unique political, economic, and social characteristics.

Over the past two decades, Saudi Arabia has relied on the experiences of international consulting companies that have designed and constructed several high-profile projects based on international best practices and management solutions. This strategy has allowed Saudi Arabia to rapidly achieve infrastructure services commensurate with developed countries. Nevertheless, there remains a need to institutionalize this knowledge and experience to facilitate the implementation of more complex projects. Considering its dwindling oil profits, the Saudi government's strategy is to increasingly invest in local firms and companies to develop infrastructure services and drive economic growth. However, there is still a need for specialized units within the government of Saudi Arabia that can regulate, monitor, and administer PPP projects. Private sector companies need to consult with and involve numerous government entities, and some PPPs require the involvement of various ministries, authorities, and entities that, at times, require lengthy bureaucratic processes. Hence, simplifying, streamlining, and reducing the burden of bureaucracy on the private sector will serve as an enabling factor that can facilitate the establishment of PPPs.

In light of other international contexts, this could be achieved by empowering a "one-stop shop" PPP unit to handle all necessary paperwork within a single ministry. More importantly, such a unit would be responsible for conducting feasibility studies and ensuring that a proposed PPP project is aligned with Saudi Arabia's economic objectives and priorities. The government of Saudi Arabia has already established the National Center for Privatization & PPP which can assume this role. Furthermore, creating a regulatory framework will also be a key enabler to ensure the success of PPP programs, as it can protect the interests of all players in a PPP agreement. A government unit empowered to play such a role would attract the interest of both public and private entities in collaborating to create public value while also protecting their rights. The technical and legal expertise necessary for administering PPPs could also be provided by such a unit, representing the public sector across the various stages of the PPP agreement.

The establishment of the proper legal and policy grounds for PPPs to deliver Saudi Arabia's school project is thus vital to its success. To date, however, the country has yet to develop a dedicated PPP law to facilitate the delivery and procurement of public infrastructure via the private sector. Although the Private Sector Participation Law was enacted in 2022, this law has not been adopted to initiate and implement PPP projects. There have also been many efforts to draft a PPP law specifically designed to cater to the interests and protect the rights of public and private institutions entering into collaborative agreements, but, as of this writing, there is still a need to develop a specific legal framework that could be referred to in the case of disputes beyond the local courts, which do not have the expertise to handle such technical and complex matters.

A dearth of necessary talent is another pressing issue facing Saudi Arabia in this regard. PPPs require advanced technical skills in identifying potential projects, drafting contracts, negotiating risk transfers, and ultimately implementing the projects. Furthermore, the public sector is usually at a comparative disadvantage in PPP contracts when it lacks the experts that could protect its rights in the case of disputes. Hence, attracting and maintaining skilled talent is essential if the country wishes to successfully implement a sustainable and comprehensive PPP program that serves the best interests of both the public and private parties forming partnerships.

An observation of international practices in administering PPPs reveals that enabling institutional factors is critical. Figure 6.3 presents the three key frameworks and enabling dynamics that Saudi Arabia's government should implement to secure a sound ecosystem for its school PPP project. First, an institutional framework must ensure the existence of an independent governmental body that will anchor the public sector's efforts and initiatives to implement successful PPP projects. A central PPP unit is thus essential in Saudi Arabia to enable a streamlined and simplified process for public and private entities intending to enter a PPP contract. Such units usually provide technical support and advisory services to private and public entities before they engage in PPP projects.

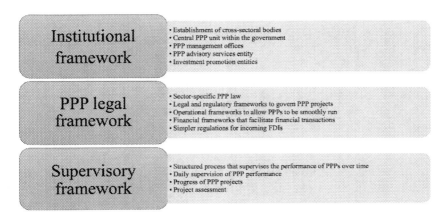

Figure 6.3 Essential requirements to support Saudi Arabia's school PPP project
Source: Adapted from Strategy& (2012)

Furthermore, given the cross-sectorial nature of infrastructure PPP projects, Saudi Arabia's school PPP program will be complex to manage. It will encompass curricula development, government entities providing educational services, and the private sector's role in operating and maintaining school facilities. Managing such a web of cross-sectorial entities requires a central governing body to facilitate collaboration and smooth the lengthy processes required by PPP contracts.

Second, a sound and transparent legal environment must be established to support PPPs, and this will serve as a key driver in encouraging private sector entities to comfortably invest in Saudi Arabia's school PPP project. A sector-specific PPP law defining the legislative, legal, and governance-related matters that secure investors' rights vis-à-vis the private and public sectors is equally essential. This can be specifically designed to address disputes that commonly emerge while administering long-term contracts. Hence, both parties can know that, in the case of a breach of contract, a legal authority exists with explicit laws that can solve their disagreements or disputes. Such an authority can instill significant confidence, especially in the private sector, which is usually the bearer of the lion's share of risks.

Third, a supervisory framework is necessary to ensure that PPP projects are monitored continuously throughout the project cycle, and this will guarantee that projects are in line with the contractual and legal agreements before their start. Moreover, following up on the public and private sector entities to meet their deadlines and achieve the milestones of their projects can act as a proactive mechanism to avoid future disputes or disagreements, especially during the project delivery period.

Lessons learned

This section presents the lessons and findings of the chapter together with recommendations that aim to address existing challenges facing the transformation of Saudi Arabia's school program from a lofty ambition into a successful reality.

There are numerous lessons that Saudi Arabia can learn from the global experiences with PPPs, and these can serve as valuable tools toward the success of its school project and the achievement of its desired objectives of quality and timeliness. On the one hand, PPPs undoubtedly offer a potential strategic option for Saudi Arabia to deliver 1,600 schools. On the other hand, it could also rely on other forms and models to raise the needed financial support to manage its public schools more efficiently. Using private finance to build 1,600 new schools is thus a pathway that Saudi Arabia can follow to generate the necessary upfront costs for a project of such magnitude. Nevertheless, as indicated previously, this will require the Saudi government to also invest in building the legal and regulatory infrastructure that will attract local and international private sector companies. As this chapter has shown, several challenges could inhibit the successful

Table 6.7 The prospects of various PPP initiatives in Saudi Arabia

PPP initiative	Prospects in Saudi Arabia
Private sector philanthropic initiative	• Saudi Arabia hosts philanthropic family businesses that can devote a share of their wealth to financing or building new schools or refurbishing existing ones. • Part of Saudi Arabia's Zakat money (almsgiving) could be strategically channeled toward the education system. • The government can introduce incentives to encourage the private sector to donate to building schools as part of their corporate social responsibility.
School management initiative	• This initiative can easily enhance the quality of management for existing schools in Saudi Arabia. • This initiative has been highly tested in the Gulf region, particularly in Qatar and the UAE, and it has substantially improved schools' overall management practices. • Best practices and knowhow from the private sector can potentially be transferred to train local talents. • The government can implement and oversee curricula while the private sector handles operational tasks.
Purchase of educational services from private schools	• This model would allow the Saudi government to pay schools' annual fees based on the number of Saudi students enrolled. • This would be more helpful in the eastern and southern areas of the Kingdom, where there is a more significant need for schools. • This model would create a strong demand in the schools' infrastructure sector and incentivize local merchant families to utilize empty land for building schools.
Vouchers and voucher-like programs	• The government can induce competition among its schools by providing parents with vouchers that would allow them to freely select those they think to offer higher education and infrastructure quality. • This model has been tested in Qatar and other Middle Eastern countries and proved effective when designed and delivered correctly.
School infrastructure initiative	• Saudi Arabia can rely on local and international private sector partners to finance, design, build, maintain, operate, and transfer schools to the government. • This model requires the existence of regulatory, legal, and supervisory frameworks to successfully attract the private sector. • If the requirements are met, this model has been proven internationally to attract private finance for schools.

Source: Author's analysis

implementation of school PPP projects, and this section provides some recommendations on how to mitigate them.

As Table 6.7 illustrates, the five listed PPP initiatives can potentially enhance the education sector in Saudi Arabia on various fronts. While the

192 *Importance of partnerships between the public and private sectors*

private sector's philanthropic initiatives can provide financial resources to improve the quality of infrastructure and educational programs, government reliance on the private sector's management of schools, purchasing of educational services, and issuance of vouchers that parents can use to enroll their children in local schools are all innovative ways in which the public and private sectors can form partnerships in Saudi Arabia.

Recommendations

The Saudi government can successfully deliver its school PPP program if it is carried out in parallel with implementing the necessary enabling environment. This can take many forms, including the following.

Establish (or amend existing) policies, regulatory, and legal frameworks

Saudi Arabia's existing policies and regulatory frameworks allow for implementing infrastructure services through the traditional EPC model. However, procurement of the school infrastructure program via the PPP model will require a significant amendment of the Government Procurement Law to enable the private sector to finance and own facilities for a period and then transfer them to the public sector.

Build capacity to manage PPP contracts

PPP projects require a sophisticated cadre of technical, legal, and financial advisers who can study the feasibility of PPP proposals, ensure effective implementation, and monitor governance and progress. International experience has shown that developing the capacity of public sector entities to enact legislation and policies that can drive the implementation of PPPs is crucial. This capacity ensures that public sector employees are trained in navigating the complexities associated with PPP agreements and are aware of the risks that might emerge throughout the process. Furthermore, a dedicated PPP unit can facilitate coordination, collaboration, and knowledge sharing across the various layers of bureaucracy.

Contract management is also a significant feature of successful service delivery via PPPs. Practitioners must therefore be well trained to develop effective and efficient contract management plans and negotiation skills. Furthermore, successful PPPs only emerge when there is clarity of purpose, sensible preparation and documentation of projects, accountability, competitive pricing, and professional contract management. To avoid failure, the parties involved in PPPs should understand a project's expected outcomes and risks and how they can maximize value for money.

Empower the role of the private sector in providing school infrastructure

The government of Saudi Arabia has traditionally funded all public infrastructure services, and thus the introduction of PPPs and attempts to engage the private sector as funders of public schools will result in a significant cultural shift in the Kingdom's infrastructure development. Hence, government provision of subsidies, encouragement of philanthropic funding for private schools, and incentives to engage the private sector in funding the school program will go a long way toward making the project a success.

Allow and enable tapping into the international market and labor importation

PPPs are inherently complex contractual agreements, and even advanced economies such as Australia, the USA, and Canada often import lawyers and financial advisors from the UK to advise them on the best contractual and legal mechanisms when using PPPs for infrastructure development. To guarantee the success of its school PPP program, the government of Saudi Arabia should facilitate granting residency visas to private entities working to build the necessary capabilities that do not yet exist within the Kingdom.

Use clearly defined and appropriate funding models

Reliance on international consultants should not deter Saudi Arabia from developing a model of funding that reflects the cultural and social characteristics of the Kingdom, as well as the unique composition of its private sector. The UK's PFI model is just one example, and funding models tailored to the Saudi environment, perhaps using Islamic Finance principles, should be investigated.

Facilitate borrowing from local banks

PPP projects entail substantial upfront investments often provided on an 80% debt, 20% equity basis. Local banks must therefore be willing to provide long-term loans, and existing insolvency legislation should be revised to enable the implementation of projects with a longer duration and greater risks. This is particularly salient in the case of international investors willing to invest in the education sector in Saudi Arabia.

Establish PPP performance and monitoring mechanisms

It is difficult to predict the performance of a PPP project; hence, performance and governance monitoring mechanisms are essential to ensure that public and private sector parties adhere to their contractual obligations. Establishing an independent auditing body that can safeguard and monitor

PPP projects across their various implementation and performance stages is thus critical for the overall success of such projects and programs.

Governance and accountability mechanisms

Governance and accountability issues are paramount if PPPs wish to achieve better results in Saudi Arabia and gain greater acceptability and trust from the private sector (Bovaird, 2004). In the initial stages of a program, it is especially important to guarantee a fair and transparent bidding process that ensures a project is allocated to the party best suited to handle it. PPPs are more likely to fail when governance risks are not carefully and thoroughly assessed, and when they do not prioritize citizens' concerns or share the outcomes of the partnership with them. Although PPPs may be commercially successful at first, such successes can eventually be limited when the partnership is a two-way affair between the government and business sectors rather than one that directly includes citizens' interests.

Incentivizing school performance

An equally important factor that the Saudi government should consider investing in is the provision of sufficient incentives for schools to perform well. International experience has shown that creating competition among schools via vouchers that parents can use to freely choose schools for their children is an effective method. This forces schools to compete in the market and provide higher quality facilities, competent staff, and creative learning methodologies.

Conclusion

This chapter presented an international overview of PPP use to deliver school infrastructure by examining countries where such policies have been tested for decades and analyzing their experiences. It is clear from this review that PPPs are used for three main reasons, and the first is to compensate for significant fiscal deficits in government budgets. In European countries, Canada, and some Middle Eastern countries like Egypt, private finances provided a valuable option for delivering much-needed schools when sufficient public funds were unavailable. Second, although PPPs promise better efficiency of service delivery, in theory, international experience reveals diverse outcomes—sometimes culminating in significant successes, such as in the UK, the USA, or Germany, but at other times failing to deliver efficiently, as in the case of Canada. Nonetheless, when PPPs' contractual and operational components are designed correctly, they have a greater potential to meet the public sector's desired financial and quality-related objectives. The third key reason for using PPPs is to ensure risk transfer to the party best qualified to shoulder it. While the private sector takes on risks associated with construction to ensure the use of high-quality materials and minimize maintenance costs at later stages, the public sector handles broader political or other risks falling beyond the scope of the private sector.

Finally, the chapter examined the potential of Saudi Arabia's ambitious school program being constructed through the PPP route. It provided a holistic picture of the conceptual arguments surrounding PPP school models in the existing literature and shed light on the readiness of Saudi Arabia's government and private sector to adopt the PPP model for a school program of such magnitude. It is ultimately concluded that Saudi Arabia must simultaneously develop the necessary legal, institutional, and supervisory frameworks essential for PPPs to successfully deliver its school PPP program. The chapter proposes the implementation of these frameworks to mitigate existing challenges and encourage the private sector's adoption of contractual arrangements and engagements to protect the interests of the two sectors.

Notes

1 www.australasianlawyer.com.au/news/australasian-firms-team-up-for-kiwi-ppp-200227.aspx
2 www.education.govt.nz/news/consortia-shortlisted-for-third-schools-ppp/
3 www.hochtief-solutions.com/htsol_en/65.jhtml?p=200&u=14
4 http://infrapppworld.com/2015/11/kuwait-issues-rfp-for-schools-ppp-project.html

References

Abu Dhabi Department of Economic Development. (2008). Education and public-private partnerships (PPPs). International experiences and lessons. Retrieved from: https://ded.abudhabi.ae/en/studies-indicators/Studies/Education%20and%20Public%20Private%20Partnership%20(PPP)%E2%80%A6%20Internation.pdf Accessed on 3 September 2022.

Accounts Commission. (2002). Taking the initiative. Using PFI contracts to renew council schools. Audit Scotland. Retrieved from: www.audit-scotland.gov.uk/docs/local/2002/nr_020612_PFI_schools.pdf Accessed on 2 September 2022.

Asian Development Bank. (2010). Public-private partnerships in ABD Education lending. 2000–2009. Retrieved from: www.adb.org/sites/default/files/publication/27484/ppp-education-2000-2009.pdf accessed on 1 September 2022.

Audit Office of New South Wales. (2006). Retrieved from: https://web-archive.cloud.audit.nsw.gov.au/publications/financial-audit-reports/2006-reports/volume-2-2006.1.html Accessed on 7 September 2022.

Banks, G. (2008). Riding The Third Wave: Some Challenges in National Reform. Productivity Commission, Melbourne, 27 March.

Broadbent, J., & Laughlin, R. (2003). Public-private partnerships: An introduction. *Accounting, Auditing and Accountability Journal*, 16 (3), 332–341.

Boardman, A., Siemiatycki, M., & Vining, A. (2016). The theory and evidence concerning public-private partnerships in Canada and elsewhere. *The School of Public Policy SPP Research Papers*, 9 (12), 1–32.

Bovaird, T. (2004). Public-private partnerships: from contested concepts to prevalent practice. *International Review of Administrative Sciences*, 70 (2), 199–215.

Caldwell, B., & Keating, J. (2004). Adding value to public education: An examination of the possibilities for public-private partnerships. Retrieved from: www.acde.edu.au/?wpdmact=process&did=MjUuaG90bGluaw Accessed on 1 September 2022.

Carpintero, S., & Siemiatycki, M. (2015). PPP projects in local infrastructure: evidence from schools in Madrid region, Spain. *Public Money & Management*, 35(6), 439–446.

Canadian Council for PPPs. (2022). Definitions and models. Retrieved from: www.pppcouncil.ca/web/Knowledge_Centre/What_are_P3s_/Definitions_Models/web/P3_Knowledge_Centre/About_P3s/Definitions_Models.aspx?hkey=79b9874d-4498-46b1-929f-37ce461ab4bc Accessed on 5 September 2022.

CfBT. (2008). Public-private partnerships in basic education: An international review. Retrieved from: www.azimpremjifoundation.org/pdf/ppp_report.pdf Accessed on 3 September 2022.

Darvish, H., Zou, P., Loosemore, M., & Zhang, G. (2006). Risk management, public interests and value for money in PPP projects: Literature review and case studies, *The CRIOCM International Symposium on Advancement of Construction Management and Real Estate*.

Department of Education and Training. (2003). New schools privately financed project: Summary of contracts, Government of New South Wales, Sydney.

Education International. (2009). Public-private partnerships in education. *Education International*. Retrieved from: http://download.ei-ie.org/docs/irisdocuments/research%20website%20documents/2009-00086-01-e.pdf Accessed on 3 September 2022.

English, L. (2006). Public private partnerships in Australia: An overview of their nature, purpose, incidence and oversight. *UNSW Law Journal*, 29(3), 250–262.

Ernst & Young (2013). Mayoral position paper on public private partnerships. Retrieved from: https://media.nzherald.co.nz/webcontent/document/pdf/201348/PPPStudyForAttachmen1.pdf Accessed on 3 September 2022.

European Commission. (2003). Guidelines for successful public-private partnerships. Retrieved from: https://ec.europa.eu/regional_policy/sources/docgener/guides/ppp_en.pdf Accessed on 8 September 2022.

Fennell, S. (2010). *Public Private Partnerships and Educational Outcomes: New Conceptual and Methodological Approaches.* Department for International Development. Retrieved from: http://ceid.educ.cam.ac.uk/researchprogrammes/recoup/publications/workingpapers/WP37-PPP_and_Educational_Outcomes.pdf.Accessed on 2 September 2021.

Forward, P. (2006). Public private partnership or conflict: Is it time for a new approach? *UNSW Law Journal*, 29(3), 263–269.

Financier World Wide. (2012). Infrastructure & project finance. Infrastructure and project finance. Retrieved from: www.financierworldwide.com/annual-review-infrastructure-project-finance-2012/#.V8q9UJh97IU Accessed on 3 September 2022.

German Federal Ministry of Finance. (2010). PPP schools Frankfurt. Case study, Partnerschaften Deutschland, OPP Deutschland. AG.

Grimsey, D., & Lewis, M. (2000). Evaluating the risks of public private partnerships for infrastructure projects. *International Journal of Project and Management*, 20, 107–118.

Grimsey, D., & Lewis, M. (2005). Are public private partnerships value for money? Evaluating alternative approaches and comparing academic practitioner views. *Accounting Forum*, 29(2005), 345–378.

Grimsey, D., & Lewis, M. (2007). Public private partnerships and public procurement. *Agenda*, 14(2), 171–188.

HM Treasury. (2003). PFI: Meeting the investment challenge, Her Majesty's Stationery Office, London.

HM Treasury. (2007). PFI signed projects list – December 2004, The Treasury, London.

HM Treasury. (2012). Private finance 2. Retrieved from: www.hm-treasury.gov.uk/infrastructure_pfireform.htm. Accessed on 10 September 2022.

HM Treasury. (2005). Application note: value for money in refinancing. Retrieved from: www.gov.uk/government/uploads/system/uploads/attachment_data/file/225371/08_application_note_value_for_money_280205.pdf Accessed 5 August 2022.

Infrastructure Ontario. (2015). Making projects happen. Value for money assessment. Retrieved from: www.infrastructureontario.ca/WorkArea/DownloadAsset.aspx?id Accessed on 3 September 2022.

Kozarovski, D. (2006). Public private partnerships – solution worth pursuing despite their complexity. *UNSW Law Journal*, 29(3), 308–317.

McKinsey & Company. (2014). Partnering for outcomes: Public private partnership for school education in Asia. McKinsey Center for Government. Retrieved from: http://www.mckinsey.com/global-locations/asia/singapore/en/our-work/mckinsey-innovation-campus Accessed on 1 September 2022.

National Infrastructure Plan. (2010). Retrieved from: https://infrastructure.planninginspectorate.gov.uk/wp-content/uploads/2010/12/nationalinfrastructurepla n251010.pdf Accessed on 3 September 2022.

NSW Office of Financial Management. (2002). Private provision of public infrastructure and services.

OECD. (2010). Flexible and alternative approaches to providing school infrastructure in Alberta, Canada. Retrieved from: www.oecd-ilibrary.org/education/flexible-and-alternative-approaches-to-providing-school-infrastructure-in-alberta-canada_5kmh36j9vwmw-en?crawler=true Accessed on 3 September 2022.

Patrinos, A. (2005). Education Contracting: Scope of Future Research, Program on Education Policy and Governance Report, 05–23, Harvard University, Cambridge, MA.

Price Water House Coopers. (2010). Public-private partnerships: US perspective. Retrieved from: www.pwc.com/us/en/capital-projects-infrastructure/publications/public-private-partnerships.html Accessed on 3 September 2022.

PPP Knowledge Lab. (2022). PPP reference guide, version 3. Retrieved from: https://ppp.worldbank.org/public-private-partnership/ppp-knowledge-lab Accessed on 3 September 2022.

Ronald, D. (2005). *Public-private partnerships offer innovative opportunities for school facilities*, The Maryland Public Policy Institute, Germantown, Maryland. Retrieved from: www.mdpolicy.org/docLib/20051112_PPPSchoolFacilities.pdf Accessed on 3 September 2022.

Ross, P. (2004). Australia's first public private partnership school project. Retrieved from: www.oecd-ilibrary.org/education/australia-s-first-public-private-partnership-school-project_616725002620?crawler=true Accessed on 3 September 2022.

Sands, V. (2006). The right to know and obligation to provide: Public private partnerships, public knowledge, public accountability, public disfranchisement and prison cases. *UNSW Law Journal,* 29(3), 334–341.

Schmold, S. (2009). Building together – It's time to act infrastructure report. Alberta School Boards Association.

Strategy&. (2012). Partnerships for transformation: Using public–private partnerships in the GCC. Retrieved from: www.strategyand.pwc.com/m1/en/ideation-center/media/private-sector-participation-in-the-gcc.pdf Accessed on 4 September 2022.

Teicher, J., Alam, Q., & Gramberg, V. (2006). Managing trust and relationships: Some Australian experiences. *International Review of Administrative Sciences,* 72(1), 85–100.

UNICEF. (2011). Non-state providers and public-private partnerships in education for the poor. Retrieved from: www.adb.org/publications/non-state-providers-and-public-private-partnerships-education-poor Accessed on 3 September 2022.

Vanourek, G. (2005). State of the charter school movement, 2005: Trends, issues, and indicators, Charter School Leadership Council, Washington, DC.

Webb, R., & Pulle, B. (2002). Public private partnerships: An introduction. Department of the Parliamentary Library.

World Bank. (2009). The role and impact of public-private partnerships in education. Retrieved from: www.ungei.org/resources/files/Role_Impact_PPP_Education.pdf Accessed on 3 September 2022.

World Bank data (2020). Retrieved from: www.worldbank.org Accessed on 11 July 2022.

Part III
Importance of effective human resource development

7 Talent management in the GCC
MENA comparisons and recommendations

Introduction

The ramifications of COVID-19 and other global economic and geopolitical shifts witnessed worldwide over the past decade have triggered financial and institutional performance problems, which in turn have sparked a serious debate about the capacity of government entities and private sector firms to develop, incorporate, and manage human capital and knowledge resources more strategically and sustainably. The Gulf Corporation Council (GCC) and the Middle East and North Africa (MENA) countries, in particular, have already historically faced critical challenges related to the formation and management of talent, given their shortage of national skill and knowledge resources, the continued need for investment in such resources, and the reliance on large numbers of foreign workers and firms to fill national skill-knowledge gaps and shoulder the burden of implementing ambitious economic development goals.

The GCC region has managed to afford that reliance in part due to its abundant financial resources, improved working and living conditions, and greater integration into the global economy. However, conditions have recently been changing as budgetary allocations for major expansion projects and human resource development shrink, talent is fleeing from a wide range of sectors, and the quest for workforce nationalization and employment opportunities for locals is in full swing. These changes further highlight the limitations of organization and management development approaches previously adopted by the GCC region's public and private sectors. As described in the Human Development Report (UNDP, 2002), talent and knowledge represent pivotal levers in the service of growth and development. Hence, effective talent management is a necessary vehicle for realizing and maximizing the potential of knowledge for sustainable performance in work organizations and society at large (UNDP & MBRF, 2020).

Therefore, effective talent management is vital to MENA and GCC countries (Singh et al., 2012). Governments there have invested generously in developing or attracting human capital and knowledge resources through education, research, and training, but despite this expansion in

DOI: 10.4324/9781003267744-10

human capital resources, the Human Development Report (UNDP, 2002) suggests low returns in terms of achieving positive results in the empowerment and management of local talent and performance improvements. One hindering factor is the endemically high level of knowledge and skill underutilization, especially in the public sector, and the advent of the COVID-19 pandemic only exacerbated the gravity of several organizational and managerial problems that public organizations have been facing in GCC countries due to the sudden departure of expatriates. The region has historically been confronted with three significant challenges: the "organizational management system challenge", the "knowledge management challenge", and the "talent management challenge". These three intertwined issues constitute a major stumbling block that hampers the success of the region's organizational reform initiatives (Biygautane & Al Yahya, 2010).

To understand these issues, it is important to note the characteristics of countries in the GCC and MENA regions, which the World Bank classifies into three categories. The first category is resource-poor, labor-abundant countries like Egypt, Jordan, Morocco, and Tunisia. These countries have little or no natural resources, but massive pools of labor primarily seeking jobs in Europe or the Gulf states. The second is resource-rich, labor-abundant countries such as Algeria, Iraq, and Iran. The third is resource-rich, labor-importing countries, which generally include the GCC countries where expatriates sometimes comprise up to 90% of the population, as is the case in the United Arab Emirates (UAE) and Qatar. Understanding these characteristics is essential to understanding how talent management can be improved in those countries.

In its exploration of how talent management challenges in those regions can be transformed into opportunities, the following section of this chapter begins by defining and providing a brief overview of global talent management and its opportunities and challenges from a general perspective. The various structural, economic, educational, and technical challenges hindering GCC and MENA governments' efforts to benefit from the young talent pools they host are then elucidated. To effectively evaluate such challenges, the chapter examines the GCC and MENA regions' socioeconomic contexts, including unemployment numbers, educational system deficiencies, literacy rates, and other indicators that highlight the issues associated with proper talent investment. The following section looks at opportunities in the region's marketplace and how talent's purposeful formation, utilization, and management can serve as a vehicle for talent empowerment. It also enumerates the efforts made by governments of the GCC and MENA regions to transform their economies based on knowledge, diversify their economies, and protect local labor forces through policies such as the GCC "nationalization" initiatives. Specifically, the case of the UAE in nationalizing its workforce is discussed in detail. The chapter then offers specific recommendations to policymakers in the region for better utilizing and managing their talent pools and identifying gaps in current policies and practices.

Definition and a brief overview of talent management

Over the past two centuries, abundant natural resources and adequate labor have achieved higher productivity and competition in domestic and international markets. However, the gradual transition to knowledge economies in the 21st century has drastically transformed the means of production, and has resulted in the scarcity of another viable source of productivity and sustainable growth that must be competed for, which is talent (Beatty & Becker, 2005; Kumari & Bahuguna, 2012).

The first difficulty researchers face when dealing with talent and global talent management is the "disturbing lack of clarity" regarding its definition, scope, and goals (Lewis & Heckman 2006; Tarique & Schuler, 2010). It has even been said that "there is not a single consistent or concise definition" of the concept (Ashton & Morton, 2005; Makram et al., 2017; Tafti et al., 2017). In this vein, Creelman (2004) defines talent management as "not a set of topics, but as a perspective or a mindset. A talent management perspective presumes talented individuals play a central role in the success of the firm" (p. 3). Meanwhile, Schweyer (2004) defines it as "what occurs at the nexus of the hiring, development and workforce management processes and can be described alternatively as talent optimization" (p. 38). Lewis and Heckman (2006) effectively addressed such inconsistencies in defining talent management by identifying major trends in how academics and practitioners tackle the subject, arguing that there are three main schools of thought in this regard (Kravariti & Johnston, 2020). The first one approaches the issue from a standard human resources (HR) viewpoint regarding the processes involved in hiring, retaining, and developing people (Farley, 2005). The second takes a talent pool perspective to identify the talents necessary to fill specific organizational positions. The third is, according to the authors, more complex and slippery to grasp, and categorizes the workforce by performance levels (Lewis & Heckman, 2006; Shulga & Busser, 2019). In addition, a fourth dimension can be added to these three: identifying not only talent, but also critical positions within an organization that can serve its long-term strategic objectives (Boudreau & Ramstad, 2005; 2007).

Furthermore, due to waves of globalization and easy mobility of people across continents, the notion of talent management is no longer considered a domestic issue, but rather an international and global one (Al Ariss et al., 2014; Sparrow et al., 2004). Concepts like "global workforce" and "global talent management" have accordingly received substantial attention from academics and corporate heads over the past two decades (Aguirre et al., 2009; Collings & Mellahi, 2009). Such global talent management involves the various processes and organizational, human, and economic factors that affect talent on a global scale (Sparrow et al., 2004). In this context, employers compete fiercely with one another to attract and retain talent, thereby gaining competitive advantages for their companies (Farndale et al., 2010; Kafetzopoulos et al., 2022).

Global talent management has thus emerged as one of the most challenging and essential strategic issues for both organizations and human resource managers in the 21st century (Ashton & Morton, 2005; Cappelli, 2008a; Mellahi & Collings, 2010). Now, both public and private organizations are increasingly faced with the difficulty of attracting, recruiting, and retaining appropriate talent (Dougherty & Van Gelder, 2015; Shulga & Busser, 2019; Tlaiss, 2021). A study entitled "The War for Talent" (Chambers et al., 1998) predicted such competition and challenges concerning talent, having surveyed 77 large corporations in the USA to find that "successful organizations tend to have a dominant talent segment, while their weaker peers have a bit of everything" (p. 4). The study offered two important lessons. First, it provided an astute analysis of the complexity of the new global economic climate and the role of talent in producing value and comparative advantages, and, second, it triggered an unprecedented interest in the topic of talent and why it needed to be a "burning" priority for organizations if they wished to survive in increasingly globalizing markets (Vecchi et al., 2021).

Since the publication of "The War for Talent", a growing body of literature has asserted that competition for talent is a phenomenon that organizations must cope with to grow and flourish effectively (Meyers & Van Woerkom, 2014; Michaels & Handfield-Jones, 2001). Athey (2008) argues that "despite millions of unemployed workers, there is an acute shortage of talent: science educators to teach the next generation of chemists, health care professionals of all stripes, design engineers with deep technical and interpersonal skills" (p. 1). Meanwhile, Cappelli (2008b) provides a systematic analysis of the history of talent in the USA, starting from excess supply during the recession of 1988 to scarcity once again during the country's economic boom of the 1990s, and considers the essence of talent management to be the proper identification of talent needs and the setting of a coherent strategy to meet them. The study looks at talent management holistically and does not consider it an end in and of itself, but rather as an instrument that supports the overall objectives of maximizing organizational profits and growth (Becker & Huselid, 2006; Phillips & Phillips, 2019).

Research conducted within major international corporations has also proven how organizations that implemented effective global talent management programs then witnessed significant improvement in their performance (Schuler et al., 2011). Hiring and developing talent are no longer the primary ingredients for organizational effectiveness and competition in the increasingly complex global economic system; instead, proper management of that talent is essential. Such management involves ensuring that the right people are in the right place at the right time with the necessary skills to produce competitively (Lane & Pollner, 2008). The challenges in managing this global talent then emerge from an array of intertwined factors and drivers. First among them is globalization, having been identified as the key element by numerous studies (Beechler & Woodward, 2009; Schuler et al., 2011; Scullion et al., 2007). The spread of multinational corporations worldwide and the mobility of labor have facilitated the emigration of talent, also known as the "brain drain" phenomenon (Stahl et al., 2007). This ease of moving from one country to another to pursue education or seek out better job opportunities has affected many developing countries and caused them to lose significant pools of talent (Guthridge & Komm, 2008). The second challenge is associated with demographic transitions and trends within developed and developing countries (Faust, 2008; Mujtaba et al., 2022). While population growth in developed economies, such as the USA, the UK, and Australia, remains relatively stable, albeit with considerable potential for a decline in the years to come, developing and emerging countries are witnessing significant baby booms. The ease of migrating from one country to another makes these young and talented generations a potential threat to workforces in more developed economies, which could be at risk of losing access to job opportunities due to increasing competition from younger (and possibly cheaper) labor forces from developing countries. A third major factor is a shift toward a knowledge economy, which entails the urgent need to train and equip "knowledge workers" with the necessary skills to operate in a dynamic and rapidly changing global environment (Hay Group, 2011; Oracle, 2012).

Benefits of talent management for the public sector

This section will discuss talent management's main benefits, including the ability to attract and empower staff in the public sector.

Attracting talented staff

The public sector is currently experiencing challenges in attracting talented staff due to budget cuts and rigid salary policies. Meanwhile, some critics argue that the strategies of talent management have the potential to attract and retain high-performing individuals and, as a result, mitigate the loss of long-term staff (Garrow & Hirsh, 2008; Poocharoen & Brillantes, 2013). These strategies involve promoting staff leadership and professional development opportunities, removing barriers in the hiring process, and creating long-term contracted positions for staff retention (Clarke & Scurry, 2017; Kock & Burke, 2008; Tafti et al., 2017). These strategies aim to create a more accessible and inclusive environment for staff, which also offers competitive benefits to attract new employees. Glenn (2012) further argues that marketing and branding are crucial in attracting public sector talent, as many candidates interested in public sector work often share the values of supporting the public. By adopting such talent management strategies, the public sector can implement policies that will attract new employees.

Empowering staff

In addition to attracting talented staff, talent management aims to support existing staff through fair and regular performance appraisals. In this regard, the concepts of "exclusive" and "inclusive" talent management are relevant in the public sector's approach to recognizing employees' performance (Sehatpour et al., 2022). This approach is usually exclusive to talent management in the public sector, where only high-performing employees are rewarded for their achievements through career progression (Gallardo-Gallardo et al., 2013). Alternatively, inclusive talent management views all employees as crucial to an organization's performance. Within the inclusive talent management approach, areas for development and support are identified for all staff, and rewards are achievable for all—not just high performers (Thunnissen & Buttiens, 2017). This inclusive approach is beneficial, as all employees become invested in the organization and undertake skill development to meet organizational aims. While inclusive talent management reflects the public sector's values of equal opportunity, Thunnissen and Buttiens (2017) find that most governments adopt a mixture of inclusive and exclusive talent management models. For example, in Malaysia, students are offered scholarships to various government programs regardless of their backgrounds, which represents an inclusive talent management approach. However, high-performing students are often given a greater choice in what areas of government they work in, and this is an exclusive form of talent management (Lawler, 2008).

In addition to talent management, Brown and Ryan (2003) argue that Human Resource Management (HRM) should be introduced in the public sector to boost career succession and employment conditions. HRM involves creating more flexible and decentralized processes that improve relationships among staff, managers, and supervisors (Gardner, 1993; Gardner & Palmer, 1997; Shim, 2001). Within HRM, there is also an emphasis on staff benefits, which are associated with staff retention and organizational sustainability (Brown, 2004, p. 307). Both talent management and HRM work to address the public sector's bureaucratic nature, which often creates systems that restrict innovative practices to encourage the movement and empowerment of staff (Kwon & Jang, 2022; Troshani et al., 2011). Talent management and HRM thus aim to implement strategies that ensure current staff can progress in their careers within the public sector.

Challenges for talent management in the GCC and MENA regions

To provide a clear picture of talent management challenges and opportunities in the MENA region, one must inevitably consider the intertwined structural, socioeconomic, and educational factors hindering the utilization of and investment in talent. While the GCC region enjoys abundant energy reserves, a strategic geographic location, and a generation below the age of 30 that comprises 60% of its population, most other countries in the MENA region are not endowed with such plentiful natural resources and struggle to enhance their performance in major economic indicators. For example, the UNDP Knowledge Development Report (2009) states that, "For nearly two and [a] half decades after 1980, the region witnessed hardly any economic growth." High unemployment rates, educational systems that fail to deliver quality programs, and a public sector that is the market's leading recruiter all constitute mounting long-term challenges that the region must take measures to address.

Talent management is strategically suited to play a vital role in the MENA region's economic progress (Abdulkarim, 2001). However, tackling it in the region goes beyond the boundaries of human resource departments and practices in public or private organizations to include government policies and strategies for youth education, training, formation, and integration into the market (Al Qershi et al., 2022). For years, talent management has been neglected by both corporations and governments, but in recent years it has taken on an added value as economic development programs have generally failed to produce tangible improvement in the wellbeing of people in the region. Talent management in the MENA region is thus a major structural and governmental issue, rather than simply an organizational and institutional one. Unlike member countries of the Organization for Economic Co-operation and Development (OECD) and other high-income countries where the challenge involves how to get the most from the "war for talent", the GCC and MENA countries still struggle with mounting socioeconomic and educational obstacles that prevent them from forming and training adequate talent pools that can be absorbed easily by their job markets.

In this respect, The Global Knowledge Index (GKI), offers a good picture of the quality of education and capacity of countries to develop research and ICT expertise (UNDP & MBRF, 2020). As shown in Table 7.1, only a handful of GCC states ranked highly in key GKI indicators in 2020. For example, the UAE topped the GCC and other MENA countries in overall GKI, ranking 15th globally, followed by Qatar at 39th. Saudi Arabia, meanwhile, ranked 42nd and Bahrain placed 43rd. Kuwait placed only 65th, and the MENA countries of Algeria, Syria, and Mauritania ranked 103rd, 130th, and 136th, respectively. In quality of pre-university education, the UAE again topped the region with a global ranking of 10th, followed by Bahrain (53rd) and Qatar (64th). Saudi Arabia placed lowest in the GCC region with a ranking of 104th. The lowest-ranking countries in the MENA region overall were Syria at 130th and Mauritania at 136th. Regarding quality of higher education, the UAE ranked 19th, followed by Qatar (24th) and Bahrain (54th). The UAE ranked 29th in research, development, and innovation, followed by Saudi Arabia (35th). Meanwhile, fellow GCC countries Kuwait and Bahrain ranked much lower at 90th and 92nd, respectively. The variation in rankings among GCC and MENA countries hints at the

Table 7.1 Rankings of GCC and MENA regions in key Global Knowledge Index indicators in 2020 *(out of 138 countries, 1= best performance, 141 = worst performance)

Country	Global knowledge index	Pre-university education	Technical and vocational education and training	Higher education	Research, development, and innovation	Information and communication technology
UAE	15	10	11	19	29	14
Kuwait	65	74	98	57	90	61
Bahrain	43	53	29	54	92	39
Qatar	39	64	49	24	39	34
Oman	58	81	81	83	60	46
Saudi Arabia	42	104	12	60	35	36
Lebanon	76	66	21	75	68	105
Syria	130	133	125	131	117	118
Jordan	79	110	85	50	75	73
Egypt	72	83	80	42	74	74
Morocco	83	100	86	85	82	75
Algeria	103	82	133	37	114	106
Tunisia	82	80	107	56	72	85
Mauritania	136	131	124	132	137	131

Source: UNDP & MBRF (2020) and World Bank Data Bank (2022)

challenges emanating from low quality of pre-university education, higher education, and technical and vocational education and training, which do not offer solid educational experiences to prepare students in the region for jobs in the private sector. This in turn reduces the chances of students landing jobs in the private sector, which requires skilled graduates equipped with the technical knowledge, critical thinking, and leadership skills needed to excel in the labor market (Crowley-Henry & Al Ariss, 2016).

Unemployment: Talent in waiting

Unemployment rates vary considerably among MENA and GCC countries. The MENA region has unemployment rates that are not only the highest worldwide, but also nearly double the world average of 6% (see Figure 7.1), with a growth rate 2.5 times faster than the global average between 2010 and 2021 (UNDP & MBRF, 2020). Despite MENA governments' persistent, yet ultimately ineffective, attempts to curtail rising unemployment rates, they only managed to reduce them by approximately 2% in the first decade of the 21st century, after which rates rose again from 2010 to 2021. In contrast, GCC countries have the lowest unemployment rates not only in the region, but in the world as well, as the oil sector's generous revenues subsidize other sectors and create job opportunities, thereby keeping rates around 5% (Razwan & Malik, 2021).

Talent management in the GCC 209

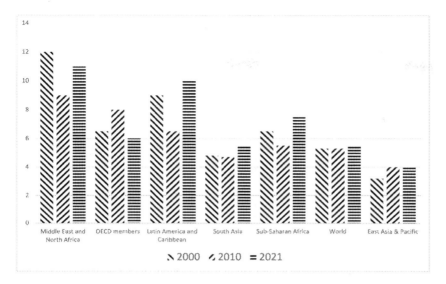

Figure 7.1 Unemployment rates around the world
Source: *Adapted from International Labor Organization (2020)*

Table 7.2 shows that total unemployment in the UAE was 2.4% in 2011, rising slightly to 3.19% in 2020. A similar trajectory was witnessed in Kuwait, rising from 2.2% in 2011 to 3.54% in 2020. On the other hand, Qatar possessed a significantly low unemployment rate of 0.5% in 2011, dropping even lower in 2020 to just 0.21%. Meanwhile, other MENA countries like Iraq, Tunisia, and Jordan topped the list of unemployment rates, ranging around 15.3%, 14%, and 13.4% in 2011, respectively. These figures changed slightly for Iraq, which achieved a total unemployment rate of 14.09% in 2020, while that in Tunisia spiked to 16.59%, and Jordan witnessed a jump to 19%. The cost of unemployment and inefficient use of talent in the MENA has reached around US$40 to 50 billion annually based on a study by McKinsey, which surveyed 1,500 employers and conducted 200 interviews. These losses resulted from governments' investment in education and preparation of individuals who then became unemployed after graduation or emigrated to other countries that offered better opportunities, thereby resulting in brain drain that further exacerbated the faltering economic development and growth of MENA countries.

The impact and magnitude of the brain drain phenomenon varies considerably between the GCC and overall MENA regions. Specifically, all GCC state lowered their brain drain rates, with the UAE dropping from 5.6% in 2011 to 2.2% in 2020. Similarly, Qatar fell from 5.7% in 2011 to 1.8% in 2020. However, rates of brain drain increased considerably in the other MENA countries, especially those with no significant natural

Table 7.2 Brain drain index and unemployment rates in the GCC and MENA regions

	Brain drain index		Total unemployment		Youth unemployment	
	2011 (1–7)	2020 (0–10)	2011	2020	2011	2020
UAE	5.6	2.2	2.4	3.19	6.3	9.01
Kuwait	5.4	3.3	2.2	3.54	23.3	19.37
Bahrain	4.7	3.1	15	1.78	20.7	7.97
Qatar	5.7	1.8	0.5	0.21	17	0.63
Oman	3.9	2.2	15	2.94	19.6	15.44
Saudi Arabia	4.6	3.6	10.8	7.45	25.9	28.17
Lebanon	---	5.9	13	13.3	22.1	27.43
Syria	2.3	8.4	8.3	10.26	18.3	25.24
Jordan	2.8	4.8	13.4	19.03	28.1	40.68
Iraq	---	6.8	15.3	14.09	43.5	27.16
Egypt	2.3	5.3	9.7	9.17	24.8	23.39
Libya	---	5.7	---	20.07	---	51.53
Morocco	3.1	7.6	9.8	11.45	17.6	26.58
Algeria	2.4	5.8	9.9	12.55	45.6	31.04
Tunisia	3.9	5.9	14	16.59	29.4	38.11
Mauritania	2.4	6.6	---	11.27	---	22.68
Sudan	---	8	---	19.65	---	35.78
Yemen	---	7	---	13.39	---	25.44

Source: World Bank Data Bank (2022), International Labor Organization (2020), and UNDP & MBRF (2020)

resources such as Egypt, which scored 2.3% in the brain drain index in 2011 and then 5.3% in 2020. Meanwhile, despite its abundant natural resources, Algeria had a brain drain rate of 2.4% in 2011, which increased to 5.8% in 2020. Jordan experienced brain drain of 2.8% in 2011, and this then rose to 4.8% in 2020, while Mauritania nearly tripled from 2.4% in 2011 to 6.6% in 2020 (see Table 7.2). The Global Competitiveness Report (World Economic Forum, 2012) found that the countries facing more challenges in retaining their talents were Lebanon and Egypt, and similar results were confirmed by the Bayt.com Middle East Salary Survey (2012) survey, which showed that 31% of individuals were ready to relocate to countries offering higher salaries and promising opportunities.

Education: Mismatch between market requirements and students' learning and skills

While MENA countries have significantly improved their literacy rates over the past two decades, the quality, contents, and applicability to market needs of their education systems remain questionable (Qari, 2013). More importantly, tertiary school enrollment stood at a meager rate of 41% in the MENA region in 2021 compared to 77% in OECD countries (World

Bank Data Bank, 2022). Businesses in the region also consistently complain about the inherent mismatch between skills required in the marketplace and the materials taught in public schools and universities.

This is because the educational systems prevalent in most MENA countries (and, to a lesser extent, in the GCC) do not effectively train or prepare students with the technical, personal, entrepreneurial, and analytical skills necessary for today's competitive world, and instead demand traditional rote memorization in order to pass tests (UNDP & MBRF, 2020). Numerous reports by international organizations have stressed the lack of practical skills taught in educational systems in the region. For example, the Arab Human Capital Challenge Report (MBRF & PricewaterhouseCoopers, 2007), based on 585 surveys among 18 Arab countries and interviews with over 40 prominent Arab senior executives, revealed crucial findings about employment and talent management in the region. Significantly, the report found that 54% of respondents claimed existing educational systems did not provide adequate skills to match the labor market's needs and expectations. Moreover, 97% of respondents in Jordan, 92% in Morocco, and 86% in Algeria all agreed that curricula were essentially based on theoretical rather than practical foundations, and were insufficient for preparing the workforce for the labor market. Moreover, the World Bank Enterprise Surveys found that many firms identified talents' lack of skills as a key stumbling block for recruitment in Lebanon (38%), Syria (36%), Jordan (33%), and Egypt (31%) (MBRF & PricewaterhouseCoopers, 2007).

Table 7.3 confirms the mismatch between graduates' skills acquired through educational systems in the region and their lack of preparation for the labor market. It also demonstrates that the performance of GCC and

Table 7.3 Rankings of GCC and MENA regions in key Global Knowledge Index indicators *(out of 138 countries, 1 = best ranking, 141 = worst ranking)

Country	Skillsets of graduates	Critical thinking in teaching	Ease of finding skilled employees
UAE	14	8	8
Kuwait	112	60	62
Bahrain	41	33	18
Qatar	8	6	3
Oman	40	15	46
Saudi Arabia	32	27	14
Lebanon	27	26	10
Jordan	69	37	24
Egypt	133	123	87
Morocco	117	121	94
Algeria	99	88	76
Tunisia	108	99	88
Mauritania	137	136	111

Source: *UNDP Arab Knowledge Development Report (2022)*

MENA countries varies considerably in the GKI, particularly in indices reflecting the graduates' skillsets and critical thinking capabilities. For example, in the skillsets of graduates indicator, the UAE is the highest-ranking country in the GCC and MENA regions with a global ranking of 14th, followed by Qatar (8th), Saudi Arabia (32nd), Oman (40th), and Bahrain (41st). Kuwait again placed lowest among all GCC states with a ranking of 112th. Razwan and Malik (2021) indicate that, although Kuwait spends the same amount on education per student as Finland, the quality of education and its impact on developing students' skills are drastically lower. Similarly, while Saudi Arabia spent 5.2% of its GDP on education compared to just 3.5% in high-income countries, Saudi students attained 7.8 years' worth of learning from their 12.4 years spent in classrooms (Razwan & Malik, 2021).

Meanwhile, the MENA countries of Egypt, Morocco, and Tunisia came in at 133rd, 117th, and 108th, respectively, thus testifying to the lack of adequate workforce equipped with the skillsets sought after by the labor market in the region. Similarly, in the index of critical thinking in teaching, Qatar ranked 6th globally, followed by the UAE at 8th, while Oman ranked 15th and Saudi Arabia placed 27th. Meanwhile, Egypt ranked 123rd and Morocco placed 121st in the MENA region, with Mauritania falling toward the bottom of the list at 136th. In ease of finding skilled employees, Kuwait was the GCC country where skilled employees were scarcest with a ranking of 62nd. By comparison, Qatar ranked 3rd and the UAE placed 8th among the easiest places to find skilled employees.

The low quality of educational programs naturally affects students' academic achievements in the GCC and MENA regions compared to other parts of the world. For example, the results of a World Bank study found that MENA students who participated in the Third International Mathematics and Sciences Studies (TIMSS) and the OECD Program for International Student Assessment (PISA) standard exams scored close to the bottom of the list among all participating countries (Salehi-Isfahani & Dhillon, 2008). In addition, the UNDP Knowledge Development Report (2009) compared test results between US and Arab students taking business administration tests. Table 7.4 shows that 26% of the students hailing from Arab countries participating in the tests scored "Poor" in comparison with only 15% of US students. Furthermore, 39% of US students scored "Good" compared to only 19% of those from Arab countries. Similarly, Boudarbat and Ajbilou (2007) report that, despite strenuous efforts made by the government of Morocco to improve the quality of its public sector education, the country remained the only one that did not meet the minimum acceptable participation rate in TIMSS examinations among eighth graders in 2007. Moreover, it had previously failed to meet the minimum requirements in 2003, particularly in math and science exams. This weakness in science and math is what principally forced students to major in the humanities, thereby missing the opportunity to pursue diverse fields of education that promise careers in the private sector.

Table 7.4 Comparison of results of tests in business administration

Grade category	Rating	Percentage of Arab country students %	Percentage of United States students %
120–130	Nil	15	0
131–140	Poor	26	15
1471–150	Fair	28	22
151–160	Good	19	39
161–170	Very Good	9	10
171–200	Excellent	3	14
Total		100	100

Source: *UNDP Knowledge Development Report (2009)*

The low performance of MENA students in these global indicators demonstrates the complex challenges for talent management in the region. Unlike the OECD and developed countries, where the main challenge involves determining how to attract talent to organizations and retain and develop them, the primary challenge for the private sector in the GCC and MENA regions involves finding adequately educated and trained employees with the essential skillsets for high performance in the job market. Since more than 70% of students with higher education degrees graduate in the humanities and social sciences in the GCC and MENA regions, many potential employees are rendered unattractive to the private sector. Their only alternative is thus to seek public sector jobs, which often offer lifetime employment and higher salary opportunities (Salehi-Isfahani & Dhillon, 2008).

Another critical element inhibiting the proper preparation and training of talent that has not been adequately researched or discussed involves teachers' skills and teaching methodologies. In this regard, Salehi-Isfahani and Dhillon (2008) have pointed to the socioeconomic characteristics of teachers in the region, who receive low salaries and insufficient or improper training, and may even use violence against students. Teachers constitute the backbone of the educational experience, and if they are not psychologically prepared to deliver such education, their impact on students will most likely be negative.

Finally, weak governance structures and the prevalence of nepotism, especially while attempting to access the job market, are talent issues that plague the MENA region. Although Islamic beliefs stress values like moderation, trustworthiness, accountability, and discipline (Eabrasu & Al Ariss, 2012), these values seem to be absent from the practices of managers working within organizations in the MENA region. For example, in a study based on fieldwork and extensive interviews, Al Ariss (2010) argues that merit is not necessarily the criterion that guarantees a job in the Lebanese market, and an analysis of the data demonstrates how religious affiliation and confessional diversity schemes play a significant role

214 *Importance of effective human resource development*

in securing a position. This obliges many talents to travel abroad for equal access to job opportunities that prioritize merit and qualifications rather than religious beliefs or connections.

National versus expatriate workforces in the GCC

The discovery of petroleum and the resultant accumulation of abundant revenues have dramatically changed the shape of GCC countries, demanding the urgent employment of expatriate employees to run their newly established institutions and organizations. As a result, since the late 1980s, Gulf countries have generally experienced an unprecedented wave of modern state construction. Nevertheless, since they lacked sufficient human capital possessing the necessary qualifications and skills to run those institutions, they have relied heavily on the expertise and knowledge of foreign consultants, experts, and advisors to fill this gap. At the same time, the GCC governments have generously invested in their citizens' education to improve local human capital resources in support of rapid economic growth.

In the meantime, GCC talents find it difficult to compete with the imported expatriate workforce, which often possesses the higher levels of education and professional experience desired by many public and private employers, supporting the GCC's development. Previous studies have confirmed that the private sector in the Middle East responds more positively to expatriate applicants than to nationals, since they generally cost less, work longer hours, and do not pose the same legal challenges to companies (Gardner, 1993). In terms of numbers, the Arab Labor Organization indicated in 2007 that the rate of the foreign labor force as a percentage of the total labor force in the UAE was 91.6%, 82.2% in Kuwait, and around 70% in other GCC countries. In the first quarter of 2020, these figures remained largely changed (see Figure 7.2). For Qatar, expatriates represented a staggering 95% of the labor force as compared to just 5% made up of locals, and the UAE followed close behind with 88% of its workforce comprised of expatriates versus just 12% being filled by locals.

Public sector as a dominant recruiter

Most graduates in the MENA region find the public sector to be a promising avenue for securing a lifetime career, especially considering their limited qualifications in the private sector. To meet its social contract obligations, the public sector absorbs as much talent as it can afford, thus raising the MENA region's percentage of government wages relative to GDP to around 9.8%, making it the highest in the world and well over the global average of 5.4% (IMF, 2022).

Meanwhile, the private sector in the MENA region does not provide sufficient incentives to recruit the best-performing talent, and thus risks losing it to other countries. Bayt.com, which runs the Middle East Salary Survey,

Talent management in the GCC 215

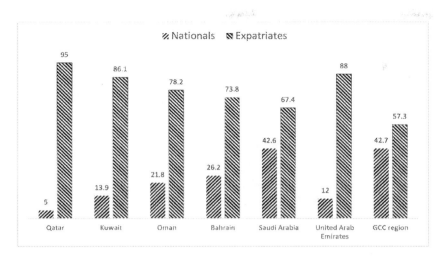

Figure 7.2 Percentage distribution of total employment by nationality in GCC countries (first quarter of 2020)
Source: *World Bank Data Bank (2022)*

found that 52% of surveyed employees were unsatisfied with their salaries and compensation packages, while 48% expressed only medium satisfaction. More importantly, only 35% believed the salary offered to men and women are equal in their company, and only 31% said that they were paid a raise in 2021. Regarding training opportunities, less than 10% of the survey respondents mentioned receiving any form of training (Bayt.com, 2022). In addition, various other factors encourage talent in the Arab world to opt for the public sector as the first employer of choice. Some of these factors include a better pay scale, more extended vacations, shorter working hours, lifelong job security, and regulations that make it difficult for employers to fire public servants. A careful examination of these factors indicates that the public sector perpetuates an environment of stagnation and a lack of motivation, development, or competition. An alarming finding of the 2020 Arab Youth Survey was that nearly half of young Arabs have considered leaving their home countries in search of better opportunities elsewhere in Europe, North America, or Gulf countries (Arab Youth Survey, 2020).

As a result, the public sector in GCC countries recruits nationals far more often than the private sector thanks to the benefits and rewards it provides, such as fewer working hours, lower expectations for productivity, and less focus on qualifications and merit. The Middle East Policy Council, for example, stated that in 2012, 72.3% of all public sector jobs in the Gulf were held by nationals, with ratios as high as 91.3% in Saudi Arabia, 90.8% in Bahrain, 80.5% in Oman, and 74.6% in Kuwait as cited in *MENA: The Great Job Rush 2012* (Al Masah Capital Limited, 2012). In

2021, these figures hardly changed for some countries, with the employment of nationals in the public sector ranging above 80% in Kuwait, Qatar, and the UAE, as opposed to 58% percent in Saudi Arabia, 43% in Oman, and 38% percent in Bahrain (The Economist, 2021).

Opportunities for talent management in the GCC and MENA regions

Economic growth and investment in talent creation

Despite its challenges, the MENA region enjoys abundant human and natural resources that can be invested effectively to propel development and growth (Abdulkarim, 2001). As of 2018, the region is home to more than 578 million people, 60% of whom are under the age of 30 (World Bank Data Bank, 2022). This vibrant, energetic, and youthful population can become the engine of economic prosperity in the region if their talent and potential are properly tapped. Specifically, to curb rising unemployment in parallel with increasing fertility rates, the World Bank estimates that the region needs to create more than 33 million jobs by 2030 (UNDP Knowledge Development Report, 2009). Furthermore, since around 60% of all global energy reserves are located within the MENA region (UNDP & MBRF, 2020) investing them in sustainable development projects will yield progressive results that can improve the overall performance of the region and employ both the unemployed and "waiting generations" (Dhillon & Yousef, 2009).

The Arab Youth Survey (2013) found that most Arab youth strongly believed that "the best days are ahead of us" (p. 7). This belief in a better future is crucial to empower, energize, and incentivize young people to give the best they can for themselves and their countries (ASDA'A Burson-Marsteller Arab Youth Survey, 2013). Job creation for such youth has become the main priority for governments in the MENA region, especially after the Arab Spring events that occurred in late 2010. The governments of Morocco, Tunisia, and Libya realized that they would eventually be voted out of power if they did not deliver on their promises to the people. Thus, they are strategizing to create jobs by empowering the development of small and medium-sized enterprises (SMEs), providing the necessary technical training for unemployed talents to facilitate their integration into the workforce, and providing them with micro-finance loans to establish small businesses. In this way, they will be able to nurture their skills and capitalize on their youth in preparation for becoming future entrepreneurs in the region. Saudi Arabia, for example, has considered the recent political turmoil and dedicated US$36 billion to job creation, benefits, and allowances for its jobless.

Gulf countries fully realize that investments in research and education are the key pillars for a successful transition into a knowledge economy. Thus, they are competing to build the necessary infrastructure to attract high talent globally and train and develop their local nationals. For instance, the government established the Qatar Foundation to "support Qatar on its journey from a carbon economy to a knowledge economy by unlocking human potential" (Qatar Foundation, 2022). The foundation invests massively in science, education, and research and has attracted top niche universities like Georgetown University, Carnegie Mellon, the University College London in Qatar, and others to create a vibrant, competitive, and innovative culture of serious scholarship in Qatar. Furthermore, hundreds of millions of US dollars are given yearly in grants to conduct scientific research in the region. In Dubai, the Mohammed Bin Rashid Al Maktoum Knowledge Foundation (MBRF) was established to create leaders with the talent, knowledge, and training to make a difference in the region. The foundation's mission is to "provide Arabs with opportunities to guide the region towards a knowledge economy through promoting entrepreneurship, research and innovation, enhancing access to quality education and professional development; and supporting the production, acquisition and dissemination of Arab knowledge sources" (MBRF, 2022). This is carried out by offering generous full scholarships for Arab students attending some of the most prestigious universities worldwide, training teachers on delivering quality education, and supporting research on and translation of notable books. Saudi Arabia has pursued a similar path by establishing the world's largest "economic city" at the cost of US$86 billion. The city is intended to become a hub of research, commerce, and environmentally friendly industry, providing more than one million jobs (SAGIA, 2013).

Gulf countries are also diversifying their economies to rely less on natural resources and to nurture the talents and skills of their people by exposing them to new market opportunities. There is thus a growing shift away from traditional channels of job creation in the region toward the provision of incentives for the private sector to create and provide jobs. Governments are also increasingly attempting to reform investment policies, facilitate business startups by young entrepreneurs, and enhance ease of doing business to attract FDI.

Nationalization as a policy to manage and empower nationals' talent: The UAE as a successful case

"Nationalization" processes are typically a response to the challenges posed by waves of globalization and the increasingly easy movement of goods and human capital from one place to another. Abdulkarim (2001) defines what nationalization means: "a multilevel process through which dependency on the expatriate labor force is reduced and nationals are prepared to take up jobs performed by expatriates. Such preparation entails enabling nationals to perform their jobs equally as [well], if not better, than expatriates in the shortest possible period" (p. 38).

"Emiratization", on the other hand, is an example of an interventionist approach that governments in the GCC region take to protect access to jobs among their local workforces, and represents one of the most successful experiences of workforce nationalization in the Gulf region (Abdulkarim, 2001). The main purpose of the Emiratization policy is to reduce the UAE's dependence on expatriate workers and enhance national participation in the workforce (Wilkins, 2001). In addition to its main function of enforcing recruitment of Emiratis, the Emiratization policy plays a role in protecting and sustaining the national identity of working Emiratis in the face of rising globalization, the integration of economies and information technologies, and the trend of spreading globalized cultures. To do this, the National Human Resource Development and Employment Authority (*Tanmia*) has been established mainly to address issues related to the nationalization of the UAE's workforce, recommend appropriate policy options to the government, and assist Emiratis in matching their skills to appropriate jobs. The emphasis on nationalization in the UAE (Emiratization) results from "serious thinking and careful policymaking that sets targets with a long-term vision" (Gulf News, 2004).

The government of the UAE announced 2013 as a year of Emiratization to further strengthen the foundations of this policy, thus demonstrating the government's willingness to gradually decrease dependence on expatriates and start building homegrown national expertise. In a decade or two, the UAE's vision is to achieve further milestones in enabling local talents, training them, and qualifying them to hold challenging and leading roles in the public and private sectors. However, to fully benefit from the experiences of a foreign labor force, it is in the best interest of the UAE's government to intensify the implementation of knowledge management (KM) programs and tools. This will allow a smooth transfer of knowledge to the national workforce and enable them to learn from the expertise of expatriates more effectively. Furthermore, to better enforce Emiratization, the UAE government introduced a new policy in 2022 that required private entities to increase their Emiratization rates annually by a minimum of 2% or face a monthly fine of 6,000 AED (US$1,600) (Khaleej Times, 2022).

Recommendations and conclusions

Curbing unemployment rates by reinvigorating the private sector's role in the economy

Among the challenges faced by the MENA region, unemployment is a universal phenomenon requiring scrupulous policymaking that identifies the impacts of education, society, and the private sector on the labor force. Given that the region has the highest unemployment rates in the world, in addition to the challenges associated with creating 33 million jobs by 2030, the implementation of carefully designed and well-informed policies to trigger economic growth is a must for MENA governments, especially considering the new tribulations of COVID-19 and geopolitical risks in the region.

Job creation must therefore be a burning priority for the MENA region in the short and medium term to mitigate the losses incurred by governments due to departure or underutilization of talent. However, in doing so, traditional channels of recruitment through public sector agencies and entities should be avoided to curtail the burden of heavy public spending that consumes substantial portions of the region's GDP.

Diversifying the economy, establishing a business-friendly environment, attracting FDI, and providing micro-finance possibilities for youth should also be fostered by governments in the MENA region. Furthermore, supporting a culture of entrepreneurship and SME creation is another path toward unlocking young talent and allowing them to be potential recruiters rather than job seekers in the market. Since the region's political uprisings in late 2010, various governmental and non-governmental organizations have provided significant support to young people, facilitating micro-finance loans and offering training sessions on entrepreneurship.

GCC countries, meanwhile, should focus on the proper training and education of their national workforces before they can expect to see the fruits of nationalization policies. The expatriate workforce is still essential for the region's economic growth, and implementing KM tools and mechanisms is thus critical to guarantee the effective transfer of knowledge and knowhow from expatriates to nationals.

Reforming educational programs and policies

Furthermore, educational systems and policies must be revisited and redesigned to align them with job market needs. New educational systems that rely on critical thinking, quantitative methods, communication skills, problem-solving, teamwork, and entrepreneurial skills need to be introduced to schooling systems in the MENA and GCC regions.

Moreover, students must be acclimatized to the working environment before they graduate via internship programs, which must become a mandatory component of their learning experience. Selection of a specific educational stream should emanate from the students' interests, who should be fully supported through proper advice and guidance well before high school so that they may better know what career path they wish to take and the best academic programs to lead them there.

On the other hand, educational policies must also stress the introduction of international best practices in developing curricula, implementing educational programs, and training teachers to deliver them adequately. Moreover, government policies should clearly indicate the importance of updating textbooks, teaching materials, and methodologies to cope with dynamic and changing job market requirements. Continuous training and support for teachers should also be emphasized through clear government policies that articulate the hours needed for training and what aspects they should focus on.

Implementing talent management programs

Finally, public and private organizations that have effectively running talent management departments naturally outperform those that do not. Hence, government policies should emphasize the need to manage talent effectively and adequately by making talent management departments an integral part of organizational charts.

References

Abdulkarim, A. (2001). The UAE Labor Market and the Problem of Employment of Nationals: The Need for Intervention in A. Abdelkarim (ed.), *Employment and Employability in a Small Oil Economy—The UAE*, Shaker Publishing, Maastricht.

Aguirre, D., Hewlett, S., & Post, L. (2009). Global talent innovation: Strategies for breakthrough performance [report], Booz and Company, San Francisco, pp. 1–25.

Al Ariss, A., Cascio, W., & Paauwe, J. (2014). Talent management: Current theories and future research directions. *Journal of World Business*, 49(2), 173–179.

Al Ariss, A. (2010). Religious Diversity in Lebanon: Lessons from a Small Country to the Global World in M. Ozbilgin & J. Seyed (Ed), *Managing Cultural Diversity in Asia: A Research Companion*, Edward Elgar Publishing, New York, pp. 56–72.

Al Qershi, N., Thurasamy, R., Ali, G., Al-Rejal, H., Al-Ganad, A., & Frhan, E. (2022). The effect of talent management and human capital on sustainable business performance: An empirical investigation in Malaysian hospitals. *International Journal of Ethics and Systems*, 38(2), 316–337.

Al Masah Capital Limited. (2012). MENA–The great job rush–the unemployment ticking time bomb and how to fix it. Retrieved from: www.scribd.com/document/93683064/MENA-The-Great-Job-Rush-The-Unemployment-Ticking-Time-Bomb-and-How-to-Fix-It-3-JULY-2011 Accessed on 8 September 2022.

Arab Youth Survey. (2013). Retrieved from: http://arabyouthsurvey.com/en/whitepaper/2013/ Accessed on 4 September 2022.

Arab Youth Survey. (2020). Retrieved from: https://arab.org/blog/arab-youth-survery-2020/ Accessed on 4 September 2022.

ASDA'A Burson-Marsteller Arab Youth Survey. (2013). Retrieved from: http://arabyouthsurvey.com/wp-content/uploads/2013/04/AYS-2013-Brochure-White-Paper-Design-ARTWORK-REV.pdf Accessed September 2021.

Ashton, C., & Morton, L. (2005). Managing talent for competitive advantage. *Strategic HR Review*, 4(5), 28–31.

Athey, R. (2008). It's 2008: do you know where your talent is? Connecting people to what matters. *Journal of Business Strategy*, 29(4), 4–14.

Bayt.com. (2012). Retrieved from: www.bayt.com Accessed on 7 September 2022.

Bayt.com. (2022). Retrieved from: www.bayt.com Accessed on 7 September 2022.

Beatty, R., & Becker, B. (2005). "A players" or "A positions"? The strategic logic of workforce management. *Harvard Business Review*, (December), 110–117.

Becker, B., & Huselid, M. (2006). Strategic talent management: Where do we go from here? *Journal of Management* 32(6), 898–925.

Beechler, S., & Woodward, I. (2009). The global "war for talent". *Journal of International Management*, 15(3), 273–285.
Biygautane, M., & Al Yahya, K. (2010). Knowledge management in Dubai's public sector: Opportunities and challenges. Policy Brief no. 27, published by the Dubai School of Government.
Boudreau, J., & Ramstad, P. (2005). Talentship, talent segmentation and sustainability: A new HR decision science paradigm for a new strategy definition. *Human Resource Management*, 44(2), 129–136.
Boudreau, J., & Ramstad, P. (2007). *Beyond HR: The New Science of Human Capital*. Harvard Business School Press, Boston.
Boudarbat, B., & Ajbilou, A. (2007). Youth exclusion in morocco: Context, consequences, and policies, middle east youth initiative working paper no. 5, Wolfensohn Center for Development at Brookings and Dubai School of Government, Washington, DC and Dubai.
Brown, K., & Ryan, N. (2003). Redefining government–community relations through service agreements. *Journal of Contemporary Issues in Business and Government*, 9(1), 21–30.
Brown, K. (2004). Human resource management in the public sector. *Public Management Review*, 6(3), 303–309.
Cappelli, P. (2008a). Talent management for the twenty-first century. *Harvard Business Review*, 74–81.
Cappelli, P. (2008b). *Talent on demand*. Harvard Business School Press, Boston.
Chambers, E., Foulon, M., Handfield-Jones, H., Hankin, S., & Michaels, E. (1998). The war for talent. *The McKinsey Quarterly*, 3(3), 1–8.
Clarke, M., & Scurry, T. (2017). The role of the psychological contract in shaping graduate experiences: A study of public sector talent management programmes in the UK and australia. *The International Journal of Human Resource Management*, 29(13), 2054–2079.
Collings, D., & Mellahi, K. (2009). Strategic talent management: A review and research agenda. *Human Resource Management Review*, 19(4), 304–313.
Creelman, D. (2004). *Return on Investment in Talent Management: Measures You Can Put to Work Right Now*, Human Capital Institute, Washington, DC.
Crowley-Henry, M., & Al Ariss, A. (2016). Talent management of skilled migrants: Propositions and an agenda for future research. *The International Journal of Human Resource Management*, 29(13), 2054–2079.
Dhillon, N., & Yousef, T. (2009). *Generation in Waiting: The Unfulfilled Promise of Young People in the Middle East*, Brookings Institution Press, Washington DC.
Dougherty, G., & Van Gelder, M. (2015). Public agency hiring, minimum qualifications, and experience. *Review of Public Personnel Administration*, 35(2), 169–92.
Eabrasu, M., & Al Ariss, A. (2012). Socially Responsible Employee Management Case Studies from Saudi Arabia and Lebanon in D. Jamali & Y. Sidani (eds.), *CSR in the Middle East*, Palgrave and Macmillan, Hampshire, pp. 93–113.
Farley, C. (2005). HR's role in talent management and driving business results. *Wiley Periodicals*, pp. 55–61.
Farndale, E., Scullion, H., & Sparrow, P. (2010). The role of corporate HR function in global talent management. *Journal of World Business*, 45, 161–168.
Faust, C. (2008). State of the global talent nation report 2008: organizations' struggle to prepare workforces to meet growth demands. Retrieved from: www.softscape.com
Gallardo-Gallardo, E., Dries, N., & González-Cruz, T. (2013). What is the meaning of "talent" in the world of work? *Human Resource Management Review*, 23(4), 290–300.

Gardner, M., & Palmer, G. (1997). *Employment Relations: Industrial Relations and Human Resource Management in Australia* (2nd edn), Macmillan, Melbourne.

Gardner, M. (1993). Introduction in M. Gardner (ed.), *Human Resource Management and Industrial Relations in the Public Sector*, Macmillan, Melbourne.

Garrow, V., & Hirsh, W. (2008). Talent management: Issues of focus and fit. *Public Personnel Management*, 37(4), 389–402.

Glenn, T. (2012). The state of talent management in canada's public sector. *Canadian Public Administration*, 55(1), 25–51.

Gulf News. (2004). Tanmia Report: Call for strong push towards emiratisation. Retrieved from: https://gulfnews.com/uae/tanmia-report-call-for-strong-push-towards-emiratisation-1.316166. Accessed on 23 january 2023.

Guthridge, M., & Komm, A. (2008). Why multinationals struggle to manage talent. *The McKinsey Quarterly*, 1–5.

Hay Group. (2011). Mind the Talent Gap. Retrieved from: http://infokf.kornferry.com/rs/494-VUC-482/images/Mind%20the%20gap%20viewpoint.pdf Accessed on 13 December 2021.

International Labor Organization. (2020). Retrieved from: www.ilo.org/global/lang--en/index.htm Accessed on 10 September 2022.

IMF. (2022). Retrieved from: www.imf.org Accessed on 10 September 2022

Kafetzopoulos, D., Psomas, E., & Bouranta, N. (2022). The influence of leadership on strategic flexibility and business performance: The mediating role of talent management. *Management Decision*, 60(9), 2532–2551.

Khaleej Times. (2022). UAE: Firms that do not comply with 2% Emiratisation rule must pay Dh6,000 monthly for every unemployed citizen. Retrieved from: www.khaleejtimes.com/government/uae-companies-defying-emiratisation-rule-to-pay-dh6000-monthly-for-every-unemployed-citizen Accessed on 30 July 2022.

Kock, R., & Burke, M. (2008). Managing talent in the south african public service. *Public Personnel Management*, 37(4), 457–470.

Kravariti, F., & Johnston, K. (2020). Talent management: A critical literature review and research agenda for public sector human resource management. *Public Management Review*, 22(1), 75–95.

Kumari, P., & Bahuguna, P. (2012). Measuring the impact of talent management on employee behaviour: An empirical study of oil and gas industry in India. *Journal of Human Resource Management* 2(2), 65–85.

Kwon, K., & Jang, S. (2022). There is no good war for talent: A critical review of the literature on talent management. *Employee Relations*, 44(1), 94–120.

Lane, K., & Pollner, F. (2008). How to address China's growing talent shortage. *McKinsey Quarterly*, (3), 33–40.

Lawler, E. (2008). Strategic talent management: Lessons from the corporate world. *Strategic Management of Human Capital*, pp. 1–34.

Lewis, R., & Heckman, R. (2006). Talent Management: A critical review. *Human Resource Management*, 16(2), 139–154.

Makram, H., Sparrow, P., & Greasley, K. (2017). How do strategic actors think about the value of talent management? Moving from talent practice to the practice of talent. *Journal of Organizational Effectiveness: People and Performance*, 4(4), 259–378.

MBRF. (2022). Retrieved from https://mbrf.ae/en Accessed on 5 September 2022.

MBRF & PricewaterhouseCoopers. (2007). The arab human capital challenge. Retrieved from: www.pwc.com/m1/en/publications/abir/ahccenglishfeb172009.pdf Accessed on 7 September 2022.

Mellahi, K., & Collings, D. (2010). The barriers to effective global talent management: The example of corporate elites in MNEs. *Journal of World Business*, 45(2), 143–149.

Meyers, M., & Van Woerkom, M. (2014). The influence of underlying philosophies on talent management: Theory, implications for practice, and research agenda. *Journal of World Business*, 49(2), 192–203.

Michaels, E., & Handfield-Jones, H. (2001). *The War for Talent*. Harvard Business School Press, Brighton.

Mujtaba, M., Mubarik, M., & Soomro, K. (2022). Measuring talent management: A proposed construct. *Employee Relations*, 44(5), 1192–1215.

Oracle. (2012). The future of talent management: Underlying drivers of change [report]. Oracle Taleo Cloud Service, pp. 1–20.

Phillips, P., & Phillips, J. (2019). The state of human capital analytics in developing countries: A focus on the Middle East. *Strategic HR Review*, 18(5), 190–198.

Poocharoen, O., & Brillantes, A. (2013). Meritocracy in asia pacific: Status, issues, and challenges. *Review of Public Personnel Administration*, 33(2), 140–163.

Qari, R. (2013). How to capitalize on human capital. *Endeavor Insight*, pp. 5–19.

Qatar Foundation. (2022). Retrieved from: www.qf.org.qa/ Accessed on 7 September 2022.

Razwan, I., & Malik, I. (2021). Tackling the public sector wage bill in the GCC. Retrieved from: https://blogs.worldbank.org/governance/tackling-public-sector-wage-bill-gcc Accessed on 30 July 2022.

SAGIA. (2013). www.sagia.sa Accessed on 15 September 2021.

Salehi-Isfahani, D., & Dhillon, N. (2008). Stalled youth transitions in the middle east: A framework for policy reform, the middle east youth initiative working paper. Retrieved from: www.researchgate.net/profile/Djavad-Salehi-Isfahani/publication/228236497_Stalled_Youth_Transitions_in_the_Middle_East_A_Framework_for_Policy_Reform/links/5badfdce45851574f7ec3f6d/Stalled-Youth-Transitions-in-the-Middle-East-A-Framework-for-Policy-Reform.pdf Accessed on 7 September 2022.

Schuler, R., Jackson, S., & Tarique, I. (2011). Global talent management and global talent challenges: Strategic opportunities for IHRM. *Journal of World Business*, 46(4), 506–516.

Schweyer, A. (2004). *Talent Management Systems: Best Practices in Technology Solutions for Recruitment, Retention and Workforce Planning*, Tri-Graphic Printing, Toronto, Canada.

Scullion, H., Collings, D., & Gunnigle, P. (2007). International HMR in the 21st century: Emerging themes and contemporary debates. *Human Resource Management*, 17(4), 309–319.

Sehatpour, M.-H., Abedin, B., & Kazemi, A. (2022). Talent management in government organizations: Identification of challenges and ranking the solutions to address them. *International Journal of Productivity and Performance Management*, 71(4), 14–44.

Shaw, R. (2012). New Public Management in Australia: Past, Present and Future, *Pouvoirs*, 142(2), 117–132.

Shim, D. (2001). Recent Human Resources Developments in OECD Member Countries. *Public Personnel Management*, 30(3), 323–47.

Shulga, L., & Busser, J. (2019). Talent management meta review: A validity network schema approach. *International Journal of Contemporary Hospitality Management*, 31(10), 3943–3969.

Singh, A., Jones, D., & Hall, N. (2012). Talent management: A research-based case study in the GCC region. *International Journal of Business and Management* 7(24), 94–107.

Sparrow, P., Brewster, C., & Harris, H. (2004). *Globalizing Human Resource Management*, Routledge, London, UK.

Stahl, G., Bjorkman, I., Farndale, E., Morris, S., Paauwe, J., Stiles, P., Trevor, J., & Wright, P. (2007). Global talent management: How leading multinationals build and sustain their talent pipeline. *INSEAD*, pp. 2–34.

Tafti, M., Mahmoudsalehi, M., & Amiri, M. (2017). Critical success factors, challenges and obstacles in talent management. *Industrial and Commercial Training*, 49(1), 15–21.

Tarique, I., & Schuler, R. (2010). Global talent management: Literature review, integrative framework, and suggestion for further research. *Journal of World Business*, (45), 122–133.

The Economist. (2021). Gulf states are trying to increase private employment. Retrieved from: www.economist.com/middle-east-and-africa/2021/10/07/gulf-states-are-trying-to-increase-private-employment Accessed on 29 July 2022.

Thunnissen, M., & Buttiens, D. (2017). Talent management in public sector organizations: A study on the impact of contextual factors on the TM approach in flemish and dutch public sector organizations. *Public Personnel Management*, 46(2), 391–418.

Tlaiss, H. (2021). Exploring talent management in practice: An Arab country-specific empirical investigation. *Employee Relations*, 43(1), 63–81.

Troshani, I., Jerram, C., & Hill, S. (2011). Exploring the public sector adoption of HRIS. *Industrial Management and Data Systems*, 111(3), 470–488.

UNDP. (2002). *Human Development Report 2002: Deepening Democracy in a Fragmented World*. Retrieved from: http://hdr.undp.org/en/content/human-deve lopment-report-2002 Accessed on 26 November 2021.

UNDP & MBRF. (2020). Global knowledge index 2020. Retrieved from: https://www.undp.org/publications/global-knowledge-index-2020. Accessed on 30 July 2022.

UNDP Knowledge development report. (2009). Fertility Rates [online]. Retrieved from: www.un.org/en/development/desa/population/publications/dataset/fertil ity/data.asp Accessed on 20 July 2022.

UNDP Arab Knowledge Development Report. (2022). Middle East and North Africa: Addressing highest rates of youth unemployment in the world. Retrieved from: https://news.un.org/en/story/2022/05/1118842 Accessed on 10 July 2022.

Vecchi, A., Della, B., Feola, R., & Crudele, C. (2021). Talent management processes and outcomes in a virtual organization. *Business Process Management Journal*, 27(7), 1937–1965.

World Bank Data Bank. (2022). Retrieved from: www.worldbank.org Accessed on 8 September 2022.

World Economic Forum. (2012). The global competitiveness report 2012–2013. Retrieved from: www3.weforum.org/docs/WEF_GlobalCompetitivenessRepo rt_2012-13.pdf Accessed on 8 September 2022.

Wilkins, S. (2001). Student and employer perceptions British higher education in the Arabian Gulf region. *Research in Post-Compulsory Education,* 6(2):157–174.

8 The impact of training on public sector organizations

Insights from the United Arab Emirates

Introduction

In the 21st century, it has become increasingly clear that governments are under considerable pressure to undertake institutional, economic, and operational reforms. Competition among countries and organizations is no longer determined by ownership of abundant natural or financial resources, but by acquiring ever-more innovative and creative ideas that can facilitate the transition to knowledge-based economies (Powell & Snellman, 2004). To maintain competitiveness within such a rapidly changing environment, public organizations are finding themselves compelled to engage in training programs to equip their employees with the necessary skills that would allow them to enhance public service quality. However, as argued by Seidle et al. (2016, p. 611), budget and debt crises continue to exact a heavy toll on governments worldwide, and thus the use of training in the public sector may be expected to decline. Nevertheless, many researchers have argued that public organizations should maintain training programs to improve government efficacy and reap the myriad benefits of well-trained organizations (Mohabbat & Islam, 2014; Poor & Plesoianu, 2010; Tawalare & Laishram, 2019; Zumrah, 2015a).

Several public management scholars have therefore called for exploration of how training and professional development programs can affect the quality of public sector services (Zumrah, 2013; 2015b). In this context, training refers to a structured and carefully designed approach to teaching individual employees, teams, and sometimes entire organizations the necessary skills to perform their roles (Goldstein & Ford, 2002; Zumrah, 2015b). Existing research examining the relationship between training programs and organizational performance has focused heavily on private sector organizations, and thus a gap exists in the current scholarly literature, which has yet to delve into the impact of training on public sector organizations and the factors that can enhance the quality of such programs.

This chapter responds to these calls for research on training and its effects on public sector organizations by analyzing the case study of Dubai in the United Arab Emirates (UAE) and how its public sector designs training programs and strategies, as well as their resultant impact on public

DOI: 10.4324/9781003267744-11

service quality. The Dubai government has realized that introducing and implementing new managerial models can enhance customer satisfaction with the services provided by its public sector entities. As a result, Dubai public sector entities have shifted from traditional bureaucratic administration models toward more managerial and result-oriented ones, and have therefore relied heavily on training their public sector employees to develop the managerial skills necessary to effectively administer public sector organizations.

The aims of this chapter are twofold. First, it explores the impact of effective training programs on organizational performance in the public sector. Second, it identifies the critical requirements for developing efficacious strategies that can lead to successful training programs. The analysis is based on primary data gathered from public sector entities in Dubai. To start, 17 semi-structured and in-depth interviews were conducted with human resources and training directors from public sector entities in Dubai, and a survey instrument was then developed and sent out to all public organizations in the Emirate. Out of the 60 surveys sent, 49 were completed and returned, representing an effective response rate of 81%. Surveyed and interviewed organizations included the Dubai Executive Council, Dubai Electricity and Water Authority (DEWA), Dubai Economic Department, Dubai Chamber of Commerce and Industry, Dubai Public Prosecution, Dubai Department of Tourism, Dubai Health Authority, Dubai Municipality, Dubai Statistics Center, Dubai Media Office, Dubai Customs, Dubai Land Department, Dubai Airports, Dubai Corporation for Ambulance Services, Dubai Culture & Arts Authority, Road & Transport Authority (RTA), Knowledge and Human Development Authority (KHDA), and the Mohammed Bin Rashid Housing Establishment (MBRHE).

This chapter is organized as follows. First, a literature review section explores the benefits of training in the public sector, enumerates the various training programs, identifies the requirements to make them effective, and describes the impact of such strategies and practices on the public sector. That section is followed by the fieldwork findings, which reveal the current state of training in Dubai's public sector, the role of effective training strategies in achieving outcomes, and the influence of training programs on organizational performance. A recommendation section then concludes the chapter with several solutions that the Dubai government could adopt to enhance the quality of its training programs.

Literature review

Benefits of training in the public sector

Enhancing employee performance

Up to the present, academic and scholarly research has established a positive correlation between training and development programs and improved employee performance, job satisfaction, and growth within organizations

(Aguinis & Kraiger, 2009; Saastamoinen et al., 2017). For example, Frayne and Geringer (2000) administered a self-management training program to 30 salespeople in the life insurance business that included classroom-style lectures, small group discussions, and case studies, and found that those who participated exhibited greater performance, such as increased sales and enhanced confidence in fulfilling their duties. Other researchers have argued that training can increase employee motivation and passion for work (Collins & Holton, 2004; Day, 2000). For example, Dvir et al. (2002, p. 739) analyzed cadets' performance in the Israel Defense Forces after group leaders had received "transformational leadership training", which involved developing leaders' ideas into achievable outcomes and focused on team engagement. Research demonstrates that leadership training improved the participants' capacity to perform tasks confidently and embody their organization's moral values (Chawla & Joshi, 2010; Dvir et al., 2002, p. 740; Gilley et al., 2009; Hooijberg & Choi, 2001; Mau, 2019; Meaklim & Sims, 2011).

Organizational growth

Several studies have explored the positive impact training has on organizational growth. For example, Aragón-Sánchez et al. (2003) explored the relationship between training and performance in organizations by surveying 457 businesses across the UK, the Netherlands, Portugal, Finland, and Spain. Certain training types, such as on-the-job training, were positively related to organizational effectiveness and profitability (Aragón-Sánchez et al., 2003).

Types of training

Classroom education

Among the various training and development methods, researchers have found that classroom education is the most common (Conger & Benjamin, 1999). Education in the classroom is simple to implement and requires few resources, as one person can teach many employees in a single session. Conversely, some critics have argued that traditional classroom education can be challenging for individuals (Bass & Vaughan, 1966; Dotlich & Noel, 1998). To mitigate this, Day (2000) asserts that a combination of training strategies should be used to yield the best results. Individuals learn differently, and providing a mixture of innovative strategies, such as traditional lectures combined with one-on-one mentoring, can be more effective (Towler & Dipboye, 2001).

Coaching and mentoring

Due to the limitations of traditional classroom education, coaching has arisen as a preferred strategy for training individuals. For example, Smither et al. (2003, p. 39) surveyed 1,361 senior managers in a large global corporation and found that coaching enabled managers to set more defined goals that they could then update and refine easily (Chun & Rainey, 2005). Furthermore, researchers have also linked coaching with greater job performance, salary growth, career advancement, and employee satisfaction (Allen & Poteet, 1999).

Technology-delivered instruction

Technology-delivered instruction (TDI) is also becoming increasingly popular in the private sector and is being adapted for public agencies (Paradise, 2007). TDI involves digitally based training videos and programs that can be viewed on computers, with training questions, or accessed via other technological devices (Aguinis, 2009; Ali & Magalhaes, 2008). This digital approach to training is highly accessible, as it enables individuals to choose their preferred platforms and times to participate in training activities. However, Noe (2008) notes that TDI also has the potential to be ineffective if individuals struggle with the training material, as it may be used in asynchronous learning environments. Similarly, DeRouin et al. (2004) found that low-ability or inexperienced learners might make poor decisions about what and how to learn without the guidance of a class instructor or mentor. Furthermore, a study by Kraiger and Jerden (2007) revealed that TDI has only a marginally positive impact on learning, while Bell and Kozlowski (2002) state that independent learning through technology should always be accompanied by guidance. For example, managers and leaders could select specific TDI activities for employees to participate in based on consultations to determine what skills they need to develop or competency gaps they need to address (Mau, 2019; Ulrich & Lake, 1990).

Personal experience and professional feedback

The field of human resource management has continuously focused on the role of individual employees in determining the overall performance of their organizations. Concentrating on the micro-level of performance allows human resource managers to identify the strengths and weaknesses of their most valuable human resources and develop them to enhance their output. Training programs offering trainees the chance to receive adequate constructive feedback and have their performance evaluated tend to lead to more positive outcomes (Smither et al., 2005).

Lived experience and personal hardship can also be seen as effective mechanisms that initiate learning. Career-defining moments, such as layoffs, downsizing, or conflict in the workplace, can increase an individual's resilience or knowledge of their job; however, replicating this experience of dealing with workplace-related hardships is a challenge when teaching and administering a training program, as it something that occurs spontaneously throughout a person's career (Moxley & Pulley, 2004; Seidle et al., 2016, p. 605). Conversely, feedback can be given to individuals through classroom education, mentoring, and other workshops. Researchers have highlighted that professional feedback has been found to improve the self-awareness and confidence of individuals initially lacking these qualities, in contrast to leaders, who already demonstrate self-awareness and thus do not require as much (Atwater et al., 2007). Furthermore, feedback can be provided in training or by managers, supervisors, and colleagues in the everyday work environment (Seidle et al., 2016, p. 605).

Requirements for effective training programs in the public sector

A significant body of literature has discussed why training programs do not always lead to their desired outcomes, and numerous studies argue that such programs fail to achieve their expected results due to the failure to target specific objectives in their design (Bartlett & Rodgers, 2004). Healy (2001), for example, found that various training programs were offered at government organizations, yet proved ineffective because they were theoretical and broad in scope rather than directed toward achieving clear-cut goals. These programs were not responsive to the needs of employees, since there was no prior identification of training needs within the organization and no coordination among the various stakeholders to identify organizational weaknesses needing to be remedied.

As a result, significant financial resources, time, and effort were invested in training programs that were poorly designed, inefficient, and lacking a preliminary training needs analysis to identify shortfalls in the knowledge and experience of participants. Ultimately, training effectiveness depends upon numerous interwoven factors that can improve employees' managerial, professional, and personal skills in a particular institution, eventually leading to enhanced performance and productivity (Malik & Lenka, 2020; Tracey & Tews, 1995). In this regard, Kirkpatrick (1967) has argued that the effectiveness of training programs can be assessed by examining four dimensions: 1) the reaction of trainees to program content, 2) the acquisition of new knowledge and skills, 3) changes in employee behavior, and 4) concrete and tangible improvement in employees' organizational loyalty and productivity.

The motivation to undergo training is also one of the most significant components in this respect, and has proven to be significant in improving an organization's working environment and training outcomes (Tracey et al., 2001). Motivation for training thus plays a crucial role in determining the overall effectiveness of any training program (Hill & Lent, 2006). For example, Campbell (1988) has argued that there is a strong relationship between trainee motivation and training effectiveness, stressing that researchers and practitioners should address and study the "individual and situational" factors impacting trainees' motivation and interest in attending training programs offered within their organizations or at training institutions. Noe (1986) has further stated that training's effectiveness improves significantly if its strategies target the enhancement of the trainees' recognition of its significance for their personal and career development. Enhanced trainee motivation is thus dependent on the following three factors: (1) whether they believe that high effort will result in higher performance in training, (2) whether they are convinced that high performance in training will ultimately lead to better job performance, and (3) whether such high job performance is linked to opportunities for promotion and achievement of personal and organizational growth (Noe, 1986; Stuart & Binsted, 1979).

Measuring and evaluating training effectiveness

The evaluation of training programs and to what extent they have succeeded or failed in bringing about desired changes within an organization is essential (Cappelli et al., 2011). It can be measured by the four factors outlined by McCourt and Sola (1999): 1) the immediate reaction of participants in a training session and whether they felt that the training helped strengthen any knowledge or skill gaps they previously had, 2) the lessons learned from the training and whether they advanced their knowledge about their areas of specialization and acquired new skills, 3) any changes in participants' behavior in identifying and solving problems, and 4) the training program's impact on the organization's overall performance—which can sometimes be much more difficult to evaluate and assess (Kraiger, 2002). Measurement of these four dimensions can contribute significantly to clarifying the extent to which a training program has effectively achieved the objectives it was set up to accomplish, and can help identify any shortfalls or areas for improvement in existing training programs.

When implementing training strategies, researchers emphasize the importance of measuring the effectiveness of each program delivery method (Wang & Wilcox, 2006). This can be facilitated by encouraging participants to reflect on their experiences, allowing practitioners to improve training activities for future employees. For example, surveys are often used after training completion to determine the course's effectiveness or coaching sessions (Hall et al., 1999). In this regard, Kirkpatrick's (1967) four-dimension approach to training evaluation has been widely adopted to measure efficacy across the various stages of a training program. In one adaptation of this system, the initial "reaction" stage measures individuals' engagement and participation in the training activity (Praslova, 2010, p. 220). Following this, the "learning" stage tests and challenges individuals' skills based on what they have studied, the "behavior" stage explores how individuals implement the skills developed through training in everyday tasks within their organization, and finally, the "results" stage examines the overall outcomes of the training activity, such as reduced costs, improved performance, and higher motivation (Praslova, 2010, p. 221). This four-step process is a method that ensures all dimensions of a training program are assessed and thus is used by many practitioners (Sugrue & Rivera, 2005; Twitchell et al., 2000).

Importance of a sound training strategy

Designing and drafting a clear and coherent training strategy is one of the most essential steps that training managers consider when planning their training programs. Such planning should start with fully understanding the objectives and reasons behind an organization's desire to invest in training. Identifying the needs of employees and their expectations should also be indicated in the training strategy (Wang et al., 2002). Training and learning can be further facilitated by adopting technological instruments to deliver the content more clearly. Two additional important steps are implementing the training programs and monitoring their performance and overall operation (Ramirez, 2008).

The existing human resource management and training literature has indicated that the design of a training strategy is the first critical component leading to effective training. A successful training strategy must be supported and backed by top management, engage all employees in training strategy formulation, be aligned with the organization's strategic objectives, and aim to enhance clearly defined areas with specifically targeted knowledge and skill gaps. Moreover, a coherent training approach is essential to successfully deliver training programs with the highest possible quality. Given the rapidly evolving nature of work environments and the constant need to alter the strategies and frameworks that organizations apply to compete in global markets, it is essential to implement training strategies that reflect specific organizational needs (Howard, 1995). If a training strategy is sound and well-designed, one can expect a positive influence on the behaviors and attitudes of employees and, consequently, organizational performance (Holton & Baldwin, 2003).

Needs assessment and pre-training

Before initiating training activities, researchers have found that needs assessment is essential to ensure that programs achieve their desired outcomes. Such assessments identify knowledge and skill areas that employees need to improve and set goals for them, increasing their interest and motivation to undergo the training sessions (Blanchard & Thacker, 2007). In addition to needs assessments, it has been discovered that pre-training sessions often increase engagement in professional development activities. For example, Tracey et al. (2001) consulted 420 hotel managers who participated in a two-and-a-half-day managerial knowledge and skills training program and found that those who joined the pre-training program were more motivated and engaged in the tasks that they were performing (Tracey et al., 2001).

Continuous training needs assessment is another essential factor contributing to the success of training programs. Brown (2002) argues that some organizations develop and implement training strategies and plans without conducting needs analysis, which exposes them to risks of "overdoing training, doing too little training, or missing the point completely" (p. 569). Conducting a needs assessment exercise can lead to several positive outcomes, including: 1) aligning organizational goals and objectives with those that the training programs expect to achieve, 2) identifying gaps between employees' current skills and those necessary to perform their duties with more effectiveness and efficiency, 3) discovering which organizational problems and weaknesses cannot be solved by training, and 4) preparing the conditions and general environment in which training activities will take place (Brown, 2002).

Impact of effective training strategies and practices on public organization performance

One of the main objectives of training programs is to build strong, competent, and qualified personnel in the private or public sectors (Healy, 2001). The central core of any organization is its human capital, and the strength or weakness of this capital is reflected in the overall performance of the organization (Becker, 1964). Mentz (1997), therefore, argues that improving the quality of public service delivery depends largely on the effectiveness of training programs provided to public sector employees. Organizations are required to constantly introduce new managerial practices and instruments to become more competitive and effective in public service delivery, as both private and public organizations aim to provide the most affordable products and the best services to the public (Rainey & Bozeman, 2000). This requires them not only to provide training programs to equip employees with the necessary skills to perform their duties, but also to ensure the effectiveness and quality of such programs in the first place (Satterfield & Hughes, 2007).

Impact of effective training on organizational performance

Regarding the link between effective training and organizational performance, it is important to develop new tools to identify less efficient units in an organization and whether their inefficaciousness could result from a malfunctioning workforce (Cho & McLean, 2004). The reasons for these workforce deficiencies could then be narrowed down, such as skills no longer matching the updated requirements of the organization or a selection process that does not successfully assess an individual's expected contribution to the organization. Campbell's (1988) study has demonstrated that individuals' behavior within an organization can be improved if the appropriate training programs are provided and shortfalls are correctly identified and addressed. A more recent study was conducted by Sahinidis and Bouris (2008) to determine what factors affect training effectiveness and organizational performance and covered 134 employees to evaluate the impact of training on their performance. As might be expected, the study's results indicated a strong correlation between training effectiveness and employees' job commitment, satisfaction, and motivation (Sahinidis & Bouris, 2008).

Furthermore, Owens (2006) established a coherent relationship between training and organizational outcomes, stating that training is a vital function for all organizations regardless of specialization or size. In examining training programs' relationship with and impact on variables like job satisfaction, organizational commitment, and employee turnover, statistical analysis confirmed a strong positive relationship between effective training and organizational success, thus significantly contributing to the existing literature by effectively demonstrating how training can affect those variables. (Owens, 2006).

Findings

This section presents the findings of the interview and survey data gathered for this chapter, which explore the relationship between effective training programs and their impact on organizational performance in the public sector and the impact of training strategies on training programs within the government of Dubai.

Role of leadership and Dubai central government in preparing and implementing training strategies

As shown in Figure 8.1, over 70% of the survey respondents indicated that their respective organizational leadership provided the necessary financial support for their training strategy. Moreover, 79.6% stated that their leadership believed that human capital was a source of competitive advantage for the organization and invested in its empowerment and improvement. When asked if leadership was involved in preparing and designing such strategies, however, only about half of the respondents agreed (53%), while the rest were either neutral (32.7%) or disagreed (14.2%). Their leadership's financial commitment to designing and preparing an effective and efficient training strategy could have a greater impact, especially in ensuring that the organization's vision, mission, and objectives are aligned with the training strategy and reflected in its programs.

Furthermore, the role of Dubai's central government in supporting its public entities' training efforts was limited to the provision of necessary funds and training policies, in addition to the recommendation of training institutions. The government did not transcend this technical role to become more directly involved in assessing the training outcomes and their impact on organizational performance, instead only drafting a broad training strategy that outlined the objectives, direction, and desired results from the training programs to achieve the strategic objectives of the Emirate on the national and federal levels. This strategy was then circulated among all public sector entities to align the objectives of their training strategies with those of the central government; however, there was little evidence of

234 Importance of effective human resource development

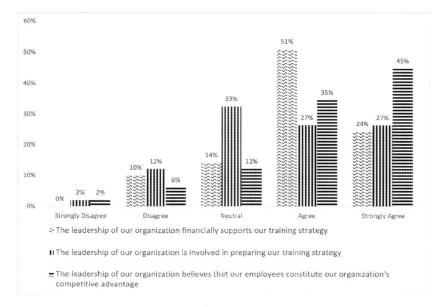

Figure 8.1 Role and involvement of the organizational leadership in preparing training strategies
Source: Designed by the author based on original survey data

follow up on the progress of its various entities in achieving those objectives, the training outcomes, or their impact on organizational performance.

The first half of Table 8.1 summarizes data from the in-depth interviews conducted with human resources and training directors in the various public sector entities covered by this study. The interviews revealed that the involvement of organizational leadership in supporting training programs was mostly realized by convincing the top management in Dubai's public sector to provide sufficient financial support and ensure training covered all levels of public organizations. Ultimately, the leadership's role was restricted to assessing the effectiveness of the training programs and reviewing the training strategy. Thus, there remained considerably more that could have been done within the various public sector entities in Dubai to ensure that the role of leadership was more influential.

Staff involvement and tools used to prepare training strategies

The participation and involvement of all staff within an organization, regardless of rank, in preparing and designing a training strategy is paramount to its success. Employees are the backbone of any organization and are the ones most directly affected by the outcomes of training programs. If their participation in preparing the strategy is minimal, there could be

Table 8.1 The role of leadership and the central government in preparing training strategies

	Current practices	Recommended practices / reforms
The role of government leadership in supporting effective training programs	• Convincing top management to provide the necessary financial support to conduct effective training programs. • Ensuring that training programs are provided across all individual, departmental, and organizational levels. • Analyzing the results of previous training programs and identifying any weaknesses that needed to be addressed to improve the quality of the programs. • Reviewing the training strategy and identifying new needs.	• Provide a vision and direction and specify outcomes the training programs should achieve. • Have leadership directly involved in preparing the training strategy. • Ensure that the provided training materials, programs, and trainers meet the highest quality, effectiveness, and efficiency levels. • Help to establish a culture of learning, knowledge sharing, and self-development and oversee the success of training programs to achieve desired results. • Establish communicational and cooperative links among all public sector entities to share training methods and exchange expertise and best practices. • Attend training sessions, share real-life experiences, and empower participants to be influential leaders. • Create a common platform and communication channels to allow all governmental entities to share training practices and exchange learning and resources. • Identify, properly manage, and train talented employees within organizations to become potential internal trainers.
The role of Dubai's central government in supporting its entities' training efforts	• Providing sufficient funds, tools, and human resources to conduct the training programs. • Issuing convenient training policies, regulations, and methodologies to ensure continuous growth and better services. • Recommending training institutions that provide the best training programs.	• Have individual entities assess the results of training programs and send reports to the central government. • Establish a team of auditors to assess the effectiveness of training programs. • Establish a world-class training organization (preferably a semi-governmental entity) based in Dubai to meet the training needs of all public sector entities. • Make effective training a criterion for awarding the "Dubai Excellent Program Award".

(*continued*)

Table 8.1 Cont.

	Current practices	Recommended practices / reforms
Training strategies of Dubai's central government and other public sector entities	• The central government issued and administered the general framework, training policies, and guidelines. • The central government's training strategy outlined the key factors to enhance its employees' productivity and make the government of Dubai one of the most effective regionally and globally. • Various public sector entities were able to develop customized training strategies based on their organizational needs in alignment with the central government's long-term objectives.	• The central government should ask its entities to submit reports outlining the results of their training practices and outcomes. • The central government should stress the importance of implementing knowledge management programs to obtain the best training methods. • Public sector entities' strategies should focus on enhancing employee satisfaction and organizational loyalty. • Each government entity should conduct an institutional analysis to evaluate the organizational effectiveness of its training programs.

Source: Designed by the author based on data from interviews with human resources and training directors in Dubai's public sector

negative consequences on the training's impact on their behavior or overall skills that it aims to strengthen.

As displayed in Figure 8.2, only 46.9% of respondents indicated that employees participate in preparing their training strategy. Of the remainder, 20.4% disagreed while 30.6% chose a neutral response. These results are much lower than those indicating the participation of supervisors in the preparation of training strategies, of which 63.3% agreed, 20.4% were neutral, and 12.2% disagreed. Supervisors' feedback, comments, and remarks regarding the strategy seem to have been taken into consideration by the organization, however, as a total of 79.6% of respondents agreed on this.

In this regard, developing a comprehensive and focused training strategy can be achieved by relying on several tools and frameworks to ensure that internal and external factors are considered. For example, Strengths, Weaknesses, Opportunities and Threats (SWOT) analysis has proven to be one of the most reliable tools in assessing an organizational environment and its training needs. However, as indicated in Figure 8.3, only 38.8% of respondents agreed that SWOT analysis was used to develop their training strategy, 12.2% strongly disagreed, and the remaining 49% either disagreed or chose neutral.

Although SWOT analysis was not utilized by more than half of all survey respondents, 77.5% stated that their training strategy's primary purpose

The impact of training on public sector organizations 237

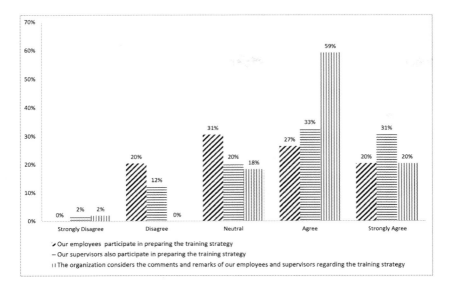

Figure 8.2 Involvement of all staff in preparing training strategies
Source: Designed by the author based on original survey data

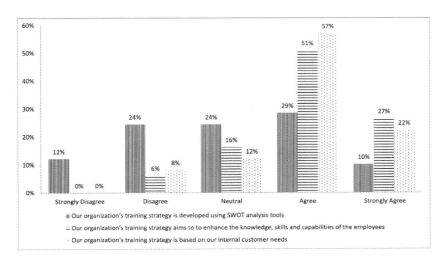

Figure 8.3 Tools used to develop training strategies
Source: Designed by the author based on original survey data

was to enhance employees' knowledge, skills, and capabilities. A total of 70.5% of respondents agreed that their organizations' internal customer needs constituted the basis of the training strategy; however, the addition of a tool like SWOT analysis could enable these organizations to develop a more thorough awareness of their own internal/external strengths and weaknesses, as well as opportunities and threats that they can incorporate when building future strategic plans.

Aside from SWOT, various methods and measures were adopted by the organizations surveyed and interviewed in this study when developing comprehensive and effective training strategies. As shown in Table 8.2, the training methods utilized by most public sector entities were coaching and mentoring for new recruits to introduce them to the organization, shadowing, on-the-job training, and reliance on case studies and practical

Table 8.2 Methods and measures taken to implement effective training strategies

	Current practices	Recommended practices / reforms
Training methods implemented to achieve effective training	• Coaching and mentoring for new recruits. • Workshops, job rotation, shadowing, and training the trainers. • Internal and external training programs. • On-the-job training. • Encouragement of e-learning programs for large groups of employees to cut costs and ensure effectiveness. • Case studies and experimental training courses.	• Organize conferences to attract regional and global experts and learn from them. • Conduct regional and international study tours to capture the public sector's best practices. • Create a virtual knowledge base/bank with all the important job-related information and training courses. • Hold brainstorming sessions and focus groups where all employees take part in identifying training needs and strategies.
Measures are taken to implement a comprehensive training strategy	• Identification of both organizational and employee needs and implementation of strategic training programs to fill gaps in their performance. • International consultants' advice and recommendations. • Regularly updated training strategy that reflects changes in the market.	• Involve all employees in the various phases of strategy creation, implementation, and evaluation. • Decrease involvement of and reliance on international consultants and foster homegrown expertise. • Utilize SWOT analysis to identify the organization's internal/external challenges and opportunities effectively.

Table 8.2 Cont.

	Current practices	Recommended practices / reforms
	• Alignment of training strategy with the vision and mission of the organization.	• Conduct pre- and post-training surveys/interviews to assess training program quality and use lessons learned to improve the following year's strategy. • Increase top management's involvement, commitment, and support in creating each year's strategy. • Establish and link strategic goals to result-based KPIs. • Set SMART goals.
Criteria for securing a training budget from the central government	• The total number of employees in the public sector entity and their role in enhancing the growth of the public sector. • The actual training needs of each entity. • The previous years' training budgets.	• Conduct a comprehensive training analysis before reaching out to the Department of Finance for the annual training budget. • Compare Dubai's training budget percentage to other regional and global governments. • Fix a minimum training budget for each employee based on their grade and increase it as their training needs arise. • Have the central government set the allocated training budget for each entity based on the level of their training effectiveness.

Source: Designed by the author based on the analysis of data from interviews with human resources and training directors in Dubai's government

training courses to expose employees to real-life scenarios and train them on how to react to and solve issues. Regarding the measures taken to implement a comprehensive training strategy, training departments aligned their strategies with the vision and mission of their respective organizations, identified both organizational and employee training needs, and hired consultants to benefit and learn from international best practices. In terms of the methods followed to calculate necessary training budgets, organizations used the total number of employees to indicate their budgetary needs and specify an amount of money for each employee concerning their rank and contribution to the organization's productivity.

240　*Importance of effective human resource development*

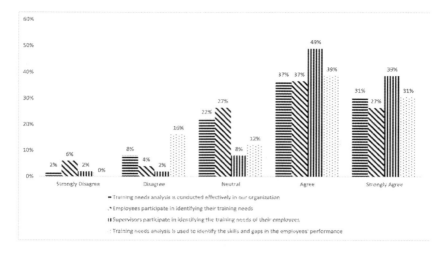

Figure 8.4 Involvement of staff and supervisors in identifying training needs
Source: *Designed by the author based on original survey data*

Conducting training needs analysis

As demonstrated in Figure 8.4, 67.3% of survey respondents confirmed that their departments conducted prior training needs assessments to identify which training programs were needed for their organizations. Among them, 63.2% indicated that employees participate in the assessment, while 87.8% agreed that supervisors were consulted while evaluating the employees' training needs. These statistics show that an organization's employees were consulted less than their supervisors when determining which training programs would be needed to strengthen employee skills and knowledge.

To further substantiate the data obtained from the survey concerning training assessment, in-depth interviews were used to offer greater insight into the methods for determining training needs. As delineated in Table 8.3, human resources and training departments in Dubai were aware of the most reliable techniques to identify the training needs of employees. For example, most of the interviewed department directors indicated that training needs assessments were carried out on three levels: individual, departmental, and organizational. Individual performance plans, annual performance appraisal results, and supervisors' reports were all utilized to identify individual training needs, and numerous methods involved employees and supervisors in this process. For example, supervisors were encouraged by human resources and training departments to hold regular meetings with employees to discuss their performance and progress and suggest training

Table 8.3 Training needs measurement and assessment

	Current practices	Recommended practices / reforms
Ways in which public sector entities defined employees' training needs	• Three levels of individual, departmental, and organizational. • Training needs analysis • Individual performance plans. • Results of annual performance appraisals. • New strategic plans of the organization and emergent needs for new training programs. • Feedback from supervisors and managers regarding the performance of their employees. • Dubai Government Excellence Program feedback.	• Ensure that employees are motivated to participate in the training program. • Base training material on the needs of trainees. • Use surveys to identify training needs.
Involvement of employees and their supervisors in identifying their training needs	• Determination of the most reliable way to identify employee training needs. • Regular meetings between supervisors and employees to discuss their performance and the training necessary to enhance it. • Suggestion of training programs by supervisors and line managers to their employees based on the performance gaps identified throughout the year. • Face-to-face meetings between human resources/training directors and employees within the entities.	• Conduct training not only to address weaknesses in performance, but also as a part of continuous learning. • Have supervisors and line managers empower their employees to be innovative in how they conduct their jobs and share best practices with their colleagues.
Types of training programs currently conducted by public sector entities in Dubai	• Strategy making and planning. • Financial management programs. • 360 leadership training. • Strategy & organizational performance. • Leadership & negotiation. • People management & emotional intelligence. • Problem-solving & decision-making.	• Train all public sector employees on research methods to construct evidence-based policies. • Focus more on cycles of policy making, implementation, and evaluation. • Implement knowledge management programs and practical skills. • Share best practices in organizational management, organizational performance, and effective benchmarking.

Source: Designed by the author based on the analysis of data from interviews with human resources and training directors in Dubai's public sector

242 *Importance of effective human resource development*

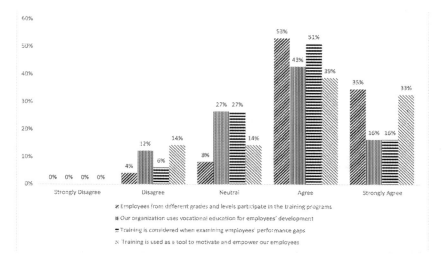

Figure 8.5 Training and employee development
Source: *Designed by the author based on original survey data*

programs to improve their productivity and accomplishments. Moreover, every department's new strategic direction within the organization was considered to identify the new skills and practical behaviors necessary for employees to achieve the desired outcomes and results.

The training programs' ultimate objectives were to strengthen employees' competencies, identify gaps in their performance, and equip them with the theoretical, practical, and behavioral skills necessary to perform their duties more effectively. The survey data (Figure 8.5) show how 87.8% of respondents indicated that all employees across the various grades and levels participated in training programs. Moreover, 59.2% of respondents said they used vocational education for employee development and skills building. More than 60% of the respondents also stated that training was not simply used to improve the skills and knowledge of employees, but also to empower and motivate them to focus on continuous learning.

The highest survey scores in this study can be found in results regarding the quality of trainers and training materials offered by Dubai public sector departments to their employees. As shown in Figure 8.6, 83.7% of respondents asserted that the primary criterion for selecting trainers was their proven command of the subjects they taught and demonstrated experience. More importantly, the training programs were designed to meet only the highest quality standards and match international best practices, as indicated by 63.3% of respondents.

Training effectiveness was monitored by the UAE's Institute of Administrative Development, which adopted a systematic approach

The impact of training on public sector organizations 243

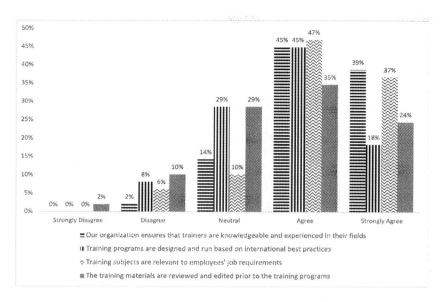

Figure 8.6 Quality of training materials, subjects, and trainers
Source: *Designed by the author based on original survey data*

to identifying the training needs of all public sector entities in Dubai. Furthermore, to deliver high-quality training programs, instructors were selected based on their seniority and capability to develop well-targeted and excellently designed programs commensurate with such high levels of quality. The training departments in Dubai public sector entities also focused on evaluating the training and ensuring it met the best international standards. They evaluated the trainees and their attendance, participation, and attention paid to the programs, and recommendations were provided to improve the overall quality of training programs in the future. The enhanced quality of training programs was reflected in an increasing number of public sector entities' training departments being awarded ISO 9001-2000 certification, which is a testament to the quality of training programs they delivered.

Naturally, the relevance of training programs to employee needs is crucial in motivating participants to do their best in learning new skills and applying them in their workplaces. Among the surveyed human resources and training directors, 83.6% stated that training programs were designed to develop new skills that public sector employees needed to perform their jobs better. Nevertheless, only 59.2% said they had reviewed the training programs and training materials before they were delivered to trainees.

Impact of a clear training strategy on training outcomes

Designing a coherent and clear training strategy is one of the first necessary steps that training managers should consider to ensure that training will deliver its expected outcomes. Planning for a training strategy should begin with a full understanding of the rationales and objectives organizations wish to achieve through the training programs. The employees' needs and expectations should also be identified and indicated in the training strategy. Training and learning can be further facilitated by technological instruments that deliver the content in an innovative and accessible manner (Ramirez, 2008).

In the case of Dubai's public sector, developing a coherent and clear training strategy positively impacted training effectiveness. As shown in Figure 8.7, 91.6% of respondents agreed that their training effectiveness measures witnessed substantial improvement due to the implementation of well-designed training strategies. A total of 85.7% of the surveyed organizations also indicated that the training methods used to deliver training programs directly impacted the quality and effectiveness of their training. Furthermore, 89.8% of respondents asserted that allocating a sufficient training budget was critical for enabling training departments to deliver high-quality training programs. A clear training strategy, diverse and purposeful training methods, and a sufficient training budget are thus identified as the three crucial components for effective training.

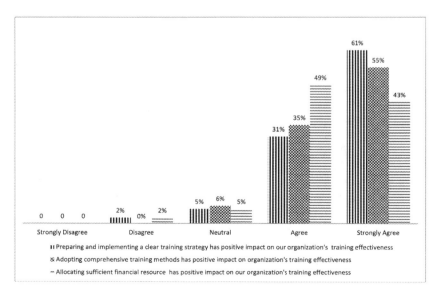

Figure 8.7 Impact of training strategy and methods on training effectiveness
Source: Designed by the author based on original survey data

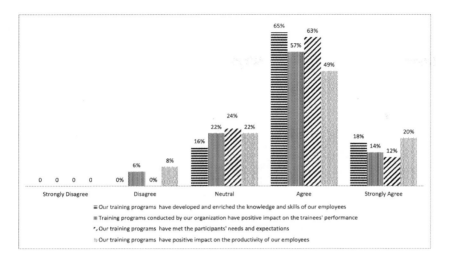

Figure 8.8 Positive outcomes of effective training on employee performance
Source: Designed by the author based on original survey data

Impact of adequate training on performance and productivity of Dubai public sector employees

The findings of this research demonstrate that training programs greatly impacted Dubai government employees' skills and knowledge. As illustrated in Figure 8.8, 83.7% of respondents indicated that evaluations conducted after employees completed their training courses indicated significant positive changes in their knowledge and skills. Furthermore, 87.8% of them stated that the training programs had met the participants' needs and expectations, which is crucial, since the leading challenge facing governments is the inefficiency of training courses that are not matched to employee needs. Moreover, 71.4% of respondents indicated that trainee performance improved after the training, and 69.4% said that the training programs positively influenced the overall productivity of employees within their organizations.

Impact of training on performance of Dubai public sector entities

The positive influence of effective training on organizational performance can be seen in Figure 8.9. A total of 89.8% of respondents affirmed that their organizational performance improved substantially due to the increased effectiveness of their workforce. Equipping public sector employees with the necessary skills and knowledge and helping them to identify their weaknesses and strengths has thus reflected positively on their performance. Moreover, 77% of human resources and training

246 *Importance of effective human resource development*

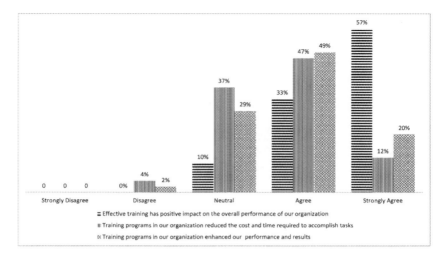

Figure 8.9 Effective training and organizational performance
Source: Designed by the author based on original survey data

directors participating in the survey stated that their organizations' output had improved gradually due to the impact of effective training programs on employee productivity.

Another indication of enhanced organizational performance due to effective training is the time required to accomplish tasks within Dubai government organizations. According to the survey results, 62.1% of respondents agreed it took their employees less time than before to accomplish the same tasks. The results in Figure 8.10 show that effective training programs conducted or funded by public sector entities improved the quality of services delivered to the public, as verified by 71.4% of respondents. Moreover, more than 50% of respondents stated that improvements in customer satisfaction could be mainly attributed to the positive effects of training programs on employee performance.

Interviews with government officials from 17 public sector entities further demonstrated that the impact of effective training on their organizations was substantial, as broken down in Table 8.4. The effects on performance were multidimensional, covering the organizational, departmental, and individual levels. Employees learned how to use new techniques to deliver their jobs more effectively, and their leadership skills helped them solve challenges encountered at work. Moreover, learning from best practices and benchmarking their performance with other organizations improved their skills and enhanced the quality of their output.

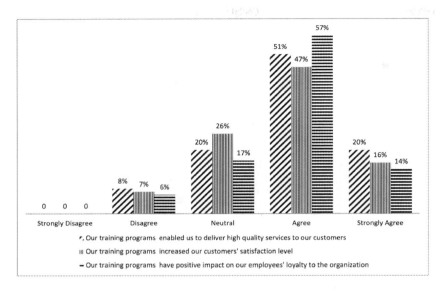

Figure 8.10 Benefits of effective training on the overall performance of public sector entities
Source: Designed by the author based on original survey data

Conclusion and recommendations

To maintain a sustainable organizational culture, public sector organizations should offer greater employee training and professional development opportunities. As this chapter has demonstrated, the government of Dubai invested in training as a vehicle for public sector excellence and efficiency in service delivery. The role of leadership within Dubai's public organizations was identified as crucial for securing the necessary financial support for training and their involvement in the building and implementation stages of training strategies. Moreover, the methods and measures put into place to secure effective implementation of the training strategies were examined, and staff involvement in training needs assessment exercises was evaluated.

Beyond this, the chapter also recommends improvements across several areas in which Dubai public sector entities must invest further effort and resources to ensure that their training strategies meet the highest international standards. First, it is essential to revitalize the role of the Dubai Institute for Human Resources Development and ensure that it provides high-quality training for Dubai public sector's employees. This organization is critical in responding to the training needs of public sector entities in Dubai and ensuring that appropriate, low-cost, and high-quality training is achieved. On the local government level, the heads of departments and entities can play an essential role in the success of training programs. They

Table 8.4 Impact of training on organizational performance in Dubai public sector entities

Impact of training on organizational performance	• Multi-level impact: 1) Organizational level—Better customer service; 2) Departmental level—Achievement of strategic goals and targets; 3) Individual level—Improved performance and higher organizational loyalty. • Introduction of innovative problem-solving skills. • Implementation of new financial management and control techniques resulting in more efficiency. • Enhanced employee satisfaction levels. • Provision of better services and higher customer satisfaction. • Improvement of leadership skills of most government employees through leadership training programs. • Less time taken by employees to perform duties. • Reception of the "Government Excellence Award". • Fewer errors and mistakes.
Proposed ways to enhance impact of training effectiveness on organizational performance	• Encourage the creation of a working environment where employees share and transmit what they learn to colleagues. • Organize meetings at least quarterly where human resources/training directors from all public sector entities discuss and exchange training strategies and practices. • Reduce governmental bureaucracy and inter-governmental conflicts. • Promote knowledge transfer of skills and tools. • Create knowledge management programs to allow employees to share what they learned and how it benefited their performance. • Improve team building and working. • Create smoother internal business processes. • Teach employees how to do more with less and engage in new responsibilities and tasks. • Focus more on training UAE nationals.

Source: Designed by the author based on the analysis of interviews conducted with human resources and training directors in Dubai's public sector

should therefore participate in the formation of training strategies and ensure that they develop ones that respond to the needs of their employees. Direct interaction with human resources departments is essential to effectively discuss such needs. Furthermore, it was revealed by this study that supervisors, rather than staff, are more often given a chance to be a part of training strategy design. Instead, all staff within organizations should be involved in preparing and implementing training strategies. Public sector entities should also utilize more tools like SWOT to study environmental factors that can impact the quality and outcomes of their training programs.

Second, the central government of Dubai (The Executive Council) should foster an environment that supports teamwork and eliminates hierarchical hindrances between employees. This will create an environment that recognizes and appreciates innovation, hard work, and accomplishments. While most of Dubai's public entities' leadership is committed to securing the necessary budget for training, they are not sufficiently involved in the design and implementation phases of the strategy. Leadership should therefore be more involved in designing and implementing training strategies and ascertaining that they are aligned with the organization's vision and mission and those of the central government of Dubai.

Third, the leadership of Dubai's public organizations should help to establish a culture of learning, knowledge sharing, and self-development, and oversee the success of training programs to achieve their desired results. This could be achieved by regularly attending training sessions, sharing real-life experiences, and empowering participants to be influential leaders rather than just passive task achievers in their departments. Training departments should also strive to create an organizational culture that supports and endorses knowledge sharing. This could be encouraged by organizing weekly or even monthly meetings where human resources and training directors meet with their employees to share their experiences of solving problems and challenges in their daily activities. The solutions that they adopt to solve these challenges should then be documented and shared with other employees.

Fourth, and finally, it is recommended that training should not be regarded as merely a tool to strengthen the weaknesses of government employees, but rather as an essential continuous learning mechanism, as doing so will foster the creation of an environment that appreciates learning and knowledge within public sector entities. The central government of Dubai should also be more involved in assessing the training strategy effectiveness of its various departments and entities. More importantly, it must trace those departments' progress in contributing to Dubai's strategic vision. The central government should thus establish or appoint a training institution to meet the training needs of all public sector entities, as the centralization of training needs provision within one institution will create homegrown expertise that is less reliant on international providers and consultants.

References

Aguinis, H. (2009). *Performance Management*, Pearson Prentice Hall, Upper Saddle River, NJ.

Aguinis, H., & Kraiger, K. (2009). Benefits of training and development for individuals and teams, organizations, and society. *Annual Review of Psychology*, 60, 451–474.

Ali, G., & Magalhaes, R. (2008). Barriers to implementing e-learning: A Kuwaiti case study. *Training and Development*, 12(1), 36–53.

Allen, T., & Poteet, M. (1999). Developing effective mentoring relationships: Strategies from the mentor's viewpoint. *Career Development Quarterly*, 48(1), 59–73.

Aragón-Sánchez, A., Barba-Aragón, I., & Sanz-Valle, R. (2003). Effects of training on business results. *International Journal of Human Resource Management*, 14, 956–980.

Atwater, L., Brett, J., & Charles, A. (2007). Multisource feedback: Lessons learned and implications for practice. *Human Resource Management*, 46(2), 285–307.

Bartlett, K., & Rodgers, J. (2004). HRD as national policy in the Pacific Islands. *Advances in Developing Human Resources*, 6, 307–14.

Bass, B., & Vaughan, J. (1966). *Training in Industry: The Management of Learning*, Brooks/Cole, Belmont, California.

Becker, G. (1964). *Human Capital: A Theoretical and Empirical Analysis, With Special Reference to Education*, Columbia University Press, New York.

Bell, B., & Kozlowski, S. (2002). Adaptive guidance: enhancing self-regulation, knowledge and performance in technology-based training. *Personnel Psychology*, 55, 267–306.

Blanchard, P., & Thacker, J. (2007). *Effective Training: Systems, Strategies, and Practices*, Pearson Prentice Hall, Upper Saddle River, NJ.

Brown, J. (2002). Training needs assessment: A must for developing an effective training program. *Journal of Public Personnel Management*, 31(4), 569–578.

Campbell, J. (1988). Training design for performance improvement in J.P. Campbell and R.J Campbell (eds.), *Productivity in Organizations*, Jossey-Bass, San Francisco.

Cappelli, L., Guglielmetti, R., Mattia, G., Merli, R., & Renzi, M. (2011). Peer evaluation to develop benchmarking in the public sector. *Benchmarking: An International Journal*, 18(4), 490–509.

Chawla, D., & Joshi, H. (2010). Knowledge management initiatives in Indian public and private sector organizations. *Journal of Knowledge Management*, 14(6), 811–827.

Cho, E., & McLean, G. (2004). What we discovered about NHRD and what it means for HRD. *Advancing in Developing Human Resources*, 6, 382–93.

Chun, Y., & Rainey, H. (2005). Goal ambiguity and organizational performance in US federal agencies. *Journal of Public Administration Research and Theory*, 15(4), 529–57.

Collins, D., & Holton, E. (2004). The effectiveness of managerial leadership development programs: a metaanalysis of studies from 1982 to 2001. *Human Resources Development Quarterly*, 15, 217–248.

Conger, J., & Benjamin, B. (1999). *Building Leaders: How Successful Companies Develop the Next Generation*, Jossey-Bass, San Francisco.

Day, D. (2000). Leadership development: A review in context. *Leadership Quarterly*, 11, 581–614.

DeRouin, R., Fritzsche, B., & Salas, E. (2004). Optimizing e-learning: research-based guidelines for learner-controlled training. *Human Resource Management Review*, 43, 147–162.

Dotlich, D., & Noel, J. (1998). *Action Learning: How the World's Top Companies Are Re-Creating Their Leaders and Themselves*, Jossey-Bass, San Francisco.

Dvir, T., Eden, D., Avolio, B., & Shamir, B. (2002). Impact of transformational leadership on follower development and performance: A field experiment. *The Academy of Management Journal*, 45(4), 735–744.

Frayne, C., & Geringer, J. (2000). Self-management training for improving job performance: A field experiment involving salespeople. *Journal of Applied Psychology*, 85, 361–72.

Gilley, A., Gilley, J., & McMillan, H. (2009). Organizational change: Motivation, communication, and leadership effectiveness. *International Society for performance Improvement*, 24(4), 75–94.

Goldstein, I., & Ford, J. (2002). *Training in Organizations*, Wadsworth, Belmont, CA.

Hall, D., Otazo, K., & Hollenbeck, G. (1999). Behind closed doors: What really happens in executive coaching. *Organizational Dynamics*, 27(3), 39–53.

Healy, P. (2001). Training and public sector reform: An integrated approach. *Public Administration and Development*, 21(4), 309–319.

Hill, C., & Lent, R. (2006). A narrative and meta-analytic review of helping skills training: Time to revive a dormant area of inquiry. *Psychotherapy*, 43, 154–172.

Holton, W., & Baldwin, B. (2003). Making Transfer Happen: An Action Perspective on Learning Transfer Systems in W. Holton and B. Baldwin (eds.), *Improving Learning Transfer in Organizations*, Jossey-Bass, San Francisco.

Hooijberg, R., & Choi, J. (2001). The impact of organizational characteristics on leadership effectiveness models: An examination of leadership in a private and a public sector organization. *Administration & Society*, 33(4), 403–431.

Howard, A. (1995). *The Changing Nature of Work*, Jossey-Bass, San Francisco, California.

Kirkpatrick, D. (1967). Evaluation of Training in R.L. Craig, & L. R. Bittel (eds.), *Training and Development Handbook*, McGraw-Hill, New York, pp.87–112.

Kraiger, K., & Jerden, E. (2007). A New Look at Learner Control: Meta-Analytic Results and Directions for Future Research, in S.M. Fiore and E .Salas (eds.), *Where is the Learning in Distance Learning? Towards a Science of Distributed Learning and Training*, APA Books, Washington, DC.

Kraiger, K. (2002). Decision-Based Evaluation, in *Creating, Implementing, and Maintaining Effective Training and Development: State-of-the-Art Lessons for Practice*, Jossey-Bass, San Francisco, CA, 331–375.

Malik, P., & Lenka, U. (2020). Identifying HRM practices for disabling destructive deviance among public sector employees using content analysis. *International Journal of Organizational Analysis*, 28(3), 719–744.

Mau, T. (2019). Enhancing leadership capacity in the public sector: branding as an employer of choice. *International Journal of Public Leadership*, 15(3), 155–169.

McCourt, W., & Sola, N. (1999). Using training to promote civil service reform: Tanzanian local government case study. *Public Administration and Development*, 19, 63–75.

Meaklim, T., & Sims, J. (2011). Leading powerful partnerships — a new model of public sector leadership development. *International Journal of Leadership in Public Services*, 7(1), 21–31.

Mentz, J. (1997). Personal and institutional factors in capacity building and institutional development, working paper 14. European Centre for Development Policy Management.

Mohabbat, M., & Islam, M. (2014). Public sector leadership development in Bangladesh: Present state and future prospect. *International Journal of Leadership in Public Services*, 10(1), 17–30.

Moxley, R., & Pulley, M. (2004). Hardships in C.D. McCauley and E. Van Velsor (eds,), *The Center for Creative Leadership Handbook of Leadership Development*, 2nd ed., Jossey-Bass, Francisco, 183–203.

Noe, R. (1986). Trainees' attributes and attitudes: Neglected influences on training effectiveness. *Academy of Management Review*, 11, 736–749.

Noe, R. (2008). *Employee Training and Development*, Irwin-McGraw, Boston, MA.

Owens, P. (2006). One more reason not to cut your training budget: The relationship between training and organizational outcomes. *Public Personnel Management*, 35(2), 163–172.

Paradise, A. (2007). *State of the Industry: ASTD's Annual Review of Trends in Workplace Learning and Performance*, ASTD, Alexandria, VA.

Poor, J., & Plesoianu, G. (2010). Human resource management under change in the Romanian civil service in an international context. *Employee Relations*, 32(3), 281–309.

Powell, C., & Snellman, Y. (2004). The Concept of Project in Motivation to Vocational Training: A Model Proposal in F. Avallone, J. Arnold, & K. De Witte (eds.), *Feelings Work in Europe. Quaderni di psicologia, 5,* pp. 282–289.

Praslova, L. (2010). Adaptation of Kirkpatrick's Four Level Model of Training Criteria to Assessment of Learning Outcomes and Program Evaluation in Higher Education, *Educational Assessment. Evaluation and Accountability*, 22(3), 215–225.

Rainey, H., & Bozeman, B. (2000). Comparing public and private organizations: Empirical research and the power of the a priori. *Journal of Public Administration Research and Theory*, 10(2), 447–470.

Ramirez, E. (2008). This bus is plugged in: Wi-Fi lets Arkansas kids study on their commute, *US News and World Report*, January 10. Retrieved from: www.usnews.com/articles/education/e-learning/2008/01/10/this-bus-is-plugged-in.html

Saastamoinen, J., Reijonen, H., & Tammi, T. (2017). The role of training in dismantling barriers to SME participation in public procurement. *Journal of Public Procurement*, 17(1), 1–30.

Sahinidis, A., & Bouris, G. (2008). *Employee Perceived Training Effectiveness Relationship to Employee Attitudes*, Emerald, Bradford, England.

Satterfield, J., & Hughes, E. (2007). Emotion skills training for medical students: A systematic review. *Medical Education*, 41, 935–941.

Seidle, B., Fernandez, S., & Perry, J. (2016). Do leadership training and development make a difference in the public sector? a panel study. *Public Administration Review*, 76(4), 603–613.

Smither, J., London, M., & Reilly, R. (2005). Does performance improve following multisource feedback? a theoretical model, meta-analysis, and review of empirical findings. *Personnel Psychology*, 58(1), 33–66.

Smither, J., London, M., Flautt, R., Vargas, Y., & Kucine, I. (2003). Can working with an executive coach improve multisource feedback ratings over time? a quasi-experimental field study. *Personnel Psychology*, 56(1), 23–44.

Stuart, R., & Binsted, D. (1979). Designing reality into management learning events. *Personnel Review*, 8(3), 5–8.

Sugrue, B., & Rivera, R. (2005). *State of the Industry: ASTD's Annual Review of Trends in Workplace Learning and Performance*, ASTD, Alexandria, VA.

Tawalare, A., & Laishram, B. (2019). Factors hindering effective partnering in Indian public sector construction organizations. *Journal of Financial Management of Property and Construction*, 25(1), 83–105.

Towler, A., & Dipboye, L. (2001). Effects of trainer expressiveness, organization, and trainee goal orientation on training outcomes. *Journal of Applied Psychology*, 86(4), 664–674.

Tracey, J., & Tews, M. (1995). Training effectiveness: Accounting for individual characteristics and the work environment. *Cornell Hotel and Restaurant Administration Quarterly*, 36(6), 36–42.

Tracey, J., Hinkin, T., Tannenbaum, S., & Mathieu, J. (2001). The influence of individual characteristics and the work environment on varying levels of training outcomes. *Human Resource Development Quarterly*, 12, 5–23.

Twitchell, K., Holton, E., & Trott, J. (2000). Technical training evaluation practices in the United States. *Performance Improvement Quarterly*, 13(1), 84–109.

Ulrich, D., & Lake, D. (1990). *Organizational Capability: Competing from the Inside Out*, John Wiley, New York.

Wang, G., & Wilcox, D. (2006). Training evaluation: Knowing more than is practiced. *Advances in Developing Human Resources*, 68, 528–539.

Wang, G., Dou, Z., & Li, N. (2002). A systems approach to measuring return on investment for HRD interventions. *Human Resource Development Quarterly*, 13, 203–224.

Zumrah, A. (2013). Is job satisfaction enhancing learning-training transfer relationship? *Journal of Workplace Learning*, 25(8), 543–555.

Zumrah, A. (2015a). Examining the relationship between perceived organizational support, transfer of training and service quality in the Malaysian public sector. *European Journal of Training and Development*, 39(2), 143–160.

Zumrah, A. (2015b). How to enhance the impact of training on service quality? Evidence from Malaysian public sector context. *Journal of Workplace Learning*, 27(7), 514–529.

9 Knowledge management in the public sector
Empirical insights from the United Arab Emirates

Introduction

In today's increasingly globalized and competitive environment, an organization's knowledge assets have become a fundamental source of wealth and a critical factor in its competitiveness, growth, and success (Hussinki et al., 2017; Holsapple & Joshi, 2000; Riege, 2005). Thus, knowledge has become a crucial element in achieving a competitive advantage and a driving force behind organizational excellence (Accenture, 2004; Bell, 1973; Drucker, 1968; Nonaka, 1994). As a result, the field of knowledge management (KM) has gained enormous popularity among both the public and private sectors, and a torrent of research has been produced, particularly concerning how knowledge creation and sharing within organizations can be fostered and how to implement systems that can protect such knowledge from being lost (Nonaka, 1994). Scarborough et al. (1999) observed that numerous articles on KM have appeared in academic and practitioner journals. Consequently, as private and public organizations increasingly realize its importance, they have ramped up their attempts to implement KM programs and strategies (Nonaka et al., 1996). Nevertheless, up until the financial crisis of 2008 and the sharp decline of oil prices in the second half of 2014, knowledge management had garnered little attention in the Gulf region, and there still exists a considerable dearth of research on this topic within this region. This chapter therefore aims to fill this gap in the existing literature by offering a comprehensive analysis of how KM has evolved in Dubai's public sector (Jain & Kelvin, 2013).

KM is vital to countries of the Gulf Cooperation Council (GCC) (Ahmad & Daghfous, 2010; Siddique, 2012; Skok & Tahir, 2010). Their governments have invested in developing and nurturing human capital and knowledge resources through education, research, and training. However, despite this expansion in capital and resources, recent studies suggest that there have been low returns in terms of capturing and transferring knowledge, and performance has not notably improved. One significant finding involves the prevalent underutilization of knowledge and skills, especially in the public sector, with underutilization levels at 47% in Saudi Arabia, 45% in Oman, and 42% in the United Arab Emirates (UAE) (Al-Yahya,

DOI: 10.4324/9781003267744-12

2009). These figures reveal that nearly half of the region's available skills and knowledge resources are not being adequately recognized and used to achieve organizational goals (Al-Yahya, 2010). Furthermore, while GCC countries have been fortunate in attracting expertise and talent from around the world, thus enabling the region to build its basic knowledge and talent infrastructure, these sources of knowledge often exist only temporarily within local markets in the form of experiences and knowhow accumulated by expatriates over the years, leading to considerable losses for local organizations when expatriates return to their countries of origin (Siddique, 2012).

This chapter covers three main topics in its exploration of KM in the public sector. First, it highlights the importance of creating, capturing, documenting, and disseminating knowledge within public organizations. Second, it assesses the extent to which Dubai's public sector relies on flexible and fixed-term employees and the policy measures adopted to protect and document their knowledge. Since KM is a protective mechanism that prevents loss of employee knowledge and knowhow (Lesser et al., 2000), the chapter evaluates the techniques used for obtaining, capturing, and storing staff knowledge and how this affects the current state of KM in Dubai's public sector, as well as its overall outcomes. Third, it presents the factors influencing the implementation of KM within public organizations. Specifically, the chapter assesses the clarity of the KM concept among Dubai's public sector entities, their ability to capture and store knowledge, and the rationales and expected benefits of KM program implementation. A set of recommendations are then addressed to policymakers and heads of KM departments in Dubai, the UAE, and the entire GCC region. This study can offer numerous lessons to guide future initiatives or programs.

The chapter is organized as follows. The next section presents a literature review that clarifies the meaning of KM and the challenges concerning its definition are presented, particularly within the context of the public sector. The literature review section then discusses the enablers and barriers of KM. This section is followed by the research methodology and tools used to acquire data for the study. The findings section then follows that elucidates the clarify of KM's concept in Dubai's public sector, challenges of capturing tacit knowledge, importance of KM for Dubai's public sector, implementing KM processes, the current state of KM in Dubai and the factors affecting KM in Dubai. Finally, the chapter presents the lessons learned and conclusions.

Literature review

KM is not a new phenomenon, yet it has only recently emerged as an explicit area of inquiry in managing organizational knowledge (Garcia-Perez et al., 2019; Wiig, 1997). Throughout the annals of history, knowledge has been transferred progressively from one generation to the next, mainly through informal channels. Wiig (1997), for example, traces the origins of knowledge transfer and sharing practices back to nomadic peoples who ensured that they transferred their hunting skills to maintain the continuity and sustainability of their groups. In terms of business, Gian et al. (2012) state that it has always been a standard practice for successful managers to use the knowhow, or the skills and experience of their employees, for effective management of their institutions (Laihonen et al., 2015). Nevertheless, it has only been during the last two decades that KM has seen systematic, methodical, and explicit development as its field. Since the early 2000s, governments in developed countries, particularly members of the Organization for Economic Co-operation and Development (OECD), have implemented many initiatives to encourage knowledge utilization in their organizations (Yee et al., 2019). These countries have also found through annual surveys of their public and private organizations that KM is a crucial driver behind organizational effectiveness and competitive advantage, as well as an effective method to address issues such as loss of organizational knowledge and memory emanating from high turnover and a retiring workforce (Laihonen et al., 2015). Organizations considering their utilization and sharing of knowledge have tended to discover that they possess far more knowledge than they realize (OECD, 2003).

What is knowledge management?

Defining KM has been a notoriously complex and complicated task. The lack of a commonly accepted definition has spawned considerable ambiguity and confusion about the concept and its significance (Demarest, 1997; Garcia-Perez et al., 2020). To this day, there remains no consensus on the concept's meaning (Cong & Pandya, 2004; Wiig, 1997). However, various definitions in the available literature agree that KM is an ongoing, persistent, and purposeful process that enables organizations to create, select, organize, conserve, disseminate, and transfer knowledge to achieve their strategic objectives and create value (Allee, 1997; Davenport & Prusak, 1998). The American Productivity and Quality Center provides a comprehensive definition that integrates the elements of the KM process, defining it as "the systematic process of identifying, capturing, and transferring information and knowledge people can use to create, compete and improve" (APQC, 2000). In this regard, Hoffman et al. (2005) define an organization's knowledge as its professional intellect or its "knowhow", "know-why", and values and beliefs. Moreover, they argue that knowledge has a substantially limited value if it is not shared within an organization. Hence, defining KM needs to consider managing an organization's knowledge via systematic and organized means. One of the shortcomings in understanding and comprehending KM is the reduction of its concept to technical terms, as most organizations tend to limit its application to information systems and automation (Schiuma, 2012). Nonetheless, KM should not be interpreted in technical terms only. Any definition of KM should consider knowledge as a dynamic and social phenomenon that is

Knowledge management in the public sector 257

embedded in individuals' social experiences and interactions. KM systems are intended to be a means, not an end in and of themselves, as they are merely tools to facilitate the capture, documentation, and dissemination of knowledge (Pauleen & Wang, 2017).

From data to knowledge

To understand the concept of KM, it is vital first to distinguish the meanings of data, information, and knowledge (Harlow, 2018; Nonaka, 1994). In the existing literature, data and information are often used interchangeably with the word knowledge, thereby exacerbating the ambiguity and vagueness associated with the concept of KM. Figure 9.1 lays out the processes by which data evolves into knowledge. Simply put, data are raw facts, such as numbers, words, or combinations of the two, but they carry no meaning in and of themselves and offer little value for decision-making or other activities (Guadamillas-Gómez & Donate-Manzanares, 2011; Serban & Luan, 2002). For data to be meaningful, they must be processed and molded in a particular context, leading to information, which is an organized and contextualized set of data (Nonaka & Peltokorpi, 2006).

Knowledge, meanwhile, is "information in action" (O'Dell & Grayson, 1998) or "meaning made by the mind" (Marakas, 1999). Knowledge without clear meaning is merely information or data. Hence, knowledge combines an individual's judgment, reflections, and analysis of perceived information. Information goes through four processes when transforming into knowledge in an individual's mind: comparison, consequence, connection,

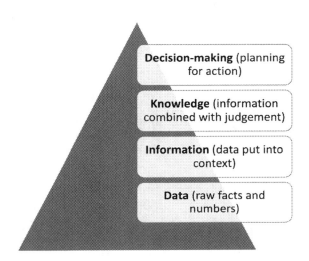

Figure 9.1 Evolution from data to knowledge
Source: Adapted from Serban and Luan 2002

and conversation (Davenport & Prusak, 1998). Thus, knowledge concerns beliefs, commitment, perspectives, intention, and action (Nonaka, 1994).

Tacit, explicit, and organizational forms of knowledge

Knowledge becomes embedded and manifests itself in various forms. It has been categorized into four main classes: individual, structural, organizational (Paulin & Suneson, 2012), and social/cultural (Jordão & Novas, 2017; Serban & Luan, 2002). Most scholarly work on KM refers to Michael Polanyi's (1967) distinction between tacit and explicit knowledge. Individual knowledge (known as tacit knowledge) resides primarily in people's minds (Edvinson & Malone, 1997), and it is the personal, unspoken, and cognitive knowledge that individuals in organizations do not readily share or communicate with one another. The most salient component of tacit knowledge is that it is "the knowhow and know-what" that individuals acquire through years of experience in a particular organization, and yet it is not well recognized, captured, or documented (Inkinen, 2016). Moreover, when such individuals (knowledge creators and carriers) leave their organizations for another, they take the knowledge they have accumulated over the years. In contrast, structural knowledge (explicit knowledge) is well documented in numerous sources such as instruction manuals, books, newsletters, or magazines, and it is captured and codified, and thus easily accessible and shared among individuals. Table 9.1 below clarifies the differences between the characteristics and sources of both tacit and explicit forms of knowledge.

On the other hand, organizational knowledge refers to the learning activities that occur within a particular organization regarding the tacit and explicit forms of knowledge, and the crux of such learning activities involves

Table 9.1 Tacit and explicit knowledge

	Tacit knowledge (not documented)	*Explicit knowledge (documented)*
Characteristics	• Highly personal • Nonverbalized and unspoken • Difficult to capture and share • Intuitive and unarticulated • Topic-specific	• Easily captured and codified • Well documented • Easily communicated and shared • Formal and systematic • Accessible
Sources	• Informal face-to-face meetings and discussions • Personal experiences • Telephone conversations • Emails	• Instruction manuals • Written procedures and books • Databases and reports • Research findings • Best practices

Source: Adapted from Bhatt (2001), Serban and Luan (2002), and Cong and Pandya (2004)

transforming the former into the latter (Ahmed & Elhag, 2017). Tacit knowledge is a critical asset to organizations, as research has shown that managers obtain two-thirds of their information and knowledge from formal and informal face-to-face meetings or phone conversations (Davenport & Prusak, 1998). Moreover, exchanging tacit knowledge provides employees firsthand experiences and ideas about successful or failed endeavors. It strengthens their confidence when they conduct their tasks, as they will have learned from their peers' successes and failures. Finally, social/cultural knowledge refers to what individuals acquire through social or cultural interactions. This knowledge affects their attitudes and behavior in the work environment and determines the level of trust among colleagues (Oliva & Kotabe, 2019). It is thus crucial to recognize this knowledge to better guide and motivate employees to share their knowledge. Hence, the role of KM is to ascertain that organizational knowledge is appreciated, systematically organized, maintained, and shared. This can then lead to effective use of the organization's intellectual capital and eventually contribute to creating new knowledge (Toffler, 1990).

Knowledge management in the public sector: Challenges and opportunities

Although KM first appeared under the umbrella of the private sector and was designed to maximize the profitability and efficiency of private companies, it was later adopted by the public sector to safeguard its knowledge capital. Nevertheless, KM is nothing new to the public sector (Anthony, 2019; Riege & Lindsay, 2006). Reliance on knowledge as a valuable source of wealth and guidance for policymaking has been an ongoing trend in most OECD countries, but recognition and implementation of the specific systems, structures, and tools of KM have been a relatively recent phenomenon in the public sector (Friis, 2002). The more public policies are grounded in scientific and knowledge-based sources, the more likely they succeed and achieve the desired outcomes (Covin & Stivers, 1997). Furthermore, when knowledge informs policy, it offers the potential to maximize opportunities and minimize challenges and risks associated with implementing new and untested policies. More pragmatically, many governments today are under increasing pressure from their citizenry, who expect better quality services at lower costs (Akhavan et al., 2014).

To meet such needs, many managerial techniques have been introduced to the public sector under new public management reforms to improve efficiency, quality of decision-making, and responsiveness to the public. At the start, results-based performance was the main driver behind organizational and operational excellence, and managers accordingly emphasized observable work and output quality (Wiig, 2002). The increasing role of information technology and the use of computers then added order and efficacy to the performance of public organizations (Guadamillas-Gómez

& Donate-Manzanares, 2011). Due to economic and cultural factors, waves of globalization, and a worldwide shift toward a "knowledge economy" or "knowledge society" (Arab Knowledge Report, 2020; Wiig, 1997; 2002), attention has now turned to KM—a new ingredient for achieving organizational excellence. Thus, the focus and efforts of decision makers have shifted toward creating mechanisms and requirements for such a society to evolve and produce the knowledge necessary to maintain a competitive advantage. For example, the experiences of OECD countries show that KM has become an essential instrument for improving the effectiveness and responsiveness of the public sector (OECD, 2003). Since 2002, the OECD has produced annual reports based on comprehensive surveys of the concept and practice of KM within their public sector entities. These reports offer recommendations that address the challenges facing these government entities and this then allows their public sector organizations to reform KM programs and initiatives and update practices to match international best practices in the field of KM, thereby enhancing their outcomes (O'Dell & Grayson, 1998).

Riege and Lindsay (2006) point out the following four main drivers motivating the recent adoption of KM in the public sector. First, effectiveness in public service delivery has been an ongoing objective for governments worldwide, and KM promises to help achieve this. Adopting KM initiatives would facilitate knowledge transfer and sharing among employees, enhancing clarity and ease of operations. Second, public organizations wish to improve, develop, or update their existing knowledge repertoires, or establish new ones to make current knowledge accessible and protected from outside the organizations. Third, relying on knowledge to inform decisions and policies increases the likelihood of their success and makes the decision-making process more straightforward. Fourth, increased responsiveness and engagement in partnerships with the public sector are expected to lead ultimately to better service delivery and higher quality of such services (Hussinki et al., 2017).

Notwithstanding the above, there remains a paucity of research on KM in the Arab public sector. This is generally due to high levels of illiteracy, mediocre investments in R&D, and insufficient Information Communication Technology (ICT) in the region. While there is a growing body of literature on KM, it stems mainly from a Western point of view. Meanwhile, most public administrative practices in Arab countries are inherited colonial legacies, and their governments faced significant challenges in making the machinery of government effective and achieving desired results and outcomes in their specific social and cultural environments. Ultimately, little research has been conducted on elements hindering the success of KM initiatives in the Arab region. However, the region now needs KM more than ever due to the changing nature of global competitiveness and shift to a knowledge economy or society in which R&D are vital requirements.

Knowledge management processes

The knowledge of individuals is an essential ingredient in developing overall organizational knowledge, but not the only one (Thomas et al., 2001). The KM literature reveals that there are several "interactive" and intertwined processes in KM, and these involve the human, technological, and operational aspects that facilitate the creation, capture, organization, access, and use of various types of knowledge (Bhatt, 2001; Jain & Kelvin, 2013; Serban & Luan, 2002). The interaction among these processes has significant implications for any KM program or initiative, and each is inimitably distinct, since they are linked to organizations and their histories and unique characteristics (McLaughlin & Stankosky, 2010). Hence, ample attention needs to be paid to the effective implementation of these processes and their operation in specific cases.

Table 9.2 summarizes the above processes and specifies the role of individuals in collaborating, finding, facilitating, and sharing knowledge. In this respect, knowledge creation refers to the ability of an organization to generate innovative solutions and ideas (Marakas, 1999). This can take many forms, such as discovering new techniques and methods of solving a problem, borrowing certain practices from external sources, and contextualizing and integrating them into the organization. Furthermore, this process requires collaboration, discussion, and articulation of new knowledge among individuals. Lynn et al. (1996) argue that motivation, inspiration, and experimentation play a pivotal role in the knowledge creation phase and determine to what extent employees share knowledge among themselves. Meanwhile, Bhatt (2001) argues that knowledge creation does not mean organizations must always generate knowledge from scratch, but rather can constantly reconfigure and assemble pieces of knowledge from within the organization based on imitation, replication, and substitution strategies. These techniques can then allow an organization to identify

Table 9.2 Knowledge management processes

		Knowledge content		
	Knowledge	*management*	*processes*	
1) Create	**2) Capture**	**3) Organize**	**4) Access**	**5) Use**
• Discover	• Document	• Structure	• Present	• Disseminate
• Realize	• Extract	• Categorize	• Display	• Improve
• Discuss	• Store	• Analyze	• Profile	• Perform
• Articulate	• Represent	• Catalog	• Find	• Learn
Collaborate	*Find*	*Facilitate*	*Augment*	*Share*
		People's processes		

Source: Adapted from Serban and Luan (2002)

existing knowledge, restructure it, and create a new set of knowledge (Bhatt, 2001).

Similarly, Pentland (1995) argues that knowledge creation involves the discovery or invention of new knowledge and the replacement of existing content within an organization's tacit and explicit knowledge. This process involves a continual interplay between those two forms of knowledge through the four modes of knowledge creation defined by Nonaka (1994): socialization, externalization, internalization, and combination. These are intertwined models, and each relies on the other. The second step is capturing that knowledge and documenting it. Research has shown that, even when organizations can create knowledge, they risk losing it (Argote et al., 1978). Hence, storing this knowledge in what is often referred to as "organizational memory" is an instrumental step toward safeguarding it and maintaining it within an organization (Stein & Zwass, 1995). At this stage the role of technology becomes especially vital in codifying and digitalizing acquired knowledge. Establishing a proper technological infrastructure can enable organizations to organize and store knowledge effectively and, at the same time, create coherent channels for accessing and displaying it (Fai & Marschan, 2003). Chen and McQueen (2010) state that advanced IT tools, such as multimedia databases and database management systems, can effectively improve organizational memory and protect an organization's knowledge from being lost. Even with such systems, however, if an organization finds it challenging to localize necessary knowledge at the right time and in the correct format or context to utilize it, any benefit from its knowledge repository may disappear.

Nevertheless, as Bhatt (2001) argues, organizations can overcome this problem by training their employees, incentivizing them, familiarizing them with the entire knowledge management process, and showing them how they can express their creativity within the organization. The final process of KM is knowledge sharing, which Bukowitz and Williams (1999, p. 10) describe as "one of the toughest nuts organizations have to crack". This stage involves a complex interaction among the organization's technological, social, and human resources. Thus, it is easy to imagine the complicated nature of sharing knowledge and the challenges that arise when organizations attempt to encourage employees. Organizations should therefore seek to create an environment that incentivizes and rewards employees for sharing their knowledge and facilitate this task by implementing the mechanisms required for that purpose.

Enablers of knowledge management in the public sector

The success of KM initiatives depends on several critical factors within the organizations adopting such programs, and an ever-broadening body of literature discusses these factors and their role in enabling KM projects to succeed and achieve their expected outcomes. Such factors range from leadership (Siddique, 2012) and technology (McAdam & McCreedy, 1999;

Riege, 2005) to organizational culture (De Long & Fahey, 2000; Sun & Scott, 2005) and financial resources (Holsapple & Joshi, 2000). Overall, the current KM literature emphasizes leadership, control, human resources, and trust as critical conditions for the success of KM programs (Ringel-Bickelmaier & Ringel, 2010).

Leadership

A study conducted by Sayyadi (2019) found that selecting a capable KM leader is the first step that an organization should take, even before putting together a plan or strategy for a KM program. The importance of the leadership role resides in effectively approaching top management to obtain the necessary support and then constructing the human and technological infrastructures needed for KM projects. Also, the leader can provide the conditions and general atmosphere that will allow the processes to be carried out efficiently. This would be achieved by empowering and incentivizing individuals to share knowledge and ensuring that the required tools are available and function according to the organization's needs.

Control

Control is concerned with the need to ensure the availability of knowledge resources at adequate levels of quality and quantity, as well as necessary information security measures (Holsapple & Joshi, 2000). KM programs are responsible for creating accurate, coherent, and valid knowledge, but such knowledge must be protected from loss and maintained in a way that makes it accessible yet still secure against unauthorized use.

Human resources

Thomas et al. (2001) argue that too much attention in the literature has been paid to the technical aspects of KM, with far less research being conducted on the importance of KM's human and social aspects. Inkinen (2016) further argues that the success of KM initiatives is fundamentally reliant on having capable individuals who know how to share knowledge. Moreover, as Storey and Quintas (2001) suggest, the success of KM initiatives requires employees who are "willing to share their knowledge and expertise" in the first place (p. 359). Creating an environment and mechanisms that allow employees to maximize the use of their talents and easily share knowledge are among the main drivers behind any successful KM program.

Barriers to knowledge management

Among the major obstacles standing in the way of effective implementation of KM programs, the people who form the very bedrock of such programs must be considered (Riege, 2005). A significant corpus of academic research and consultancy reports have addressed the factors inhibiting knowledge sharing in public and private organizations, and the key elements commonly identified are organizational culture and trust among individuals and institutions. Each of these factors has a significant influence on the adoption and sustainability of KM programs.

Organizational culture

Numerous studies have found that knowledge and organizational culture are inextricably linked (De Long & Fahey, 2000; McDermott & O'Dell, 2001; Robertson & O'Malley-Hammersley, 2000; Scarborough et al., 1999). Culture shapes the understanding of knowledge and its dissemination within organizations and groups of individuals. For example, a cultural context that does not emphasize the value of knowledge or does not allow its utilization through increased participation in decision-making and vertical interaction among social and organizational groups will experience difficulties when implementing KM programs and reaping their benefits. In many ways, culture sets the stage for the social and collective orientations that make accumulating and sharing knowledge a pattern of behavior both within and outside the workplace.

Numerous studies have closely examined how the cultural setting of an organization can play a role in determining the fate of its KM programs. For example, Robertson and O'Malley-Hammersley (2000) found that when workers' expectations are satisfied via fair HR practices and the organizational culture promotes knowledge sharing, employees are more eager to share knowledge and allow others to benefit from what they know. Similarly, McDermott and O'Dell (2001) found that employees are more likely to share knowledge when the organizational culture rewards knowledge sharing. This can take the form of financial or moral support, as well as acknowledgment of those who have made extra efforts to disseminate what they have learned to others within the organization. One of the most critical factors described in the existing research that can influence knowledge sharing is the level of organizational commitment among employees (Hussinki et al., 2017). For example, Storey and Quintas (2001) argue that securing employees' trust, commitment, and motivation to share knowledge is one of the main factors that must be considered when implementing KM projects.

Unfortunately, the organizational culture in most Arab organizations creates numerous challenges that stand in the way of effective sharing and transfer of knowledge (Ahmad & Daghfous, 2010), resulting in a severe aversion to knowledge sharing. While history has shown that Arabs and Muslims have certainly engaged in knowledge sharing, and the Islamic holy book, the Qur'an, requires all Muslims to learn and spread knowledge among themselves, current research findings have proven that Arabs are among the most resistant to knowledge sharing for various reasons (Hussinki et al., 2017; Siddique, 2012). Skok and Tahir (2010), for example, have confirmed the complexity and difficulty of sharing knowledge in the Arab world, explaining that people's social and cultural beliefs can be the primary hindrances to knowledge sharing.

Trust

Lack of trust among individuals and between employees and management constitutes a significant challenge for knowledge sharing, especially in the Arab world, where knowledge is considered a form of power. Trust is fundamental in knowledge creation, acquisition, and dissemination (Harlow, 2018; Riege, 2005), as individuals cannot share what they know when they fear that others might misuse their knowledge or attribute it to themselves. When employees lack interpersonal trust, they refrain from sharing what they know with each other, thereby drastically blocking the processes of KM (Sun & Scott, 2005). This phenomenon is particularly pertinent in the Arab world, where establishing trust and connections is the first step before engaging in any collaborative and sustainable exchange. People are often reluctant to share their tacit knowledge with anyone unless firm confidence and an expected level of trustworthiness have been well-established, and thus Ahmad and Daghfous (2010) indicate the importance of building trust by creating legal frameworks to protect individuals who share knowledge and incentivize them to do so.

Research methodology and data analysis

This chapter relies on primary data collected from the Dubai government through structured interviews and a survey tool. The first stage of data collection involved personal in-depth and onsite interviews conducted in five major government entities with a running KM program such as the Dubai Electricity and Water Authority (DEWA), Dubai Courts, Knowledge and Human Development Authority (KHDA), Roads and Transportation Authority (RTA), and the Dubai Police. These interviews were intended to identify critical challenges in defining, implementing, and running KM programs in Dubai. Structured questions were asked to the five organizations to discover their challenges, and their answers were then used to design the survey tool. Interviews were transcribed, summarized, and analyzed by comparing the answers of each organization to the same question. This allowed identification of patterns, similarities, and differences in each organization's approach to knowledge management. Such an approach to analyzing interviews has proven reliable and thus is used regularly in qualitative research (Guba & Lincoln, 1994).

In the second stage of data collection, a comprehensive survey tool was created by adapting the OECD knowledge management survey with permission and incorporating elements related specifically to Middle Eastern cultures. Since Arabic is the official language of the UAE, the survey was translated from English into Arabic and thoroughly proofread to identify

266 *Importance of effective human resource development*

and eliminate any contextual and grammatical mistakes. Both English and Arabic versions of the survey were then mailed to human resources, KM, and strategy managers across all government entities in Dubai, with a response rate of 66%. Respondents were asked to state their opinions on statements that described sources of information and knowledge, incentives for sharing knowledge, instruments used to share and disseminate knowledge, and the challenges of implementing and running KM programs. Answers mainly used a five-point Likert scale, with one representing "strongly disagree" and five representing "strongly agree".

Findings

Clarity of the knowledge management concept among Dubai's public sector entities

Successful implementation of KM programs is contingent on the clarity of its concept among all members of an organization. One of the most significant obstacles government entities have faced when running KM programs in Dubai is the vagueness and lack of clarity concerning the concept among their people, and this challenge was common among all interviewed and surveyed organizations. For example, the Dubai Courts stated that it was challenging to explain and clarify what KM meant to everyone within their organization, and it was also quite difficult to decide which department to run it. KM was a new concept upon its introduction, and employees at the Dubai Court had received no training on such programs. This created difficulties when initially implementing the KM program, but with the addition of training programs, workshops, and lectures, the meaning of KM gradually became clearer. Similarly, the Dubai Police asserted that the concept of KM was vague to most of its employees despite persistent efforts to clarify it. The Dubai Police, therefore, organized workshops and training sessions to inform employees about the importance and meaning of KM, and felt confident that its efforts would lead to the desired outcomes.

Analysis of the survey data shows that, when asked about the main difficulties in their attempts to implement KM programs, 30% of the respondents strongly agreed and 36% agreed that lack of awareness and understanding of the KM concept was high among them (Figure 9.2). Moreover, 19% of the respondents strongly agreed and 53% agreed that another challenging factor was a lack of awareness concerning how to use KM tools.

Most government entities in Dubai were aware of KM, but used different terms interchangeably to refer to the concept. Figure 9.3 shows the four terms predominantly used by those entities in their strategy and general management documents. Respondents were asked to indicate which of the terms they used and were allowed to choose more than one response. A total of 51% of respondents confirmed that they used the

Knowledge management in the public sector 267

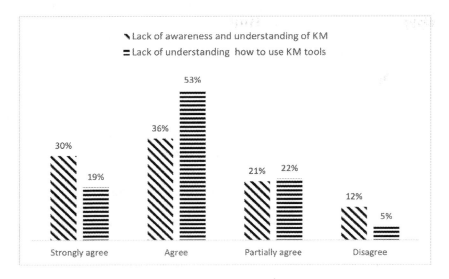

Figure 9.2 Awareness of KM in Dubai's public sector
Source: *Designed by the author based on original survey data*

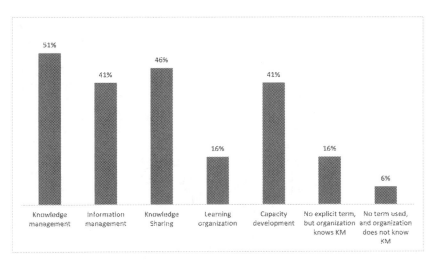

Figure 9.3 Terms used for KM in Dubai's public sector
Note: *These figures do not total 100%, as respondents were allowed to provide multiple responses.*
Source: *Designed by the author based on original survey data*

268 *Importance of effective human resource development*

term "knowledge management", 46% used "knowledge sharing", and 41% indicated that they used "information management" and "capacity development".

Using these various terms in this way can result in ambiguity and confusion among individuals in an organization and hinder any attempts to foster KM program implementation. Therefore, it is crucial to clearly define the concept of KM and distinguish it among the related terminology to avoid such confusion.

The challenge of capturing tacit knowledge within Dubai government entities

Dubai government entities vary in their capabilities and efforts to capture and store tacit knowledge. Figure 9.4 reveals that 19% of respondents strongly agreed and 47% agreed that capturing tacit knowledge was a difficulty they faced in their organizations. Insufficient time did not appear to be a major contributing factor, as only 19% strongly agreed, and 22% agreed that lack of time was a reason for the difficulties encountered while attempting to capture the tacit knowledge of their employees. Interviews with the public organizations also offered similar results to those from the survey analysis. For example, the Dubai Police recognized the significance of tacit knowledge and were aware of its complexity, thus establishing mechanisms to capture and store it. The Japanese model of KM was adopted for sharing and transferring knowledge within the organization by establishing cross-organizational and self-managing teams, arranging

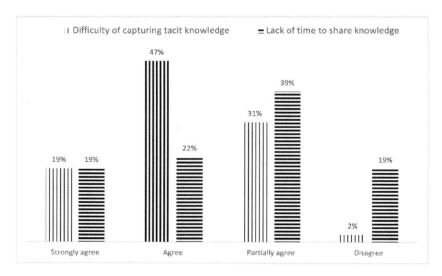

Figure 9.4 Challenges of knowledge sharing in Dubai public organizations
Source: *Designed by the author based on original survey data*

Knowledge management in the public sector 269

weekly meetings among its employees, organizing workshops and lectures targeting specific skills, and calling upon each police officer to share their experiences and ways in which they dealt with particular issues. More specifically, employees were required to meet every Thursday for two hours to discuss the new techniques they had learned and share them with recruits.

Furthermore, officers were strongly encouraged to write about new cases and how they solved them, and financial incentives were provided for those who regularly wrote articles about their experiences. Pilots in the Police Aviation Department were required to document their experiences and mistakes and explain how they resolved them. Regular training workshops were also held where pilots were introduced to new practices and needed to use specific manuals that carefully captured details concerning the most recent techniques in the aviation industry. This then allowed knowledge transfer from experienced individuals to those less experienced among the police and ensured that tacit knowledge was exchanged among all employees.

The Dubai Courts also adopted efficient practices for the sharing and storing its employees' tacit knowledge. For example, judges were required to meet regularly to discuss their cases and share their experiences and opinions with others, particularly new judges. This technique helped the judges to learn from each other and, more importantly, gave new judges the chance to acquire skills and expertise from older and more experienced judges in the Dubai Courts. Moreover, when judges finalized a case and announced a verdict, they were required to electronically store the case details and explain how they reached their decision. This way, when other judges dealt with a similar case, they could refer to the precedent set by previous judges when forming their judgments. Other techniques of storing judges' tacit knowledge included informal seminars, weekly meetings, training workshops, and booklets published frequently by judges. Based on interviews with the Dubai Courts, if a judge permanently resigned or retired, their knowledge and experience would be appropriately stored and easily accessible to other judges. The Dubai Courts' performance increased significantly after implementing these procedures, with 86% of the cases finalized within three months and the remaining 14% determined within six months.

Dubai's RTA also raised critical points regarding the crucial role of tacit knowledge in their organization. They stated that their heavy reliance on international consultants made the knowledge created vulnerable to loss once those consultants departed. Although consultants were a rich source of "rented knowledge", if their experiences, observations, and recommendations were not well documented, the organization risked losing an invaluable source of "costly" knowledge. RTA thus attempted to establish a system that captured the tacit knowledge of such consultants through various methods such as mentoring, coaching, and informal meetings. KM champions were hired to facilitate the transfer of knowledge from these experts to the organization and hold weekly presentations lasting two to four hours to teach RTA employees how to share knowledge.

DEWA, meanwhile, acknowledged that they had no formal internal systems or procedures to capture tacit knowledge due to a lack of awareness about its significance among most employees. However, the organization recognized the importance of this knowledge and intended to invest in it in the future. Furthermore, as a relatively new organization, KHDA argued that it needed to focus on developing the capacity and human resources to generate knowledge within the organization. The next step would be to create the necessary mechanisms to store such generated knowledge and establish a robust KM program.

Importance of knowledge management for Dubai's public sector

There are several reasons why adopting KM programs in Dubai is necessary. Shrinking budgetary allocations, the need to invest in significant expansion projects and human resource development, the departure of talent from many sectors, and the quest for workforce nationalization and employment opportunities for locals all exert considerable pressure on the public sector bureaucracy's capacity to function more efficiently. Indeed, 66% of the surveyed organizations in Dubai asserted that they had lost core competencies when their staff members moved to other organizations or units. More importantly, Dubai relies heavily on the expertise of consultants who provide "rented knowledge" to various private and government entities, and this knowledge has often been lost due to the lack of a well-structured and developed KM system.

Implementing KM in Dubai's public organizations also creates benefits and opportunities at individual and organizational levels. At the individual level, employees can share their experiences and knowledge and learn from each other's mistakes, enhancing performance and improving their skills. At the organizational level, efficiency, quality, productivity, and better decision-making are the fruits of KM. In this way, organizations can witness substantial improvement in the quality and cost-effectiveness of their operations and public satisfaction (Cong & Pandya, 2004).

More specifically, Table 9.3 shows that the five organizations interviewed for this research all had similar reasons for implementing KM programs. They all aimed to enhance their organizational performance, improve internal efficiency and service delivery, facilitate communication among individuals and departments within or outside their organizations, and better store their knowledge capital through proper mechanisms. Dubai's RTA, the Dubai Courts, and Dubai Police were fully aware of the importance of the KM for their organizations and implemented it accordingly. DEWA and KHDA, however, implemented their KM programs not only for organizational reasons but also to satisfy the Dubai Government Excellence Program (DGEP) requirements, which considered the presence of KM tools one of the main criteria for winning the award. The DGEP, therefore, succeeded in encouraging public organizations in Dubai to adopt the best practices to enhance their effectiveness and service delivery.

Table 9.3 Rationales for KM implementation among Dubai's government entities

Public entity	Public entity rational for deciding to adopt knowledge management
Dubai Electricity and Water Authority	• Fulfill the requirements of the DGEP. • Follow recommendations by external consultancy firms to enhance performance. • Improve internal efficiency, productivity, and service delivery.
Knowledge and Human Development Authority	• Fulfill the requirements of the DGEP. • Facilitate communication of knowledge among all employees. • Avoid overlap in performance of specific duties. • Sound policymaking, improving internal decision-making and increasing transparency.
Road and Transportation Authority	• Capture knowledge through study, training, and best practice sharing. • Share knowledge with colleagues within RTA. • Classify, index, store, and retrieve knowledge.
Dubai Courts	• Enhance knowledge transfer and creation and, more importantly, organizational effectiveness. • Increase productivity and quality of service delivery.
Dubai Police	• Create, transfer, and share knowledge with everyone within the organization. • Facilitate E-Government initiatives and, more importantly, make use of good practices within the organization. • Facilitate communication between Dubai Police and Dubai government.

Source: Compiled by the author based on original interview data

Implementing knowledge management processes in Dubai

Dubai government entities differed in their institutionalization and implementation of a structured process for creating, capturing, organizing, and sharing knowledge, which significantly impacted the respective outcomes of their KM programs. For instance, the Dubai Courts, Dubai Police, and RTA were pioneers in adopting well-established KM processes. The Dubai Courts fostered knowledge creation by incentivizing judges and employees to be innovative in handling the cases they dealt with and requiring them to document how they reached a particular verdict or decision in a well-systematized internal portal that included extensive information about everything taking place within the Courts. Judges had direct access to this portal and could upload their ideas, opinions, or suggestions regarding their cases and learn from others' experiences.

Likewise, the Dubai Police utilized a straightforward process for its KM program, adopting the Japanese model to capture, store, and share knowledge by frequently organizing meetings, workshops, and seminars where the police exchanged experiences and shared knowledge. Creative ideas and new practices were documented in a report published every six months and shared among all departments. Another method to create knowledge involved applied research conducted by student employees. The Dubai Police strongly encouraged and supported its employees to pursue higher education and participate in national or international training workshops to acquire new skills and insights. The recommendations of the dissertations and reports produced by those student employees were then taken seriously to improve efficiency in service delivery.

In the case of RTA, their KM team developed a methodical process framework based on best practices that aimed to capture, evaluate, categorize, and share knowledge across the organization. Like the Dubai Courts and Dubai Police, knowledge within RTA was captured through training sessions, meetings, workshops, and personal discussions. Newly created knowledge was classified, indexed, stored, and shared through monthly newsletters and an intranet portal. In addition, an electronic data management system (EDMS) was created to facilitate sharing documents and knowledge among RTA employees. DEWA and KHDA indicated that they had not yet adopted any institutionalized processes for their KM programs, but they had incorporated many practices to foster knowledge sharing among their employees, including holding occasional meetings and organizing lectures and workshops.

The current state of knowledge management in Dubai's public sector organizations

Knowledge loss risk due to staff mobility or departure

Recently, government entities in Dubai have engaged in decentralizing authority and allowed for more flexibility and mobility of staff within and outside of their organizations. While these changes promised improved performance and enhanced efficiency, they also created new challenges and risks. For example, organizational memory and intellectual capital can suffer when employees move from one department or organization to another without adequate documentation and storage of their experiences and knowledge.

Moreover, financial pressures have obliged some government entities to hire more part-time employees to cut costs. As shown in Figure 9.5, the survey conducted among government entities in Dubai revealed that 24% and 38% of respondents claimed to systematically or occasionally employ staff in temporary positions, respectively. Meanwhile, 50% indicated they offered internships to new graduates, and 27% said they had transferees from other organizations working for them. Organizations with more temporary staff faced greater risks of losing knowledge, as their employees had fewer incentives to store and share knowledge and less organizational

Knowledge management in the public sector 273

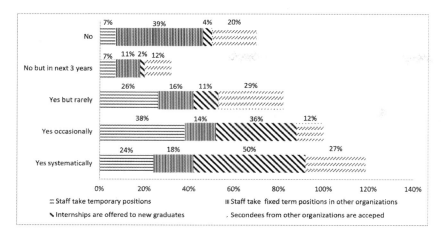

Figure 9.5 Mobility of staff in Dubai's public sector
Source: Designed by the author based on original survey data

commitment, which are among the main prerequisites to motivate employees to share their knowledge with others.

Furthermore, Dubai relies heavily on the experience and knowledge of consultants for developmental and operational matters, and Figure 9.6 shows that 49% of temporary staff in Dubai's public sector were consultants. Their role was instrumental in providing "rented knowledge", yet if they left without adequately documenting their experiences, organizations risked losing that costly knowledge and wasting significant amounts of money on consultancies.

Temporarily hired consultants, contractors, and advisors represented the knowledge and knowhow suppliers of most Dubai government entities. Data analysis for the survey administered among those entities revealed that 45% of temporary staff were advisors, 44% were contractors, and 55% were interns. These figures demonstrate the precariousness of the public sector's position and the risks of losing competencies if they are not effectively stored.

Moreover, the 2008 global financial crisis resulted in a significant downturn in Dubai's economy and a considerable uptake in its employee turnover. Figure 9.7 reveals how government entities in Dubai lost a significant portion of their senior and middle management, with 47% of senior staff, 87% of government officers, and 21% of consultants leaving. Among these, officers comprised the most significant portion at 87%. Some left for other institutions in Dubai or other Emirates, while others left the country entirely in search of better and more rewarding opportunities. Hence, there has been a dire necessity to implement KM strategies and programs that can motivate employees to share knowledge and establish the necessary

274 *Importance of effective human resource development*

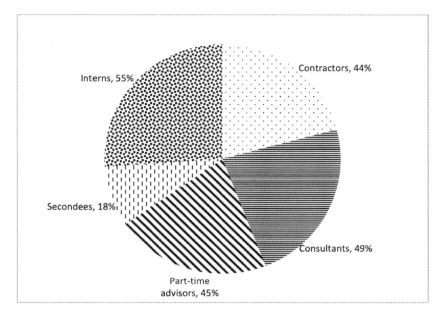

Figure 9.6 Temporary staff with limited period contracts in Dubai government entities
Note: These figures do not total 100%, as respondents were allowed to provide multiple responses
Source: Designed by the author based on original survey data

tools to keep knowledge and experience stored within organizations for future use.

Strategies adopted to protect organizational knowledge

Given its high levels of employee turnover, it would behoove the Dubai public sector to implement strategies that safeguard the knowledge and experience of employees in a systematic and accessible manner. One of the first steps toward reflecting the importance of KM in government entities is placing it among their top five priorities. However, the survey data shows that less than half of the entities considered KM one of their top five, and 52% indicated that it was not now but could be in the future (see Figure 9.8).

Similar results were found for written KM policies or strategies, with only 44% indicating that they had clear and articulate KM policies, and the remaining 56% stating that they did not but intended to develop them in the future. It is clear from the statistics in Figures 9.8 and 9.9 that the organizations that considered KM one of their top five priorities were those already possessing written KM policies or strategies.

Knowledge management in the public sector 275

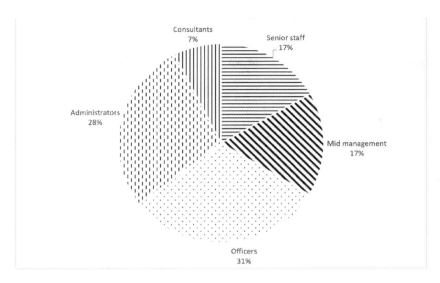

Figure 9.7 Staff turnover
Source: Designed by the author based on original survey data

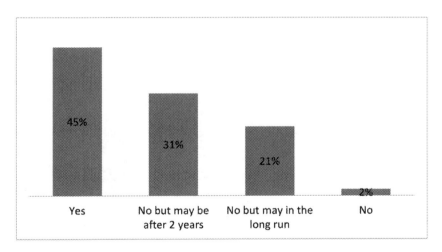

Figure 9.8 KM is one of the top five priorities of the organizations
Source: Designed by the author based on original survey data

Furthermore, 47% of respondents stated that the policies or strategies that their organizations had implemented focused mainly on HR aspects, while 40% said they focused on information management, and 37% claimed they focused on IT (see Figure 9.10). The earlier stages of KM program

276 *Importance of effective human resource development*

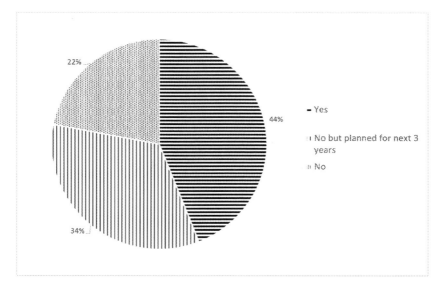

Figure 9.9 Existence of written KM policy or strategy
Source: *Designed by the author based on original survey data*

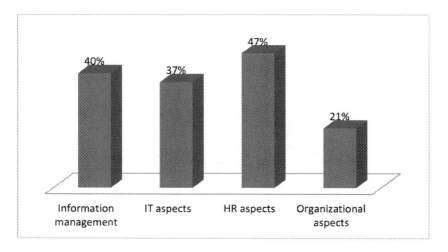

Figure 9.10 KM policy/strategy focus areas
Source: *Designed by the author based on original survey data*

implementation in Dubai witnessed over-reliance on automation and digitalization of KM processes, as information management and IT were the main areas in which most Dubai government entities initially established their KM programs and policies.

Knowledge management in the public sector 277

However, as analysis of the interviews confirmed, major government entities in Dubai later realized that because KM is about people, HR policies are the correct means to incentivize and encourage staff to share their knowledge and become dynamic in facilitating the KM process. As such, they gradually shifted their focus from IT to HR.

Sources and documentation of knowledge in Dubai's public sector

To clearly understand KM in Dubai, it is essential to trace government entities' sources of information and knowledge and how they document it. This can elucidate how information is relied upon and used, its credibility, and reveal whether it was stored and documented correctly. As Figure 9.11 shows, 86% of respondents pointed out that they systematically relied on Dubai's government agencies and entities to obtain their required information. The second important source was federal ministries or agencies, which were relied upon by 54% of respondents. Meanwhile, only 23% regularly relied on think tanks or research centers, and just 35% sought out universities for information. These findings are consistent with the interviews conducted with major government entities, such as DEWA, Dubai Courts, and the RTA, which revealed that the public sector in Dubai still had a long way to go before research centers and universities became one of its primary sources of information, as is also the case in most OECD countries. Government entities instead circulated information among each

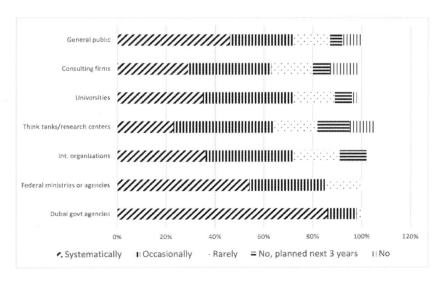

Figure 9.11 Sources of information for government entities in Dubai
Source: Designed by the author based on original survey data

278 *Importance of effective human resource development*

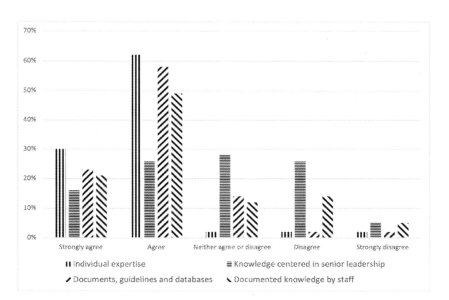

Figure 9.12 Sources of knowledge for Dubai government entities
Source: Designed by the author based on original survey data

other and, to some extent, sought out the public's input. A total of 46% of respondents indicated that the public was a valuable source of information, and their suggestions, opinions, and recommendations were welcomed via online channels and the media that voiced their needs and concerns.

As shown in Figure 9.12, 62% of respondents agreed that they sourced their knowledge from the individual expertise of consultants, experts, or advisors. This result is consistent with the interview findings and other survey sections that assessed the level of reliance on external consultants and experts. It reinforces the necessity of capturing and documenting such tacit knowledge and providing the mechanisms to properly document it and make it accessible to other employees within the organization. Meanwhile, 58% of respondents indicated that their second source of knowledge was documents, guidelines, and databases, which only reflect an organization's explicit knowledge. It was also found that 49% of the surveyed organizations agreed that they relied on knowledge documented by their staff.

The public organizations that participated in the survey were also asked whether their knowledge and good practices were captured, and in what form they were documented. Interestingly, it was found that 72% of respondents considered business mapping and surveys as equally important in capturing the knowledge of employees. Furthermore, another significant source of organizational knowledge was post-project or action reviews, which comprised 49% of the responses.

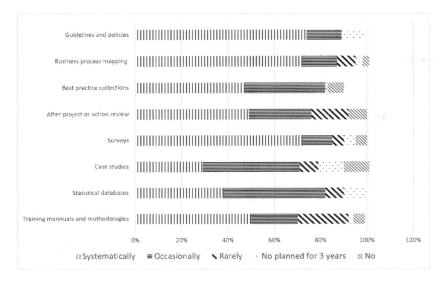

Figure 9.13 Methods of capturing knowledge and forms of documentation
Source: Designed by the author based on original survey data

Regarding documentation of that knowledge, 74% of respondents said they systematically translated the captured knowledge into guidelines and policies implemented and institutionalized within their government entities. In addition, best practice collections and statistical databases constituted 47% and 38% of the total responses, respectively (see Figure 9.13).

Means of sharing or transferring knowledge

After creating and documenting knowledge, sharing it and transferring it to others within or outside of the organization is the next step. Sophisticated technological devices, especially since the advent of the Internet, and the accessibility of computers, have made knowledge sharing far more manageable and straightforward. However, these technological instruments do not constitute the core of KM programs, as they are only a means to facilitate access and sharing of knowledge. Instead, a wide array of organizational, technological, and personal techniques must facilitate knowledge transfer. As shown in Figure 9.14, 72% of respondents reported that they systematically relied on document management systems like electronic shared folders, 65% used an intranet, and 62% indicated that they used the Internet. Thus, the government seemed overly reliant on automation and digitalization, as methods for conveying tacit knowledge like video or telephone conferences were not used to share knowledge. Lessons learned databases also accounted for a mere 14%. These findings are consistent with

280 *Importance of effective human resource development*

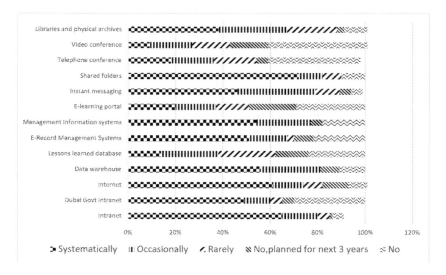

Figure 9.14 Means of sharing knowledge within Dubai's public sector
Source: Designed by the author based on original survey data

the interviews; for example, DEWA, RTA, and the Dubai Courts affirmed that IT companies implemented a system-centered approach to run their KM programs. Although technology has been instrumental to the success of KM programs, it can also become an impediment if organizations are overly reliant on it and ignore the human aspects of knowledge sharing. More importantly, tacit knowledge is often transferred through informal discussions, such as phone calls or casual meetings, and not necessarily through formal channels like those discussed above.

Goals for establishing KM programs in Dubai's public sector

To evaluate the outcomes of KM programs in Dubai's public sector, it is first necessary to highlight the goals of their establishment. In this study, 19 government entities were surveyed to compare KM's goals with the success level they achieved. Results from the survey demonstrated that achieving enhanced efficiency, productivity, and service delivery through more systematic knowledge sharing were the main drivers behind the establishment of KM programs within Dubai's public sector entities. As displayed in Figure 9.15, 73% of respondents indicated that the first and most important reason for implementing KM programs was to improve work efficiency and productivity by facilitating access to and sharing knowledge within their organizations. After this, the second most essential rationales were to protect the organization against loss of knowledge due to staff departure

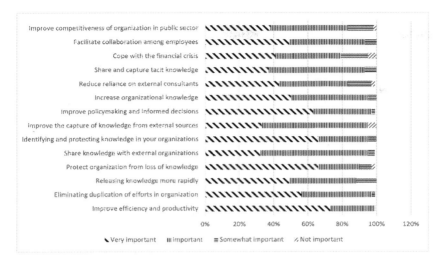

Figure 9.15 Goals of implementing KM programs in Dubai's public sector
Source: Designed by the author based on original survey data

and to identify and secure the organization's current strategic knowledge (66%). The third significant reason was to improve policymaking within the organization and make more informed decisions (62%). In the end, only 37% of respondents indicated that capturing and sharing tacit knowledge was very important in establishing a KM program, and it was not among the top four factors. Indeed, Dubai government entities' objectives in setting up KM programs are consistent with those of OECD countries, whose primary goals were to improve the efficiency and productivity of public service delivery (90%) (OECD 2003).

Results of current KM programs in Dubai's public sector

Overall, analysis of the data in this study has revealed some poignant insights concerning the current state of KM in Dubai's public sector, as the surveyed organizations indicated that they had not achieved significant success in reaching the primary objectives they intended to achieve by establishing KM programs. For example, improving work efficiency and productivity by facilitating access to and sharing knowledge was the most important factor in establishing KM programs in Dubai government entities (73%). Nevertheless, as Figure 9.16 shows, only 23% pointed out they were very successful and 43% of respondents said they succeeded in achieving this goal. Similarly, the current KM program did not achieve significant success in protecting the organization from loss of knowledge due to the

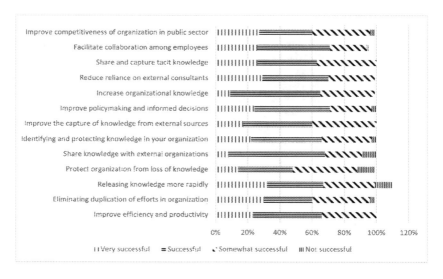

Figure 9.16 Factors that would facilitate the implementation of Dubai's public sector

Source: Designed by the author based on original survey data

departure of staff, as just 14% and 34% of respondents indicated that they were very successful or successful in attaining this objective, respectively. The same mediocre results were reached in identifying and protecting the knowledge residing within the organization, as 22% and 44% reported they were very successful or successful, respectively. Regarding the improvement of informed policymaking decisions, only 47% claimed they succeeded in achieving this objective.

Notwithstanding the above, Dubai's current KM programs appear to have achieved significant success in other elements. For example, 32% of respondents indicated that they successfully released knowledge more rapidly, and 30% reported successfully eliminating redundant tasks among government organizations and agencies. Improving knowledge sharing with external organizations was the top achievement of the current KM project, as 60% of respondents pointed out that they were successful in this aspect. Likewise, 56% indicated that, through the current KM program, they had successfully managed to increase their organizational knowledge.

The survey respondents were also asked to determine to what extent their KM programs had successfully achieved their primary objectives. Figure 9.17 illustrates that 49% of respondents considered their programs only reasonably successful, and 38% considered them unsuccessful. The reasons behind such mediocre results are numerous.

Knowledge management in the public sector 283

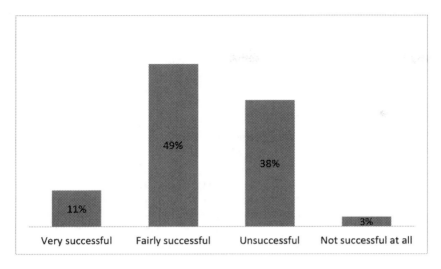

Figure 9.17 Overall results of implementing KM in Dubai's public sector
Source: Designed by the author based on original survey data

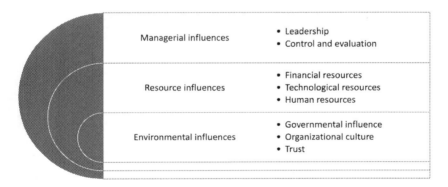

Figure 9.18 Factors influencing the management of knowledge
Source: Adapted from Holsapple and Joshi (2000)

Factors affecting knowledge management programs in Dubai

As demonstrated in Figure 9.18, managerial influences, resource influences, and environmental influences all contribute to the overall outcomes of KM programs. This framework of tracing influences was thus applied to the context of Dubai's public sector to assess how such influences play out in managing knowledge in Dubai.

284 *Importance of effective human resource development*

Managerial influences

Managerial influences are the dynamic drivers that catalyze implementation of KM within organizations and take on a leading role throughout the process. These influences comprise four elements that differ in importance and functionality.

LEADERSHIP

The survey data clearly shows the important role of leadership in KM programs within Dubai's public sector. Previous studies have indicated three primary sources of leadership that can steer KM programs: 1) a central unit for KM, 2) chief officers responsible for overseeing the implementation and effective operation of KM processes, and 3) knowledge champions who work directly with employees and facilitate the creation, documentation, and sharing of knowledge. Organizations were asked to specify whether they had any of these elements in the Dubai public sector survey. As shown in Figure 9.19, 66% of the surveyed organizations did not have a central unit for KM programs, 67% did not have chief KM officers, and 80% did not have KM champions. These results offer a clear picture of how government entities in Dubai were not fully aware of the instrumental role played by leadership in driving KM programs and establishing a proper environment that would allow them to function effectively.

To explore this issue further, it is important to turn to the in-depth interviews conducted among five organizations in Dubai: the RTA, Dubai Courts, Dubai Police, DEWA, and the KHDA. Some of these

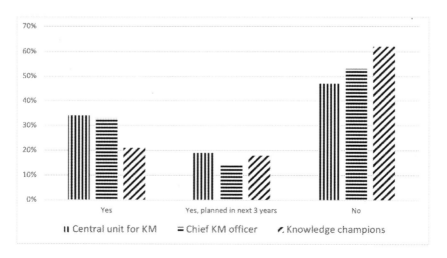

Figure 9.19 Role of leadership in Dubai's KM programs
Source: *Designed by the author based on original survey data*

Knowledge management in the public sector

organizations demonstrated a clear direction guided by effective leadership. For example, the RTA had nine KM champions to lead the implementation and knowledge-sharing processes. These champions integrated with and clarified the concept with employees, facilitated knowledge sharing, and ensured that the organization followed the correct path toward making KM an integrative part of the organization. Similarly, the Dubai Courts had 11 administrative directors who oversaw the progress of their KM programs and met annually to discuss their achievements and progress. This set an example for other entities to appoint KM leaders who could help their organizations move in the right direction and achieve their desired results.

CONTROL AND EVALUATION

No matter the context, KM programs' performance should always be subject to continuous evaluation. In Dubai, government entities used various instruments to assess the performance of their KM programs. Figure 9.20 shows that 39% used international KM best practice indicators to assess their practices and compare performance with that of other organizations. Moreover, 27% of respondents relied on written feedback about KM achievements, while only 14% used a balance scorecard. Interviews with the Dubai Courts revealed that they relied on annual surveys among all their employees, including judges, to identify and assess successes, challenges, failures, and opportunities for improvement. The results of these surveys helped the Dubai Courts realize where they stood in achieving the KM program's expected outcomes.

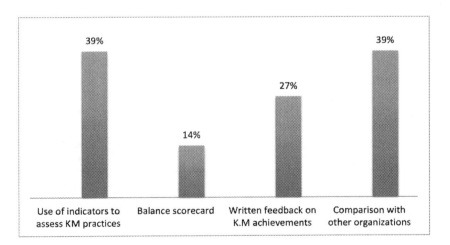

Figure 9.20 Assessment of KM performance in Dubai's public sector
Source: Designed by the author based on original survey data

286 *Importance of effective human resource development*

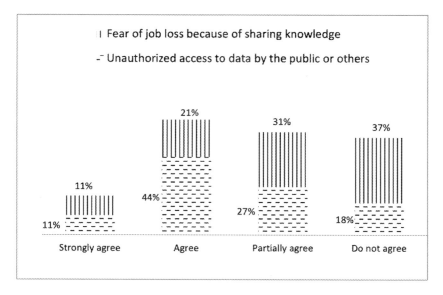

Figure 9.21 Protection of employees and data
Source: *Designed by the author based on original survey data*

Regarding concerns about the willingness to share knowledge, Figure 9.21 shows that 11% of respondents strongly agreed and 21% agreed when asked whether they were worried about losing their jobs due to knowledge sharing. Meanwhile, 11% strongly agreed and 44% agreed that they were worried about unauthorized access to data by the public or other competing organizations.

These results reveal that the environment of the organizations did not threaten the security of employees if sensitive knowledge was shared, but they had yet to establish the necessary instruments to protect their data from unauthorized use.

Resource influences

For the successful implementation of KM initiatives, financial and human capacities are required. Allocation of sufficient financial resources for KM projects determines their efficiency and overall quality, and also establishes the human, technological, and institutional capabilities necessary for the KM program to operate successfully. Public organizations should, therefore, assign a sufficient annual budget for KM. Since knowledge is a source locked in the human mind (Kim & Mauborgne, 1998), it is imperative to create the necessary conditions and incentivizing mechanisms that would encourage individuals within an organization to share their knowledge.

FINANCIAL RESOURCES

In this regard, the advent of the global financial crisis had a tremendous effect on the government of Dubai and resulted in cuts to government spending and the reordering of priorities. This also had implications for KM activities in some organizations, as it was one of the critical areas affected by budget cuts. Survey data could not precisely reflect the percentage each organization spent on KM programs because only seven organizations answered the question related to the budget allocated to KM. Among them, four indicated that they spent 5% of their overall budget on KM, one spent 4%, and the remaining two spent 2%. These findings provide little insight into KM's current state and perceived importance; however, many surveyed organizations did emphasize KM in their future work plans. When asked what they expected to happen to their KM budgets over the coming five years, 4% of the respondents said that it would increase by 100%, 21% said it would increase by 50% to 99%, 48% said it would increase by 0% to 49%, 8% said that it would remain the same, and 16% indicated that it would decrease.

Interviews, meanwhile, provided a clearer image of the KM budgetary issues facing most public organizations since the 2008 financial crisis began. For example, half of the interviewed government agencies stated that the budgets they allocated for KM programs were significantly cut due to budgetary restrictions stemming from the financial crisis that saw the government permanently reducing its spending. This then limited their capability to organize workshops, provide training on KM for employees, and even translate KM material from English to Arabic.

TECHNOLOGICAL RESOURCES

After capturing and codifying data comes the task of documenting and storing it. The availability of necessary technological instruments for this purpose is thus an instrumental element in the overall success of any KM program, and survey findings indicate that Dubai government entities relied on sophisticated IT systems to store their captured knowledge. Figure 9.22 shows that 54% of respondents stated that they systematically used data warehousing and data mining tools to facilitate knowledge storing and sharing, 49% used the Dubai Government Intranet for knowledge sharing and communication, and 47% used other online collaboration tools. However, 38% did not use lessons learned databases, where tacit knowledge could be effectively stored.

The perception of KM in most of Dubai's public organizations was that it was synonymous with Knowledge Management Systems (KMS). Most employees thus had a limited and narrow understanding of KM, and often thought that implementing state-of-the-art technological instruments to store knowledge was the only salient feature of KM, thereby overlooking the other structural, cultural, and managerial elements without which a KM program would likely fail to succeed and bring about desired outcomes.

288 *Importance of effective human resource development*

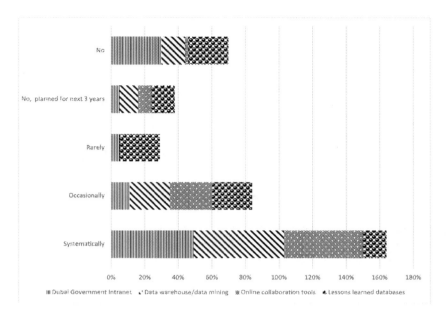

Figure 9.22 IT systems for KM in Dubai's public sector
Source: Designed by the author based on original survey data

HUMAN RESOURCES

The survey administered to participant organizations also focused on measuring the effectiveness of human resource development (HRD) activities in building skills and how these resources are effectively utilized in the workplace. Regarding HRD effectiveness, the results in Figure 9.23 indicate that 54% of respondents considered the training and skill building provided by the organizations to be successful and 17% thought it to be very successful in enhancing staff skills, abilities, and knowledge.

However, the results showed different patterns in terms of actual utilization of competence, and it was found that employees' skills, abilities, and experience were not fully recognized or utilized by most public organizations in Dubai. Figure 9.24 shows that none of the respondents indicated that their skills were fully utilized, 37% claimed they were highly utilized, 39% said they were utilized, and 17% reported poor utilization. To some extent, these figures reveal that their organizations did not recognize employee skills well. This is consistent with other cross-national studies conducted in the region. For example, the underutilization of nationals' labor capacity is one of the leading human capital challenges facing the UAE, Qatar, and Oman (Al-Yahya, 2009). Another study was conducted by Al-Yahya (2010) in Saudi Arabia, Oman, and the UAE. It found that underutilization of human capital resources (knowledge, skills,

Knowledge management in the public sector 289

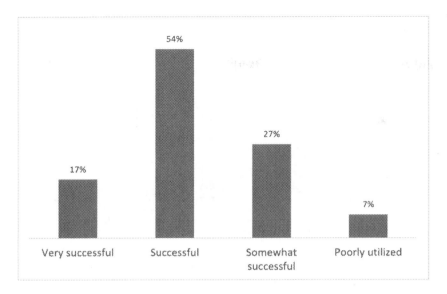

Figure 9.23 Training effects on staff skills and knowledge
Source: *Designed by the author based on original survey data*

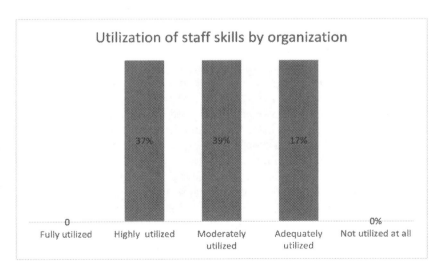

Figure 9.24 Utilization of staff skills, abilities, and experience by organizations
Source: *Designed by the author based on original survey data*

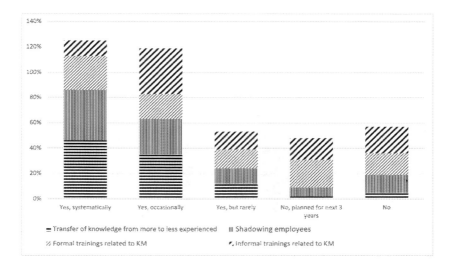

Figure 9.25 Techniques for transferring knowledge
Source: *Designed by the author based on original survey data*

and abilities) in the public sector averaged 47% in Saudi Arabia, 44% in Oman, and 40% in the UAE. These findings concluded that, although skills and competencies were increasingly abundant, they were invariably underutilized and un-activated, and thus their potential contributions to performance went largely unrealized.

To facilitate the transfer and sharing of knowledge among their employees, government entities in Dubai experimented to varying degrees with several techniques such as shadowing and, to a lesser extent, formal and informal meetings. For example, as Figure 9.25 shows, 46% of respondents sought to systematically transfer knowledge from more experienced staff to those less experienced, and 40% used shadowing employees to capture and benefit from their tacit knowledge.

However, only 27% and 12%, indicated that they systematically organized KM-related training on a formal or informal basis, respectively. This lack of awareness of KM and its importance, which was one of government entities' main challenges, could partly be explained by this insufficient formal and informal training.

Regarding providing adequate incentives to encourage employees to share knowledge, the survey data shown in Figure 9.26 reveals that 39% of respondents confirmed a lack of incentives for sharing knowledge. More significantly, 65% indicated that sharing knowledge was not a criterion for assessing the individual performance of employees. Meanwhile, the DGEP seems to have positively influenced employees' sharing of knowledge, as 34% considered it a motivating factor. Regarding monetary

Knowledge management in the public sector 291

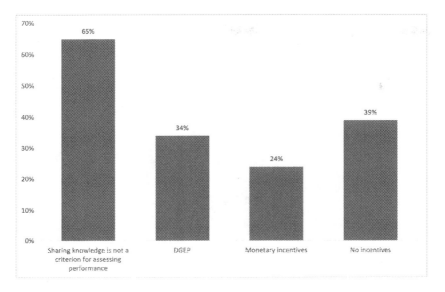

Figure 9.26 Incentives for sharing knowledge within organizations
Source: Designed by the author based on original survey data

incentives, only 25% of respondents indicated their use as motivation to share knowledge.

As can be seen, aspiring for an effective KM program without incentivizing mechanisms is challenging. Employees have no reason to share what they know if their efforts are not appreciated and rewarded, especially if this is accompanied by a fear of losing their jobs when this asset and source of employment is given to others.

Environmental influences

The managerial and resource influences discussed above are internal factors affecting KM's success, but environmental influences are typically external and not necessarily under the direct control of an organization's management. In the public sector, political influence and macro-institutional arrangements can limit knowledge sharing and cap what can be shared inside and outside the organization. This is more prevalent in the MENA region, where governments are either suspicious of sharing information and knowledge or find it impossible due to poor and fragmented inter-governmental relations systems. Furthermore, the social and cultural environment in which an organization operates is an external factor that can influence a knowledge-sharing culture, as will be explained below.

292 *Importance of effective human resource development*

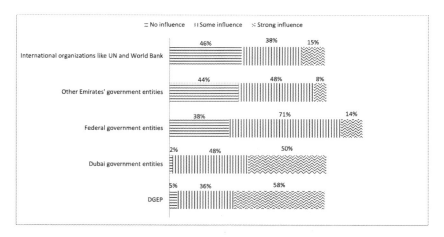

Figure 9.27 Governmental influences on KM programs in Dubai
Source: Designed by the author based on original survey data

Governmental influence

Dubai's public sector has been under pressure from various governmental bodies and programs to implement KM. Notably, as shown in Figure 9.27, 58% of respondents indicated that the DGEP was the main driver substantially influencing government entities to consider KM programs. Similar results were also drawn from interviews with the organizations that had begun experimenting with KM.

Strengthening cooperation and coordination with other local and federal authorities also motivated to adopt KM systems. International organizations, however, were not significantly influential, as only 15% of respondents said their role was enormously influential, and 38% said they had only some influence.

Surveyed organizations were asked to indicate the importance of some practices in improving the performance of their KM programs, which revealed what government entities in Dubai thought they should focus on to make their programs successful. As Figure 9.28 shows, respondents agreed that allocation of sufficient funds, reward systems, staff involvement, and management support and commitment were essential requisites for KM systems to succeed. In particular, the direct involvement of staff in implementing and running KM programs scored the highest with 56%. Allocating sufficient funds (53%) and high prioritization by top management (50%) came in second and third, respectively. These findings are consistent with the interviews conducted with major government entities in Dubai, which indicated that sufficient fund allocation and involvement of staff and top management were most important in adopting KM programs.

Knowledge management in the public sector 293

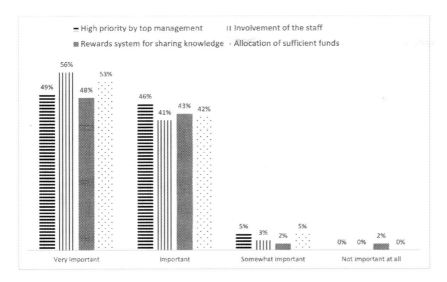

Figure 9.28 Important factors for improving KM programs
Source: Designed by the author based on original survey data

Organizational culture

Organizational culture also plays a considerable role in the outcomes of KM programs, particularly regarding the resistance to sharing knowledge. The study's interviews found considerable pushback among some employees concerning the idea of KM on the one hand, and sharing what they know with others on the other. Figure 9.29 shows that middle management and administrators and officers ranked highest as the primary sources of resistance within government organizations, scoring 31% and 30%, respectively. Moreover, 50% of respondents indicated that comfort with the status quo and fear of the unknown were major concerns that discouraged adopting new practices since their outcomes were uncertain. DEWA, KHDA, and the Dubai Courts respondents stated that they witnessed varying degrees of resistance among employees who were habitually attached to and defensive of their former ways of doing things. Difficulties in changing their behavior and attitudes represented a major hindrance to successful KM programs. Lastly, the diverse cultural and linguistic backgrounds of individuals within single organizations, which is endemic to Dubai's public sector workforce, were cited by 38% of respondents as a challenge facing knowledge sharing.

Trust

The interviews with Dubai's government entities clearly illustrated how lacking trust in organizations could lead to inadequate knowledge exchange.

294 *Importance of effective human resource development*

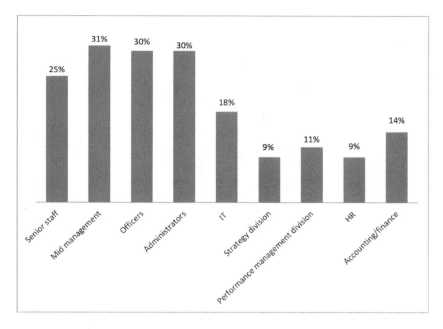

Figure 9.29 Groups resisting KM and knowledge sharing
Source: Designed by the author based on original survey data

Employees often refrained from sharing what they knew with each other out of fear that sharing their knowledge might counter their best interests in the future. Lack of confidence in and loyalty to their organization due to low job security and tenuous residency rights among expatriates may also have been a factor. Moreover, employees in most cases did not receive training on the value of sharing knowledge for the institution and individuals, nor were they assured that sharing knowledge would not threaten the security of their jobs and instead be an asset.

Lessons learned and conclusions

This chapter has discussed the importance of KM in Dubai's public sector and identified a range of drivers and obstacles standing against it, showing the extent to which current orientations and practices among such organizations became manifest in KM's practical and mature institutionalization. In its findings, the research identified several shortfalls in terms of the content of managing and sharing knowledge. It also offers a set of conclusions and recommendations that can be useful to public sector organizations in building and operating knowledge-based functions that can deliver superior results. The following is a summary of these main conclusions and recommendations.

One of the main challenges facing Dubai's government entities in their KM programs is the vagueness and ambiguity of the concept among most of their employees. This phenomenon can also be found in other countries, and only time and focused strategies can remedy it. In the case of the Middle East, KM was only recently introduced and required more time to mature and become clearer to public organizations. Such organizations, however, also need to invest more effort into organizing workshops and training sessions and involving their employees in understanding what KM stands for and its crucial role in the development and sustainability of organizations. In doing so, rather than interchangeably using a wide range of terminology, a single term should be used to avoid confusion and uncertainty about the meaning of the KM concept. Significantly, KM can enhance interaction and communication among individuals across organizational units and levels, and thus the tendency to reduce KM's definition to technical terms using new IT solutions and automation should be avoided. KM is a dynamic and social system, and its success hinges mainly on the quality and thickness of human interactions both within and outside the workplace.

Among the five interviewed government entities in Dubai, only two (the Dubai Police and the Dubai Courts) seem to have recognized the crucial role of tacit knowledge and implemented the necessary tools to capture, document, and share it. The other three organizations are still lagging and must therefore take the necessary steps to implement a process ensuring that tacit knowledge is adequately maintained and easily accessible. KM programs are mainly designed to protect tacit knowledge from loss and ensure that it resides in an organization even after the departure of employees. As such, organizations in Dubai should strongly consider the importance of such knowledge and create the tools to share it. This is an essential requirement for any successful KM program.

Furthermore, most public organizations in Dubai are not adequately aware of the vital role leadership plays in generating the proper conditions to create, select, organize, conserve, disseminate, and transfer knowledge to achieve an organization's strategic objectives. This lack of effective leadership negatively affects the adoption and success of KM as a pathway toward sustainable progress. Therefore, before establishing a KM department, program, or even initiative, government entities should select competent leaders who genuinely believe in and promote the values and practices associated with KM, whether as heads of organizations, managers of central units for KM, knowledge champions, or knowledge officers. This will guarantee that the programs follow a systematic, coherent, and well-established structure.

It should be noted that Dubai government entities did pursue advanced technological instruments to store created or captured explicit knowledge; however, lessons learned from this study establish that such instruments do not always adequately unpack the tacit knowledge embedded within individuals. Tackling this challenge involves the removal of specific barriers to sharing tacit knowledge such as belief in the hierarchical nature of knowledge (i.e., those with more significant organizational titles are wiser and more knowledgeable). Moreover, it is imperative to establish mechanisms that ensure the knowhow of employees is safely stored and remains in the organization by focusing more on developing and utilizing the human aspect of KM processes.

Dubai's government entities must also fully recognize the risks associated with hiring employees temporarily and establish sufficient mechanisms to protect their knowledge, store it, and make it accessible to others within the organization. Employees with temporary contracts tend to be less motivated, driven, and committed to the organization in which they work, and this could hinder not only the process of knowledge sharing but also the establishment of KM as one of the five main priorities of the organization. Thus, it is necessary to center attention and efforts on the establishment of proper human, technological, and organizational tools that would safeguard the creation, documentation, and sharing of knowledge.

Finally, government entities should establish written policies and strategies for KM programs. It is crucial to create formal guidelines, requirements, and obligations that encourage employees within organizations to document and share their knowledge. These entities should also consider universities and think tanks among the sources of knowledge and information they avail themselves of. Currently, government entities in Dubai rely heavily on each other's knowledge, consultants, and experts. In Western countries, for example, public policy schools are the primary sources of policy advice and guidance which is important to provide evidence-based policymaking. Finally, government entities should focus on achieving the goals of KM programs. The current KM programs did not achieve the primary objectives set before their establishment, and it is therefore vital to set clear objectives and closely monitor their progress.

References

Accenture. (2004). E-Government leadership: high performance, maximum value. *The Government Executive Series.* Chicago, IL.

Ahmad, N., & Daghfous, A. (2010). Knowledge sharing through inter-organizational knowledge networks. *European Business Review*, 22(2), 153–174.

Ahmed, A., & Elhag, M. (2017). SMART KM model: The integrated knowledge management framework for organisational excellence. *World Journal of Science, Technology and Sustainable Development*, 14(2/3), 172–193.

Akhavan, P., Reza Zahedi, M., & Hosein, S. (2014). A conceptual framework to address barriers to knowledge management in project-based organizations. *Education, Business and Society: Contemporary Middle Eastern Issues*, 7(2/3), 98–119.

Al-Yahya, K. (2009). Human capital strategy in the Gulf firms: Challenges and opportunities. *Tharawat Magazine*, 6, 56–61.

Al-Yahya, K. (2010). Challenges Facing Workforce Nationalization in the Gulf in *Human Resources and Development in the Arabian Gulf*, The Emirates Center for Strategic Studies and Research, Abh Dhabi, UAE.

Allee, V. (1997). *The Knowledge Evolution: Expanding Organizational Intelligence*, Butterworth-Heinemann, Oxford.

American Productivity and Quality Center. (2000). Knowledge management, www.apqc.org/knowledge-management

Anthony, B. (2019). A developed software agent-knowledge-assisted procurement management tool for retailing enterprise: A feasibility study. *VINE Journal of Information and Knowledge Management Systems*, 49(1), 54–75.

Arab Knowledge Report. (2020). United Nations Development Programme and Mohammed bin Rashid Rashid Al Maktoum Foundation.

Argote, L., Bechman, S., & Epple, D. (1978). The persistence and transfer of learning in industrial settings. *Management Science*, 36, 1750–1763.

Bell, D. (1973). *The Coming of Post-Industrial Society Forecasting*, Basic Books, New York.

Bhatt, G. (2001). Knowledge management in organizations: Examining the interaction between technologies, techniques, and people. *Journal of Knowledge Management*, 5(1), 68–75.

Bukowitz, W., & Williams, R. (1999). *The Knowledge Management Fieldbook*, Financial Times/Prentice Hall, London.

Chen, J., & McQueen, R. (2010), Knowledge transfer processes for different experience levels of knowledge recipients at an offshore technical support center. *Information Technology & People*, 23(1), 54–79.

Cong, X., & Pandya, V. (2004). Issues of knowledge management in the public sector. *Electronic Journal of Knowledge Management*, 1(2), 25–33.

Covin, T. J., & Stivers, B. (1997). Knowledge management in focus in UK and Canadian firms. *Creativity and Innovation Management*, 6(3), 140–50.

Davenport, T., & Prusak, L. (1998). *Working Knowledge: How Organizations Manage What They Know*, Harvard Business School Press, Cambridge, MA.

De Long, D., & Fahey, L. (2000). Diagnosing cultural barriers to knowledge management. *The Academy of Management Executive*, 14(4), 113–127.

Demarest, M. (1997). Understanding knowledge management. *Long Range Planning*, 30(3), 374–384.

Drucker, P. (1968). *The Age of Discontinuity: Guidelines to Our Changing Society*, Harper and Row, New York.

Edvinson, L., & Malone, M. (1997). *Intellectual Capital: Realizing your Company's True Value by Finding its Hidden Brainpower*, Harper Business, New York.

Fai, F., & Marschan, R. (2003). Language issues in cross border strategic alliances: An investigation of technological knowledge transfers. *Annual Meeting of the European International Business Academy*. Copenhagen.

Friis, C. (2002). Knowledge in public administration. *Conference Proceedings of the 3rd International Workshop by International Federation for Information Proceeding*, Copenhagen.

Garcia-Perez, A., Gheriss, F., & Bedford, D. (2019). *Metrics for Knowledge Management Capabilities, Designing and Tracking Knowledge Management Metrics (Working Methods for Knowledge Management)*, Emerald Publishing Limited, Bingley, pp. 129–143.

Garcia-Perez, A., Ghio, A., Occhipinti, Z., & Verona, R. (2020). Knowledge management and intellectual capital in knowledge-based organisations: A review and theoretical perspectives. *Journal of Knowledge Management*, 24(7), 1719–1754.

Gian, G., Lee, K., & Loon, M. (2012). Knowledge sharing: Influences of trust, commitment and cost. *Journal of Knowledge Management*, 16(5), 740–753.

Guadamillas-Gómez, F., & Donate-Manzanares, M. (2011). Ethics and corporate social responsibility integrated into knowledge management and innovation technology: A case study. *Journal of Management Development*, 30(6), 569–581.

Guba, E.G., & Lincoln, Y.S. (1994). Competing Paradigms in Qualitative Research in N.K. Denzin & Y.S. Lincoln (eds.), *Handbook of Qualitative Research*, Sage Publications, Inc, pp. 105–117.

Harlow, H. (2018). Developing a knowledge management strategy for data analytics and intellectual capital. *Meditari Accountancy Research*, 26(3), 400–419.

Hussinki, H., Ritala, P., Vanhala, M., & Kianto, A. (2017). Intellectual capital, knowledge management practices and firm performance. *Journal of Intellectual Capital*, 18(4), 904–922.

Hoffman, J., Hoelscher, M., & Sheriff, K. (2005). Social capital, knowledge management and sustained superior performance. *Journal of Knowledge Management*, 9(3), 93–100.

Holsapple, C., & Joshi, K. (2000). An investigation of factors that influence the management of knowledge in organizations. *The Journal of Strategic Information Systems*, 9(2–3), 235–261.

Inkinen, H. (2016). Review of empirical research on knowledge management practices and firm performance. *Journal of Knowledge Management*, 20(2), 230–257.

Jain, P., & Kelvin, B. (2013). Knowledge management portals as enablers for institutional competitiveness: Surveying universities in Southern African Development Community (SADC). *VINE*, 43(4), 400–423.

Jordão, R., & Novas, J. (2017). Knowledge management and intellectual capital in networks of small–and medium-sized enterprises. *Journal of Intellectual Capital*, 18(3), 667–692.

Kim, W., & Mauborgne, R. (1998). Procedural justice, strategic decision making, and the knowledge economy. *Strategic Management Journal*, 19, 323–338.

Laihonen, H., Lönnqvist, A., & Metsälä, J. (2015). Two knowledge perspectives to growth management. *VINE*, 45(4), 473–494.

Lesser, E., Mandel, D., & Wiecha, C. (2000). Managing customer knowledge. *Journal of Knowledge Strategy*, 21(6), 34–37.

Lynn, G., Morone, G., & Paulson, A. (1996). Marketing and discontinuous innovation: the probe and learn process. *California Management Review*, 38, 8–37.

McDermott, R., & O'Dell, C. (2001). Overcoming cultural barriers to sharing knowledge. *Journal of Knowledge Management*, 5(1), 76–85.

Marakas, G. (1999). *Decision Support Systems in the Twenty-First Century*, Prentice-Hall, Engelwood Cliffs, NJ.

McAdam, R., & McCreedy, S. (1999). The process of knowledge management within organizations: A critical assessment of both theory and practice. *Knowledge and Process Management*, 6(2), 101–113.

McLaughlin, G., & Stankosky, M. (2010). Knowledge has legs: Personal knowledge strategies shape the future of knowledge work and knowledge management. *On the Horizon*, 18(3), 204–212.

Nonaka, I. (1994). Dynamic theory of organizational knowledge creation. *Organization Science*, 5(1), 14–37.

Nonaka, I., & Peltokorpi, V. (2006). Objectivity and subjectivity in knowledge management: A review of 20 top articles. *Knowledge and Process Management*, 13(2), 73–82.

Nonaka, I., Umemoto, K., & Senoo, D. (1996). From information processing to knowledge creation: A paradigm shift in business management. *Technology in Society*, 18(2) 203–18.

O'Dell, C., & Grayson, J. (1998). If only we knew what we know: Identification and transfer of internal best practices. *California Management Review*, 40(3), 154–65.

OECD. (2003). Conclusions from the results of the survey of knowledge management practices for ministries/departments/agencies of central government in oecd member countries, 3–4.

Oliva, F., & Kotabe, M. (2019). Barriers, practices, methods and knowledge management tools in startups. *Journal of Knowledge Management*, 23(9), 1838–1856.

Pauleen, D., & Wang, W. (2017). Does big data mean big knowledge? KM perspectives on big data and analytics. *Journal of Knowledge Management*, 21(1), 1–6.

Paulin, D., & Suneson, K. (2012). Knowledge transfer, knowledge sharing and knowledge barriers: Three blurry terms in KM. *Electronic Journal of Knowledge Management*, 10(1).

Pentland, B. (1995). Information systems and organizational learning: The social epistemology of organizational knowledge systems. *Accounting, Management and Information Technologies*, 5(1), 1–21.

Polanyi, M. (1967). *The Tacit Knowledge Dimension*, Routledge & Kegan Paul, London.

Riege, A. (2005). Three dozen knowledge sharing barriers managers must consider. *Journal of Knowledge management*, 9(3), 18–35.

Riege, A., & Lindsay, N. (2006). Knowledge Management in the Public Sector: Stakeholder Partnerships in the Public Policy Development. *Journal of Knowledge Management*, 10(3), 24–39.

Ringel-Bickelmaier, C., & Ringel, M. (2010). Knowledge management in international organisations. *Journal of Knowledge Management*, 14(4), 524–539.

Robertson, M., & O'Malley-Hammersley, G. (2000). Knowledge management practices within a knowledge-intensive firm: The significance of the people management dimension. *Journal of European Industrial Training*, 24, 241–253.

Sayyadi, M. (2019). How effective leadership of knowledge management impacts organizational performance. *Business Information Review*, 36(1), 30–38.

Scarborough, H., Swan, J., & Preston, J. (1999). *Knowledge management: A literature review*, Institute of Personnel and Development, London

Schiuma, G. (2012). Managing knowledge for business performance improvement. *Journal of Knowledge Management*, 16(4), 515–522.

Serban, A., & Luan, J. (2002). Overview of knowledge management. *New Directions for Institutional Research*, 11, 5–16.

Siddique, C. (2012). Knowledge management initiatives in the United Arab Emirates: A baseline study. *Journal of Knowledge Management*, 16(5), 702–723.

Stein, E., & Zwass, V. (1995). Actualizing organizational memory with information systems. *Information Systems Research*, 6(2), 85–117.

Storey, J., & Quintas, P. (2001). Knowledge Management and HRM in J. Storey (ed.), *Human Resource Management: A Critical Text*, Thomson Learning, London.

Skok, W., & Tahir, S. (2010). Developing a knowledge management strategy for the Arab world. *Electronic Journal of Information Systems in Developing Countries*, 41.

Sun, P., & Scott, J. (2005). An investigation of barriers to knowledge transfer. *Journal of Knowledge Management,* 9, 75–90.
Thomas, J., Watts, A., & Henderson, J. (2001). Understanding strategic learning: Linking organizational learning, knowledge management, and sensemaking. *Organizational Science,* 12(3), 331–345.
Toffler, A. (1990). *Powershift: Knowledge, Wealth and Violence at the Edge of 21st Century,* Bantam Books, New York.
Wiig, K. (1997). Knowledge management: Where did it come from and where will it go? *Expert Systems with Applications,* 13(1), 1–14.
Wiig, K. (2002). Knowledge management in public administration. *Journal of Knowledge Management,* 6(3), 224–239.
Yee, Y., Tan, C., & Thurasamy, R. (2019). Back to basics: Building a knowledge management system. *Strategic Direction,* 35 (2), 1–3.

10 Conclusion

Translating institutional and human constraints into opportunities

The importance of enhancing the quality and efficiency of the public sector

In Chapter Two, the book demonstrated how to address the weak role of political accountability in the GCC and Middle East and North Africa (MENA) region through a managerial accountability model. New forms of public management can reform how the public sector operates and improve the accountability of governments and their agencies to the people. If political accountability witnesses substantial improvement under managerial reforms as politicians and administrators work more closely together, accountability to citizens can also be enhanced. Establishing independent agencies that work with governments on a contractual or quasi-contractual basis can create many opportunities for enhanced political accountability. The involvement of the private sector in the provision of public services can improve the quality of services and enhance the transparency of tendering and award processes—an aspect that still requires considerable development in the GCC and MENA regions.

Furthermore, the chapter showed how initiating administrative reforms could effectively enable efficient public budgeting. Performance budgeting can also enhance communication between governmental organizations that design budgets and citizens by clarifying goals and identifying performance targets. Moreover, it can improve government agencies' management, identify problems, and facilitate solutions. The chapter also stressed the significance of performance-based and decentralized budgets, arguing that there is a need for an institutional environment that allows managers to manage with flexibility and autonomy and to make decisions focused on achieving results and outcomes within their agencies. To put it simply, achieving an adequate budget requires wise spending and, since the government cannot steer and row simultaneously and is, moreover, less efficient at rowing, it could become more effective by focusing on the steering and leaving the rowing to other private sector actors.

The book also recommended implementing a straightforward process for strategic and performance planning to enhance the quality of government. Strategic planning ultimately sets out to identify an organizational

DOI: 10.4324/9781003267744-13

mission, perform a thorough environmental scan, specify a set of objectives, and develop a strategic plan to achieve these objectives, and this type of planning can take three different forms. The first is strategic business planning, which has short- and long-term objectives. The second is corporate strategic planning, which is more concerned with the higher levels of the organization than strategic business planning. The third form is strategic management, which aims to produce strategic results such as new markets, products, and technologies. The techniques employed in such strategic planning and management provide the private sector with instruments to anticipate the future and prepare its business platform for unexpected circumstances or market changes. The benefits associated with strategic planning range from enhanced control and accountability to reduced uncertainty and information asymmetry in the public sector.

The book proposes shifting from the hierarchical administrative bureaucracy which still characterizes most GCC states to a more managerial government. Excessive centralization of public administration, weak institutional development, lack of results appraisal, unprofessional public services, and political culture of patronage are potent inhibitors against any holistic administrative change in the region. The proposed solution to changing this mentality is adopting a long-term, purposeful, methodical, and progressive approach to administrative change. Such an approach should be holistic and focus on cultivating future bureaucrats and administrators in their education and when they begin work. As it stands, current educational systems in the GCC region do not fully prepare future leaders with the capacity to administer innovative solutions to ongoing problems. Instead, they replicate old systems of governance, administration, and management, and thus the governments lack the necessary skills, governance structures, and administrative ecosystem that could encourage change.

Chapter Three highlighted the need for more effective bureaucratic systems as shown in the case of Saudi Arabia, where the government has already begun reforming its bureaucracy and restructured some of its key ministries to align their objectives and performance with its Vision 2030. Providing adequate training programs to government officials will better support their efforts to implement policies that serve the private sector's needs, especially given Vision 2030's focus on facilitating dialogue and cooperation between the public and private sectors. Furthermore, a streamlined and efficient public sector will mean a faster and more accountable decision-making process that will assist the private sector's operations.

Chapter Four analyzed how Qatar and the UAE (viewed as the least corrupt countries in the GCC) have successfully implemented effective institutional and structural governance mechanisms that tackle corruption within the public sector. The chapter's central research question is what makes these two countries unique in their approach toward successfully tackling corruption despite sharing political, cultural, and historical similarities with their neighboring states? The chapter illustrated the current state of corruption within the government sector of the six GCC states, and demonstrated the uneven performance of these states in curbing corruption. The chapter presented the various mechanisms each GCC state adopted to address and combat corruption in the public sector. These included enacting legislation and anti-corruption laws, establishing various anti-corruption agencies, formulating national anti-corruption strategies, and forming regional networks and collaborations to share best practices in controlling corruption.

The importance of establishing partnerships between the public and private sectors

Chapter Five showed that the abrupt drop in oil prices has resulted in a sudden interest in infrastructure public-private partnerships (PPPs), but attracting foreign investors to the Gulf region might not be so smooth and fast. Some of the challenges identified in this chapter are structural and deeply rooted in the local culture, and these issues will require time and resolute efforts to overcome. Experience from past fluctuations of oil prices shows that once these prices ascend, the motivation for administrative reform will gradually diminish. Hence, committed political will and serious determination to achieve administrative and economic reforms will be the key ingredients to transform existing challenges into opportunities and provide the prerequisites for infrastructure PPPs to flourish in the GCC region.

Chapter Six illustrated the advantages and drawbacks of using PPPs in social infrastructure projects as debated in the PPP literature, and presented the factors generally leading to either success or failure of PPP agreements as demonstrated by international experience. The multifarious models, types, and formats assumed by PPPs in schools were discussed in detail to reveal that the most prominently used model is infrastructure PPPs, with the primary rationale among countries around the world being to compensate for financial constraints preventing the public sector from meeting increased demand for schools. The experiences of Australia, New Zealand, Alberta in Canada, the USA, and European countries represent the highly successful use of infrastructure PPPs to deliver school infrastructure or operations-related services. The chapter also discussed some Middle Eastern countries' experiences with management contracts for operating schools and universities in the United Arab Emirates and Qatar. However, the case of Egypt remains the only one in which PPPs were extensively adopted to successfully deliver public schools. Also commented on was the impact of each PPP model on certain performance indicators, such as access to schools, risk, and quality of education, as well as evaluations of existing PPP projects in Western countries.

The importance of addressing the human capital challenges within the GCC region

The book also explained why it is critical to address the human capital challenges that the GCC region faces via macro-level and long-term strategies such as talent management, and micro-level and shorter-term ones such as targeted training and knowledge management programs within public sector organizations.

Chapter Seven reviewed the challenges and opportunities associated with global talent management in the MENA region and concluded that, while the Organization for Economic Cooperation and Development (OECD) and high-income countries struggled to identify mechanisms to attract, retain, and develop talent pools in a fierce war over such talent, the MENA region is still hampered by chronic socioeconomic challenges, which are essentially due to the failure of policymakers to appreciate the importance of educational system quality and its applicability to job market needs. To support the use of talent management going forward, more research on how the public sector is struggling under new public management's corporate-oriented ideals will be necessary. Further studies are required to show how austerity and cost-cutting measures have limited the public sector's capacity to attract new staff. Such research might then inform the decisions of government actors to shift toward enhanced talent management measures. Furthermore, greater exploration of talent management's implementation in the public sector is required. Specifically, the analysis of internal structures, such as salary and staff selection procedures, will highlight the scope of talent management to be incorporated within different public agencies.

Chapter Eight analyzed the current state of training in Dubai's public sector and offered four main recommendations. First, it found that it was essential to revitalize the role of the Dubai Institute for Human Resources Development and ensure that it provides high-quality training for Dubai public sector employees. Second, it recommends that the central government of Dubai (The Executive Council) foster an environment that supports teamwork and eliminates hierarchical hindrances between employees. Third, the chapter recommends that the leadership of Dubai's public organizations should help to establish a culture of learning, knowledge sharing, and self-development, and oversee the success of training programs to achieve their desired results. Fourth, and finally, it recommends that training should not be regarded as merely a tool to strengthen the weaknesses of government employees, but rather as an essential continuous learning mechanism, as doing so will foster the creation of an environment that appreciates learning and knowledge within public sector entities.

Chapter Nine explored how to manage knowledge, particularly within the Dubai government and found that the main challenge facing Dubai's government entities in their KM programs is the vagueness and ambiguity of the concept among most of their employees. Furthermore, the chapter argued that most public organizations in Dubai are not adequately aware of leadership's vital role in generating the proper conditions to create, select, organize, conserve, disseminate, and transfer knowledge to achieve an organization's strategic objectives. The chapter also found that Dubai government entities did pursue advanced technological instruments to store created or captured explicit knowledge; however, lessons learned from this study establish that such instruments do not always adequately unpack the tacit knowledge embedded within individuals. The chapter recommended that Dubai's government entities fully recognize the risks associated with hiring employees temporarily and establish sufficient mechanisms to protect their knowledge, store it, and make it accessible to others within the organization. Finally, the chapter recommended that Dubai public organizations establish written policies and strategies for KM programs. It is crucial to create formal guidelines, requirements, and obligations that encourage employees within organizations to document and share their knowledge.

Index

Note: Tables are indicated by **bold** page numbers and illustrations by *italicised* ones.

Abdulkarim, A. 217
Abu Dhabi 96, 183
accountability 5, 6, 10, 11, 29, 32, 34, 59–60, 61, **124**, **125**, 130, 149, 150, 301; managerial model of 59–60; and PPPs 139, 140, 141, 166–168, **167**, **169**; *see also* voice and accountability
Adams, J. 155
Africa 34, 176
Ahmad, N. 265
Ajbilou, A. 212
Akçay, S. 13
Al Ariss, A. 213
Al-Ghurair Foundation 172
Al Mansouri, Sultan 96
Al-Yahya, K. 288–290
Algeria 36, *39*, *40*, *43*, *44*, *49*, *55*, *57*, 202, 211; brain drain 210, **210**; corruption control indicator 42, *42*; customs and border management 52, *53*; ease of doing business 46, *47*, *48*; global innovation index 54, *54*; Global Knowledge Index 207, **208**, **211**; government effectiveness 35–36, *35*; infrastructure, quality of 51, *51*, *52*; political stability and absence of violence 44, *45*; regulatory environment 41, *41*; rule of law 45, *46*; scientists and engineers, availability of 58, *58*; starting a business 48–49, *48*, *49*; talent retention 58, *59*, **210**; tax and contribution rate 50, *50*
Altenburg, T. 69–70
Arab Labor Organization 214
Arab League 127, 128
Arab Spring (2010) 216, 219

Arab Youth Surveys (2013 and 2020) 216
Aragón-Sánchez, A. 227
Argentina 12
Athey, R. 204
Australia 7, 9, 168–169, **171**, 173, 177–178, 185, 193, 205, 303
Automotive Manufacturers Association (OSD) 90–91
Az-Zour North project (Kuwait) 146

Bahrain 35, *37*, *48*, *49*, *53*, 55, *57*, 104, **210**; corruption 116, **118**, 120, **124**, 129; corruption control indicator 42, *42*, **113**, 114; Corruption Perceptions Index (CPI) 43, *43*, 111, **112**; ease of doing business 46, 47, *47*, *48*, **115**, 116; education 207, **208**; expatriates 215, *215*, 216; favoritism 115, 129; GDP 110, **111**; global innovation index 54, *54*; Global Knowledge Index 96, 207, **208**, **211**, 212; government effectiveness **113**, 114; government inefficiency 36, *36*; Human Development Index (HDI) *39*, *39*, 40, *40*; infrastructure, quality of 51, *51*, 52, *52*; political stability and absence of violence 44, *45*; port infrastructure 52, *52*; quality of government 18, 29, **115**; R&D 55, *55*, *56*, *57*; regulatory environment 18, 29, 41, *41*, **113**; rule of law 29, 45, *46*, **113**; scientists and engineers, availability of 58, *58*; talent retention 58, *59*; tax and contribution rate 50, *50*; transparency of policymaking **115**, 129; voice and accountability

43–44, *44*, **113**; wastefulness of government spending **115**, 129
bankruptcy 141, 145, **156**, 157
Bauer, M. 62
Bayt.com 210, 214–215
Beh, L. S. 154
Bell, B. 228
Bettcher, K. 68
Bhatt, G. 261–262
Bill and Melinda Gates Foundation 171
Bouckaert, G. 3, 4, 5–6
Boudarbat, B. 212
Bouris, G. 232–233
Bovaird, T. 166–167
brain drain 205, 209–210, **210**
Brown, J. 231–232
Brown, K. 9, 206
Build, Operate, and Transfer (BOT) 145, **171**, 173, **175**, 183
Build, Own, and Operate (BOO) 14, 165, 175, **175**
Build, Own, Operate, and Transfer (BOOT) 14, 165, 166, 168
Bukowitz, W. 262
bureaucracy 2, 6, 9, 15, 19, 30, 31, 32, **33**, 60, 62, 66, 70–71, 99, 114, 138, 141; Chile 86–87; Ireland 85; knowledge management 226, **248**, 270; Kuwait 145, 146–147, **147**; Malaysia 83, 91–92, 99; meritocratic 67–68, 70, 84; PPPs 152–153, 154, **156**, 157–158, 188, 192; Qatar 151; Saudi Arabia 99, 148, 149–150, 157, 188, 302; South Korea 84; *see also* inefficient government bureaucracy
business associations 19, 66, 68, 74, 82, 87–91, 99–100
business-friendly environments 2, 29, 30, 40, 46–53, *47*, *48*, *49*, *50*, *51*, *52*, *53*, 68, 80–82, **81**, 116, 219; and PPPs 119, 155, **156**, 157; United Arab Emirates 80, **81**, 82, 97
Buttiens, D. 17, 206

Caiden, G. 31
Calderón, C. 12
Campbell, J. 229, 232
Canada 7, **170**, **171**, 173, 179–180, 193, 194, 303
capitalism 12, 32
Cappelli, P. 204
centralization 8, 62, 84, 96, 249, 302
Chen, J. 262

Chile **72**, 74, 77, *77*, *78*, *79*, **81**, 86–87, 99; business and peak associations 88–89, 99; credit, ease of obtaining **81**, 82; GDP 75, *76*; R&D expenditure 80, *80*; services, value-added 77, *78*
China 14, 109, 142, 155
Chong, A. 11, 12
civil society 3, 10, 105, 108, **124**, 141–142
Clarke, J. 4, 8
coaching and mentoring 227–228, **238**
collaboration 2, 8, 19, 30, 55, 67, 70, 73, 105, 128, 261, **261**, 265, 303; *see also* public-private partnerships (PPPs); university-industry collaboration
Comoros *35*, *39*, *40*, *41*, *42*, *43*, *44*, *45*, *46*, *48*, *49*
competition 2, 8, 52–53, 68, 69, 107–108, 141–142, 225; education sector 173–174, 185, **186**, **191**, 194; knowledge management 254, 260; PPPs 16, 32, **33**, 138, 141–142, 153, 154, 155, **156**, 157–158, 165, 168, **169**, 173–174, 185, 192; public sector 5, 7, 9, 32, **33**, 215, 232, *281*; talent management 203, 204, 205, 210, 216–217, 233
consultants, reliance on 18, 193, 214, **238**, 239, 269, 270, 273, 278, *281*
contract enforcement 44–45, **81**, 82, **145**, 150; PPPs 141, 142, 155, 156–157, **156**
control of corruption indicator 10, 34, 41–42, *42*, 111–114, **113**, 128, 129, **144**, 146, 149, 150, 302–303
corruption 2, 19, 29–30, 62, 67, 104–133, **117–118**, **124–126**, 154–155, 302–303; Bahrain 116, **118**, 120, **124**, 129; definition 12–13; and democracy 11; and good governance 12–13, 104–133; Kuwait 116–119, **117**, 120, 121, **124**, 129, 146, **147**; MENA countries 29–30, 41–43, *42*, *43*; Oman 116, **118–119**, 120, 121–122, **125**, 129, 130; and PPPs 139–140, 141, 142, 152, 157, 167; private sector 107–108, 127, 149–150; Qatar 19, 104, 105, 116, **119**, 120, 122–123, **125**, 128–129, 130, 131, 302–303; regional anti-corruption agencies 19, 105, **126**, 127–128, 303; Saudi Arabia 116, **117–118**, 120, 123, **125**, 129, 130, 149–150, 157; United

308   Index

Arab Emirates 19, 104, 105, 116, **118**, 120, **124**, 127, 128–129, 130, 131, 302–303
Corruption Perceptions Index (CPI) 13, 19, 34, 43, *43*, 104, 105, 111, **112**, 128
Costa, A. 13
Côte d'Ivoire 172
COVID-19 1, 75, 97–99, 201, 202, 218
credit, ease of obtaining 80–82, **81**, **145**, 157
credit ratings 153
Creelman, D. 203
cronyism 12–13, 62, 106
cultural factors 62, 108, 109, 128, 131, 154–155, **156**, 157–158, 193, 258, 259, 260, 264–265, 291, 293
customs and border management 46, 52, *53*

Daghfous, A. 265
Darvish, H. 168
Day, D. 227
days required to start businesses 46, 49, *49*
decentralization 182, 206, 272, 301
Deininger, K. 11
democracy 10, 11–12, **33**, 141, 143
DeRouin, R. 228
Design, Build, Finance, and Operate (DBFO) 178, 181, 184
Design, Build, Finance, Operate, Transfer (DBFOT) **171**
Design, Construct and Maintain (DCM) 14, 165
Dhillon, N. 213
Diamond, L. 11
disaggregation 5, 7
discrimination 10, 12–13, 152
dispute resolution 15, 140, 148, 150, 152, 155–156, **156**, 189, 190
diversification 55, **73**, 74, 82–83, 93, 116, 119, 130, 138, 217; Saudi Arabia 75, 79, 82, 100; United Arab Emirates **73**, 74, 75, 82, 97
Djibouti *35*, *39*, *41*, *42*, *44*, *45*, *46*, *48*, *49*, *50*
Doing Business Database (World Bank) 80, **81**, 138, 145, **145**, 146, **147**, 148, 151
Dougherty, G. 8
Dubai 20–21, **73**, 75, 96, 97, 101, 104, 171–172, 217; knowledge management in public sector 21, 254, 255, 265–296, *267*, *268*, **271**, *275*, *276*, *277*, *278*, *279*, *280*, *281*, *282*, *283*, *284*, *285*, *286*, *288*, *289*, *290*, *291*, *292*, *293*, *294*, 304–305; productivity 270, **271**, 280, 281, *281*; training programs 20–21, 225–226, 233–249, *234*, **235**–**236**, *237*, **238**–**239**, *240*, **241**, *242*, *243*, *244*, *245*, *246*, *247*, **248**, 304
Dubai Courts 265, 266, 269, 270, **271**, **271**, 277, 280, 285, 293, 295
Dubai Electricity and Water Authority (DEWA) 226, 265, 270, **271**, 272, 277, 280, 293
Dubai Government Excellence Program (DGEP) 270, **271**, *292*
Dubai Institute for Human Resources Development 247, 304
Dubai Police 265, 266, 268–269, 270, 271–272, **271**, 295
Dunleavy, P. 5
Dvir, T. 227

ease of doing business 1, 30, 46–47, *47*, *48*, **115**, 116, **145**, 147
education 13, 84, 105, 108, 151, 207–208, **208**, 210–214, *213*, 219–220, 304; free 1, 86, 95, 163; Global Knowledge Index 207–208, **208**, **211**; Ireland 74, 86; Kuwait 184, 207, **208**; Malaysia 83, 91, 206; and market requirements 57–58, 69, 74, 83, 84, 86, 91, 100, 151; philanthropic model 169–172, **170**; Saudi Arabia 100, 163, 184, *189*, **191**, 207, **208**, 212; United Arab Emirates 95, 96, 183, **191**, 207, **208**, 303; United States **170**, 171; *see also* school infrastructure and public-private partnerships (PPPs); training programs for the public sector; universities
Education and HR Index 96
Education International 176
Egypt *39*, *40*, *46*, *48*, *51*, *52*, *53*, *55*, *58*, *59*, 202, **210**, 211; brain drain 209–210, **210**; corruption control indicator 42, *42*; Corruption Perceptions Index (CPI) 43, *43*; ease of doing business 47, *47*, *48*; global innovation index 54, *54*; Global Knowledge Index **208**, **211**, 212; government effectiveness 35–36, *35*; government inefficiency *36*, 37; graduate skillsets 57, *57*; political stability and absence of violence

44, *45*; PPPs **171**, 183, 194; public sector expenses 37, *37*; regulatory environment 41, *41*; starting a business 49, *49*; talent management 210, **210**; tax and contribution rate 50, *50*; university-industry collaboration 56, *56*; voice and accountability 44, *44*
embedded autonomy 67, 70
Emiratization 217–218
Engineering, Procurement, and Construction (EPC) 175, 179, 185, 187, 192
entrepreneurship 217, 219
European Union 89
Evans, P. 67, 84
evidence-based policymaking 68, 70, 88, **241**, 296
expatriates 152, 154, 202, 214, *215*, 219
explicit knowledge 258, **258**, 262, 278
exports 100; high-tech 79–80, *79*, 100; Malaysia 79–80, *79*, 91, 92; processing 51, 52; Saudi Arabia 79, *79*, 100, 148; Turkey 79, 90, 93–94, *94*, *95*; United Arab Emirates 79, 100; *see also* oil

facility availability model 173–174, **174**
favoritism 9, 11, 114, **115**, 129, 142, 151, 157–158
feedback 228–229, 236, **241**, 285, *285*
FIFA World Cup (2022) 137
final consumption expenditure as percentage of GDP 77, *77*
financial crisis (2007–2009) 1, 14, 18, 75, 78, 127, 273, 287
Finland 212, 227
Flinders, M. 140
foreign direct investment (FDI) 19, 21, 47, 51, 53, 66, **73**, 74, 80, 85, 86, 104, 110, 116, 119, 130, 217, 219; FDI Confidence Index 97, *98*; Qatar 130, 150–151; United Arab Emirates 82, 97, **98**, *98*, 101, 130
foreign workers 17, 18, 56, 193, 214, **238**, 239, 269, 270, 273, 278, *281*
fragmentation 8, 152, 166, 291
Frayne, C. 227
free trade 87, 91, 109
Free Zones **73**
Fruytier, B. 9

Gallop, G. 61
Garavan, T. 8
gas 1, 21, 38, 97, 137, 164

Geringer, J. 227
Germany 55, 173, 182
Gian, G. 256
Glenn, T. 205
Global Competitiveness Report 210
global innovation index 53–55, *54*
Global Knowledge Index (GKI) 95–96, **96**, 207–208, **208**, 211–212, **211**
globalization 203, 204–205, 218, 260
Goldsmith, A. 12, 34
good governance 29, 34–53, 104–133, **126**; and corruption 12–13, 104–133; definition 10–11, 34–35; and democracy 10, 11–12; and economic development 12; and PPPs 140, 143, 151–152, 153, **156**; quality of government, interchangeability with 10; and rule of law 13–14, 140; *see also* quality of government; Worldwide Governance Indicators
government effectiveness 10, 11, 18, 19, 29, 34, 35–36, *35*, 111, **113**, 114, 120
Gradstein, M. 11
Grimsey, D. 15
Grindle, M. 12
Gross Domestic Product (GDP) **110**; final consumption expenditure as percentage of 77, *77*; growth 75, *76*; Malaysia 75, *76*, 83–84; oil rents as percentage of 75, *76*; public sector expenses as percentage of 37–38, *37*, *39*, 219; Saudi Arabia 75, *76*, 110, **111**, 149; services, value-added as percentage of 77, *78*
Gulf Cooperation Council (GCC) region 1, 202; current state of government 35–40, *35*, *36*, *38*, *39*, *40*; good governance 40–46, *41*, *42*, *43*, *44*, *45*, *46*

Healy, P. 229
Heavy Chemical and Industry Development Plan (HCIDP) 92–93, 100
Heckman, R. 203
hierarchies within public administration 4, 31, 32, **33**, 248, 302, 304
high-tech 84, 94; exports 79–80, *79*, 100; Saudi Arabia 79, *79*, 100; United Arab Emirates 79, *79*, 100
Hoffman, J. 256
Holmberg, S. 10, 11–13
Hong Kong 11, 91, 108, 120
Hudson, P. 8, 9

310 *Index*

Hughes, O. 59–60
human capital 1–2, 20–21, 74, 163, 288–290, 304–305; *see also* foreign workers; talent management
Human Development Index (HDI) 18, 29, 34, 38–40, *39*, *40*
human resource development (HRD) 17, 201, 270, 288, *289*
Human Resource Management (HRM) 206

India 106, 171
industrial policies 69–70, **73**, 74, 85, 91, 92, 93–94
industry, value-added 77–78, *78*
inefficient government bureaucracy 31, 32, **33**, 34, 36–37, *36*, 146–147, **147**, 149, 151, 152–153
Information and Communication Technology (ICT) 95, 260, 262, *276*, 277, 279–280, *280*, 287, *288*; expertise 207, **208**; Index 96; Ireland 85, 86; knowledge management 295
information flow 68, 70–71, 85, 87, 99
infrastructure 18, 137–138, 148, 188, 216–217; government provision 1, 16, 154, 163, 184, 193; Kuwait 51, *51*, *52*, 137–138, 143–147, 155; port 46, 51–52, *52*; PPPs 14–16, 19, 137–158, 163, 165–166, 168, 169, 193, 303; Qatar 51–52, *51*, *52*, 137, 150–151, 155; quality of 30, 46, 50–52, *51*, *52*, **191**; Saudi Arabia 19, 20, 51, *51*, *52*, 137, 138, 147–150, 155, 157, 163–164, 184, 185–195, **191**; United Arab Emirates 51–52, *51*, *52*, 75; *see also* school infrastructure and public-private partnerships (PPPs)
Inkinen, H. 263
innovation 4, 30–31, 32, **33**, 35, 53–59, 69, **72**, 80, 85, 95, 96, 187, 207–208, **208**, 217, 248
insolvency resolution **81**, 82, **145**, 148, 150, 152, **156**, 157, 193
International Monetary Fund (IMF) 11, 34, 148
Iran 202
Iraq *35*, *44*, *48*, *49*, *50*, *55*, 202; corruption control indicator 42, *42*; Corruption Perceptions Index (CPI) 43, *43*; ease of doing business 46, 47, *47*, *48*; Human Development Index (HDI) 39, *39*, *40*; regulatory environment 41, *41*; rule of law 45, *45*; unemployment 209, **210**
Ireland **72**, 74, *76*, 77, *77*, **81**, 100; business-friendly environment 80, **81**; contract enforcement **81**, 82; education 85–86; FDIs 86; GDP 75, *76*; high-tech exports 79, *79*; industry, value-added 77, *78*; R&D 79–80, *80*, 85, 86; services, value-added 77, *78*, *78*
Islamic heritage 137, 148, 155, 193, 213, 264
Israel Defense Forces 227

Japan 84, 91, 92, 268, 271
Jerden, E. 228
Jordan *35*, *37*, *39*, *41*, *43*, 45, *47*, *48*, *55*, *57*, *58*, 202, 211, **211**; brain drain 210, **210**; corruption control indicator 42, *42*; customs and border management 52, *53*; global innovation index 54–55, *54*; government inefficiency *36*, 37; Human Development Index (HDI) 39, *39*, *40*; infrastructure, quality of 51, *51*, *52*; political stability and absence of violence 44, *45*; starting a business 49, *49*; talent retention 58, *59*; tax and contribution rate 50, *50*; unemployment 209, **210**; voice and accountability 44, *44*

Kaufmann, D. 12
Keating, M. 6, 7
Kirkpatrick, D. 229, 230
knowledge 257–259, *257*, **258**
Knowledge and Human Development Authority (KHDA) 226, 265, 270, **271**, 272, 293
Knowledge Economic Index 95
knowledge economies 95–96, **96**, 104, 203, 205, 216–217, 225, 260; and FDIs 97; Ireland **72**, 74; Kuwait 137–138; Malaysia 83; Saudi Arabia 164; United Arab Emirates 95–97, **96**, 101
knowledge management (KM) 2, 3, 17–18, 219, 254–265, *257*, **258**, **261**, 304; definitions 256–259, 266–268, *267*, 295, 304; Dubai 21, **241**, 254, 255, 265–296, *267*, *268*, **271**, *275*, *276*, *277*, *278*, *279*, *280*, *281*, *282*, *283*, *284*, *285*, *286*, *288*, *289*, *290*, *291*, *292*, *293*, *294*, 304–305; and trust 259, 263, 264, 265, *283*,

293–294; United Arab Emirates 21, 218, 255
König, K. 4
Kozarovski, D. 168
Kozlowski, S. 228
Kraemer, K. 3
Kraiger, K. 228
Kurer, O. 13
Kuwait 48, 53, 57, 59, 100, 154, **210**; 2035 Economic Vision 137–138; bureaucracy 145, 146–147, **147**; contract enforcement 145, **145**; corruption 116–119, **117**, 120, 121, **124**, 129, 146, **147**; corruption control indicator 42, 42, **113**, 114, 128, **144**, 146; Corruption Perceptions Index (CPI) 43, 43, 104, 111, **112**, 128, 129; ease of doing business 46, 47, 47, 48, **115**, 116, 145–146, **145**, **147**; education 184, 207, **208**; expatriates 152, 214, 215–216, 215; favoritism 114, **115**; GDP **111**; global innovation index 54, 54; Global Knowledge Index **96**, 207, **208**, **211**, 212; government effectiveness 35, 35, **113**, 114, **144**; Human Development Index (HDI) 39, 39, 40, 40; inefficient government bureaucracy 36, 36, 146–147, **147**, 153; infrastructure 51, 51, 52, 137–138, 143–147, 155; knowledge-based economy 137–138; legal rights 145, **145**; oil, dependency on 137, 146; port infrastructure 52, 52; PPPs 19, 100, 137–138, 143–147, 151–158, 184; procurement 100, 146, **147**, 153, 157, 184; public sector expenses 37, 37; quality of government 114, **115**; R&D 55, 55, 56, 57; regulatory environment 41, 41, 114–116, **115**, 144, **144**; restrictive labor regulations 147, **147**; rule of law 45, 45, **113**, 143–145, **144**; scientists and engineers, availability of 58, 58; starting a business 49, 49, **145**; tax and contribution rate 50, 50; transparency of policymaking 114, **115**; trust in politicians **115**, 116; unemployment 209, 209, **210**; university-industry collaboration 56, 56; voice and accountability 44, 44, **113**, 114, 143, **144**; wastefulness of government spending 114, **115**

leadership 173, 247, 248–249, **248**; Dubai's public sector 20, 233–235, 234, **235**, **241**, 246, 247, 248–249, **248**; knowledge management 262–263, 283, 284–285, 284, 294, 295, 304–305; skill development **156**, 205, 208, 227, **241**, 246, **248**
leadership, political 29, 62, 70, 75, 90, 105, 130; and corruption 119, 120, 129, 130, 131
Lease or Own, Develop, and Operate (L/ODO) 175, **175**
Lebanon 35, 36, 39, 40, 41, 42, 46, 50, 58, 59; Corruption Perceptions Index (CPI) 43, 43; customs and border management 52, 53; ease of doing business 46, 47, 48; global innovation index 54–55, 54; graduate skillsets 57, 57; infrastructure, quality of 51, 51, 52, 52; political stability and absence of violence 44, 45; port infrastructure 52, 52; public sector expenses 37, 37; public sector wage bills 38, 38, 39; starting a business 49, 49; talent management 210, **210**, 211, **211**, 213; voice and accountability 44, 44
legal rights 145, **145**, 152, 155–156, **156**; Kuwait **145**, 148; Qatar **145**, 150; Saudi Arabia **145**, 148
Lewis, M. 15
Lewis, R. 203
Li, H. 11
Libya 39, 40, 43, 59, **210**, 216; corruption control indicator 42, 42; ease of doing business 47, 47, 48; government effectiveness 35, 36; government inefficiency 36, 37; infrastructure, quality of 51, 51, 52; regulatory environment 41, 41; rule of law 45, 45; scientists and engineers, availability of 58, 58; starting a business 49, 49; tax and contribution rate 50, 50; voice and accountability 44, 44
Lindsay, N. 260
loans 93, 95, 100–101, 193, 216, 219
lobbying 68, 87, 88, 89–90
Lukea, S. 8
Lynn, G. 261

macroeconomics 66, 69, 71–77, 108–109, 116
Malaysia 74, **81**, 82–84, 101; bureaucracy 83, 91–92, 99; business-friendly environment 80, **81**, 100;

credit, ease of obtaining 80–82, **81**; education 83, 91, 206; exports 79–80, *79*, 91, 92; FDIs **73**, 74; final consumption expenditure 77, *77*; GDP 75, *76*, 83–84; industrial planning 91–92; industry, value-added 77–78, *78*; oil rents as percentage of GDP 75, *76*; PPPs 154–155; R&D **73**, 79–80, *80*; services, value-added 77–78, *78*
Malik, I. 212
managerialism **33**, 226, 259, 283–284, *283*; definition 4; managerial accountability 59–60; and PPPs 151–155; private sector, tools from 3, 4, 32, 164
Mauritania *36*, *42*, *43*, *44*, *53*; brain drain 210, **210**; customs and border management 52, *53*; ease of doing business 46–47, *47*, *48*; Global Knowledge Index 207, **208**, **211**, 212; government effectiveness 35–36, *35*; graduate skillsets 57, *57*; Human Development Index (HDI) 39, *39*, 40, *40*; infrastructure, quality of 51, *51*, 52, *52*; port infrastructure 52, *52*; regulatory environment 41, *41*; rule of law 45, *45*; scientists and engineers, availability of 58, *58*; starting a business 49, *49*; talent retention 58, *59*, **210**; tax and contribution rate 50, *50*
Mauro, P. 13
Maxfield, S. 70–71
McCourt, W. 230
McCusker, R. 109–110
McDermott, R. 264
McQueen, R. 262
Medina airport 155
Mentz, J. 232
meritocratic bureaucracy 67–68, 70, 84
Messick, R. 14
Metcalfe, L. 3, 4
Middle East and North Africa (MENA) countries 2, 202, 216; business-friendly environments 46–53, *47*, *48*, *49*, *50*, *51*, *52*, *53*; corruption 29–30, 41–43, *42*, *43*; education **208**, 210–213, **213**, 304; governance and public management 18, 20–45, *35*, *36*, *38*, *39*, *40*, *41*, *42*, *43*, *44*, *45*, *46*, 59–62, 213; innovation 30–31, 53–59, *54*, *55*, *56*, *57*, *58*, 207–208, **208**; knowledge management 290; PPPs 176–177; public sector employment 214–216, *215*; R&D 30–31, *55*, *57*, *58*, 62, 207–208, **208**; talent management 20, 58–59, 201–224, **208**, *209*, **210**, **211**, 304; unemployment 208–209, *209*, **210**, 216, 218–219; *see also individual countries*
Middle East Policy Council 215
Mohamad, Mahathir 83
Mohammed Bin Rashid Al Maktoum Knowledge Foundation (MBRF) 171–172, 217
Morocco *35*, *41*, 45, *49*, *55*, *57*, *58*, 202, 211, 212, 216; corruption control indicator 42, *42*; Corruption Perceptions Index (CPI) 43, *43*; customs and border management 52, *53*; ease of doing business 46, 47, *47*, *48*; global innovation index 54, *54*; Global Knowledge Index **208**, **211**, 212; government inefficiency *36*, 37; Human Development Index (HDI) 39, *39*, 40, *40*; infrastructure, quality of 51, *51*, *52*; political stability and absence of violence 44, *45*; public sector expenses 37–38, *37*; public sector wage bills 38, *38*, *39*; R&D 56, *56*, *57*; talent retention 58, *59*, **210**; tax and contribution rate 50, *50*; university-industry collaboration 56, *56*; voice and accountability 44, *44*
Mpuga, P. 11

nationalization of workforce 17, 201, 202, 217–218, 219, 270
needs assessments 231–232, 240, 247
neoliberalism 12, 74
nepotism 12–13, 29, 62, 106, 107, **117**, 154, 213
Netherlands **170**, 173, 182, 227
new public management (NPM) 2, 3, 5, 16, **33**, 61–62, 163–164; emergence 5, 31–34; post-NPM reforms 8–9; and PPPs 14, 163–164
New Zealand 7, **170**, 172, 173, 178–179, 185, 303
Newman, J. 4
Noe, R. 228, 229–230
non-governmental organizations (NGOs) 108, 172
Nonaka, I. 262

O'Dell, C. 264
oil 1, 2, 18, 38, 104, 110, 143, 163; prices 1, 19, 75, 97–99, 146, 148, 153, 154, 163, 164, 185–187, 254, 303

oil, GCC dependency on 1, 21, 75, 119, 153, 154, 208; Kuwait 137, 146; Qatar 137; Saudi Arabia 75, 79, 97–99, 137, 148, 163–164, 184; United Arab Emirates 75, 76, 96–97
O'Malley-Hammersley, G. 264
Oman 35, 42, 46, 53, 55, 57, 58, 59, 100, **113**, **210**, **211**, *215*, 288–290; corruption 116, **118–119**, 120, 121–122, **125**, 129, 130; corruption control indicator **113**, 128; Corruption Perceptions Index (CPI) 43, *43*, 111, **112**, 128; ease of doing business 46, 47, *47*, *48*; expatriates 215, *215*, 216; GDP **111**; global innovation index 54, *54*; Global Knowledge Index **96**, **211**, 212; government effectiveness **113**, 114; government inefficiency 36, *36*; Human Development Index (HDI) 39, *39*, *40*; infrastructure, quality of 51, *51*, *52*; knowledge management 254; political stability and absence of violence 44, *45*; quality of government **115**; regulatory environment 41, *41*, **113**; starting a business 48, *48*, 49, *49*; tax and contribution rate 50, *50*; voice and accountability 43–44, *44*
Organization of Economic and Cooperation Development (OECD) 1, 5, 6, 7, 29, 61, 86, 87, 97, 100, 128, *209*; corruption control indicator 42, *42*; education 210–211; good governance 34, *35*; Human Development Index (HDI) 38, *39*; knowledge management 256, 259, 260, 265, 277, 281; policymaking 69, 114, 259; political stability and absence of violence 44, *45*; quality of government 114; regulatory environment 41, *41*; rule of law 45, *46*; talent management 207, 210, 212, 304; voice and accountability 43, *44*; *see also individual countries*
Owens, P. 233

Pakistan **170**, 171
Palestine 35, *39*, *40*, *41*, 42, *42*, 44, *44*, *45*, *46*
Park Chung-hee 84, 87, 88, 92–93
patronage 12–13, 67–68, 141, 142, 154–155, 167, 302
peak associations 19, 66, 68, 74, 82, 87–88, 89, 99–100

Penang 91–92
Pentland, B. 262
performance budgeting 30, 301
Perry, J. 3
Peru 11
Peters, B. 4
philanthropy 169–172, **170–171**, 191–192, **191**, 193
Philippines 171, 172
Pierre, J. 3
Poland **72**, *76*, *77*, *79*, **81**; business associations 89–90; business-friendly environment 80, **81**; contract enforcement **81**, 82; credit, ease of obtaining 80–82, **81**; industry, value-added 78, *78*; services, value-added 77, 78, *78*; starting a business 80, **81**; trading across borders **81**, 82
Polanyi, M. 258
policymaking 6–7, 68, 71, 74, 82, 83; business and peak associations 87–91; evidence-based 68, 70, 88, **241**, 296; and knowledge management 259, **271**, 280, 281, *281*, 282; policy capacity 6; public involvement 40, 43, 147; transparency 114, **115**, 129
political stability 10, 34, 44, *45*
Pollitt, C. 3, 4, 5–6
port infrastructure 46, 51–52, *52*, 97
Portugal 227
private sector 1–2, 4, 8, 9, 17, 60, 66–71, **73**, 99, 137–158, **156**; business associations 19, 66, 68, 74, 82, 87–91, 99–100; corruption 107–108, 127, 149–150; knowledge management 254, 259; and the local workforce 2, 38, 147, 151, 154, 208, 213, 214, 215–216; planning 61; talent management 16–17, 214–215; training programs 225, 228; transparency 16, 60, 68, 71; *see also* public-private partnerships (PPPs); state-business relations
privatization 32, 86, 107–108, 142
procurement 106, 154; Kuwait 100, 146, **147**, 153, 157, 184; length of process 143, 146, **147**, 148, 153, 157; and PPPs 16, 143, 148, 150, 153, **156**, 167, **169**, 181, 183, 184, 188, 192; Qatar 150, 151; Saudi Arabia 148, 149, 188, 192
productivity 70, 71, 203, 219, 239, 240–242, 246–247; Dubai 270, **271**, 280, 281, *281*; and knowledge

314 Index

management 270, **271**, 280, 281, *281*;
public sector **33**, 83, 215, **236**, 245, 270, **271**, 280, 281, *281*
Program for International Student Assessment (PISA) 212
public administration 3, 4, 8, 30, 60, 226, 302; and public management 31–34, **33**; weaknesses 62
public management 1–21; current state in the GCC 29–62; definitions 3–4; emergence 30, 60; and public administration 31–34, **33**; *see also* new public management (NPM); *individual indicators*
public-private dialogue 19, 68
public-private partnerships (PPPs) 2–3, 14–16, 19–20, 32, 68, 71, 119, 130, 135–198, **156**, **167**, **169**, 303; corruption 139–140, 141, 142, 152, 157, 167; definitions 139, 164–165; Egypt **171**, 183, 194; emergence 165–166; and good governance 140, 143, 151–152, 153, **156**; Kuwait 19, 100, 137–138, 143–147, 151–158, 184; Malaysia 154–155; Qatar 19, 137, 150–158, 184, **191**, 303; Saudi Arabia 19, 20, 138, 147–150, 155, 157, 164, 184, 185–195, *189*, **191**, 302; skills 147, **156**, **167**, 189, 192; transparency 139, 140, 141, 146, 152, 154, 157, 166–168, **167**, **169**; trust 142, 153, **156**, 157, **169**, 194; United Arab Emirates 183, **191**, 303; *see also* school infrastructure and public-private partnerships (PPPs)
public sector: dominant recruiter in the GCC 1–2, 30, 67–68, 151, 214–216, 219; expenses 37, *37*; productivity **33**, 83, 215, **236**, 245, 270, **271**, 280, 281, *281*; wages 34, 38, *38*, *39*, 77, 107, 214; *see also* bureaucracy
Public Sector Comparator (PSC) 15, 139

Qatar 104, **111**, 154, **210**, 217, 288; brain drain 209, **210**; bureaucracy 151; contract enforcement **145**, 150; corruption 19, 104, 105, 116, **119**, 120, 122–123, **125**, 128–129, 130, 131, 302–303; corruption control indicator 42, *42*, 111–114, **113**, 128, **144**; Corruption Perceptions Index (CPI) 43, *43*, 111, **112**; credit, ease of obtaining **145**, 151; customs and border management 52, *53*; ease of doing business 46, *47*, *48*, **145**, **147**, 151; education 151, **170**, 184, **191**, 207, **208**, 217, 303; expatriates 202, 214, *215*, 216; global innovation index 54, *54*; Global Knowledge Index **96**, 207, **208**, **211**, 212; government effectiveness 35, *35*, **113**, 114, 120, 128, **144**; government inefficiency 36, *36*; graduate skillsets 56, *57*; Human Development Index (HDI) 39, *39*, 40, *40*; inefficient government bureaucracy **147**, 151; infrastructure 51–52, *51*, *52*, 137, 150–151, 155; insolvency resolution **145**, 150; legal rights **145**, 150; oil 137; political stability and absence of violence 44, *45*; port infrastructure 52, *52*; PPPs 19, 137, 150–158, 184, **191**, 303; procurement 150, 151; quality of government 18, 29, 114, **115**; R&D 55, *55*, *56*, *57*; regulatory environment 18, 29, 41, *41*, **113**, 114, **115**, **144**; rule of law 29, 45, *46*, **113**, **144**, 150; scientists and engineers, availability of 58, *58*; starting a business 49, *49*, **145**, 151; talent retention 58, *59*; tax and contribution rate 50, *50*; transparency of policymaking 114, **115**; trust in politicians **115**, 116; unemployment 209, *209*, **210**; universities 55, *56*, 184, 217, 303; university-industry collaboration 55, *56*; voice and accountability 43–44, *44*, **144**; wastefulness of government spending 114, **115**
Qatar Vision 2030 137
Quah, J. 107
quality of government 2, 10–14, 18; assessing 29–65; and corruption 12–13, 104–133; and democracy 10, 11–12; enhancing 104–133, 301; good governance, interchangeability with 10; Saudi Arabia 66–103; *see also* good governance
Quintas, P. 263, 264

Rashid, Sheikh 97
Razwan, I. 212
red tape 67, 69, 142, 146, 152
regional anti-corruption agencies 19, 105, **126**, 127–128, 303
regions, industrial policy in 12, 69, 93, 94, 100–101, 172

Index   315

regulatory environments 8, 18, 19, 29, 30, 34, 80–82, **81**, 91, 92, 93, 104, 105–106, 150; burden of government 114–116, **115**; PPPs 19, 20, 137, 138, 141–143, 145, 148, 151–152, 154–157, **156**, 163, 164, 177, 188, 190, **191**, 192; regulatory quality 10, 34, 40–41, *41*, **113, 144**, 148, 152; regulatory reform 6, 8, 69, 148, 192; *see also individual indicators*
rented knowledge 269, 270, 273
research and development (R&D) 30–31, 53–54, 55, *55*, *56*, *57*, 62, **73**, 74, 79–80, *80*, 260; Bahrain 55, *55*, *56*, *57*; Ireland 79–80, *80*, 85, 86; Kuwait 55, *55*, *56*, *57*; Malaysia **73**, 79–80, *80*; Qatar 55, *55*, *56*, *57*; Saudi Arabia 55, *55*, *56*, *57*, 80, *80*, 100; South Korea 79–80, *80*; United Arab Emirates 55, *55*, 56, *57*, 80, *80*, 96
restrictive labor regulations 147, **147**, 149
Richards, S. 3, 4
Riege, A. 260
Riley, S. 116
risk transfer 15, 139, 166, **167**, 168–169, 174–176, **175**, 194–195
Road & Transport Authority (RTA), Dubai 226, 265, 269, 270, 271, **271**, 272, 277, 280, 284–285
Robertson, M. 264
Rotberg, R. 10
Rothstein, B. 10, 11, 13
rule of law 2, 10, 11, 18, 29, 30, 34, 44–45, *45*, 111, **113**, 143–145, **144**, 152; definition 13; and PPPs 138, 140; and quality of government 13–14, 44–45
Ryan, N. 9, 206

Sahinidis, A. 232–233
Salehi-Isfahani, D. 213
Salman, Crown Prince Mohammed bin 123
Sands, V. 198
Saudi Arabia *49*, *53*, *57*, *59*, 66–103, 154, 172, **210**, 216, 217, 288–289; bureaucracy 99, 148, 149–150, 157, 188, 302; business-friendly environment 80, **81**; corruption 116, **117–118**, 120, 123, **125**, 129, 130, 149–150, 157; corruption control indicator 42, *42*, **113, 144**, 149; Corruption Perceptions Index (CPI) 104, 111, **112**; credit, ease of obtaining **81**, 82; credit ratings 153; diversification 75, 79, 82, 100; ease of doing business 46, *47*, *48*, **145, 147**; education 100, 163, 184, 207, **208**, 212; expatriates 215, *215*, 216; exports 79, *79*, 100, 148; final consumption expenditure 77, *77*; GDP 75, *76*, 110, **111**, 149; global innovation index 54, *54*; Global Knowledge Index 95, **96**, 207, **208**, **211**, 212; government effectiveness 35, *35*, **113, 144**; government inefficiency 36, *36*; high-tech field 79, *79*, 100; Human Development Index (HDI) 38–39, *39*, 40, *40*; industry, value-added 77–78, *78*; inefficient government bureaucracy **147**, 149; infrastructure 19, 20, 51, *51*, *52*, 137, 138, 147–150, 155, 157, 163–164, 184, 185–195, **191**; insolvency resolution **81**, 82, **145**, 148, 157; Kingdom of Saudi Arabia Vision 2030 (2016) 138; knowledge-based economy 164; Knowledge Economic Index 95, **96**; knowledge management 254; legal rights **145**, 148; National Transformation Plan 20; oil 75, *76*, 79, 97–99, 137, 148, 163–164, 184; PPPs 19, 20, 138, 147–150, 155, 157, 164, 184, 185–195, *189*, **191**, 302; procurement 148, 149, 188, 192; R&D 55, *55*, *56*, *57*, 80, *80*, 100; regulatory environment 41, *41*, **113**, 114, **115, 144**, 148; restrictive labor regulations **147**, 149; rule of law 45, **113, 144**; school infrastructure and PPPs 185–195, *189*, **191**; scientists and engineers, availability of 58, *58*; services, value-added 77, *78*; Sharia law 148, 155; starting a business 48, *48*, **145**; state-business relations 18–19, 66–103, **73**; tax and contribution rate 50, *50*; trading across borders **81**, 82; Vision 2030 18–19, 20, 66, 157, 187, 302; voice and accountability 43–44, *44*, **113**, 114, **144**, 147
Savas, E. 141
Sayyadi, M. 263
Scarborough, H. 254
Schneider, B. 70–71
Schomaker, R. 62

school infrastructure and public-private partnerships (PPPs) 20, 163–198, **170–171**, **174**, **175**, *176*, *177*, **186**, **191**, 303; Saudi Arabia 185–195, *189*, **191**
Schweyer, A. 203
scientists and engineers, availability of 54, 58, *58*, 83, 86, 204
Scurry, T. 8
Seidle, B. 225
services, value-added 77–79, *78*
Silva, E. 88–89
Singapore 11, 120, 171
skills 147, 151; graduate skillsets 54, 56–58, *57*, 208, 211–212, **211**; Ireland 85, 86; Malaysia **73**, 92; mismatch with market requirements 210–214, 228, 232; PPPs 147, **156**, **167**, 189, 192; Saudi Arabia 79, 187, 189, 254; shortages 17, 18, 147, 151, 189, 201, 204, 211–214, **211**; testing 9, **213**; underutilization 202, 254–255, 288–290, *289*
Skok, W. 264–265
small and medium-sized enterprises (SMEs) 93, 95, 100, 216, 219
Smither, J. 227
social contract 154, 163, 214
Sola, N. 230
Somalia *35*, 41, *41*, 44, *44*, *48*
South Korea **73**, 74, 75, *76*, *77*, *78*, **81**, 91, 92–93, 99, 100, 109; bureaucracy 84; business-friendly environment 80, **81**; contract enforcement **81**, 82; GDP 84; high-tech exports 79, *79*; peak associations 87–88; R&D 79–80, *80*; services, value-added 77, *78*; trading across borders **81**, 82
Spain **171**, 182–183, 227
starting a business 80, **81**, **145**, 146, 149, 151, 157; days required 46, 49, *49*; procedures to register 46, 47–49, *48*
state-business relations 18–19, 66–103; definition 67; and successful industrial policies 69–71, 74, 91–94; *see also* public-private partnerships (PPPs)
Storey, J. 263, 264
Strengths, Weaknesses, Opportunities and Threats (SWOT) analysis 236–238, **238**, 248
subsidies 71, **73**, 77, 90, 93, 94, 109, **170**, **171**, 181, 185, 193
Sudan *35*, *43*, *46*, *49*, *50*, **210**; corruption control indicator 42, *42*;

ease of doing business 47, *47*, *48*; Human Development Index (HDI) 39–40, *39*, *40*; starting a business 48, *48*
Syria *36*, *40*, *48*, *49*, *51*, *52*, *58*, **210**, 211; corruption control indicator 42, *42*; Corruption Perceptions Index (CPI) 43, *43*; Global Knowledge Index 207, **208**; government effectiveness *35*, 36; Human Development Index (HDI) 39–40, *39*; political stability and absence of violence 44, *45*; regulatory environment 41, *41*; rule of law 45, *46*; voice and accountability 44, *44*

tacit knowledge 255, 258–259, **258**, 262, 268–270, *268*, 278, 280, *281*, 290, 295–296, 305
Tahir, S. 264–265
talent management: definition 16–17, 203–205; private sector 16, 20, 187, 204, 208, 213, 214–215, 217, 218; public sector 2, 3, 8, 16–17, 54, 58–59, *59*, 95, 104, 154, 157, 189, 201–224, 304
tax 7, 88; incentives 30, 50, **73**, 85, 89, 90, 93, 94, 100, 180; rates 46, 49–50, *50*, 89
teachers **170**, 172, 182, 213, 217, 219
technology-delivered instruction (TDI) 228
Teorell, J. 10, 11, 13
Third International Mathematics and Sciences Studies (TIMSS) 212
Thomas, J. 263
Thunnissen, M. 17, 206
Tracey, J. 231
trading across borders **81**, 82
training programs for the public sector 2, 20, 69, 99; Dubai 20–21, 225–226, 233–249, *234*, **235–236**, *237*, **238–239**, *240*, **241**, *242*, *243*, *244*, *245*, *246*, *247*, **248**, 304; knowledge management 262, 290; Malaysia 92
transparency 16, 30, 31, 71, 106, 121, **124**, **125**, **126**, 142, 158; of government policymaking 114, **115**, 129; PPPs 139, 140, 141, 146, 152, 154, 157, 166–168, **167**, **169**
Transparency International 42; Corruption Perceptions Index (CPI) 13, 19, 34, 43, *43*, 104, 105, **112**, 128; National Integrity System 106

tribal heritage 137, 154
trust: in government 8, **115**, 116, 119; knowledge management 259, 263, 264, 265, *283*, 293–294; and PPPs 142, 153, **156**, 157, **169**, 194
Tunisia 35, 37, *39*, *41*, *42*, *43*, *45*, 46, 53, *54*, 55, *57*, *58*, *59*, 202, 216; ease of doing business 46, *47*, *48*; Global Knowledge Index **211**, 212; government inefficiency 36–37, *36*; infrastructure, quality of 51, *51*, *52*; public sector expenses 37, *37*; public sector wage bills 38, *38*, *39*; R&D 56, *56*, *57*; tax and contribution rate 50, *50*; unemployment 209; voice and accountability 44, *44*
Turkey **72**, 74, 77, *77*, *79*, **81**, 93–94, *94*, *95*, 100; business associations 90–91, 99; credit, ease of obtaining 80–82, **81**; exports *79*, 90, 93–94, *94*, *95*; GDP 75, *76*; industry, value-added 78, *78*; services, value-added 77, 78, *78*

Uganda 106, 172
unemployment 85, 202, 204, 207, 208–210, *209*, **210**, 216, 218–219; private sector 38, 91, 216; public service reduces 30, 67–68; youth 30, 38, 91, **210**
United Arab Emirates (UAE) *36*, **73**, 75, 77, *77*, **81**, 100, 101, 265, 288–290; brain drain 209, **210**; business-friendly environment 80, **81**, 82, 97; corruption 19, 104, 105, 116, **118**, 120, **124**, 127, 128–129, 130, 131, 302–303; corruption control indicator 41–42, *42*, 111–114, **113**, 128; Corruption Perceptions Index (CPI) 43, *43*, 104, 111, **112**; customs and border management 52, *53*; diversification **73**, 74, 75, 82, 97; ease of doing business 46, 47, *47*, *48*, **115**, 116; education 95, 96, 183, **191**, 207, **208**, 303; Emiratization 217–218; expatriates 202, 214, *215*, 216, 218; exports *79*, 100; FDIs 82, 97, **98**, *98*, 101, 130; GDP 75, 76, *76*, 110, **111**; global innovation index 54, *54*; Global Knowledge Index 95, **96**, 207, **208**, **211**, 212; government effectiveness 35, *35*, **113**, 114, 120, 128; graduate skillsets 56–57, *57*; high-tech 79, *79*, 100; Human Development Index (HDI) 38–39, *39*, 40, *40*; infrastructure 51–52, *51*, *52*, 75; knowledge-based economy 95–97, **96**, 101; knowledge management 21, 218, 255; nationalization of workforce 202; oil 75, 76, 78, 96–97; political stability and absence of violence 44, *45*; port infrastructure 51–52, *52*; PPPs 183, **191**, 303; public sector expenses 37, *37*; quality of government 18, 29, 114, **115**; R&D 55, *55*, 56, *56*, *57*, 80, *80*, 96; regulatory environment 18, 29, 41, *41*, 114, **115**; rule of law 29, 45, *46*; scientists and engineers, availability of 58, *58*; starting a business 48, *48*, 49, *49*, 80, **81**; talent retention 58, *59*; transparency of policymaking 114, **115**; trust in politicians **115**, 116; unemployment 209, *209*, **210**; universities 56, 96, 183, 277, 303; university-industry collaboration 55–56, *56*; voice and accountability 43–44, *44*, **113**, 114; wastefulness of government spending 114, **115**; *see also* Dubai
United Kingdom (UK) 7, 31, *48*, **171**, 193, 205, 227; education **170**, **171**, 173, 180, 181, 185; PPPs 18, 140, 142, **170**, **171**, 173, 180, 181, 185, 193, 194; starting a business 47–48
United Nations Development Programme (UNDP) 29, **126**, 127–128; Arab Knowledge Development Report (2022) 17; Knowledge Development Report (2009) 207, 212, 216
United Nations (UN) 11, *292*; Convention against Corruption (UNCAC) 105–106, 120, 121, 122, **125**, 129; Human Development Report 201–202; Office on Drugs and Crime 128
United States (USA) 12, *37*, 92, 97, 193, 204, 205; education **170**, 171, 172, 173, 180–181, 212; R&D 55; starting a business 47–48
universities 9, 30, 53, 86, 172, 211, 277, 296; Qatar 55, *56*, 184, 217, 303; United Arab Emirates 56, 96, 183, 277, 303
university-industry collaboration 53–54, 55–56, *56*

value-added services 77–79, *78*
Van den Brink, M. 9

318 *Index*

Van Gelder, M. 8
violence, absence of 34, 44, *45*
Vision 2030 18–19, 75, 99, 100
voice and accountability 29, 34, 43–44, *44*, 111, **113**, 114, 143, **144**, 147, 152
vouchers and voucher-like programs **170**, 172–173, 185, **191**, 192, 194

wage bills 77, 107; as percentage of GDP 38, *39*, 214; as percentage of public expenditure 34, 38, *38*
"The War for Talent" (Chambers) 204
Washington Consensus model 12
wastefulness of government spending 114, **115**, 129
whistleblowing 107
Wiig, K. 255–256
Williams, R. 262
World Bank 1, 10–11, 29, 38, 42, 109, 128, 146–147, 212, 216; Doing Business Database 80, **81**, 138, 145, **145**, 146, **147**, 148, 151; Enterprise Surveys 211; GCC and MENA country characteristics 202; Global Knowledge Index 95–96, **96**, 207–208, **208**, 211–212, **211**; good governance, definition of 10–11, 34–35; governance, definition of 10; investment climate reforms 69; and new public management (NPM) 5; PPPs 163, 173–174; Report on Africa (1989) 34; *see also* good governance; Worldwide Governance Indicators
World Economic Forum 19, 69, 105
World Trade Organization (WTO) 93
Worldwide Governance Indicators 10, 11, 13–14, 19, 105, **113**, 129, 138; *see also individual indicators*

Yemen 36, *47*, *51*, *52*, *54*; corruption control indicator 42, *42*; Corruption Perceptions Index (CPI) 43, *43*; ease of doing business 47, *48*; government effectiveness *35*, 36; graduate skillsets 57, *57*; Human Development Index (HDI) 39–40, *39*, *40*; political stability and absence of violence 44, *45*; regulatory environment 41, *41*; rule of law 45, *46*; scientists and engineers, availability of 58, *58*; starting a business 49, *49*; talent retention 58, *59*, **210**; voice and accountability 44, *44*
youth (un)employment 30, 38, 79, 91, 100, 207, **210**, 215, 216

Zhang, X. 142

Printed in the United States
by Baker & Taylor Publisher Services